THE LANGUAGE OF HISTORY

The Language of History

SANSKRIT NARRATIVES OF INDO-MUSLIM RULE

Audrey Truschke

Columbia University Press
New York

Columbia University Press
Publishers Since 1893
New York Chichester, West Sussex
cup.columbia.edu

Library of Congress Cataloging-in-Publication Data
Names: Truschke, Audrey, author.
Title: The language of history : Sanskrit narratives of Indo-Muslim rule / Audrey Truschke.
Description: New York : Columbia University Press, [2021] |
Includes bibliographical references and index.
Identifiers: LCCN 2020021927 (print) | LCCN 2020021928 (ebook) |
ISBN 9780231197045 (hardback) | ISBN 9780231197052 (trade paperback) |
ISBN 9780231551953 (ebook)
Subjects: LCSH: India—Civilization—Islamic influences—Sources. |
India—Civilization—1200-1765—Sources. | India—History—Sources. |
India—Historiography. | Sanskrit language—History. | Sanskrit literature—History
and criticism. | Literature and history—India. | Muslims—India—History—Sources. |
Islam—India—History—Sources.
Classification: LCC DS427 .T78 2021 (print) | LCC DS427 (ebook) | DDC 954.02072—dc23
LC record available at https://lccn.loc.gov/2020021927
LC ebook record available at https://lccn.loc.gov/2020021928

Cover image: Madhuravijaya of Gangadevi, Punjab University Library, Lahore, ms. no. 8579
Cover design: Chang Jae Lee

For Allison Busch,
a mentor, role model, inspiration, and friend, always

بول، کہ سچ زندہ ہے اب تک
بول، جو کچھ کہنا ہے کہہ لے

Speak, the truth is still alive;
Speak: say what you have to say.

—FAIZ AHMAD FAIZ, TRANSLATED BY YASMIN HOSAIN

Contents

List of Illustrations xiii

List of Tables xv

Acknowledgments xvii

Note on Translations and Scholarly Conventions xxi

Select Time Line of Political Events, ca. 1190–1720 xxiii

Introduction: Controversial History 1

I Before Indo-Persian Rule: Many Sanskrit Ways to Write About Muslims 27

II Difference That Mattered: Defining the Ghurid Threat 44

III Indo-Muslim Rulers: Expanding the World of Indian Kingship 66

IV Local Stories in Fourteenth-Century Gujarat and Fifteenth-Century Kashmir 99

V Meeting the Mughals and Reformulating Jain Identity 133

VI Rajput and Maratha Kingships in an Indo-Persian Political Order 161

VII Mughal Political Histories 189

Epilogue: Starting Points 212

Appendix: Select Translations from Sanskrit Histories 223
Glossary 245
Notes 251
Bibliography 305
Index 333

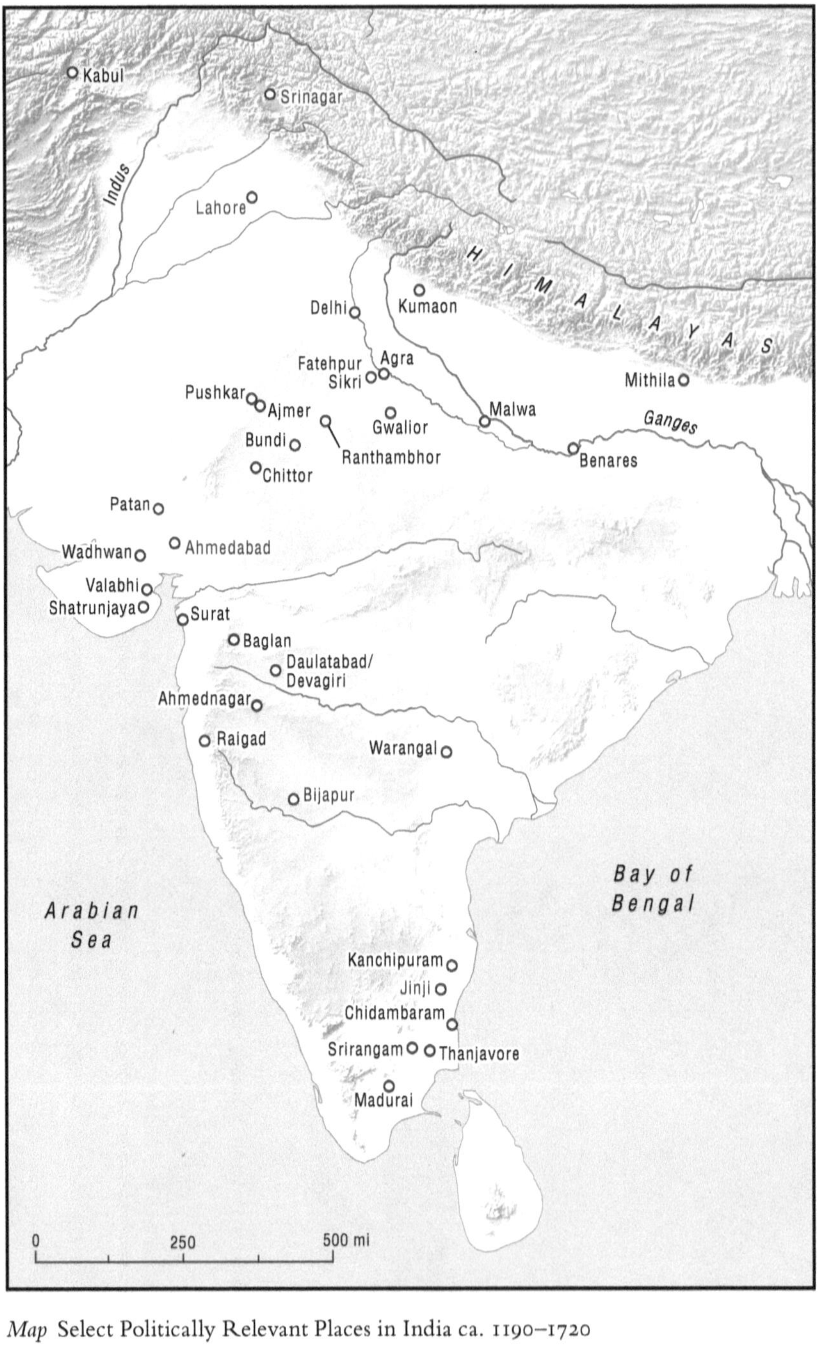

Map Select Politically Relevant Places in India ca. 1190–1720

Illustrations

2.1. Adhai-din-ka-Jhompra mosque, Ajmer, Rajasthan 50

3.1. Two-faced rider, Kalyana Mandapa, Varadaraja temple, Kanchipuram, clean-shaven side 71

3.2. Two-faced rider, Kalyana Mandapa, Varadaraja temple, Kanchipuram, mustached side 72

3.3. Goripalayam Dargah, Madurai, site of two graves of the sultans of Madurai 87

3.4. Thiruparankundram Dargah, outside of Madurai, site of grave of Sultan Alauddin Sikandar Shah, the last sultan of Madurai, external view 88

3.5. Thiruparankundram Dargah, outside of Madurai, site of grave of Sultan Alauddin Sikandar Shah, the last sultan of Madurai, internal view 88

3.6. Wall of Ranthambhor Fort, Rajasthan 93

6.1. Surjan of Hada submitting to Akbar, *Akbarnāma*, ca. 1590–95 176

7.1. Burning of the Rajput women during the siege of Chittor, *Akbarnāma*, ca. 1590–95 196

Tables

1.1. Sanskrit inscriptions before 1000 CE that mention historical encounters with Muslims 29

4.1. Jain prabandhas 1305–49 that refer to Muslim political figures 103

4.2. Kashmiri rajataranginis in premodernity 113

5.1. Individual biographies 1589–1652 featuring Jain activities at the Mughal court 136

6.1. Sanskrit histories sponsored by the Maratha Bhonsle family, 1673–1690 178

7.1. Sanskrit-language Mughal political histories 191

7.2. Time lines of the establishment of Mughal power 192

Acknowledgments

I argue in this book that a hitherto unrecognized archive, Sanskrit histories of Indo-Muslim rule, ought to be acknowledged as crucial to the study of Indo-Persian political history and Sanskrit intellectual culture in the second millennium CE. Among the things I highlight are the variety of views held by premodern India's traditional learned elite of the Muslim Other (most often depicted as not particularly Muslim and, often, as not particularly Other). I also demonstrate some analytical approaches for how to navigate literary aspects of writing about political pasts that are compelling for the study of South Asia and beyond. Some premoderns wrote history as poetry, and, I argue, the texts that they produced might prompt us to think in dynamic ways about the definition and practice of history today.

Both the texts and the political events that I resurrect here unfolded in the past, primarily between 1191 and 1721 CE. But the telling of this past occurs in the twenty-first century. The narrative as I have crafted it is a modern phenomenon. One of my core arguments in this book is that storytelling, albeit truthful storytelling, is a critical and still-underappreciated dimension of the historian's craft. And so, let me begin with part of my story, namely how I came to write this book and how I benefited from the generosity and skills of many colleagues and institutions along the way.

I began work on this project a number of years ago, but then put it on the back burner, because I was interrupted by Aurangzeb Alamgir. The sixth Mughal emperor has been dead for more than three centuries, but he has commanded an immense amount of attention in recent times. In my case, the interruption consumed several years, as I researched, wrote, and dealt with the aftermath of having produced a historical biography of Aurangzeb, India's most hated king. Along the path of writing *Aurangzeb: The Life and Legacy of India's Most Controversial King* (2017), I developed new skills and sensitivities as a historian. Most relevant here is that writing *Aurangzeb* and living through its reception brought home to me, in visceral, immediate, and sometimes terrifying ways, how the past lives in the present. As a result, I embarked on my next book project (resulting in this monograph) highly attuned to questions of narrative, the nuances of identities, and the emotions often wrapped up in how people interpret the Indian past. I think I am a better historian for this set of experiences, painful as some of them were, and I hope that, as a result, this is a better book than it might otherwise have been.

In researching and writing this book, I acquired many debts of gratitude. I am thankful to the numerous colleagues who commented on chapters, batted around ideas at various stages, and made interventions in this project. I could not have written this book without you. That said, all views and errors in this book are my own.

For feedback and assistance, I especially thank Dean Accardi, Daud Ali, Debjani Bhattacharyya, Allison Busch, Pratik Chakrabarti, Divya Cherian, John Cort, Whitney Cox, Daniele Cuneo, Purnima Dhavan, Richard Eaton, Finbarr Barry Flood, Kashi Gomez, Sumit Guha, Jack Hawley, Sander Hens, Tony Joseph, Sunila Kale, Aparna Kapadia, Sudipta Kaviraj, Pasha M. Khan, Mana Kia, Corinne Lefèvre, Christian Novetzke, Luther Obrock, Satoshi Ogura, Kiyokazu Okita, Andrew Ollett, Parimal Patil, Sheldon Pollock, Frances Pritchett, Ajay Rao, Tamara Sears, Anna Seastrand, Dan Sheffield, Fabrizio Speziale, Hamsa Stainton, Cynthia Talbot, Sarah Pierce Taylor, Anand Venkatkrishnan, Steven Vose, Erica Wald, Taymiya Zaman, and Ines Županov.

For sharing unpublished work, I thank Tillo Detige, Sarah Pierce Taylor, and Taymiya Zaman. For various kinds of archival research assistance, I thank Hamid Ali, Richard Eaton, Finbarr Barry Flood, Rima Hooja, and Giles Tillotson. I also extend my gratitude to the following institutions: the Punjab University Library, in Lahore; the Pothikhana, in Jaipur's City Palace; and the British Library, in London.

The National Endowment for the Humanities provided me with a yearlong fellowship that was instrumental in writing this book. I also benefited immensely from a Visiting Professor Fellowship at the École des Hautes Études en Sciences Sociales (EHESS), in Paris. My home institution, Rutgers University, has stood behind me from top to bottom and given me incredible support throughout the researching and writing of this book; I am grateful.

I presented and received feedback on various parts of this project at many places. In this regard, I thank Aligarh Muslim University, Columbia University, EHESS, Jawaharlal Nehru University, Princeton University, the Seagull Foundation for the Arts, Tokyo University of Foreign Studies (a special shout-out to Typhoon Hagibis for some enforced work time), the University of Pennsylvania, the University of Toronto's Jainism Summer School, and the University of Washington in Seattle. Part of chapter 7 appeared, in an earlier form, in my 2012 article "Setting the Record Wrong: A Sanskrit Vision of Mughal Conquests."

I warmly thank the staff at Rutgers Interlibrary Loan Services and everyone at the Dana Library who assisted me in obtaining the many, many books required for this project. S. Anwar in Chennai and Rajni Malhotra at Bahrisons Booksellers were essential to procuring important secondary sources.

My family is my rock. To them go my deepest thanks and my love.

Note on Translations and Scholarly Conventions

I forgo diacritics for the names of people (including authors), places, and Indian-origin terms now part of English. But I retain them for titles of texts and transliterations of phrases, usually from Sanskrit, out of dedication to textual fidelity and accuracy. For potentially unfamiliar terms from Sanskrit and other languages, I generally provide diacritics on first use, and thereafter I omit both diacritics and italics. I make some exceptions and repeat diacritics when I am discussing the linguistic origins or meanings of specific words. Readers can find a glossary of non-English (and newly English) terms at the end of the book. This is an imperfect set of compromises that attempts to reconcile two scholarly commitments—precision and accessibility—that I hold equally dear.

For Sanskrit diacritics, we have an established system that all specialists will recognize. Persian is another story. Here, I use the IJMES transliteration system, with some modifications. I represent *al-* with approximate pronunciation where appropriate. Citations refer to page numbers unless otherwise marked; I cite some Sanskrit texts using book, chapter, and verse numbers, in accordance with convention (e.g., *Mahābhārata* 12.200.40–41). Sometimes, in pursuit of clarity, I give both page and verse numbers.

In this book I translate a wide variety of Sanskrit texts, inscriptions, and poetry. In so doing, I strive to be faithful to the meaning, sense, and poetry of the original texts. Sanskrit poetry has long suffered from bad translators. In recent decades, many modern Sanskritists have favored overly literal translations that transmorph refined Sanskrit verses into clunky, sometimes nearly unintelligible English. I avoid that failed approach here. Instead I strive to create readable, even appealing English renderings that at least nod at the aesthetic beauty of the Sanskrit original. I also prioritize clarity, which sometimes means that I move around clauses and repeat words, especially names. I do not shy away from idiomatic translations when I feel that they capture something important about the original Sanskrit poetry.

I invite readers to be critical of my translations (and of everything else that I write in this book). I also caution that looking up every word in a dictionary and tossing in minimal English grammar, without a thought to aesthetics in the target language, often comes closer to mutilating the original text rather than the art of translation.

Select Time Line of Political Events, ca. 1190–1720

1191 Prithviraj Chauhan triumphs over the Ghurids at Tarain
1192 Shihabuddin Muhammad Ghori triumphs over the Chauhans at Tarain
1299 Muhammad Shah defects from the Khaljis to the Chauhans
1301 Alauddin Khalji assaults Ranthambhor and ends the Chauhan dynasty
1311 Malik Kafur, on Alauddin Khalji's orders, raids several places within Pandya territory
1323 Ulugh Khan, on Tughluq orders, sacks Warangal and ends the Kakatiya dynasty
1328 Jinaprabha enters the court of Muhammad bin Tughluq
1333 Sultanate of Madurai established
1339 Shah Miri dynasty established in Kashmir
1371 Vijayanagara attack ends the Sultanate of Madurai
1398 Timur sacks Delhi
1402 Virama Tomar ascends the throne in Gwalior
1407 Muzaffar Shah establishes the Sultanate of Gujarat
1418 Sultan Zayn al-Abidin ascends the Shah Miri throne in Kashmir
1459 Sultan Mahmud Begada begins to rule in Gujarat
1526 Babur takes Delhi from the Lodis and establishes the Mughal Empire

1540 Sher Shah Suri ousts Humayun and establishes the Sur dynasty in northern India

1555 Humayun retakes Delhi from the Sur dynasty

1556 Akbar ascends the Mughal throne

1569 Mughals assault Ranthambhor and Surjan of Hada capitulates

1595 Baglan assists the Mughal assault on Ahmadnagar led by Prince Murad

1658 Aurangzeb ascends the Mughal throne

1673 Shivaji's forces seize Panhal Fort from Bijapur

1674 Shivaji undergoes coronation and ritual ceremony at Raigad

1707 Aurangzeb Alamgir dies

1712 Jahandar Shah ascends the Mughal throne

1713 Farrukh Siyar kills Jahandar Shah and ascends the Mughal throne

1719 Sayyid brothers, Abdullah Khan and Husain Ali Khan, assassinate Farrukh Siyar

1720 Husain Ali Khan is assassinated, and Abdullah Khan is imprisoned

Introduction

Controversial History

> You must have the courage to break out of your own image. At each stage you go on breaking. That is the key.
>
> —M. F. HUSAIN, 2010 INTERVIEW

In August 2018, Hindutva extremists prevented me from delivering an academic lecture on premodern Indian history in Hyderabad, in southern India. A few weeks before the scheduled event, self-described members of Hindu nationalist groups—including the Bajrang Dal, RSS, and BJP—wrote letters to the police threatening violence if I were to take the stage. The police refused to provide protection, which I sometimes need to speak in India and even in the West.[1] And so the lecture, titled, in a nice bit of unintentional irony, "Unpopular Stories," was canceled over my objections.[2] The silencing of academic voices is an increasingly common outcome in India, where a political swerve to the hard right has been accompanied by a feverish devotion to a bastardized vision of India's past.[3] In short, Indian right-wingers are trying to cook the history books. This means that historians—who call out such shenanigans by insisting on evidence, solid arguments, and professional ethics—face mounting pressure to remain mute. Sometimes the bullying works, such as in Hyderabad, but other times it does not, such as in this book.

I cannot promise that the narratives I share in what follows will be any more or less popular than those I was prevented from sharing in Hyderabad. But I can reasonably predict that the stories I resurrect here—many of them long tucked away in old, little-read Sanskrit texts—will surprise you, dear reader. For while the premodern Indian past is vibrantly alive and debated in modern times, premodern Sanskrit historical writings remain largely inaccessible and unknown to all but specialists. Even scholars partial to reading premodern Sanskrit texts may find that I analyze stories in unexpected ways and so bring out aspects of the Sanskrit tradition that are usually overlooked. The lack of visibility of Sanskrit histories of Muslim-led rule, to my colleagues and to a general audience, is part of why I decided to write about this subject. This robust body of narrative texts expands our historical and conceptual resources for understanding Sanskrit literature, early modern history, and premodern and modern Indian identities.

In this book, I present and analyze a hitherto-overlooked group of histories on Indo-Persian political events, namely a few dozen Sanskrit texts that date from the 1190s until 1721. As soon as Muslim political figures established themselves in northern India in the 1190s—when the Ghurids overthrew the Chauhans and ruled part of northern India from Delhi—Indian intellectuals wrote about that political development in Sanskrit. Indian men (and at least one woman) produced dozens of Sanskrit texts on Indo-Persian political events. These works span Delhi Sultanate and Mughal rule, and some deal with the Deccan Sultanates and other Muslim-led polities in the subcontinent's deep south. India's premodern learned elite only ceased to write on Indo-Muslim powers in Sanskrit when the Mughal Empire began to fracture beyond repair, in the early eighteenth century. In other words, Sanskrit writers produced histories of Indo-Muslim rule—meaning political power wielded over parts of the Indian subcontinent by people who happened to be Muslim—throughout nearly the entire time span of that political experience. This book seeks, for the first time, to collect, analyze, and theorize Sanskrit histories of Muslim-led and—later, as Muslims became an integral part of the Indian cultural and political worlds—Indo-Muslim rule as a body of historical materials. My main focus is historiography, or history writing, as opposed to political history (although there is more than a little of that, too, in these pages). This new archive has wide-reaching implications for specialist scholarship on premodern South Asia. The works therein lend insight into, among other things, formulations and expressions of premodern political, social, cultural, and religious identities. Given the current political climate, where nationalist claims are often grounded on fabricated visions of India's premodernity, this book also contributes to ongoing debates in the Indian public sphere.

In what follows I offer a substantial revision to Sanskrit intellectual history. I argue that Sanskrit authors marshaled the full resources of their layered literary heritage to comment on what we now identify as the single biggest set of cultural, political, and social changes of the second millennium in South Asia: Muslim-led rule. This means that some Sanskrit authors, far from being oblivious to their day-to-day realities, as many modern scholars have presumed, were keenly interested in writing about political events, on occasion in real time. The fact that premodern Sanskrit intellectuals wrote histories matters for how we understand the contours of the Sanskrit tradition and its relationship to political realities. Moreover, in the following pages, I explore *how* premodern thinkers recounted the political past in Sanskrit and what purposes these narratives served for their authors and readers.

I also investigate what these Sanskrit histories can tell us about premodern identities. This is a tradition defined by writing about an Other, a time-honored way of also writing about the Self.[4] I will tip my hand at the outset: if you are looking for the origins of "Hindu" and "Muslim" identities in premodern India or the roots of Hindu-Muslim conflict or, to be frank, Hindu-Muslim anything, then you might want to try a different book. Few, if any, of the dozens of authors I discuss here offer categories remotely approaching our modern dichotomy of broad-based religious identities. In fact, I use the general categories of "Hindu" and "Muslim" throughout this book, in part, because they do not offer strong interpretive frameworks for premodernity. Such categories are broad enough to enable us to recover the highly variegated identities expressed by premodern Sanskrit intellectuals. Sanskrit intellectuals who wrote about what we now call Indo-Muslim or Indo-Persian political history circa 1190–1721 defined peoples and communities by place of origin, place of residence, caste, class, style of rulership, and often not by the god(s) people worshipped so much as by the political power(s) they served.

Sanskrit thinkers evinced a wide range of responses to political power wielded by Muslims, including formulations that I did not expect to find. In their works we meet outcaste Ghurids who can never be proper northern Indian rulers and Mughal kings who speak flawless Sanskrit. We encounter Vijayanagara rulers who, despite not being Muslim, declare themselves sultans superior to mere Hindu kings. We stumble across Maratha and Rajput *yavana*s (a Sanskrit word most commonly translated as "Muslim") who fight proudly for a host of Indo-Persian dynasties. We have a whole lot of groups that I struggle to succinctly describe in modern English. While I wallow a little here in the glorious confusion of this rich tapestry, in the substantive chapters of this book I prioritize context and specificity. I parse the identities expressed in individual texts that generally feature an Other, who is often, although not always, an Indo-Muslim political figure or dynasty. I am interested in the definition of that Other and also in the Self, as formulated by each author, right up through the moments, in the sixteenth through eighteenth centuries, when the distinction ceased to exist for some Sanskrit intellectuals.

In this book, I am interested precisely in the intersection between an elite learned tradition (Sanskrit thought) and a disruptive set of political changes (Indo-Muslim rule). Only a thin upper crust of premodern Indians participated in Sanskrit literary and intellectual culture. Accordingly, we should not conflate Sanskrit with India at large and certainly not with "Indian civilization" (if such things even existed in premodernity).[5] Similarly, Indo-Persian rule was not an enterprise exclusive to Muslims, nor did it involve all Muslims. From the start, Muslim-led polities on the subcontinent were both elite and diverse, and included Hindus, among others. Accordingly, my questions here concern Sanskrit literary culture and its commentary on specific incarnations of Indo-Muslim rule. How did premodern Sanskrit intellectuals relate writing about new types of political power to their inherited literary tradition? Why did they write in Sanskrit? How did Sanskrit intellectuals think about rulers who happened to be Muslim? Did they always (or ever) conceptualize political actors as "Muslim" or "Other"? How did specific thinkers reformulate their own community identities through writing about Indo-Muslim political history in Sanskrit?

It is difficult to cultivate within ourselves the capacity to imagine the premodern Indian past, which looks so radically different in many ways from our present. Part of the challenge lies in lacking a cluster of familiar concepts that might order our understanding of this long-lost world. A few short paragraphs in, and I have already thrown out "Hindu" and "Muslim" as analytical identities. I am talking about Sanskrit histories, a category that may confuse people who think that these do not exist. Below I suggest some ways to muddle through and develop new analytical concepts that enable us to unpack how premodern Sanskrit intellectuals narrate aspects of the Indo-Muslim past. Ultimately, this project may empower us to think more creatively and critically about writing history in our own present, an exciting possibility that I discuss later in this introduction and to which I return in the epilogue. But we ought not to put the cart before the horse. In order to begin, we must dismantle the bad ideas that have blocked most modern scholars from seeing the rich archive of premodern Sanskrit historical materials on Indo-Muslim polities.

Finding What We Are Not Looking For

The Sanskrit historical works that I analyze in this book—"evidence" in the historian's lingo and "texts" for the philologists among us—are neither singular nor hard to find. Sanskrit intellectuals penned dozens of such histories. And they are not squirreled away in manuscript archives that are off the beaten path, where they might be understandably, if regrettably, overlooked. Rather, the overwhelming majority of texts that I mention in the following chapters have been printed. In short, a plethora of works have been available to scholars for decades (for more than a century, in some cases).[6] So, why has nobody written a book on Sanskrit historical accounts of Indo-Muslim rule until now? Scholars have worked on individual texts, and even on small collections of them, and a few thinkers have made notable attempts to catalog Sanskrit views of Muslims.[7] But no one has collated these works together and analyzed them, as I do here, as histories. This neglect of texts lying in plain sight is explained by modern scholarly biases, which I identify and counter here because, despite our best efforts to date, they still exert varying degrees of sway over academic thinking.

An earlier generation of Sanskritists thought that after they published Sanskrit literary histories, a cascade of Indological interest and awareness would follow. For instance, in 1877 Georg Bühler wrote to his colleague Theodor Nöldeke: "You are a little behind the age with your notion that the Indians have no historical literature. In the last 20 years, five fairly voluminous works have been discovered . . . I am on the track of more than a dozen more."[8] As C. H. Tawney noted, Bühler's "lifelong aspiration" was removing the idea that, aside from Kalhana's *Rājataraṅgiṇī* (River of kings), Sanskrit literature had "no work meriting the title of history."[9] I honor Bühler's efforts here, but he did not change scholarship as he dreamed, not yet anyway. A handful of books have appeared over the decades that promise to analyze Sanskrit histories, defined in various ways.[10] I draw upon some of them, but all these prior works overlook significant texts that I discuss here. Printing texts alone did not render them visible to most Sanskrit scholars, who remained—in Bühler's time and, to a lesser degree, today—attached to unfounded assumptions. Specifically, two persistent wrongheaded ideas have prevented a book like this one from being written until now: the first myth is that there is no history in Sanskrit, and the second myth is that there is nothing on Islam in Sanskrit. By failing to overturn these two durable fictions, scholars have blinded themselves, and everyone else, from seeing, analyzing, and theorizing Sanskrit historical works on Indo-Muslim political events.

The postulation that there is no history written in Sanskrit is an old trope, which most twenty-first-century scholars dare not utter but which constricts modern thinking all the same. This Orientalist slight is a subset of the earlier Orientalist dismissal that India had no history at all.[11] Arthur MacDonell, a household name for Sanskritists even today, summed up the connection between the two ideas as follows: "Early India wrote no history because it never made any."[12] The India-has-no-history (real or written) thesis possesses a precolonial lineage as well, dating back to the tenth-century polymath al-Biruni, who was sometimes cited approvingly by colonial-era scholars.[13] In both premodern and colonial India, this blatantly bad idea was partly due to straight-up bigotry and partly followed from overreliance on Brahmin interpreters, a point that will come up again in this introduction.[14] One scholar tried saying it in French, and even so it sounds every bit as prejudiced as it does in English: "L'Inde n'a pas d'histoire."[15] It has been decades since most respectable academics aired the "India has no history" line in print (although I dug up a number of exceptions, those of which from the 1980s onward I list in the note to this sentence).[16] Still, our scholarship has yet to reflect our supposed change of heart. Inside the ivory tower, India's alleged lack of history is a bias evidenced and entrenched in recent decades by omission, by what scholars do not research.

Absence constitutes the most potent evidence that history continues to be sidelined in contemporary Sanskrit-based research. It is difficult to glimpse what is not there and definitionally impossible to cite a dearth; but consider a few indications. In July 2018, thousands of Sanskrit scholars descended on Vancouver, Canada, for the 17th World Sanskrit Conference. The conference hosted twenty-four separate sessions, but the word "history" appeared in the title of only one, where it was paired with art, architecture, and epigraphy.[17] The 18th World Sanskrit Conference, originally scheduled for 2021 in Canberra, Australia, and now postponed until 2022 due to the COVID-19 pandemic, has announced a similar lineup of sessions that marginalize history.[18] More generally, Sanskritists write and teach a lot about poetry, philosophy, mythology, and religion but only much more sporadically about historical works. A solid strand of Indological thought posits that premodern Sanskrit intellectuals expressed historical impulses in inscriptions, a claim that is true but often marshaled to wrongly allege a lack of narrative histories.[19]

While few contemporary scholars wish to go on record as saying that there is no history written in Sanskrit, plenty have proclaimed that there is no *real* history written in Sanskrit. The general idea behind this line of argumentation is that in order to count as "history," a text must be sufficiently close to modern Western history. Usually this means that the text must use dates and express a historical causality palatable to modern Western sensibilities (i.e., without too much agency assigned to divine beings). This modern standard is rarely laid bare in this manner, but do not overlook its ever-lurking presence and catastrophic effects. The problem here is quite straightforward: if you look for modern Western history anywhere except in the modern West, you are doomed to find only deficiency. This is true regarding the premodern West as well, although this gap gets less airtime, because of a tendency "to idolize and fossilize the 'norm' (here, the Western model of historiography), while failing to note the diversity and historicity within itself."[20] Regarding premodern India, Romila Thapar has put the blunt reality of our own historical contingency thus: "We cannot find an Enlightenment view of history from early Indian writing."[21]

The inevitability that no premodern society could have produced modern Western historiography is borne out in the great lengths to which some scholars have gone to declare certain Sanskrit texts, which narrate real events and contain clear facts, to be nonhistories. Others have described some of the texts I analyze in this book as bad histories, folklore, hagiography, hagiology, inauthentic historical literature, legend, historical memory, mythology, pseudohistory, stories, and so forth. Such characterizations are not de facto problematic or wrong, but they are red flags when prompted by a field-wide aversion to admitting that premodern Sanskrit intellectuals wrote historical narratives. As Ronald Inden put it when talking about the importance of admitting diversity in the production of history, "To strip a community of this capacity to textualize its past or deny that they possess it, as in the case of India, is to strip those people of the knowledge to articulate themselves as polities. We call this colonialism."[22]

In its core structure, injudiciously applying modern Western standards to premodern India is a rigged game. Also, the results have proven to be analytically bankrupt. What possible insight might be gained by pointing out that premodern Indian texts are neither modern nor Western? But worse than being dull is that this line of thinking marginalizes Sanskrit narratives about Indo-Muslim political events as nonhistories or not-quite-histories or bad histories that therefore cannot be used, evaluated, and analyzed in the same way as historical works that are foundational to humanities research in many fields. In describing Sanskrit narratives as histories, I do not attempt to "scramble for coevality with the Western world and its disciplinary parameters" or gain an "exalted status" for these works, projects that other scholars have rightly criticized.[23] In fact, I think that modern Western ways of defining history need reevaluation, and premodern Sanskrit literary histories might be just the ticket to jump-start that process (for more on this, see the epilogue). The first step is to level the playing field or, to return to my earlier metaphor, derig the game. We ought to acknowledge that premodern Sanskrit poets wrote histories, not as a way of saying that they are equal to modern Western historians but rather as a way of saying that they have as much right to define what it means to write about the political past as anybody else.

A cautionary tale of what happens when scholars privilege Western ideas about historicity is the much-discussed book by Velcheru Narayana Rao, David Shulman, and Sanjay Subrahmanyam, *Textures of Time: Writing History in South India, 1600–1800*. First published in 2001, *Textures of Time* was a seminal work in many ways. For instance, it points out that written history survives in many genres in premodern India, an astute observation others have praised and upon which I build here.[24] But the authors went astray in trying to find modern Western-style history writing in the wrong time and place. They sliced and diced Indian texts according to "subgeneric markers" of their own invention and then shoved raw textual fragments into categories for which they were never intended.[25] These philological acrobatics convinced few readers, and they straitjacketed both the skillful scholars who authored the book and the rich premodern texts they analyzed, some of which had for decades prior been subjected to dismemberment into history and nonhistory.[26] In my reading, at the heart of a book like *Textures of Time* lies a deep discomfort with subjectivity. That angst is decidedly a modern, not a premodern, problem. And I no longer want to write our contemporary anxieties onto the premodern past. Rather I wish to explore how premodern Indians wrote narratives about political events, and I want to do so without being chagrined about what I might find. Sheldon Pollock, in a discussion of Indian modernity that focused on questions of historiography, wrote: "There is no shame in premodernity."[27] I agree, and moreover I want to know what it is, exactly, of which we ought not be ashamed. What kinds of political history writing did premodern Sanskrit intellectuals develop in order to talk about and think through aspects of Indo-Muslim rule?

Indologists have been ill-served by starting out with a heavy theory of what qualifies a work as written history and then seeing which premodern texts fit the bill. So, I try a different method here. I loosely define historical writing below and intentionally leave its contours flexible around the edges. Through careful textual analysis in this book, I attempt to describe the philosophies of and approaches to history writing cultivated by various Sanskrit intellectuals, along with their views of different political groups, formulations of their own community identities, and more. In declining to begin with my feet planted upon a strong definition of history writing, I aim to avoid the reductive pattern, succinctly described by Anjali Arondekar and Geeta Patel in a different context (queer theory) that "geopolitics provides the exemplars, but rarely the epistemologies."[28] I want to recover how premodern Sanskrit intellectuals defined history writing, as a methodological contribution to the broader field that can inform and challenge how we write history today.[29]

I never complete the historical-analysis circle by offering a final, clearcut delineation of what constitutes historical writing in premodern India. For readers who ache for all-encompassing definitions, I urge you to consider how poorly this impulse has served us in the past. As detailed in the prior paragraphs, ideas about historical writing that are rooted in the nineteenth-century West have resulted in earlier generations of scholars neglecting premodern Sanskrit histories, discarding them, or mutilating them. In contrast, my posture of openness and flexibility has the potential to allow us to conceptualize and analyze a body of written historical materials in one of the world's most sophisticated premodern literary traditions in ways relevant for historians today. This is a worthy prize, in pursuit of which it is worth breaking out of the cage of our own theoretical scaffolding.

Another powerful myth that has blocked scholars from investigating Sanskrit histories of Muslim political figures to the extent that I do so here is the assumption that Sanskrit intellectuals had nothing to say about Islam. This claim has been repeated ad nauseam, even in recent decades. For instance, in 1988, Wilhelm Halbfass wrote, "Even the Muslims, who were not only present in India for many centuries, but were its actual rulers, appear only in vague and marginal references [in Sanskrit literature]."[30] In 1992, Carl Ernst declared, "The Sanskrit tradition has never taken official notice of the existence of Islam."[31] It is generally, although not universally, correct that Sanskrit thinkers had limited interest in Islamic theology.[32] But do we not all agree by now that Islam consists of so much more than theology? Perhaps not. Much of our scholarship is still weighed down by the baggage of reifying Islam into religious aspects, above all high theology, while separating out Islamic cultures. Even our vocabulary meant to displace attention from religion does so by making theology the measuring stick of Islam. The best example is the term "Islamicate," which denotes nonreligious aspects of Muslim societies by adding letters to and thus distancing itself from the term "Islamic."[33] Many of my colleagues are fond of "Islamicate," because the term directs academic attention to nontheological features of Muslim societies. I agree with this emphasis, but I think we need to reassess the bad assumptions that require analyses of Islamic cultures to be labeled as distinct from the study of Islam.

From where I stand, you cannot study Islam outside of Islamic cultures. I see neither sense nor purchase in distinguishing between two things that are one and the same. And so, I reject a theology-centric definition of Islam, along with all vocabulary distinctions—"Muslim" versus "Islamic" versus "Islamicate"—premised on that bias.[34] Once we take this step of clarifying that studying Islam in history is the study of Islamic cultures, no separate vocabulary being required, and once we poke around a bit in Sanskrit texts, something emerges quite starkly. Sanskrit thinkers working in different times, places, and contexts wrote about Islam in some detail, specifically about Muslim political figures and events.

While Sanskrit thinkers wrote a great deal about Muslims who wielded political power, they rarely wrote about those figures' distinct religious beliefs. Seeking to capture the frequent nonemphasis on religious identities in premodern India, many scholars have attempted to replace the vocabulary of "Muslim" or "Indo-Muslim" with terms centered around ethnicity (e.g., "Indo-Turkic") or, more commonly, literary and ruling culture (e.g., "Persianate"). It is tempting to think that new words alone could give us better ideas, but it is hardly that straightforward. Both "Indo-Turkic" and "Persianate" are clunky terms, bewildering to most nonacademics. Even more opaque, including to scholars who have rarely bothered to theorize such terms, are the various elaborations upon "Persianate" that have proliferated in recent academic writing, including the "Persianate world," "Persianate ecumene," "Persianate cultural zone," "Persianate cosmopolis" (sometimes the "Persian cosmopolis," sans *-ate*) and "Indo-Persianate."[35] Also, neither "Indo-Turkic" nor "Persianate" is broad enough to capture the longue durée of political and intellectual histories that I investigate here. I am interested in how Sanskrit thinkers imagined and wrote about various aspects of the wide-ranging set of historical processes that we now place under the umbrella phrase "Indo-Muslim rule," which included Muslims who were not Turkish and, distinctly, Muslims who did not speak Persian. Even when Sanskrit thinkers used pseudoethnic terms, such as *turuṣka* (Turk), they generally used them to refer to groups of Muslims of various ethnic backgrounds rather than to Turks specifically (see chapter 1). I agree with the general impulse behind trying out alternative vocabulary that might displace "Muslim" as an organizing category, namely because we ought not to presume that religion always mattered most in premodern India. But our phraseological cacophony has often obscured more than it clarified on this front.

Modern scholars should take heart that premodern Sanskrit intellectuals, too, had vocabulary problems when it came to describing Muslim or Indo-Persian or Persianate kings. They used a smorgasbord of terms over the centuries—some of which could mean Muslims generally, others of which referred only to circumscribed groups of Muslim political figures, and all of which had slightly different valences that shifted in each usage. Their terminology included *cāṇḍāla, hammīra, janaṅgama, mausula, mleccha, mudgala, pulinda, saida, śāhi, śaka, śakendra, suratrāṇa, tājika, tāmra,* "turushka," "yavana," and more. Alongside this specific vocabulary that they developed or repurposed, Sanskrit thinkers also identified mleccha or turushka or shahi rulers using more general Sanskrit terms for sovereigns (e.g., *cakravārtin, mahārāja, rāja*). Here I take a similar approach of varied vocabulary. I find, not without a hefty dose of irony, that a trifecta of terms—"Muslim," "Muslim-led," and "Indo-Muslim"—are capacious enough to capture a wide array of political groups perceived by Sanskrit intellectuals as somehow different and worthy of comment as such from 736 CE onward. Each term has unique advantages. "Muslim" is the broadest and most succinct. "Muslim-led" is the most inclusive of non-Muslims who also participated in establishing and shaping a ruling culture that differed from others on the subcontinent. "Indo-Muslim" foregrounds the long-standing integration of Muslim communities into Indian society. None of these terms is good enough, however, and so I use other words as appropriate, especially "Indo-Persian," which indicates the cultural affiliations of many Indo-Muslim dynasties from the 1190s onward. In pursuit of accessibility beyond the ivory tower, I shy away from the scholarly favorite of "Persianate."

Premodern Sanskrit intellectuals never settled on a decisive vocabulary for Muslim rulers, and, even in the seventeenth century, authors were still inventing new terms and changing the meanings of old ones (see chapter 6). These twinned approaches—coining fresh vocabulary and redefining established terms—appear to be our fate in modern scholarship also. Here, I participate in the latter project of expanding and remaking the categories that we already have, especially "Muslim" and "Indo-Muslim," to be elastic enough to cover a broad set of political changes and communities about which premodern Sanskrit intellectuals wrote in remarkable ways.

It is an improbable argument that premodern Sanskrit authors wrote about everything under the sun except history and somehow failed to respond in any way to the seismic set of political, cultural, and social shifts brought on by Indo-Muslim rule. This book aims to overthrow both notions, long criticized but persistent nonetheless in the restrictions they place on our modern capacity to imagine the past. I lay the groundwork for this paradigm shift through the theoretical criticisms I have leveled here. But, going forward, I take a different tack. In the rest of this book, I endeavor to bury these scholarly prejudices under a mountain of textual evidence.

Historical Narrative Without Genre

Relying on genre divisions has led many prior scholars to seek written history in Sanskrit in the wrong places, and so I forgo a genre-specific approach here. Most commonly, modern thinkers have scoured *itihāsa* and *purāṇa* texts for Sanskrit records of the past. Daud Ali, James Fitzgerald, Sheldon Pollock, Romila Thapar, and others have given serious attention to works situated within the itihasa-purana tradition as potential written histories.[36] The term "itihasa" literally means something like "thus it was," and "purana" refers to the ancient past, so perhaps both sound like history at first blush. But, as others have pointed out, the terms are probably better translated, at least much of the time, as "lore" and "myth," respectively.[37] Plenty of scholars may object to those translations (or any single-word translation of these terms) as oversimplified. But the core point stands that itihasa-purana texts generally tell stories about historically unverified and historically unverifiable people and events. Accordingly, in this book, I include no itihasa works and analyze a single *anupurāṇa* ("new purana," Paramananda's *Sūryavaṃśa*; see chapter 6). However, I found no substitute genre that might order the disparate texts collected together here. Many of the histories that occupy my attention in the following pages cite as a model and predecessor the ur-itihasa work, the great epic Mahabharata. Some also cite puranas.[38] But they themselves offer something else: history unbound by genre.

In the absence of genre, I begin with a bare-bones definition of written history, based on what I see in the writings of premodern Sanskrit intellectuals. I consider as history selective narratives about the past, which are more or less true and hold relevance in their present. My focus on narrative is a conscious twist on the boilerplate modern line that history is concerned with change over time.[39] Narrative allows for different types of historical causality, not only those palatable to modern academic sensibilities. Moreover, it allows us to locate history "*inside* the text," rather than by measuring it against our own ideas about proper plot development or facticity.[40] I focus here on Sanskrit texts that feature Muslim political figures, and so the narratives I consider are typically about the formulation of political power and/or the articulation of identities within spaces circumscribed by political authority. Earlier thinkers have linked the production of history and the state, both generally and in India specifically.[41] I share that emphasis on political context while also considering what writing about Indo-Muslim rule meant for nonstate actors. I include only Sanskrit texts, a restriction that allows me to pose some specific questions about premodern India's most extensive literary and intellectual tradition. My broad definition captures several dozen texts, and its flexibility, rather than rigidity, around the edges enables us to glimpse a variegated tradition of writing about the past in descriptive and prescriptive ways that indicate how premodern Sanskrit thinkers thought about the Self and the Other during Indo-Muslim rule.

Because there is no demarcated genre of history writing in Sanskrit, there is no *śāstra* or technical treatise on it, either. Despite claims to encompass all knowable things in the world, many Sanskrit shastras do not match what people did in real life, and so perhaps we are not missing all that much in lacking a theoretical account of how to write history in premodern Sanskrit.[42] To give one example, Sanskrit shastras on architecture vary widely in how closely they relate to how premodern people constructed buildings.[43] Shastras also contain curious omissions of what people did in intellectual practice. For instance, despite an almost unfathomable depth of literary criticism, Sanskrit poets seemingly never articulated the importance of social conventions to grasping Sanskrit poetry.[44] In short, the absence of a reliable shastra, or any shastra, hardly meant the absence of practice.

Premodern Indians wrote Sanskrit histories within a variety of literary genres, including *ākhyāna*, *akhyāyikā*, *charita*, *paṭṭāvalī*, *prabandha*, *praśasti*, *rājāvalī*, *vaṃśāvalī*, *vijaya*, *vṛtta*, and, perhaps most importantly, *kāvya*. Other have analyzed individual texts as kavya, as prabandha, and so forth, and those analyses have proved fruitful to pursuing questions about literary styles, Jain religious narratives, and more. I cite such studies throughout this book. But, from where I stand, genre is not a useful leading interpretive lens, because there is no single Sanskrit genre that allows me to group together Sanskrit histories of Muslim-led rule. My claim that certain Sanskrit texts are histories is not exclusive; they are many other things, also. But considering them as histories allows us to do things with these works and talk about them in ways that we have not done so previously.

Sanskrit histories of Indo-Muslim rule constitute a fragmented tradition, meaning that the authors did not generally build upon or even read one another. Within regional branches of this tradition, things were more connected. For instance, the later Kashmiri rajatarangini authors modeled their works on earlier text(s) of the same title (chapter 4). Gujarati prabandha authors sometimes read each other's compositions (chapters 4 and 5). But, overwhelmingly, I have little evidence that the premodern intellectuals who fill the pages of this book even knew about prior Sanskrit histories of Indo-Muslim rule. Some cite earlier political narratives about non-Muslim rulers, most commonly the Mahabharata (mentioned above) and Kalidasa's *Raghuvaṃśa* (Raghu's lineage; ca. fifth century), another foundational text of Sanskrit literature. It remains an open question whether Sanskrit history writing, in general, was boosted by the rise of Indo-Persian rule. But, at the very least, instead of disrupting Sanskrit interest in writing about the past or continuing a preexisting "willful amnesia" regarding political facts, as some scholars have suggested, Indo-Muslim rule provided creative fodder for numerous Sanskrit thinkers who elected to write about instantiations of Indo-Muslim power.[45] That Sanskrit intellectuals kept reinventing this wheel underscores their deep and abiding interest, across time and space, in writing about political events, including of the Indo-Muslim variety. In so doing, premodern intellectuals judged Sanskrit literature, time and time again, as appropriate and efficacious for commenting on real-world political developments.

Premodern Indian historians chose to write about political reality against the backdrop of possibly the most extensive set of myths in existence, waiting to be retold. A premodern Sanskrit poet could always rework Krishna stories, or craft another Ramayana, or invent a tale entirely.[46] And many did these things, including several of the poet-historians that I discuss in this book. In the texts that occupy my attention here, premodern thinkers focus on historically verifiable events as something meaningful to write about in their presents. In so doing, they evince a "historical consciousness."[47] Like modern historians, premoderns were selective in their narratives, only sharing details as relevant to their interests in a given text. Contrary to the mistaken views of even some sophisticated thinkers, historians, be they modern or premodern, do not seek "to bare the past completely."[48] For our part, we—similar to our premodern counterparts—focus a given narrative in a book, a journal article, or, increasingly, a Twitter thread according to a set of criteria depending on what we want to know and thereby leave out many (we think) irrelevant details. Sometimes, premodern Sanskrit thinkers seem less interested in brute accuracy and more interested in twisting the facts, a trend in premodern historical traditions across the world. Still, Sanskrit historians evince (to varying degrees, admittedly) "interest in facts,"[49] which distinguishes their historical narratives, in my modern eyes, from premodern Sanskrit mythology.

Modern distinctions notwithstanding, one wonders: What, if anything, did premodern Indian intellectuals think was different about focusing on historical events, versus writing solely about myths? To put the question a nonbinary way: When premodern Indians wrote Indo-Muslim histories in Sanskrit, what did they intend to do? I think there are as many answers to that question as there are premodern Sanskrit-language historians. Even after completing this book project, I feel quite dubious about my ability to use written texts in order to discern the internal thought processes of intellectuals who lived hundreds of years ago in social, political, and cultural contexts that differ radically not only from my own but also from those inhabited by any modern.[50] And so, I focus here on what is far more knowable, namely the historical texts that premodern Sanskrit intellectuals composed, complete with their delightfully varied visions of causality, Indo-Muslim rule, and change over time.

Embracing the Poetry of History

Sanskrit narratives of Indo-Muslim rule are fully histories and fully poetry, in a way that does not mesh with the modern tendency to distinguish the two. One might argue that the Western desire to separate historical from poetic ways of writing goes far back, to the likes of Aristotle, who wrote that the major difference between the genres was scale, with poetry being about universals whereas history is mired in specifics.[51] But such a division was quite foreign to premodern India. Rather, the prevailing view was that poetry was how you wrote political history. Shrivara, one of the authors I discuss in this book, expresses this view with a rhetorical question:

> On this earth that is plagued by anarchy and dark with constant turmoil,
> who can shed light on the things of the past without the light of poetry?[52]

Practically speaking, the overwhelming majority of premodern Sanskrit texts, across topics and genres, are in metered verse. This includes most of the political histories I discuss here, with a few prose works and one *campū* (a mixture of prose and verse) thrown into the mix. But the Sanskrit history-poetry nexus extends far beyond counting long and short syllables. Sanskrit historians drank liberally from the well of literary conventions when crafting narratives of political events. In so doing, they wrote history *as* poetry.

I reject the notion that literary conventions necessarily compromise representing reality, because Sanskrit historians expressed confluence, not conflict, between the literary and representational aspects of writing about the past. If we dig into colonial-era writings, there are some real doozies on this subject. For instance, William Taylor wrote, in 1857: "From the prevalence of poetry in Hindu composition, the simplicity of truth is almost always disguised. The painful result is that the Hindu mind has become familiarized with lying. Truth is insipid. Evidence loses its force."[53] Taylor grounded his bigotry in what passed for science in his day, referring a few lines later to the inferior "phrenological construction of the Hindu skull." Or to summarize Hegel, who put it a bit more obscurely in his *Philosophy of History*, Hindus are inclined by spirit to Ideality, which "makes them incapable of writing history."[54] Hopefully everyone today rejects the racist, Indians-are-less-than-Europeans dimensions of these statements. But many people still think that poetry and fact necessarily conflict.[55] To overcome the presumed clash between literature and historical writing, we first need a clear-eyed view of the work this false dichotomy does for us.

The pretend literature-history division allows modern scholars to deny the ongoing importance of narrative and conventions within modern history writing and so makes what we write, in the twenty-first century, seem more objective, even scientific. To quote Hayden White on this fallacy: "History as a discipline is in bad shape today because it has lost sight of its origins in the literary imagination. In the interest of *appearing* scientific and objective, it has repressed and denied to itself its own greatest source of strength and renewal."[56] In the aftermath of White's formidable scholarship, most historians, when pressed, will admit their own subjectivity and the importance of narrative, and of some literary pizzazz to keep it readable. This interpretation of White does not capture the full sophistication of his analyses and their range of implications for the practice and ethics of history.[57] But, even this more basic reading of White's argument—namely, that historians should pay attention to narrative—arguably did not pierce historical thinking as deeply as we sometimes imagine it did. As Gabrielle Spiegel has noted, in the two decades after the publication of White's seminal *Metahistory* (1973), most historians declined to read the book beyond its introduction and conclusion.[58]

I think many historians, even today, prefer not to delve too deeply into the critical role that narrative plays in our craft, out of fear that it will prove destabilizing to claims about the veracity of our scholarship. Some reasons for this hesitancy are rather understandable. Most notably from where I sit, the history-is-somewhat-subjective thesis is often inappropriately weaponized to proclaim political rewritings of the past as equal to evidence-based arguments about the past (and those two are decidedly unequal).[59] In the epilogue, I return to this subject and lay out at greater length why embracing narrative and tropes as core parts of the historian's craft might actually help our ongoing quest to tell more insightful, accurate stories about the past. Here I am more interested in naming our modern anxieties so that we might set them aside in pursuit of analyzing premodern histories and premodern anxieties.

The strong presence of literary conventions and tropes in premodern Sanskrit histories means that we need a fine-tuned set of literary-critical tools for reading these works. Sometimes, novelty was a subtle art in premodern Sanskrit, and we must be attuned to precise words and turns of phrase as well as their specific contextual uses in order to see innovation. Authors also expressed historical specificity through tropes. However, many modern thinkers have seen incompatibility rather than confluence between tropes and history. As Brajadulal Chattopadhyaya, who wrote an insightful succinct book on Sanskrit views on Muslims, put it: "What was accommodated within available concepts, conventions and vocabularies, can hardly be taken as a statement made for the communication of historical reality."[60] I disagree. After all, Sanskrit boasts arguably the most extensive collection of conventions and tropes in literary history. And so, readers, premodern and modern like, could and should always ask why a poet is employing *this* trope as opposed to his myriad of other options.[61] Ultimately, the proof is in the pudding. Conventions run throughout the histories I analyze in this book, and I invite readers to judge for themselves the limits and virtues of my attempt to recover historical specificity expressed through literary tropes.

Sanskrit histories invite us to perceive more crisply the literary aspects of written histories in other linguistic traditions, chief among them Indo-Persian works. Indo-Persian texts constitute the main archive used by modern historians to reconstruct the history of Muslim-led rule in India and the views of those who enacted and lived through it. I do not seek to change the dominance of Indo-Persian sources for the hard political history of India circa 1200–1720, although I do intend to press on how scholars sometimes use these texts. Others have pointed out the varying accuracy of specific Indo-Persian chronicles.[62] Arguably this point has not gotten through to a lot of scholars who still cite Abul Fazl, Firishta, and others as if they always wrote the truth. It remains a bad assumption that, for the second millennium CE, Persian histories are always more reliable than Sanskrit ones.[63] But Sanskrit historical sources prompt a more precise and sorely needed argument that premodern Indo-Persian histories are literature too, both in their poetry and in their prose. Translators of an earlier generation sometimes cut out parts of Indo-Persian histories that they deemed irrelevant, including mythological sections and poetry, in order to make these works appear more factual to modern eyes.[64] These changes blatantly misrepresent the Indo-Persian tradition of historical writing, and they have conditioned generations of scholars to be less attuned than they ought to be to poetic features of Indo-Persian chronicles. For those who work with Indo-Persian archives, this book can provide some ideas about how to more effectively analyze, rather than sweep under the rug, literary features of their premodern historical materials.

Elite Diversity

Sanskrit histories of Indo-Muslim rule embody considerable geographic, political, and religious diversity. The authors hailed from all corners of the Indian subcontinent, from Kashmir to Tamil Nadu and from Gujarat to Bengal. They worked across nearly as broad an area (for the exception of Bengal, see the epilogue). Many texts were written by court poets, working for Muslim and Hindu kings; the works' writers and patrons also include merchants, religious leaders, and other nonimperial actors. Both Brahmins and Jains number among the authors. Brahmins get plenty of attention in contemporary Sanskrit scholarship, but Jains are often relegated to footnotes, literally. More than one scholar has repeated and so entrenched a Brahmin-centric view of the premodern Sanskrit tradition in which Jains are presented as interlopers rather than full participants.[65] By putting Jains and Brahmins on equal footing, I make a small contribution to the larger project of calling out and undermining Brahminical claims to define Sanskrit intellectual production, an issue that contemporary Sanskrit studies has not left in the past.[66]

While Sanskrit histories of Indo-Muslim rule are diverse in some ways, their authors were elite in terms of language, gender, and social status. These poet-historians all wrote in Sanskrit or (in a few cases) Prakrit, a set of Sanskrit-adjacent literary mediums, languages unknown to the vast majority of Indians, past and present. The authors were nearly all men. A sole historical text considered here was authored by a woman (Gangadevi's *Madhurāvijaya*), a small bit of diversity that, while important, points up the overarching gender exclusion that defined premodern Sanskrit textual production. The authors were often high caste, and, following the tight link between gender and caste, many express extreme levels of misogyny and casteism in their histories.[67] They are unapologetic about all of this. Exclusivity and privilege structured premodern Sanskrit intellectual culture and the social spheres in which it operated, which in turn informed what people chose to say in Sanskrit.

Again, I will give away something of my findings: elite authors often express harsh, elite ideas. I present these below in an unvarnished manner and attempt to contextualize premodern views, no matter how distasteful and bigoted we may find them today. Brahminical privilege is one notion to which I return several times, because it was a borderline obsession among several authors (e.g., Jayanaka, Jonaraja, and several writers working for Rajput and Maratha courts). We also see recurrent attention given to Kshatriya kingship, a flexible institution that rulers and intellectuals defined in many different ways. Being a Kshatriya ruler was, for most thinkers, a *varṇa* distinction and typically involved certain kinds of relations with Brahmins. But, for numerous premodern Sanskrit thinkers, the advent and expansion of Indo-Muslim rule provided new foils for thinking about what it could mean to be a Kshatriya king or warrior. Some of the results were stunning. For instance, writing in the fifteenth century, Nayachandra upholds a Muslim Mongol, somebody outside of the varna system, as an exemplar of Kshatriya heroism (chapter 3). Writing in the sixteenth century, Chandrashekhara lauds as an ideal Kshatriya king a man who neither ruled nor fought (chapter 6). There remained more traditional views as well, such as Paramananda's seventeenth-century vision of a Kshatriya ruler who took every conceivable action to assist Brahmins (chapter 6). Arguably, though, even Paramananda was innovative in his historical context, since the Kshatriya ruler in question was widely believed to have been born a Shudra. Instead of Kshatriya kingship, some thinkers reworked other kinds of local and sectarian identities in the context of Indo-Muslim rule, sometimes through contrast and other times through likening. Over time, Sanskrit poet-historians made a general move away from seeing Muslim political figures as Other, although the trajectory approximates a windy path more than a smooth arc. In short, within their elite diversity, India's traditional learned men cultivated a rather astonishing number of ways to write about Indo-Muslim political history and the key figures therein, and to articulate the relevance of this past for their communities.

I did not set out looking for diversity, even elite diversity, in this book project, and so I think it is worth reflecting briefly on how I found it. I articulated a different set of questions than most modern Sanskritists. In recent and ongoing research, a few other modern Sanskrit scholars have similarly highlighted alternative and minority voices precisely through formulating their research questions in innovative ways.[68] There is a lesson here about the need to expand the topics that we study in modern Western Indology as a way to see underappreciated aspects of the premodern Sanskrit tradition. But there is another issue, too, which is that by being a woman I stand apart from most modern Sanskritists. As Anand Venkatkrishnan described the field's jaw-dropping lack of gender representation in 2019, "If you encounter Sanskrit scholarship in America, you're likely to find it littered with men, a patriarchal lineage rivaling that of any Sanskrit epic."[69] Writing in 2018 and positioned outside the field, Karla Mallette called out the inexcusable dominance of male authors, who constituted over 90 percent of authors in a 2014 edited volume on Sanskrit literature. She noted, powerfully, that the erasure of female agency in modern times mirrored its premodern counterpart in Sanskrit erotic poetry: "Women are there, yet they are not actors. Perhaps this is not striking given the fact that the majority of the texts discussed in the book were premodern. But even the scholars who contribute to the [2014] book are men."[70] Homogeneity rarely provides fertile ground for creativity. And so, perhaps, our failure to see different viewpoints in premodern Sanskrit begins at home, in our failure to value and embody meaningful diversity in our modern field of study.

Not Writing About Hindu-Muslim Conflict

Sanskrit thinkers wrote about both the political violence and cross-cultural relations associated with Indo-Muslim kings. These two aspects are correlated, since the advent and expansion of Indo-Muslim rule, achieved in large part through force, created social and cultural conditions that allowed for exchanges across literary, linguistic, religious, and cultural lines. But the violence, in particular, sits ill with many people today. Especially striking to modern eyes are accounts of total annihilation, where one political dynasty destroyed another, which pop up several times during the first few centuries in which Sanskrit thinkers wrote about Muslim-led polities, roughly 1190 through 1420. Speaking of fourteenth-century poetry concerning political violence enacted by Indo-Muslim polities in southern India, Ajay Rao wrote, "[These violent narratives] are painful to read, sometimes depicting violence in graphic detail, and are filled with images that may lead many of us to avert our eyes."[71] Some historians, such as Taymiya Zaman, are doing important, innovative work that investigates and wrestles with modern emotions about the past.[72] Elsewhere I have confronted and reflected upon my own encounters with the emotionally charged rants and violent threats of those who promote the hateful ideology of

Hindutva.[73] I offer something a tad more conventional here, which is a non-injury-based framework that empowers us to interpret premodern narratives of political violence on their own terms rather than through a contemporary emotive lens.

For those who are interested in understanding what Sanskrit historical narratives of violence meant for those who crafted and read them in premodernity, Sanskrit literary norms of depicting bloodshed serve as our bedrock. Premodern Sanskrit poets and readers shared a nearly insatiable appetite for gore. They relished images of ghosts traversing battlefields crisscrossed by rivers of human blood, animals feasting on the entrails of the newly dead, decapitated bodies spurting blood as they staggered about tripping over fallen corpses, and the like. Such repulsive imagery was poetry in premodern Sanskrit, theorized under the aesthetic emotions of fear (*bhaya*), the macabre (*bībhatsa*), and revulsion (*jugupsā*).[74] Also, the ability to enact gratuitous carnage demonstrated political authority. In many cases, Sanskrit depictions of Muslim-enacted political violence also reflected reality. After all, when Muslim would-be rulers showed up on the subcontinent, they proved no exception to the general rule that premodern Indian politics was a bloody affair. That said, those primed to find Muslim-enacted atrocities in India's past (generally as a doomed attempt to justify their unjustifiable hatred of Muslims in India's present) should note that material evidence furnishes a mixed picture of Hindu-Muslim interaction and exchange, even in the early days of Indo-Muslim rule.[75] Sanskrit texts give us only one perspective in hard-history terms. More relevant to my purposes here is that, in textualized accounts of violence, Sanskrit intellectuals treated Muslim political figures no differently than other sorts of subcontinental political actors. As I discuss further in chapter 3, Sanskrit thinkers used violent imagery to integrate Muslim political figures within traditional Sanskrit ways of expressing political power, including through showcasing martial strength.

While Sanskrit thinkers wrote a lot about violence, it was not the communal violence of Hindutva extremists attacking Muslims that plagues India today. It is unclear that the Hindu-Muslim binary was operative—or that both of its constituent parts even existed—for much of the second millennium CE. As many scholars have pointed out, "Hindu" is a Perso-Arabic term, not a Sanskrit word, and its premodern uses often refer to residents of India ("Indians," in modern terminology).[76] The earliest usage of "Hindu" in Sanskrit dates to the mid-fourteenth century, more than six hundred years after the earliest Sanskrit texts and inscriptions that mention Muslims. Even after the 1350s, "Hindu" was more commonly used by Muslims writing in Persian rather than by anybody—Brahmin, Kshatriya, Rajput, Jain, etc.—writing in Sanskrit. Muslims, too, identified themselves and were described by Sanskrit intellectuals according to terms and norms that were often based on culture, region, and even pseudoethnicity rather than religion. Richard Eaton has argued, rather persuasively, that we ought to understand Indo-Muslim rulers as participants in Persianate culture, which was grounded in a prestige language and model of political power rather than religion.[77] I concur, even if I choose to subsume that, in terms of vocabulary, within a broad category of Muslim-led rule (as detailed above).

The Hindu-Muslim binary assumes the primacy of religious identities, which is arguably inaccurate in many instances in modernity and certainly so in premodernity. In short, to talk about Hindu-Muslim violence in premodern India is anachronism. As Eric Hobsbawm reminds us, "The most usual ideological abuse of history is based on anachronism rather than lies."[78] Sometimes I think that term, "anachronism," cloaks in scholarly language the fear, oppression, and violence fueled by crudely misreading the past through the lens of the present. There are serious stakes, in terms of human livelihoods and lives, in current politico-ideological abuses of premodern Indian history. Historians ought to call out the factual paucity of Hindutva narratives that insert Hindu-Muslim conflict into India's past, and some of us do so regularly.[79] Here, I advance a parallel project of cultivating alternative, historically grounded frameworks to the modern categories of "Hindu" and "Muslim" that might serve us better for making sense of conflicts and narratives thereof in premodern India and also might add nuance to those modern categories.

Vernaculars and Sanskrit

The vernacular swims in the background throughout this book, and I endeavor to bring it out at key points as a crucial context for Sanskrit narratives of Indo-Muslim rule. I take to heart Francesca Orsini's argument: "We need to remember that even texts in High languages were written by people who were still part of the vernacular world."[80] Sanskrit thinkers were aware of and engaged with Persian, which doubled as a vernacular and a high literary language for many Indo-Muslim dynasties, and the panoply of Indian vernaculars (and registers within individual vernaculars). Early on, writers such as Jayanaka and Gangadevi identified Persian as a major point of difference that marked Muslim-led dynasties as Other and rendered Muslims incapable of expressing poetry or, relatedly, proper political power. Later Sanskrit intellectuals tended to see more syncretic, even dynamic possibilities between Persian and Sanskrit. For instance, in the seventeenth century, somebody translated the Persian *Akbarnāma* into Sanskrit; and in the eighteenth century, Lakshmipati used hundreds of Persian words in Sanskrit, sometimes to compelling poetic effects (see chapter 7). Indian vernaculars come up more sparingly in Sanskrit histories at first, especially in narratives penned in northern India, where literary vernaculars emerged later than in the south. In southern India and in later centuries across the subcontinent, Sanskrit poet-historians sometimes expressed that they faced a real choice regarding whether to pen history in Sanskrit or a vernacular. Yet, all the poets I discuss here decided to write in a cosmopolitan literary language that could speak across time and space in South Asia, even as many texts were directed to quite local audiences. Among other things that I aim for in the pages that follow is to uncover the agency and meaning behind the choice to write about Indo-Muslim rule in Sanskrit.

Sanskrit thinkers wrote about Muslims for over a thousand years, and they wrote about Muslim-led rule for slightly more than five hundred years. I cover this time span largely chronologically, with some topical organization for later centuries. I speak most commonly about full-length texts, but I supplement with inscriptions, especially for earlier periods, when our textual sources are sometimes lean. I begin, in chapter 1, with Sanskrit mentions of Muslims before Indo-Persian rule existed on the subcontinent. This chapter centers around two distinct types of materials: Sanskrit inscriptions sponsored by western Indian kings circa 736–1190 and Kalachakra Buddhist texts circa 1025–1040. The two sources have little in common, and collectively they attest that, even early on, Sanskrit thinkers cultivated multiple contexts and ways of writing about Muslims, especially Muslims who sought political power. Such diversity proved definitional to the Sanskrit tradition of historical writing on Muslim-led rule, which began in earnest in the 1190s. I devote chapter 2 to the earliest Sanskrit work that details Muslim political activities on the subcontinent in any detail: Jayanaka's *Pṛthvīrājavijaya* (Victory of Prithviraj Chauhan). In the work, Jayanaka marks the Ghurids as irremediably and hazardously alien within a

Chauhan-protected Brahminical ritual and social order. In the wider Sanskrit historical tradition, Jayanaka represents one extreme pole in his excoriating condemnation of the Ghurid political presence in and around former Chauhan territory. Subsequent authors took a range of different views, up to and including full acceptance of Indo-Persian political power as a game changer for Kshatriya kingship. Chapter 3 analyzes two texts, and a handful of inscriptions, written between 1200 and 1450 CE. During this period, Sanskrit intellectuals explored how Indo-Muslim figures might fit within and alter Indian kingship, an already variegated and elastic tradition. Chapter 3 also includes the sole text authored by a woman that features in these pages: Gangadevi's *Madhurāvijaya*.

Chapter 4 charts two regional incarnations of the Sanskrit historical imagination, in fourteenth-century Gujarat and fifteenth-century Kashmir, respectively. I investigate how writers used a cosmopolitan literary tradition, expressed in prabandhas and rajataranginis, respectively, to speak to local concerns. This chapter also addresses Kalhana's *Rājataraṅgiṇī* (River of kings, 1149), easily the most well-known text that I discuss in the book. Crucially, I treat Kalhana's chronicle not as an unparalleled work of hard history but rather as part of a larger tradition of Sanskrit literary histories. Chapter 5 concentrates on Jain-authored histories of Jain monks' experiences at the courts of Akbar and Jahangir. This body of works arguably constitutes the most intense proliferation of historical energy in premodern Sanskrit. The texts themselves continued to be written into the late seventeenth century, decades after continuous Mughal relations with Jain monks had ceased in the late 1610s. I argue that Jain authors working within specific sects wrote about the Mughals, not as an Other, but rather as a model for themselves.

Chapter 6 looks at sixteenth- and seventeenth-century texts that emerged from Rajput and Maratha courts. I focus here on how different authors articulated claims to Kshatriya kingship on behalf of rulers who operated in a political world dominated by Indo-Persian dynasties. Among other figures I discuss is Shivaji, a Maratha Bhonsle leader who seems to grow in importance and controversy every year in twenty-first-century India. The Shivaji who features in these pages, seen through the eyes of Sanskrit historians of his era and shortly thereafter, will likely appear unfamiliar to many readers. One value of touring premodern Indian ways of seeing the world is precisely seeing old characters through fresh lenses and thereby expanding our knowledge of historical figures and how popular imaginations thereof have changed over time. Chapter 7 explores how Sanskrit writers working between 1589 and 1721 narrated Mughal political history, a subject more commonly found in Persian-language texts. I investigate four texts, which cluster around the beginning and end of the Mughal Empire and which collectively constitute the final incarnation of Sanskrit historical writing that I consider in this book. I emphasize how Sanskrit authors incorporated the topics, approaches, and even styles of Perso-Islamic historiography into the already incredibly rich universe of Sanskrit literature. I conclude chapter 7 by discussing the larger political and literary trends that brought a close to the remarkably fertile tradition of Sanskrit historical writing on Indo-Muslim rule.

The epilogue draws out some wider implications of my arguments and outlines some promising starting points for future scholarship. I address here the exception of Bengal, a region from which a few poets who feature in these pages hailed but that did not, as a region, witness the production of Sanskrit histories of Indo-Muslim rule. I end where I began: in the present day. I bring out some of the challenges and promises of these premodern materials for modern thinkers interested in how we narrate the past and how we might further diversify the modern discipline of history.

Throughout the book, I prioritize analyzing historical narratives, rather than extracting political history from these works. I indicate some points where other thinkers, asking different questions, might come along and use certain texts in pursuit of political facts and other historical questions.[81] But I am most interested in the stories themselves, why they were told, what purposes they served, and what identities they helped to formulate. Premodern Sanskrit narratives on Indo-Muslim rule mattered in a wide variety of ways for the people who wrote and read them. I also think that they hold relevance for us today, by stretching our historical and conceptual imaginations far beyond the restrictive parameters of modernity.

CHAPTER I

Before Indo-Persian Rule

Many Sanskrit Ways to Write About Muslims

When we reject the single story, when we realize that there is never a single story about any place, we regain a kind of paradise.

—CHIMAMANDA NGOZI ADICHIE, 2009 TED TALK

Muslims appear in Sanskrit inscriptions beginning in the early eighth century CE, nearly half a millennium before the establishment of Indo-Persian rule based in Delhi. Before the late twelfth century, Muslims entered India through two major paths and for two, rather distinct, reasons. By 700, Arab and Turkish Muslims traded in parts of India, probably following sea routes that accompanied the better-known, land-based Silk Routes. By 1000, if not earlier, some of these traders had built small communities along the Malabar and Konkan Coasts, which line the southwest of the Indian subcontinent.[1] Separately, traveling by land from Central Asia, some Muslims raided Hindu, Jain, and Buddhist temples in northern and northwestern India.[2] Such raids occurred periodically from the late tenth century onward and aimed primarily to extract wealth from temples, which served, among other functions, as banks in ancient India. Before 1192, Muslims did not exercise political power over any part of India aside from Sindh, in the northwest, which was under Arab-led rule starting in 711.[3] Elsewhere in India, a handful of Muslims participated in Hindu-led governments starting in the late first millennium.[4] Still, Muslims were a severe minority in pockets of India and unknown across large swathes of the subcontinent before the 1190s. With the exception of Sindh, Indo-Muslim rule did not yet exist, and, with no exceptions, Indo-Persian rule did not exist.

During this initial five hundred years in which Muslims entered the Indian subcontinent, roughly the late seventh century until the late twelfth century, they appear somewhat infrequently in Sanskrit inscriptions and texts. The relevant materials largely fall into two groups that targeted starkly different audiences and showcase radically different ways of defining these newcomers to India. Muslims are mentioned in numerous public encomia written for kings of western India that stretch across more than a four-hundred-year span. These stray remarks labeled groups of Muslims as outsiders, often as a military threat, although generally without detailing precise markers of difference. On the other hand, a small but robust collection of esoteric Buddhist materials known as the Kalachakra tradition furnishes substantive commentary on Muslim religious practices and beliefs. These eleventh-century Buddhist works took a largely unique approach in the history of Sanskrit literature by conceptualizing Muslims (or, at least, one group of Muslims) as a religious community and detailing their theological precepts. The two sets of materials had dissimilar purposes, outlooks, and circulations. In fact, they have little in common, except that both are written in Sanskrit and both talk about Muslims. Their divergence from each other exemplifies a theme that recurs throughout this book, namely the diversity of Sanskrit materials on Muslim-led incursions and rule. The plurality of this tradition of historical writing, even in its nascent stages, is further underscored by a single pre-1190 Jain and a single pre-1190 Brahmin textual reference to Muslims, respectively, that come into my discussion below. Even before the advent of Indo-Persian rule, there was no single Sanskrit way of writing about Muslim communities.

Undefined Muslims in Sanskrit Inscriptions Circa 736 to 1000 CE

Between 700 and 1000 CE, roughly the first three hundred years during which Muslim people lived in and traveled to India, they appear sparingly in Sanskrit sources. By my count, there are seven known Sanskrit inscriptions before 1000 that mention historical encounters with Muslims, and they are mostly thin on content.[5] Five of the inscriptions allude briefly to groups of Muslims and give no additional information, and the remaining two are hardly extensive.[6] The inscriptions are limited geographically—with one exception—to a band stretching from the northwest down along the western coast, halting in central India.[7] They feature only a handful of dynasties, namely the Gurjara-Pratiharas, Gujarati Chaulukyas, and Rashtrakutas.[8] A few Sanskrit texts mention Muslims in this early period, but they generally lack historical context and are also terse. The limited evidence available indicates that, in the later centuries of the first millennium, Sanskrit intellectuals recognized and wrote about specific groups of Muslims, mostly in governance contexts and as foes on the frontlines of battle, but they showed limited interest in the cultural, much less religious, practices of these new communities.

Between roughly 700 and 1000, Sanskrit thinkers referred to groups of Muslims most commonly with vague ethnonyms, especially *turuṣka* and *tājika*. The earliest known Sanskrit uses of "turushka" and "tajika" date to the seventh century and eighth century CE, respectively.[9] Sanskrit intellectuals adapted both terms from other languages, "turushka" probably from Altaic *turuk* and "tajika" from Pahlavi *tāzīg*.[10] Based on usages in their original languages, one might guess that "turushka" refers to Turks and

TABLE 1.1
Sanskrit inscriptions before 1000 CE that mention historical encounters with Muslims

Date	Location where found	Description / modern title
736	Bharuch district, Gujarat	Kavi plate
738	unknown	Navsari plate
ca. 750–800	Hund, Attock District	Fragmentary Hund inscription
795	northwest	Pratihara Vatsaraja inscription
ca. 800s–early 900s	near Gwalior	Gwalior inscription of the Pratihara ruler Bhoja
926	Chinchani, Thane district, Maharashtra	Chinchani Rashtrakuta grant
ca. mid-900s	Chinchani, Thane district, Maharashtra	Chinchani plate of the Rashtrakuta ruler Krishna II

"tajika" to Arabs. Indeed, even hundreds of years later, Persian and Arabic sources treated Turks and Tajiks as distinct ethnic groups.[11] But both "turushka" and "tajika" (and the variants *tājiya* and *tāyika*) appear to have typically described Muslim groups more generally in Sanskrit inscriptions.[12] Most often, the terms denoted otherwise undelineated military adversaries, sometimes referred to as "the Turks" or "the Tajikas" and other times, for example, as "the tajika army."[13] The wide ethnic range of these words perhaps accurately reflected the ethnic heterogeneity of many Muslim-led military forces in the early centuries of Islam.[14]

Although we lack a good sense of the precise contours of "tajika" and "turushka" in early inscriptions and how their valences may have changed over time, we can say this: Indian intellectuals introduced new Sanskrit terms for Muslim groups. Sanskrit has no dearth of words for foreigners and outsiders, some of which became repurposed as standard Sanskrit words for Muslims (e.g., *yavana*, *mleccha*). For instance, the *Pṛthvīrājavijaya* (Victory of Prithviraj Chauhan; ca. 1191–1200), which I discuss in the following chapter, used more than a dozen known Sanskrit words to describe the Ghurids. Such a wide range of inbuilt options makes it all the more remarkable that, during the early centuries of Muslims arriving on the Indian subcontinent, authors coined the terms "turushka" and "tajika" to describe the new arrivals. Rather than draw exclusively on their own tradition's deep vocabulary, Sanskrit intellectuals borrowed from other languages—an activity often frowned upon in Sanskrit intellectual discourse—to characterize groups of Muslims. In so doing, they created new Sanskrit words. This innovation suggests recognition, within the Sanskrit tradition, of some novelty embodied by Muslim communities on the subcontinent, although the precise nature of that perceived novelty is difficult to reconstruct.

While the Sanskrit terms "tajika" and "turushka" share much in common, their fates within Sanskrit discourse diverged after 1000 and hint at some of the later possibilities for how Sanskrit intellectuals thought and wrote about Muslims. Use of "tajika" for Muslims tapered off in Sanskrit after the eleventh century as other words took over.[15] After 1100, "tajika" usually indicates a specific branch of Sanskrit astrology that borrowed heavily from Persian and Arabic sources.[16] In contrast, "turushka" remained a common Sanskrit descriptor for Muslims, whether of Turkish descent or otherwise, through the early modern period and appears in many poetic, historical, and pseudohistorical texts.[17] The meaning of "turushka" hardly remained immutable, however, and the term is occasionally used for non-Muslims, also. Early on, the *Amarakośa* (ca. sixth–eighth centuries CE) mentions turushkas when discussing a type of incense, and it is not clear whether they are Muslim.[18] Half a millennium later, in the mid-twelfth century, Kalhana uses "turushka" to refer to both Muslim and non-Muslim Turks (see chapter 4).

Early Sanskrit inscriptions treated Muslims variably as military foes, allies, and subsidiary rulers but generally portrayed them as no different from other Indian political actors. Numerous inscriptions mention tajika and turushka armed threats alongside other rivals. For instance, a circa 900 inscription of the Pratihara king Bhoja, found near Gwalior, lists the turushkas among other rulers whose hill forts had been seized by Nagabhata II.[19] A 795 inscription from northwest India lauds, in the same verse, the victory of Shrivarmaka, who ruled under the Pratihara king Vatsaraja, over the tajikas and the Tomaras.[20] The inscription refers to the "lord of tajikas" (*tājikeśa*) and saw no need to explain this new type of sovereign. Other inscriptions list Muslim kings as having recognized the authority of a specific local ruler. For example, a circa 950 Rashtrakuta grant found in Maharashtra advertises that many bowed to Krishna II, including tajikas: "The Pandyas, Odras, Simhalas, Cholas, Persians [*pārasīka*], Ruler of Andhra, Dravidas, Varvaras, Tajikas, Vankinas, Hunas, Khasas, Gurjaras, and those in Malwa bowed to the lotus-like feet of [Krishna II]."[21] This list features rulers from a wide range of territory across and slightly beyond the subcontinent, including the Sinhalas in Ceylon (south), the Odras in Orissa (east), and the Khasas in Kashmir/Nepal (north/northeast). Perhaps tajikas are included to refer to northwest regions, notably without any need to further gloss or contextualize their status as rulers alongside more established Indian lineages, such as the Cholas and Gurjaras. Similarly, more than a century later, a Maharashtrian inscription described an individual as a tajika and a king (*nṛpati*).[22] In short, Sanskrit intellectuals treated Muslims as a new part of the medieval Indian landscape that merited inclusion but no special comment.

Especially when describing military adversaries who were Muslim, Sanskrit intellectuals drew on the rich imagery of their inherited tradition. For example, the 736 Kavi plate from Bharuch—the earliest Sanskrit source that mentions a historical encounter with Muslims—fancies the Gurjara king Jayabhata IV as a rain cloud extinguishing the fire that is the tajikas at Valabhi:

> In the city of Valabhi's ruler, Jayabhata wields his sword forcibly,
> like a raincloud unleashes destructive torrents of water,
> and thereby he extinguishes the tajjika fire that scorches the earth.[23]

The 738 Navsari plate is especially robust in poetic conventions and contains several long compounds that describe "the tajika army" (*tājikānīka*) as it was defeated by the Gujarati Chaulukyas in the 730s. For instance:

> The [tajika army] vomited forth arrows, maces, and other weapons. With glittering swords, they shredded the lofty kings of Sindh, Kacchella, Saurashtra, the Chavotakas, the Mauryas, Gurjaras, and others. They wanted to enter into southern India in order to conquer all southern rulers, and first they approached Navasarika. They darkened the sky with dust thrown up by the pounding hooves of their galloping horses. Their bodies were disfigured and their armor reddened by gushing blood from their entrails that spilled out of holes in their large stomachs as they rushed into battle and were ripped apart by spears . . . [24]

The grotesque imagery of the inscription continues (see appendix A.1 for a translation), culminating in the tajika troops' defeat at the hands of Pulakeshiraja: "When the tajika army was vanquished in battle [by Pulakeshiraja], their headless trunks began to dance in a circle while loud drums were struck repeatedly, seeming to rejoice at the thought that [the tajikas] had finally repaid their debt to their master [*svāmi*] at the price of their own heads."[25] The Navsari plate goes on to say that after defeating the tajikas, the Chaulukyan ruler Pulakeshiraja was honored with four titles, the final of which is "Repeller of the Unrepellable."[26] Steeped as we are in the contemporary rhetoric and reality of Hindutva-initiated violence against Muslims, moderns are liable to misread such vivid images of nearly undefeatable enemies' headless corpses dancing around blood-soaked battlefields and entrails spilling out of sliced-open stomachs as suggesting that early Indian clashes with Arabs were notably violent. On the contrary, such gory descriptions are standard, even generic, in Sanskrit literature on war.[27] It marks perceived similarity, not difference, when early inscriptions depict the tajikas as a formidable force in battle.

Only one pre-1000 Sanskrit inscription names a specific Muslim: a 926 Rashtrakuta grant found in Maharashtra. The inscription records a donation to a Brahmin monastery made by Madhumati, a Muslim administrator under the Rashtrakutas in the early tenth century. The inscription includes several Perso-Arabic names adapted into Sanskrit. In addition to Madhumati, a Sanskrit representation of Muhammad that means "honey-minded," the inscription says he was also known as Sugatipa (Subakta or Sebuktigin), meaning "lord of the virtuous" in Sanskrit, and was the son of Sahiyarahara (*sahiyārahāra*, Shahriyar).[28] The inscription furnishes significant information about Madhumati, including that he administered the division of Samyan (*saṃyāna*), established a free ferry and feeding house, and gave land along with the right to collect revenue to a Brahmin monastery (*maṭha*).[29] But what is most noteworthy about this inscription is how little it comments on Madhumati's ethnicity, religion, or any other point of difference. The author saw no need to explain a Muslim sponsoring the religious activity of Brahmins or a Muslim political figure in India at all. We moderns may find this cross-cultural situation in need of explication, but premoderns saw it as unremarkable.

Another way to grasp the extent to which early Sanskrit inscriptions describe Muslims in ordinary, nonexceptional ways is to note that we are uncertain about whether several early Sanskrit inscriptions are, in fact, about Muslims. In addition to the new terms "turushka" and "tajika," premodern Sanskrit authors also used old Sanskrit terms for outsiders (e.g., *mleccha*, *yavana*, *pārasīka*, meaning barbarian, Greek, and Persian, respectively) to delineate Muslims. Over time, by slotting Muslims into old Sanskrit categories for outsiders, Sanskrit authors redefined these terms. But, in early inscriptions, it is often unclear whether a specific mention of a mleccha, yavana, or parasika does or does not refer to a Muslim, because there is no distinctive imagery associated with Muslims in early Sanskrit representations thereof.[30] For instance, a 852 Dholpur inscription mentions *mlecchādipa*s (barbarian kings), whose identity is unclear.[31] The ca. mid-900s Chinchani plate of Rashtrakuta Krishna II, quoted above, mentions Persians (parasika) in the same verse as tajikas, but we do not know if the Persians were Muslims.[32] The list goes on for possible early Sanskrit mentions of Muslims and grows more numerous if we add terms such as *cāṇḍāla/caṇḍāla*, which was used unambiguously by several pre-1200 Sanskrit sources to refer to Muslims.[33]

No Sanskrit word for Muslims as such appears in these early inscriptions, and this calls for some comment. This absence is not, entirely, a concern that originates with modern ideas about religious identity. Leonard van der Kuijp has shown that the Sanskrit term *musalamāna* (Muslim, adapted from Perso-Arabic *musulmān*) was used in a 700 CE Buddhist commentary.[34] On the basis of this ca. 700 usage, Van der Kuijp argues that there was social awareness of Islam on the Indian subcontinent. This argument is buttressed by physical evidence that mosques were built in parts of India as early as the eighth century CE.[35] Given the ca. 700 Sanskrit usage of "musalamana" especially, we can pose the historical question: Why did most Sanskrit intellectuals before 1000 decline to use the word "musalamana" or another term of religious identity when speaking about historical events involving Muslims and resort instead to vague ethnonyms and general terms for outsiders?

Sanskrit authors did not generally use religious descriptors to identify specific adversaries or allies. This point is so obvious that it is often overlooked. Premodern Sanskrit sources typically describe political conflicts as between dynasties, such as the Rashtrakutas, Cholas, and Chaulukyas (rather than, say, Vaishnavas, Shaivites, and Jains). Between the eighth and twelfth centuries, however, Sanskrit thinkers generally did not name specific lineages of Muslim kings (e.g., the Ghaznavids), but rather used pseudoethnic and outsider descriptors. In this sense, Sanskrit intellectuals treated Muslim rulers differently than what we might now call "Hindu" dynasties. Still, by and large, they did not define political groups—whether "Hindu" or "Muslim"—with religious terms.

It remains opaque what, exactly, Sanskrit intellectuals found distinctive about the people they often termed "turushka" or "tajika" that merited new, quasi ethnonyms but not a more precise breakdown by dynasty or ruler. Small bits of evidence crop up periodically that might suggest new cultural norms, but our resources here are meager. The 738 Navsari plate mentions a svami whom the tajikas and, as I read it, the Chaulukyas serve, but the inscription is unclear about whether this is an earthly master, a Heavenly Master, or both. More concretely, one of the later uses of "tajika" for Muslim is found on a bilingual Arabic-Sanskrit coin of Mahmud of Ghazni, struck in 1027/1028, that deploys the term to refer to the Hijri calendar (*tājikīyena saṃvatī*).[36] Here, we may see something approaching a recognition of shared Islamic cultural norms, although, notably, in a coin produced by a Muslim ruler.

Many Muslims in Sanskrit Inscriptions
Circa 1000–1190 CE

After the turn of the first millennium, more Muslims entered the Indian subcontinent as migrants, traders, and raiders. Sanskrit inscriptions that mention Muslims accelerated apace with their increased presence in parts of India, and dozens of such inscriptions were written between 1000 and 1190 CE.[37] Often, eleventh- and twelfth-century Sanskrit inscriptions depict military adversaries who were Muslim, similar to pre-1000 Sanskrit sources. Sanskrit authors also began to explore new ways of talking about Muslims, sometimes with slightly increased specificity.

Some Sanskrit inscriptions from the early second millennium feature Muslims as an integrated part of local society. For example, a 1059 copperplate discusses a prominent Muslim (*tāyika*) family that became wealthy from the sea trade and served the Kadamba rulers of Goa.[38] The record names several individuals in this family, including Aliya (*āliyama*, Ali), Madhumada (Muhammad), and Sadhana (*saḍhana*, also known as Sadano).[39] Other inscriptions refer to Muslim individuals by title, especially Sanskrit renderings of *amīr* (usually *hammīra*, also *haṃvīra* and *hambīra*).[40] Groups of Muslims appear as residents of parts of India. For example, several Gahadavala inscriptions in northern India cite a *turuṣkadaṇḍa*, a Muslim tax. This phrase has been interpreted in different ways, including as a tax by Muslims and a tax to fight Muslims, but it was, most likely, a tax levied on Muslim settlers in the region.[41] Finbarr Barry Flood has described the tax as "an Indic adaptation of the *jizya*."[42]

Sanskrit inscriptions continued to dwell on the martial strength of Muslim foes, both generally and regarding specific military technologies. For example, a 1167 verse that was repeated a few times in subsequent decades lauds a Kalachuri king as follows:

> Upon hearing about the coronation of King Jayasimha,
> the Gurjara king vanished, the turushka gave up the strength of his arms,
> Kuntala's lord suddenly renounced all love sports,
> and the other kings abandoned the earth out of fear and fled across the ocean.[43]

The sentiment of the verse is conventional enough, namely that one king inspired terror in all others. And yet, it is perhaps noteworthy that the Muslim ruler is associated with military strength. Several twelfth-century Sanskrit inscriptions link Muslims with horses, especially in war.[44] This may reflect the historical reality that Muslim-led forces often boasted strong cavalries. For instance, Mahmud of Ghazni is said to have hit the Somanatha temple in 1025 with a cavalry 30,000 strong in tow.[45] But Sanskrit poets often expressed this reality through conventional descriptions. For instance, a Malwa inscription from the early twelfth century borrowed imagery from Kalidasa's classic Sanskrit poem *Raghuvaṃśa* (Raghu's lineage) to describe a Muslim's (turushka) horses trampling saffron on a field.[46] Sanskrit sources during this period still contained hardly any trace or comment on Islam as a religious tradition, with one major exception.

Theorizing Islam in a Buddhist Tradition

The *Kālacakratantra* (Tantra of the wheel of time) is perhaps the single most important pre-1190 CE Sanskrit source that talks about Islam, but it is little discussed beyond specialist circles. The Kalachakra is a late Vajrayana Buddhist tradition that thrived in India for a few centuries. A series of texts, especially the *Kālacakratantra* (sometimes called *Śrīkālacakra*) and its *Vimalaprabhā* commentary, were completed between 1025 and 1040 CE in Sanskrit and soon translated into Tibetan.[47] The Kalachakra tradition is fairly well known among Buddhist specialists, and several individuals have worked on the discussion of Islam in the *Kālacakratantra* and associated texts.[48] But these materials remain unappreciated in broader discussions of Muslims in Sanskrit sources, which so often carry a bias toward Brahminical materials.[49] The Kalachakra tradition projected Islam as central to its own self-articulation, and numerous texts proffer extensive information about Muslim social and religious practices and Islamic theology.

The Kalachakra texts frame their tradition against the alleged threat posed by Islamic teachings. Most notably, the *Vimalaprabhā* commentary pitches the entire Kalachakra as needed precisely in order to prevent oneself and one's descendants from becoming Muslims. In a passage that is as critical of upper-class Hindus as it is of Muslims, the text says that Brahmins and Kshatriyas are on the fast track to following Islam because they all use violence: "In both Islam [*mlecchadharme*] and Vedic traditions [*vedadharme*], killing is required for the sake of the gods and one's ancestors. It is the same for Kshatriyas [*kṣatradharme*]. The Brahmin sages said, 'Having pleased your forefathers and gods, it is not an error to eat meat' and 'I see no error in a person who would injure an evil man.' Therefore, those who consider Vedic traditions authoritative will embrace Islam."[50] The two quotes attributed to Brahmin sages are found, with some variants, in multiple places in Sanskrit literature, including the *Yājñavalkyasmṛti* (quote 1), the *Pañcatantra* (quote 2), and the *Garuḍapurāṇa* (quote 2).[51] The *Vimalaprabhā* cites them as proof that Brahmins and Kshatriyas have a history of endorsing violence and are thus prime candidates to become Muslim. The text goes on: "For this very reason, I have outlined this set of rules to prevent you from following Islam in the future. Therefore, you ought to follow what I teach!"[52] In other words, the Kalachakra tradition is useful because it prevents misguided conversion to Islam.[53] Furthermore, the *Kālacakratantra* prophesies a future battle between Muslims and Buddhists in the mythical kingdom of Shambhala. The battle will take place during the last stage of the current, degenerate age, when Islam (*mlecchadharma*) has spread. According to the text, a Buddhist emperor will rise up, eradicate Islam, and thus usher in a golden age.[54] That Muslims serve a crucial role in the transition to this new era signals the centrality of Islam and perhaps specifically Muslim-led military assaults to the articulators of the Kalachakra tradition.[55] The Kalachakra treats Islam and its presumed future expansion as a foil for communicating its own reasons for being needed at a particular moment in history.

Given that the Kalachakra argues for its own importance by referring to Islam, perhaps it ought to be unsurprising that these Buddhist sources detail an array of Islamic social and religious practices and beliefs. The Sanskrit texts discuss Muslim dietary restrictions and how Muslims slaughter animals. They note consumption habits, including that Muslims eat at night and periodically fast. Marriage customs are mentioned, as well as the habit of five daily prayers and circumcision. Equally of interest are theological aspects of Islam, including the major prophets of Islam and that Muslims worship a God known as Rahman. The *Kālacakratantra* notes the use of *bismillah*, a common Arabic blessing attested in the Quran, meaning "in God's name." The texts outline the basic Islamic concepts of heaven and hell and mention Mecca as the homeland of Islam and its final prophet, Muhammad.[56]

In addition to offering a plethora of details, the Kalachakra materials further theorize Islam as an independent tradition that is separate from and roughly comparable to other religious traditions. The texts speak of *mleccha-dharma*, which we might roughly translate as "Islamic social and religious practices" or, more succinctly, "Islam." While "mleccha" is a broad Sanskrit term for outsiders, the Kalachakra texts apply it more narrowly.[57] Notably, the texts do not label Tibetans as mlecchas, despite the fact that Tibetans had eating and hygiene habits—objectionable to Indian Buddhists—comparable to those of Muslims.[58] The *Kālacakratantra* describes Islam, negatively, as a religion of violence (*hiṃsādharma*) that inspires savage behavior (*raudrakarman*).[59] In their encouragement of violence, according to the Kalachakra authors, Islamic and Vedic practices were comparable. Nonetheless, the Kalachakra texts marked Islam, more so than other religious traditions, as incompatible with Buddhism. The texts prohibit Buddhist followers from partaking in Islamic practices, whereas they allow participation in some Hindu and Jain activities.[60] The texts overtly praise those able to convert Muslims to the Kalachakra path.[61]

Taken as a whole, the Kalachakra texts offer a fairly detailed, if judgmental, overview of Islam. The *Kālacakratantra* misstates certain pieces of information, such as when it portrays Mecca as a large area (*viṣaya*), rather than as a city.[62] The work contains a mildly puzzling list of eight prophets; while most of the prophets are familiar, the exact list does not correspond to any known branch of Islam.[63] The Kalachakra misunderstands Muslim animal slaughter protocols as a type of animal sacrifice.[64] Such errors may suggest that the Buddhists who wrote the *Kālacakratantra* and related works lacked first-hand experience with Muslims. Misinterpretations are also a common peril of cross-cultural meetings, especially in the early phases of being introduced to a new tradition. But the most important point about Islam in the Kalachakra texts is not the blunders or oddities but rather that Islam was discussed in rich detail and as a key foil for a Buddhist tradition.

The Kalachakra authors wrote in response to, although not specifically about, their social realities. The production of Kalachakra texts that mention Islam roughly coincided with Mahmud of Ghazni's raids in the northwest part of the subcontinent. The texts do not mention these events explicitly, but they refer to assaults on temples and iconoclasm in generic terms.[65] That said, I caution against the widespread but largely unsubstantiated narrative that Muslim-led military assaults killed off Indian

Buddhism. As Johan Elverskog has succinctly observed of the prevalence of this story line: "Whenever the topic of Buddhism and Islam is ever mentioned it almost invariably revolves around the Muslim destruction of the Dharma."[66] I have written elsewhere about the shaky historical evidence behind this presumed antagonistic relationship, which is fueled by modern biases about both Islam and Buddhism.[67] Here my interest is not determining the historical trajectory or causality of what happened to Indian Buddhism in the early second millennium CE. I remain focused on contextualizing the Kalachakra authors' decision to write in response to raids led by the Ghaznavids.

Brahmin Silence as the Exception

Contemporary Brahmin thinkers did not, so far as we know, write about Ghaznavid-led assaults. For example, Mahmud of Ghazni sacked Gujarat's Somanatha temple in 1025 CE, and we know of no contemporary Brahmin-authored account of the episode, or specifically in response to it, in Sanskrit. The sacking of the Somanatha temple, considered cataclysmic in modern popular discussions of Hindu-Muslim conflict, may have passed unremarked upon in Sanskrit by a major group who suffered from it at the time.[68] Perhaps the event was unremarkable to local Brahmins, who were accustomed to temple raids from Indian kings across the board. For instance, only three years earlier, in 1022, the army of Rajendra Chola I (r. 1014–44) had sacked another Shiva temple, in the Pala kingdom of Bengal in that case, and carted off its central image as a war trophy.[69] Also, Mahmud of Ghazni's raid did not obliterate the Somanatha temple, at least not for long; we have a record of a royal pilgrimage there just over a decade after 1025.[70] That said, the Buddhist Kalachakra texts demonstrate unambiguously that Brahminical silence was a choice. Brahmin agency in electing to remain mute is further underlined by comparison with a little-known Jain work.

Within roughly a decade of 1025, Dhanapala, a Digambara Jain monk, wrote about Mahmud of Ghazni's raids even more explicitly than his Buddhist counterparts. Dhanapala authored a short, fifteen-verse poem, titled "Saccaürivīraucchāhu" (Strength of Satyapuri's Mahavira), in Apabhramsha, a language "largely continuous with Prakrit," about the failure of Mahmud of Ghazni's troops to seize an icon of Mahavira from Sanchore, Rajasthan.[71] The work describes Ghaznavid forces as *turukka*, Prakrit for turushka, and offers fairly precise information on Ghaznavid campaigns. For instance, verses three and four read:

> They destroyed the region of Bhinmal and Anhilwad,
> and ravaged Chaddavalli, Saurashtra, and Dilwara.
> They destroyed Someshwar, which brought joy to people's hearts.
> But they did not destroy Satyapuri's Mahavira, delight of those who have achieved their aims.
> Is the light of the sun destroyed by constellations, however numerous they may be?
> Is Garuda felled when he meets with serpents, however numerous they may be?
> Do antelopes, however numerous they may be, menace the Lord of Beasts?
> Can the Turks, however numerous they may be, touch Satyapuri's Lord Jina?[72]

When taken together, the Kalachakra texts and Dhanapala's poem suggest that we might turn the tables, as it were, and see Brahmins as the exception, rather than the rule, in declining to respond directly to Ghaznavid political activities in Sanskrit.

Even Brahmin intellectuals in Sindh, the one area of the subcontinent under Arab-led rule from the early eighth century onward, generally did not write about Muslims. One exception is the *Devalasmṛti*, a Sanskrit legal text written in Sindh circa 800–1000, which discusses how Hindus who have become polluted from engaging in Muslim social and religious activities can purify themselves for reentry into their appropriate social class (varna).[73] In addition to being the exception that proves the rule, the *Devalasmṛti* does not offer many details about Muslims as such (called *mleccha* and *caṇḍāla*). The text parcels out a few morsels of information, such as that Muslims (presumably Arab Muslims, given the social context) like to eat meat. Nonetheless, like most Sanskrit thinkers of the period, the *Devalasmṛti*'s author saw little intellectual value, for his community's needs and self-identity, in theorizing Islam. Kalachakra thinkers, however, thought about this new religion vigorously and integrated it into the very foundation of their own tradition.

It is a telling lapse that modern scholars have overlooked the *Kālacakratantra* and related texts when analyzing Sanskrit sources on Islam and Muslims. In fact, scholars have pronounced—repeatedly and recently—that Sanskrit thinkers never talked about or theorized Islam as such.[74] The Kalachakra texts on Islam are not vague, singular, or difficult to locate. On the contrary, there are several that discuss Islam, often in great detail. The texts are published, and the relevant sections are translated into English. The *Kālacakratantra* and related works were translated into Tibetan many times in premodernity—perhaps more than any other premodern Buddhist work—and the Kalachakra is still a living tradition today.[75] How have such rich and readily available materials been neglected, except by Buddhism specialists? We see quite sharply here how when scholars talk about the Sanskrit literary tradition, they so often mean the Brahminical Sanskrit literary tradition, a much narrower formulation. The widespread assumption that Brahmins define the contours of premodern Sanskrit thought owes a great deal to both precolonial and colonial-era assumptions that we are still struggling to overcome. So often modern thinkers cut out contributions by Jains and Buddhists without justification and, critically, without communicating or even recognizing their own blinkers and thereby perpetuate a trend of silencing non-Brahminical voices in the narration of Indian history.[76] We can and should still ask why Brahmin men who wrote in Sanskrit from the eighth through the twelfth century declined to comment on Islamic theology. But scholars should stop asking why nobody ever wrote about Islam or Muslims in Sanskrit, because the answer is that people did.

Scarce and Abundant Evidence

The evidence I discuss above, especially the early inscriptions, has come down to us, in part, through happenstance, and this constricts, to some degree, the conclusions that we can draw from these early sources. For example, two of the seven inscriptions that mention Muslim between 736 and 1000 CE had been thrown away. One of these was found in a rubbish heap, and the other surfaced when a mid-twentieth-century farmer was plowing his field.[77] A third inscription was preserved because the marble on which it was inscribed was reused as building material.[78] This haphazard preservation makes one wonder what other early inscriptions on similar topics might have been lost. Historians rarely indulge in the tantalizing possibilities of lost evidence, and I certainly cannot make an argument on the basis of presumed lacuna. But the aleatory circumstances that have preserved nearly half of the known Sanskrit inscriptions between 736 and 1000 that mention Muslims suggest, even more strongly than usual in premodern history, that we do not have the full picture. In this vein, it is worth underscoring the ample number of surviving Sanskrit sources dated between 1000 and 1190 that refer to Muslims, including dozens of inscriptions, numerous Buddhist texts, and a few scattered Jain and Brahminical works.

Sanskrit inscriptions circa 736 to 1190 and the Kalachakra materials treat Muslims in starkly different manners. Early Sanskrit inscriptions from certain regions and select dynasties refer to Muslims briefly and never as Muslims. In contrast, the Kalachakra texts detail Islamic social practices and theological precepts and posit the spread of Islam as crucial to justifying the very existence of a new Buddhist tantra. There is a substantial divergence between mentions of Muslims so brief they are easy to miss, in early Sanskrit inscriptions, and the Kalachakra's positioning of Islam as foundational to a Buddhist tradition. This contrast is softened by Sanskrit works that seem to fall between these two extreme poles. Notably, the *Devalasmṛti* mentions Arab Muslims specifically, if briefly, when discussing religious practices. Still, the two main groups of materials I analyze above—Sanskrit inscriptions and the Kalachakra texts—offer a striking contrast regarding how India's traditional learned elite elected to describe Muslim communities in different contexts and for different audiences.

The two sets of materials also diverge in how they identify and signal the novelty embodied by Muslim communities. Most Sanskrit inscriptions from this period reused old imagery for Muslims, to the point where it can be unclear whether they are talking about Muslims or another group. In contrast, the Kalachakra tradition recognized Islam as a distinctive tradition with specific social and theological markers. Neither set of materials pursued their respective approaches exclusively. The inscriptions sometimes used old imagery to comment on specific aspects of Muslim groups, and so, as discussed in the introduction, we ought to ask: Why *this* trope? Additionally, Sanskrit inscriptions used newly crafted Sanskrit ethnonyms for Muslims, namely "tajika" and "turushka." On the other hand, the Kalachakra writers did not perceive Islam as without precedent and, in fact, posited continuity between Vedic and Islamic practices. In addition to recognizing the diversity found in medieval Sanskrit approaches to thinking and writing about Muslims, we ought to underscore the nuance and complexity within each approach. Even within a relative paucity of sources, early Sanskrit thinkers demonstrated remarkable sophistication and dexterity in depicting Muslims, a set of communities still an extreme minority with little political power on the subcontinent before 1190.

CHAPTER II

Difference That Mattered

Defining the Ghurid Threat

I do not belong anywhere. I have an accent in every language I speak.

—SHOLEH WOLPÉ, *THE OUTSIDER*, 2008

Sanskrit thinkers began writing about Indo-Muslim rule at the moment it began: the Ghurid incursions of the late twelfth century. A branch of the Ghurids—originally from the region of Ghur, of Persian descent, and Muslims—campaigned in northern India starting in the mid-1170s. Under the leadership of Shihabuddin Muhammad Ghori, they gained a foothold in the Punjab about a decade later and, from a base in Lahore seized from the Ghaznavids, warred against numerous rulers further south from 1186 onward. In 1192, the Ghurids defeated the Chauhans at Tarain, an event that paved the way for their seizure of Delhi later that same year and marked the inauguration of over five hundred years of Indo-Persian dynasties ruling over parts of northern India.[1] By the time of the Ghurid-led assaults, northern India was no stranger to Muslim-led military offensives. Most notably, the Ghaznavids, Turkish Muslims from Central Asia, had raided towns and temples in the region beginning nearly two centuries earlier. But, whereas the Ghaznavids returned up north with their looted wealth, the Ghurids pressed further into the subcontinent and ruled from Delhi. The Ghurids brought with them new languages (Persian, Turkish, and Arabic), a religion (Islam) still uncommon in most parts of India, and a culture of rulership that was markedly different from the Sanskrit-based one shared by most Indian rulers of the time. Sanskrit intellectuals of the late twelfth century wrote about Ghurid-led assaults and these associated types of difference in real time.

Rulers of regional dynasties in northern India perceived the Ghurids, correctly, as a potent military threat, and this assessment found expression in Sanskrit, the premier literary and political language of late-twelfth-century northern India. A view of the Ghurids as strong foes looms large, for example, in inscriptions that mention them warring against the Chaulukyas of Gujarat (also known as the Solankis).[2] One inscription written circa 1200 CE at Dabhoi, in Gujarat, invokes harsh language to describe a battle, probably from a decade or two earlier, where the troops of Bhimadeva, a Gujarati Chaulukya ruler, overpowered those of the Ghurids. In addition to noting the bloodshed involved, the inscription proclaims that kings "become uneasy and afraid even from stories of the Ghurid king [*turuṣkarāja*]."[3] Another Sanskrit inscription from roughly the same period laments that the Ghurid army had "crushed the entire world."[4]

While there is little doubt that Sanskrit writers of the late twelfth century understood the Ghurids as a military threat to specific kingdoms in northern India, it is more difficult to capture the operative terms of difference. There are many ways we moderns might contrast the Ghurids to dynasties such as the Chaulukyas of Gujarat or the Chauhans. The Ghurids differed from their northern Indian political adversaries in terms of origin, religion, languages, social norms, and more. But the question that occupies my attention here is more precise: What were the differences that mattered to Sanskrit intellectuals of the day? Too often modern thinkers have zeroed in on a religious angle of Ghurid conflict with the Chauhans and other Indian dynasties, blithely assuming a battle of Muslims versus Hindus.[5] This framing reflects an active, sometimes antagonistic dynamic in the twentieth and twenty-first centuries, but it finds a precarious, if any, basis in premodernity. The Chauhans did not call themselves "Hindus," and the Ghurids adhered through 1199 to an obscure sect of Islam known as the Karramiya, considered aberrant by mainstream Sunnis.[6] Even if we fudge the religious identities, we lack evidence that either dynasty fought, in any meaningful sense, in the name of religion within what was, first and foremost, a struggle for political power. In short, perhaps unsurprisingly, the historically contingent terms of our time prevent us from grasping the categories that were active among a certain group of northern Indian thinkers eight hundred years ago.

Jayanaka's *Pṛthvīrājavijaya* (Victory of Prithviraj Chauhan) stands out as a largely unique text that can help us begin to recover how India's traditional learned elite thought about Ghurid military strikes, the advent of

Ghurid rule, and the accompanying social, political, and cultural changes. Jayanaka authored his *Pṛthvīrājavijaya* during the 1190s, a decade that witnessed the birth of the Ghurids as a dynasty based in Delhi. It is the earliest Sanskrit work to discuss Indian encounters with Muslim political figures in any depth. In many ways, it is the foundational text for a Sanskrit tradition of historical narratives on Indo-Persian rule. In what follows, I argue that Jayanaka projected the Ghurids as hazardous to an established ritual and social order and that they—by virtue of being a new danger—allowed Jayanaka to imagine his own political and cultural traditions, alongside their royal protectors, with renewed potency.

Writing About the Ghurids and for the Chauhans

Jayanaka wrote the *Pṛthvīrājavijaya* under Chauhan patronage and therein details several Chauhan conflicts over more than a century, including clashes with the Ghaznavids and with various Hindu rulers. But the work centers around clashes between the Ghurids and the Chauhans at the end of the twelfth century. A key aspect that makes the *Pṛthvīrājavijaya* valuable for my project here is Jayanaka's basis in traditional Sanskrit learning. Jayanaka did not merely record what he saw happening around him but also synthesized and reflected upon Ghurid identity, using the conventions of Sanskrit literary discourse. In so doing, he considered how the identities of himself and his patron might be reconstituted against the backdrop of this new rival. Put another way, Jayanaka wrote history in all its narrative and literary glory that was intended to be read in its own cultural context.

The *Pṛthvīrājavijaya* as we have it is fragmentary and incomplete, breaking off in the middle of the twelfth chapter. But the work likely climaxed by describing or implying Prithviraj Chauhan's triumph over Muhammad Ghori at Tarain in 1191 (the *vijaya* or victory of the title).[7] Jayanaka must have completed his *Pṛthvīrājavijaya* by 1200 because the work is quoted in Jayaratha's circa 1200 *Vimarśinī* commentary on Ruyyaka's *Alaṃkārasarvasva* (Totality of ornaments), a work of literary theory. The 1191 Chauhan victory at Tarain delayed Ghurid troops from pressing further into northern India, albeit only for a matter of months. In a rematch the following year, Muhammad Ghori vanquished Prithviraj and, probably, made the former

Chauhan king a vassal for a while, before executing him for treachery and appointing Prithviraj's son instead. The son was probably overthrown shortly thereafter by Prithviraj's brother, Hariraja.[8] Earlier scholars have suggested that Jayanaka wrote in late 1191 or early 1192, before Prithviraj's defeat at Tarain.[9] This dating is possible, but it leaves a rather narrow window in which Jayanaka is supposed to have written his robust poem. I think it is equally plausible that Jayanaka wrote later in the 1190s, when Prithviraj or another Chauhan successor was ruling under Ghurid sovereignty, and simply chose to omit Prithviraj's 1192 defeat.[10] Selective recording was common for poets and historians of the period across literary traditions. For example, in his *Tāj al-Ma'āṡir*, written in Persian around 1217, Tajuddin Hasan Nizami omitted Muhammad Ghori's 1191 defeat at Tarain and only narrated his 1192 victory.[11] Jayanaka's core goal in the *Pṛthvīrājavijaya*, as I argue below, was a sociopolitical argument about kingship, which depended upon his narration of historical events but did not require a comprehensive recording of battles.

Jayanaka wrote for two major audiences: poets and kings. He tells his readers as much in some of his opening verses. He declares that only fellow poets can judge his skills and immodestly predicts that they will be inflamed with jealousy at his literary creation.[12] Jayanaka equally emphasizes his position within a royal court. In this regard, he distinguishes himself from Valmiki, the purported author of the Ramayana, who was, in Jayanaka's view, free of desires. In contrast, Jayanaka asks rhetorically: "How could the likes of me, who has been honored by the king, possibly be dispassionate regarding poetry?"[13] Additionally, Jayanaka narrates in the twelfth chapter of the *Pṛthvīrājavijaya* how he left Kashmir, his homeland, and entered into Prithviraj's Ajmer-based court, thus spotlighting his royal context. This narrative, during which the only known surviving manuscript of the *Pṛthvīrājavijaya* breaks off, perhaps also echoes Bilhana, another Kashmiri who had left his homeland a century earlier to seek patronage opportunities in northern India. Bilhana describes his wanderings at the end of his *Vikramāṅkadevacarita* (King Vikrama's deeds).[14]

Jayanaka underscores the importance of his main topic, namely historical military feats. He imagines the sun and the moon enhancing their own lineages, in which Indian kings from many dynasties often claimed to partake, by exposure to his poetic retelling of Prithviraj's heroism.[15] He flanks his prediction of the jealousy of other poets (mentioned above) by noting that King Prithviraj, who ordered him to write this work, arouses envy in other rulers. In short, Jayanaka proclaims his literary achievements possible because of the famous (and, largely, true) martial deeds that he narrates. The historical nature of the poem distinguishes the *Pṛthvīrājavijaya* from other earlier "victory" texts, such as the myth-based *Harivijaya* (Victory of Vishnu), now lost, and *Haravijaya* (Victory of Shiva), extant.[16] Jayanaka's emphasis on his patron's activities places his poem squarely in the genre of "patron-sponsored court epics," popularized and, in some ways, exemplified by Bilhana's *Vikramāṅkadevacarita* (King Vikrama's deeds), written for the Chaulukya king Vikramaditya VI (r. 1075–1126) in the 1080s.[17] Bilhana's *Vikramāṅkadevacarita* was incredibly popular and ultimately became one of the most widely quoted Sanskrit poems ever written.[18] Jayanaka's *Pṛthvīrājavijaya* bears stylistic similarities to the *Vikramāṅkadevacarita*.[19]

The *Pṛthvīrājavijaya* has come down to us along with a commentary by Jonaraja, which further indicates that the historical subject matter was vital, rather than incidental, to Jayanaka's poem. Jonaraja was a fifteenth-century Sanskrit author based in Kashmir. He is most well known for his *Rājataraṅgiṇī* (River of kings), a work that he pitched as a continuation of Kalhana's mid-twelfth-century text of the same title. Both Kalhana and Jonaraja wrote about historical subjects, including Indo-Muslim rule (see chapter 4). In other words, Indo-Muslim rule and history are the common factors between Jonaraja's *Rājataraṅgiṇī*, Kalhana's *Rājataraṅgiṇī*, and Jayanaka's *Pṛthvīrājavijaya*. Jonaraja had an enduring interest in Indo-Muslim political events, it would appear, and his commentary helps mark the *Pṛthvīrājavijaya* as an early contribution to a tradition of Sanskrit historical writing on Indo-Persian rule.[20]

For Jayanaka, writing about the Ghurids in Sanskrit was an opportunity to talk about social and political changes, more or less as they happened, and to remake himself. These two processes are closely related. As Romila Thapar reminds us, "However different, the Other demands recognition in every society."[21] A dichotomy of us versus them does not aptly capture the viewpoints expressed in most of the Sanskrit texts that I discuss in this book, but the glove fits for Jayanaka. Nonetheless, we should be wary of modern biases in assuming who constitutes the "us" and who constitutes the "them" in the *Pṛthvīrājavijaya*. In terms of the military clash, there were two clear sides: the Chauhans and the Ghurids. However, as we shall see, Jayanaka unpacks the Ghurid threat in terms of their ritual impurity, outcaste status, and linguistic limitations, rather than focusing exclusively on military might. He lauds Prithviraj Chauhan as a savior who will restore elite social practices that the Ghurids have compromised. Here, our clunky modern terminology fails us. Jayanaka did not see a Rajput warrior ethos, a Hindu struggle against Muslims, or Indians warding off invaders. And, really, how could he have? In the 1190s, the term "Rajput" as we mean it today had not been coined, the Persian term "Hindu" was not used self-referentially, and there was no Indian nation-state, in reality or imagination, to invade or protect. Rather, Jayanaka promotes a specific type of kingship, articulated through Sanskrit, freshly redefined and crystallized in response to the behaviors, status, and language of the Ghurids.

Ghurid Polluters of Brahminical Ritual Activity

Jayanaka talks a great deal in his poem about Ghurid troops spoiling sacred places within Chauhan territory, and this discussion ought to be read against the backdrop of the Ghurid penchant for altering the built religious landscape of areas under their control. In the 1170s and 1180s, the Ghurids constructed multiple mosques in Iran and Central Asia, some of which still stand today.[22] By the late twelfth century, Muslim communities had been erecting mosques in parts of India for several hundred years.[23] But, after the Ghurids took Delhi in 1192, they raised mosques that were far larger in size and situated them in more politically prominent locations. Parts of the Qutb Mosque near Delhi were built in the 1190s; the Adhai-din-ka-Jhompra mosque at Ajmer, Prithviraj's former capital, was erected in the 1190s.[24] Alka Patel has suggested that the Ghurids broke ground for a mosque at Sadadi, Rajasthan, in 1196–97.[25] The Ghurids reused temple materials in some of these building projects.[26] Closer to home for Jayanaka, Muinuddin Chishti, a Sufi leader, is thought to have arrived in Ajmer in the 1190s and set up an active Sufi dargah.[27] Without knowing when in the 1190s Jayanaka wrote the *Pṛthvīrājavijaya*, we cannot peg his poem to a specific moment in the Ghurid's aggressive building agenda. But, generally, Jayanaka's literary preoccupation with displaced ritual activity responded to the landscape changes known to accompany the institution of Ghurid-led rule.

Jayanaka opens his story, not with Prithviraj's heroism, but rather with a rich depiction of the Ghurid desecration of Pushkar, a pilgrimage

Figure 2.1 Adhai-din-ka-Jhompra mosque, Ajmer, Rajasthan
Photo by author, 2007

destination near Prithviraj's capital, Ajmer. Pushkar had long been associated with the Hindu god Brahma.[28] Jayanaka plays on that link and imagines Brahma asking Vishnu to reincarnate himself in order to save Pushkar. In Jayanaka's imagination, Brahma begins by decrying the dismal state of ritual practice in Pushkar:

> Before this place was full of sacrifices to me.
> Where once there were three pits full of fire,
> with the passage of time,
> those very pits are full of water.[29]

Brahma next points out that none of the other Hindu gods are up to the task of liberating Pushkar, as a buildup to his request for Vishnu to, again, take on human form to rescue the world. For example, Indra is weakened due to a lack of sacrifices, and Shiva is indifferent.[30] Even prior Vishnu avatars, such as the Buddha, cannot tackle the Ghurid threat. As Jayanaka puts it (in Brahma's voice):

O Vishnu, while you adopted asceticism as the Buddha incarnation
and took to being friendly with deer,
my homeland, Pushkar, has been overrun by the terror of the
Ghurids [*mātaṅga*]
as if being trampled by elephants.[31]

According to the commentator Jonaraja on this verse, "when a lion becomes peaceful," land will be crushed by elephants. This comparison brings to mind a stark image of Ghurid troops running roughshod over Pushkar, wreaking mass destruction as elephants are wont to do.

In the following verses, Jayanaka defines the devastating impact of the Ghurids as compromising Brahminical ritual purity and practice. He says that the Ghurids have conducted "violent assaults on temples and Brahmin lands" (*devagṛhāgrahārahiṃsā*).[32] That verse and several subsequent ones adhere to a pattern of comparing the glory of Pushkar's past as a holy place with its present desecration at Ghurid hands. Brahma bemoans that waters, once used ritually in the great sacrifice that created the world, now refresh the violent Ghurid army.[33] Similarly, he says to Vishnu:

Your tears of joy that comprise the Narmada
and Yamuna rivers used to enter Pushkar.
But now only the waste of the Ghurids [*janaṅgama*]
who live nearby enters again and again.[34]

Pushkar's shores were once warmed by fire from Shiva's third eye but are now heated by the "tears of Brahmins imprisoned by the Ghurids" (*mātaṅgavandīkṛtaviprabāṣpaiḥ*).[35] A comment on bathing at Pushkar is perhaps designed to be the most poignant:

In the past, heavenly courtesans smiled to themselves
that Shachi had forbidden them from bathing in Pushkar
so that she alone—Indra's beloved—could bathe there.
Now, the menstruating wives of these vile men plunge in.[36]

This image contrasts Pushkar's prior purity, so extreme that only a goddess could dip into its waters, to its present state, literally awash in Ghurid women's menstrual blood. Jayanaka summarizes at one point, still in Brahma's voice, that while holy men used to practice asceticism in Pushkar, sinners have transformed the place into *avīci*, a "special hell" (*narakaviśeṣa*) in the gloss of the commentator Jonaraja.[37] In short, a key problem for Jayanaka was that the Ghurids displaced Brahminical ritual activity from a sacred area.

In this opening scene, Brahma next elaborates that the gods, too, are at risk, and he ticks through an impressive lineup of Hindu deities who have been drawn to Pushkar as a holy place. For example, playing on the meaning of *puṣkara* as lotus, Jayanaka says that Indra came to Pushkar to cleanse the sin of sleeping with Ahalya and thereby transformed the thousand vaginas that covered his body due to the curse of Gautama, Ahalya's husband, into one thousand lotus-like eyes.[38] Vayu, god of the wind, was enticed by Pushkar's purity and now the deer that he rides refuses to leave.[39] Kubera and others have their own reasons for residing in Pushkar, Brahma says, and they require Vishnu's protection (see appendix A.2 for a translation).[40] Brahma sums up Pushkar's purity with a series of verses that play on the name of Pushkar (*tripuṣkara* in Sanskrit, meaning "Place of the Three Lotuses).[41] These verses may read as trite to modern eyes, but the approach carried significant emotional weight in the world of Sanskrit aesthetics. Brahma concludes his speech by predicting that Vishnu will turn back the clock, purging the earth of the horrors of the Kali Yuga, and making it as pure as it was in the prior era, the Dvapar Yuga. This idea of cleansing the earth is well-worn in Sanskrit poetry, and yet an important contextual detail should not escape our notice: there were no Ghurids in the Dvapar Yuga.

In the narrative of the *Pṛthvīrājavijaya*, Brahma's speech convinces Vishnu to reincarnate himself as Prithviraj and vanquish Muhammad Ghori at Tarain in 1191. Indeed, when Jayanaka describes Prithviraj's birth, in chapter 8, he explicitly refers to the prince's destiny of defeating the Ghurids. The power of Jayanaka's praise comes to the forefront when we read some of these later verses against the defilement chronicled in the poem's initial chapter. For instance, Jayanaka rejoices that the newborn Prithviraj is a "man with a cause" (*kāraṇamānuṣa*), and the commentator Jonaraja clarifies that this cause is "killing the Ghurids" (*mlecchavadhena*).[42] In the same scene of Prithviraj's birth, Jayanaka highlights the future king's role in restoring sacrifice to the earth (*dharmakarmakriyāvighnahare*), an act that will prompt sacrificers (*yajamāna*) to rejoice.[43] The divine realm, too, celebrates Prithviraj's birth, with singing apsaras and heavenly women who dance until their necklaces break and rain down pearls.[44] The lush description at the poem's outset of depravity and harm outlines the terms and playing field of Prithviraj's victory later on.

Crucial to grasping the import of Jayanaka's contrast here is the association in Sanskrit poetry of royal power with the proper maintenance of premodern India's four-fold class system (*varṇāśramadharma*). Sanskrit political theory posits that kings ought to be Kshatriyas, the second of four social classes, but Brahmins hold the exclusive ability to conduct most religious rituals, including royal consecrations.[45] The reality of social and political life in premodern India was far messier than these neat categories and theoretical symbiotic Kshatriya-Brahmin relationship would suggest. It was arguably further upset by the introduction of Indo-Muslim rule, a tradition of sovereignty that existed outside the varna system. Perhaps a confused reality—even an increasingly confused reality as the Ghurids rolled into northern India—helps to explain the need for an idealized theory, to achieve in thought what was unimaginable in real life. In the *Pṛthvīrājavijaya*, Jayanaka seizes upon the palpable military danger of Ghurid incursions in order to inject new life into this class-based ideal of the social order, especially kingship. In other words, Jayanaka's concern with ritual purity is best understood as an analysis of the Ghurids as political enemies.

Jayanaka's emphasis on Pushkar adds further depth to his image of Ghurid-Chauhan conflict as concerning ritual purity and thus proper kingship. To grasp this point, it helps to state explicitly that Jayanaka focuses in his frame story on Pushkar, a pilgrimage destination, rather than on Ajmer, Prithviraj's capital. One might think that it would make sense for Jayanaka to forefront the threat to Ajmer, since the Ghurid military objective in attacking the Chauhans was to unseat Prithviraj as ruler. Jayanaka mentions Ajmer several times in his poem. He narrates Ajmer's founding, by Ajayaraja (Prithviraj's great-grandfather, according to Jayanaka), in chapter 5, and names Ajmer as the location of Prithviraj's court in chapter 10.[46] Even if Jayanaka was concerned about the Ghurids altering northern India's built religious landscape he might have done well to focus on Ajmer. In 1192, Qutbuddin Aibak ordered the construction of a mosque on Muhammad Ghori's orders in Ajmer.[47] But Jayanaka frames Vishnu-incarnate Prithviraj as the savior, not of Ajmer, but of the pilgrimage destination and divine residence of Pushkar. This reflects Jayanaka's idealized worldview that held Prithviraj to be king, in part, insofar as he safeguarded Brahminical ritual activity and a place important to Hindu gods. Thus, Jayanaka could best express the Ghurid political threat as wreaking havoc on a sacred landscape, rather than on a mundane, administrative one.

Jayanaka's displacement of the Ghurid threat from Ajmer to Pushkar in the opening sequence of his poem also has the effect of casting the Ghurids as a danger to an entire political order rather than to a single kingdom. The Chauhans were one polity among many in northern India in the late twelfth century. Accordingly, the sacking of Ajmer, Prithviraj's political capital, would represent merely the decline of a specific lineage, a quite normal occurrence in premodern India. But Jayanaka projected Pushkar as a sacred center in the way that Mircea Eliade theorized a center from which emanated the cosmos in which one wishes to live.[48] As such, a Ghurid attack on Pushkar could be made, in Jayanaka's poem, to constitute an emergency threatening to a sacred-cum-political reality broader than independent Chauhan rule. Later Sanskrit works also mention Chauhan links with Pushkar as representing something larger than a single ruling lineage. For example, Nayachandra's early fifteenth-century *Hammīramahākāvya*—a text sponsored by the Tomars more than a century after the death of the last Chauhan, at Ranthambhor—says that the first Chauhan king descended on earth in order to protect Brahma's sacrifice at Pushkar from demons.[49]

Jayanaka develops a striking contrast between the Ghurids as destructive marauders and Prithviraj as Vishnu incarnate, savior of a *tīrtha* (pilgrimage site). Several scholars have pointed out the importance of Jayanaka casting Prithviraj as a Rama-like character, elaborating upon the inbuilt othering possibilities of the Ramayana narrative, in which a royal incarnation of Vishnu defeats a menacing demon enemy.[50] I agree and would underscore that other Sanskrit authors, especially from the 1100s onward, pursued a similar tactic of imagining political opponents, whether Muslim or not, as enemies of Vishnu who had reincarnated as a specific king.[51] Like numerous Sanskrit texts and inscriptions, the *Pṛthvīrājavijaya* recasts Vishnu and his salvific posture to speak to specific historical circumstances; in its case, Ghurid military assaults.

Outcaste Ghurids

Jayanaka rarely uses the word "Ghurid" or a Sanskrit equivalent, and instead cobbles together a rich set of Sanskrit terms to describe these would-be rulers. He refers to the Ghurids as low-caste (*mātaṅga, janaṅgama, cāṇḍāla*), demons (*asura, rākṣasa, piśāca*), vile (*adhama, pāpa*), barbarians (*mleccha, pulinda*), and Turks (*turuṣka*).[52] "Turk" is potentially neutral, but the other terms are all flagrantly derogatory. In later centuries, many though not all Sanskrit authors settled on a smaller set of Sanskrit words for Muslims that, for some writers, lost their negative connotations, mainly "mleccha," "turushka," and "yavana." Indeed, in Jonaraja's fifteenth-century commentary on the *Pṛthvīrājavijaya*, he glosses Jayanaka's myriad of terms for the Ghurids as "mleccha."[53] But Jayanaka was an early pioneer in writing about Muslim-led incursions against non-Muslim Indian dynasties. His only arguable predecessor was Kalhana, whose 1149 *Rājataraṅgiṇī* Jayanaka may have known, especially since both men were from Kashmir. Kalhana mentions Muslim political figures, such as the Ghaznavids, several times in his text, typically using a vocabulary that overlapped with but was more restricted in comparison to that of Jayanaka (e.g., "turushka," "chandala," "mleccha," and "hammira").[54] Since the question of vocabulary to capture the Ghurids was not determined by convention for Jayanaka, we are justified in giving substantial weight to the terms he selected.

Some of Jayanaka's terms for the Ghurids primarily mark that they were enemies of Prithviraj, rather than calling attention to anything specific about this group. For instance, Jayanaka uses "asura" (demon) to malign other foes of Prithviraj, such as the troops of Nagarjuna, a cousin of Prithviraj's who had seized some Chauhan territory.[55] Thus, while Jayanaka's generally negative terminology for the Ghurids places them in a conflictual relationship with the Chauhans, we can only look to certain identifiers in order to glimpse the specific terms of difference for Jayanaka. Additionally, Jayanaka's varied vocabulary does not appear designed to reflect the heterogenous and fractured nature of the Ghurid polity, aspects that have interested modern scholars.[56] Rather, Jayanaka seems to have accepted the Ghurids as a cohesive group fairly readily, even if he remained a bit uncertain about the best vocabulary for describing them in Sanskrit.

Many of Jayanaka's terms underscore that the Ghurids stood outside any social order that he deemed acceptable. For example, the terms "matanga," "janangama," and "chandala" mark the Ghurids as external to the four-fold Hindu class system and thus ritually impure and unable to be kings. In a sense, this representation of the Ghurids as strangers to the varna system actually incorporates them into a traditional Indian understanding of the world. But it only assigns them the unenviable position of outcastes.

Similarly, the term "mleccha" had long been used in Sanskrit for outsiders, both those from beyond the subcontinent and tribal peoples.[57] Sanskrit texts often describe mlecchas as living in their own separate territory and according to their own cultural norms. A circa seventh-century Sanskrit lawbook specifies that "any place that lacks the four-fold class system is to be known as the land of the barbarians [*mlecchadeśa*]. Beyond that is the land of the pure [*āryavarta*]."[58]

In descriptions of the Ghurids, Jayanaka criticizes the dietary habits of this group as unacceptable within caste-based norms. For example, he remarks that thirsty Ghurid troops slaughtered their horses and drank their blood during the long journey from Central Asia to India.[59] This accusation may be true, since consuming horse blood is an attested Mongol practice.[60] Jayanaka singled it out, perhaps, to showcase the barbarism of the Ghurids when judged by late twelfth-century Brahminical norms. Indeed, in the following verse, Jayanaka castigates the same troops for roasting still-live fish.[61] Notably, these criticisms of the Ghurids traded on their treatment and consumption of animals, a concern that had more to do with Brahminical bodily purity than Ghurid violence. Indeed, Jayanaka harbored no objections to harsh battle tactics against humans. Jayanaka represented—complimentarily, in his view—Prithviraj as decorating Ajmer with wreaths fashioned from the decapitated heads of his enemies and thereby imprisoning Lakshmi, the Goddess of Royalty and Wealth (*śrī*).[62]

In the Sanskrit imagination of this time, consuming blood was also known to challenge class-based norms. Beginning in the tenth and eleventh centuries, tantric practices in Kashmir, the poet Jayanaka's homeland, sometimes involved ingesting blood (sometimes specifically menstrual blood), precisely because exposing the body to such a polluting substance was thought to prompt an individual to overcome the powerful (and, in the tantric view, limiting) social mores of class and caste.[63] Jayanaka promotes the same basic incompatibility between drinking blood and maintaining class boundaries, but he condemns the Ghurids on these grounds. Indeed, when narrating a clash earlier in the twelfth century featuring Arnoraja (one of Prithviraj's ancestors), Jayanaka similarly vilifies the Ghaznavids for slitting their horses' throats and gulping down the animals' blood as they perished on the battlefield.[64]

Jayanaka also talks about the blood of the Ghurids and the Ghaznavids as being impure. In addition to lamenting how menstruating Ghurid women polluted Pushkar's waters (quoted above), Jayanaka wrote in a description of a battle between the Chauhan ruler Arnoraja and some Ghaznavid invaders:

> The earth was purified for a moment
> by the army of heroes of King Arnoraja's soldiers.
> But after a while it drowned in the rasa of revulsion,
> dirtied by the blood of the Ghaznavids [chandala].[65]

Next Jayanaka narrates how, after defeating Ghaznavid forces, Arnoraja ordered the creation of a large lake at Ajmer in order to wash the earth of Ghaznavid blood.[66]

Jayanaka even encodes the view of the Ghurids as bodily impure at the level of language. In a rare use of the term "Gori," the Sanskrit representation of "Ghurid," Jayanaka glosses the name as a Sanskrit word (*go-ari*, cow killer), which he says aptly characterizes Muhammad Ghori, who "enjoys foul foods."[67] False etymology was a favorite activity among premodern Sanskrit intellectuals. In this case, positing a Sanskrit meaning of "Gori" slotted the Ghurids into a larger discourse about class purity. Starting in the mid-first millennium CE, upper-caste Hindus began to criticize cow slaughter (something they had previously practiced).[68] In Sanskrit lawbooks and narrative, many thinkers subsequently maligned as impure a wide range of outsider groups who continued to consume beef.[69] In emphasizing the Ghurid penchant for slaughtering cows, Jayanaka draws on this wider discourse and identifies the Ghurids with other kinds of outcastes.

As mentioned above, one major upshot of painting the Ghurids as impure and destructive was to condemn them as illegitimate rulers and encourage recognition of Prithviraj as a proper king. This political reading does not clash with admitting Jayanaka's prima facie concern with Brahminical ritual purity as such. Any suggestion of a conflict here arises from the modern separation of politics and religion, a distinction foreign to premodern India. Narrowing in on the implications of Jayanaka's portrayal of the Ghurids regarding religious practice, the question arises: Which religions were involved? Jayanaka gives no indication that he saw the Ghurids, primarily, in terms of their religious tradition. In fact, some of his descriptions of the Ghurids, such as their consumption of animal blood, slur them for decidedly un-Islamic activities. Also, Jayanaka does not seem to have understood the Ghurids as threatening "Hinduism" writ large, to the extent we can even meaningfully use this anachronistic term to talk about a demarcated religious tradition at this point in time. Jayanaka limits his interests to a narrow band of ritual activity that concerned an elite upper-class group within Chauhan territory and was threatened by another elite group, Turkish Muslims with military might and political ambitions in northern India.

In his dichotomy, Jayanaka lumped the Ghurids and Ghaznavids together to some extent, using similar imagery and unfavorable terminology for both groups, but he also recognized an important degree of difference. In a passage in chapter 10, Jayanaka contrasts the Ghaznavids, described as vigorous, powerful lords of horses, to the Ghurids, maligned as evil, voracious cow killers.[70] A key distinction between the two is that the Ghaznavids generally raided and returned up north, whereas the Ghurids aimed to hold and rule parts of the subcontinent. In addition, as Jayanaka mentions, the Ghurids had defeated the Ghaznavids.[71] This signals that Jayanaka was concerned with the Ghurids as posing a military threat rather than with the two groups' shared religious identity. For Jayanaka, the operative cultural contrast between the Chauhan and Ghurid dynasties was not that the former was Hindu and the latter Muslim. Rather, the crucial distinction was between Kshatriya kings who upheld the specific requirements of Brahminical ritual purity versus polluted outcastes who undercut them.

Unlettered Ghurids

The Ghurids could not speak Sanskrit, and, for Jayanaka, this was a damning flaw. For premodern Indian kings across the board, language was deeply tied to political power. Sheldon Pollock has written at length about the web of connections between Sanskrit literature, grammar, and political authority.[72] However, whereas earlier Indian rulers chose Sanskrit as a language of political expression primarily in contrast to Prakrits and Indian vernaculars, Jayanaka wrote within the setting of the Ghurid selection of Persian as their prized vehicle for literary and political ideas. Jayanaka demonstrates his awareness of this relatively new language option in India and his view about its incompatibility with virtuous rulership in both his denunciation of the Ghurids and his praise of Prithviraj.

Regarding the Ghurids, Jayanaka characterizes an ambassador of Muhammad Ghori who visited Prithviraj's court as unable to speak properly. The description occurs in the tenth chapter and is worth quoting in full for its extreme othering:

> [The Ghurid ambassador's] head was so bald and his forehead was almost impossibly broad. It was as if The Creator had intentionally made them thus to inscribe on them his deeds of slaughtering countless cows. It was as if the color black had shunned his hair, beard, and eyelashes out of fear of being stained by his bad reputation. All his hair was tawny, like bunches of grapes that grow in his native land. Damn his dark speech, which lacked retroflex sounds and so squawked like the cry of wild birds. His phonemes were as pallid as his complexion. He had what looked like an unspeakable skin disease, so ghastly white was he, whiter than bleached cloth, whiter than the snow of the Himalayan region where he was born.[73]

In this passage, everything about Muhammad Ghori's ambassador—especially his appearance, diet, and speech—is depicted as foreign and revolting. Jayanaka further advances this point by twisting tropes that are usually positive in Sanskrit literature into markers of the Ghurids' irremediable alterity. For instance, he says that white—a color usually associated with fame, purity, and other virtuous things in Sanskrit poetry—makes the ambassador look diseased. Even being born in the Himalayas, a sacred place often imagined as a divine residence in Sanskrit texts, serves only to mark the ambassador as repulsive.

Jayanaka recoils at the ambassador's language, most likely Persian, specifically calling out his lack of retroflex sounds. There are moments in Sanskrit literature where kings or poets abandoned certain sounds by choice. For instance, in his *Kāvyamīmāṃsā* (Analysis of literature; tenth century CE), Rajashekhara says that King Shishunaga of Magadha demanded that nobody in his harem should use retroflexes.[74] But King Shishunaga's goal, according to Rajashekhara, was to "extinguish harsh sounds" (*duruccārāṇaṣṭau*) in favor of Prakrit. In the *Daśakumāracarita* (Stories of ten young men; seventh century CE), Dandin shows off his poetic talent by having one of the characters tell his tale without uttering any labials, in order to save his lips, which were bruised and bitten from sex games. The effect is a charming contrast between a lover's story and an onslaught of harsh consonants, usually considered more appropriate for martial sentiments in Sanskrit literature.[75] In contrast, Jayanaka raises the matter of retroflexes in order to declare that Muhammad Ghori's ambassador was incapable of proper speech, namely Sanskrit. An inability to pronounce retroflex sounds would have rendered the Ghurids unable to properly speak northern Indian vernacular languages as well. This secondary implication was perhaps a practical issue. Nonetheless, the primary contrast that packed political punch, for Jayanaka, was between Persian and Sanskrit, the latter being the language for expressing sovereignty among many northern Indian rulers at the time.

Criticizing outsiders as incapable of proper speech has deep roots in Sanskrit thought and could also gain a particular edge given specific historical circumstances. In Sanskrit religious and ethical texts, mlecchas—a word that Jayanaka uses for the Ghurids—were often described as having their own, inferior language (*mleccha-vāc*) and as unlearned in Sanskrit.[76] The Sanskrit verb *mlech-* means to speak indistinctly.[77] Jayanaka's portrayal of Muhammad Ghori's ambassador plays on this idea of the mleccha as ill-spoken, in rather vivid language. The contrast of Sanskrit to Persian also adds a certain degree of specificity, especially considering that the Ghurids championed their court language of Persian as a sophisticated medium for political expression. The language of the Ghurid envoy is singled out for praise in a Persian-language account of the same meeting with Prithviraj Chauhan. The Persian text, penned in the 1210s, remarks that: "[The Ghurid] ambassador . . . conveyed the king's message in a refined and graceful manner, putting subtle ideas into elegant language. He strung the pearls of counsel and admonition onto the thread of fine expressions."[78]

Jayanaka portrays Prithviraj as offering a stark contrast to the inability of the Ghurids to speak. In his first chapter, Jayanaka praises Prithviraj as follows:

> Even in childhood, Someshvara's son [Prithviraj],
> who knows six languages, was famed for his glorious deeds
> that were like twinkling stars shimmering in the Ganges,
> just like in childhood, Someshvara's six-faced son [Karttikeya]
> was famed for his glorious deeds,
> such as leading an army of gods in easily overcoming Taraka.[79]

Several things are compelling about this verse, including the likening of Prithviraj to Karttikeya, a recurrent comparison throughout the

Pṛthvīrājavijaya that plays on Karttikeya's battle skills.[80] But what most concerns me here is the phrase that sets off the *śleṣa* (double entendre) comparison to Karttikeya: *ṣaṇām girām śaktimato*, "knows six languages" or "six-faced." In his commentary, Jonaraja specifies that this expression, in its primary reading of "knows six languages," refers to Prithviraj's knowledge of the set of six languages beginning with Sanskrit, meaning Sanskrit, three Prakrits, Paishachi, and Apabhramsha.[81] This schema was introduced into Sanskrit thought around the ninth century, replacing an earlier configuration of three languages. Crucially, the six-fold set admitted no vernaculars, and this structured omission communicated the linguistic limitations on knowledge in premodern Sanskrit thought.[82]

In the context of the *Pṛthvīrājavijaya*, Prithviraj's purported fluency in six languages also constitutes a specific politico-historical claim. In Sanskrit texts, poets most commonly deployed the praise of knowing six languages to describe intellectuals rather than kings. When I went searching for places where Sanskrit thinkers address how different languages relate to specific rulers, I found Bhoja's *Sarasvatīkaṇṭhābharaṇa* (Necklace of Sarasvati), an eleventh-century work of literary criticism. Bhoja tells his readers that social status, regional context, topic, and so forth determine whether a literary character is depicted speaking Sanskrit, Apabhramsha, etc.[83] In one verse he introduces a certain sort of historicism, writing "regarding the appropriateness of era" (*samayaucitīṃ*):

> Who did not speak Prakrit in the kingdom of Shalivahana?
> Who did not speak Sanskrit in the days of Vikramaditya?[84]

When read alongside this idea, labeling Prithviraj as master of all languages is another way of saying that he embodies an entire laudable tradition of kingship in a single ruler. Unlike that of the great kings of old, Prithviraj's rule was not demarcated by a single language. This idea finds limited precedent in Sanskrit literary theory. For example, Rajashekhara argued that an ideal king's throne ought to be flanked by poets divided according to their linguistic proficiency, and he selected the same languages for inclusion, namely Sanskrit, Prakrits, Apabhramsha, and Paishachi.[85] Going further, Jayanaka declares that all learned languages were known by Prithviraj himself. The elevation of Prithviraj as superior to even his most illustrious predecessors is heightened by the comparison of Prithviraj to the Ghurids, who cannot master even the basic sounds of Sanskrit.

On the eve of Indo-Muslim rule, Jayanaka posited unbridgeable purity, status, and linguistic differences between the Chauhans and the Ghurids. He praises Prithviraj according to an array of Sanskrit (and often specifically upper-caste Hindu) cultural norms. Prithviraj is Vishnu incarnate and as fierce in battle as Karttikeya. He is a great Chauhan king, poised to resurrect Pushkar's glory by ushering in a golden age that will outshine the reigns of all prior Indian rulers. He knows Sanskrit and related tongues. Such praises gain potency and immediacy when read against Jayanaka's harsh depiction of the Ghurids as filthy, destructive, and linguistically inept. If translating into modern English, we might well say that Jayanaka viewed the Ghurids as pariahs, in the negative sense conveyed by that modern English slur. Implied in Jayanaka's binary of the Ghurids versus Prithviraj is that there was no possibility that the Ghurids could become integrated into the rich tapestry of northern Indian ruling culture, except as outcastes.

Jayanaka's unwillingness to forge an entry point for Islamic political figures into northern Indian society was not a foregone conclusion for Sanskrit intellectuals of Jayanaka's time, including those associated with the Chauhans. Vigraharaja IV (also known as Visaladeva), Prithviraj's uncle who ruled in the 1150s and 1160s, patronized a poet known as Somadeva. In the 1150s, Somadeva wrote a play titled *Lalitavigraharāja* (Lovely Vigraharaja), about Vigraharaja IV defeating a Muslim foe.[86] In the work, Somadeva refers to Muslim characters with respectful titles, such as "hammira" (the Sanskrit version of "amir") and "king of the Turks" (*turuṣkarāja, turuṣkendra, turuṣkeśvara*).[87] In the play's fourth act, an ambassador of the amir speaks in Sanskrit and even cites the puranas.[88] This vision issues a sharp contrast to *Pṛthvīrājavijaya*'s depiction of Muhammad Ghori's ambassador as unable to vocalize basic Sanskrit consonants.

Even beyond the high culture of kingship, Somadeva indicates that he viewed Muslim figures as incorporated, to some degree, within Indian society. For instance, in the play, a few Turkish prisoners are brought to court and, in the end, are treated similarly to Hindu prisoners of war.[89] Somadeva's *Lalitavigraharāja* was engraved on stone slabs and publicly displayed in Ajmer.[90] In contravention to this prominent example, Jayanaka took a hard line that the Ghurids could not be integrated into northern India's cultural landscape, because they posed a tangible threat to the current ritual and linguistic orders upon which proper kingship rested. Although he wrote to commemorate military events, cultural and political differences mattered to Jayanaka.

Jayanaka's harsh othering of the Ghurids was arguably contradicted by the reality, on the ground, of layered sovereignty in premodern South Asia. After the Ghurids defeated Prithviraj, they reinstated the Chauhans as vassals who ruled under the Ghurids. In this strategy, the Ghurids adhered to a well-established subcontinental pattern of conquest followed by restoration, witnessed in many prior India-based kingdoms. It is hard to know how much actually changed at the local level when Prithviraj's status was amended from an independent ruler to a subsidiary one. Certainly, we lack contemporary evidence of a religious or political crisis on the level imagined by Jayanaka. That the history of ideas does not always map onto social realities does not undermine the worth of Sanskrit historical materials. Rather, noting this gap between reality and textual representation underscores the agency embedded within Jayanaka's decision to pitch the Ghurids as a danger to a moral universe, not merely as would-be conquerors of the Chauhan dynasty.

It remains an open question whether premodern readers of Jayanaka's *Pṛthvīrājavijaya* ascribed importance to its innovative attention to Muslim-led incursions into India. Our knowledge of the reception history of the *Pṛthvīrājavijaya* is sparse, and two pieces of evidence point in contradictory directions. In 1200, Jayaratha quoted seven verses from the *Pṛthvīrājavijaya* in his commentary on Ruyyaka's *Alaṃkārasarvasva*.[91] Jayaratha took his quotations from the *Pṛthvīrājavijaya*'s fifth chapter, which narratively concerns the king's genealogy and poetically was an opportunity for Jayanaka to demonstrate his dexterity by dedicating each verse to exemplifying a different figure of speech. Jayaratha quotes no verses that concern Islamic figures, although the poem's fifth chapter mentions a few military conflicts with the Ghaznavids (referred to as "matanga").[92] Jayaratha seemed to value Jayanaka's poem for reasons other than its historical topic matter.

In contrast, in the fifteenth century, the Kashmiri Jonaraja composed a commentary for the *Pṛthvīrājavijaya*. Jonaraja's interest in Indo-Muslim political history as seen in his *Rājataraṅgiṇī* (see chapter 4) suggests that Jayanaka's topic is what drew Jonaraja to this work. We have no evidence that the *Pṛthvīrājavijaya* was read outside Kashmir. However, we do know that there were multiple copies of the work available in Kashmir in the fifteenth century, since Jonaraja refers in his commentary to variant readings.[93] The only surviving manuscript of the poem today comes from Kashmir and is written in Sharada script.[94] Perhaps the *Pṛthvīrājavijaya* was especially compelling to Kashmiri intellectuals, like Jonaraja, who were working in a region that had witnessed dramatic social and political changes associated with Muslim migrations and Indo-Muslim rule.

Regardless of whether later readers appreciated or valued the text, Jayanaka formulated an innovative royal praise that utilized Sanskrit tools of othering in the service of commenting on new circumstances. On the one hand, Jayanaka responded to a fresh threat by reasserting old Sanskrit ways of organizing the world. He describes the Ghurids by reference to the varna system, labeling them as outcastes, and he exalts Prithviraj as a just king because he upholds Brahminical ritual practice and protects Hindu gods. Similarly, Jayanaka rejoices that Prithviraj possesses fluency in all six languages in which the Sanskrit tradition dictated that knowledge, including political knowledge, could be communicated. On the other hand, Jayanaka contrasts Prithviraj with a new group, namely the Ghurids, citing certain types of culturally specific behaviors. Here Jayanaka uses the powerful tool of comparison to redefine himself and his patron. He brings into sharp focus a tradition of Sanskrit-based kingship precisely by rejecting another, all-too-real Persian-medium option. In other words, Jayanaka's building blocks were, to a significant degree, generic Sanskrit ways of depicting an Other. But Jayanaka imbued his inherited ideas with specificity by contrasting Prithviraj with the Ghurids, a new political force within northern India.

Few other Sanskrit writers of the period pursued projects similar to Jayanaka's extended meditation on difference in the *Pṛthvīrājavijaya*, even those affiliated with the Chauhans. Seven Sanskrit inscriptions are known from Prithviraj's lifetime that name that king.[95] Of these, several commemorate Prithviraj's defeat of a King Paramardi, a Chandella ruler of Bundelkhand (and a "Hindu" king, in modern parlance), but none appear to refer to Chauhan clashes with the Ghurids. This omission is all the more striking given that some earlier inscriptions mention Chauhan conflicts with the Ghaznavids. For example, an 1164 inscription praises Vigraharaja IV for having repeatedly restored "the land of the Aryans" by "exterminating barbarians [mleccha]."[96] Prithviraj's court, too, does not seem to have supported other Sanskrit intellectuals who shared Jayanaka's interests. We have limited knowledge about Prithviraj's patronage, but a few tidbits surface in Jayanaka's work and in later literature that suggest that the king's court hosted a largely unexceptional lineup of bards and Sanskrit poets.[97] Jayanaka was atypical in his focus, at such an early date, on Indo-Persian rule, a topic that drew the attention of more Sanskrit writers in subsequent centuries.

CHAPTER III

Indo-Muslim Rulers

Expanding the World of Indian Kingship

Ravana's reputation was trashed,
and Rama became revered,
all due to Valmiki's poetic prowess.
Kings should not raise the ire of poets.

—BILHANA, *VIKRAMĀṄKADEVACARITA* (KING VIKRAMA'S DEEDS), CA. ELEVENTH CENTURY

Between roughly 1200 and 1450, Muslim rulers—or, at any rate, rulers who happened to be Muslim—gained control over areas of land from Kashmir down to Tamil Nadu, and Sanskrit intellectuals stretching across the same space wrote about these political changes. In northern India, the Delhi Sultanate constituted the most prominent group of Indo-Persian kings during this period, and I discuss below Sanskrit representations of the Khalji and Tughluq dynasties (I leave Kashmir for chapter 4). Muslim-led rule also spread to southern India, especially through Delhi Sultanate campaigns in the early fourteenth century. Around 1371, Vijayanagara troops destroyed the Sultanate of Madurai, an independent Muslim-led kingdom in Tamil Nadu that had broken away from Delhi Sultanate control nearly forty years earlier, and an account of this political annihilation forms the core story of a text analyzed in this chapter. Indian intellectuals who worked circa 1200–1450 inherited a range of options from the preceding half millennium for how to write about groups of Muslims in Sanskrit. But there were precious few Sanskrit precedents for how to think about what we now call Indo-Muslim or Indo-Persian kings. Jayanaka's *Pṛthvīrājavijaya*, the subject of the previous chapter, was written between 1191 and 1200, at the moment when Muslims began moving from Central Asia into northern India with the ambition of ruling areas of the subcontinent beyond Sindh. Accordingly, Jayanaka understood the Ghurids, in no uncertain terms, as outsiders. In contrast, one hundred years later, rulers who were Indian, Muslim, and, culturally, Persian were a political fact across parts of the northern, central, and southern subcontinent. From the thirteenth century to the mid-fifteenth century, Sanskrit thinkers wrote about this political reality and in so doing explored how Indo-Muslim rule might further expand the already capacious world of Indian kingship as articulated in Sanskrit literature.

There was never a single formula for how to rule or express royal identity as an Indian king, and so Indo-Muslim rulers joined a plural, polyglot tradition of subcontinental sovereignty. In real-world terms, India had long accommodated kings from various regional, religious, social, and ethnic backgrounds. To this already diverse universe, Indo-Muslim kings added their own robust ruling cultures, complete with new languages, norms of comportment, battle strategies, legitimation needs, patronage practices, building campaigns, and more. In literature, Sanskrit thinkers had long written about all sorts of Indian political figures using tropes that incorporated rulers, no matter how weak their power in reality, into grand visions of subcontinental kingship and also expressed cultural and political specificity. They did likewise for Indo-Muslim rulers. Sanskrit writers of this period generally articulated the political ambitions of Indo-Muslim kings using traditional, Sanskrit-based idioms of sovereignty. Some authors also offered glimpses of the Islamic and Persian traditions embraced by specific dynasties and leaders. In brief, in writing about Indo-Muslim kings, Sanskrit intellectuals drew upon their tradition's astonishing breadth regarding the possibilities for expressing sovereignty, which were further extended by imagining a new type of ruler.

The diversity—in region, religion, and gender—of Sanskrit intellectuals who wrote about Muslim-led rule between 1200 and 1450 enriches this body of materials. In this chapter, I draw upon Sanskrit inscriptions from across the period and two longer texts written within a few decades of each other: Gangadevi's *Madhurāvijaya* (Victory at Madurai; ca. 1380) and Nayachandra's *Hammīramahākāvya* (Great poem on Hammira Chauhan; ca. 1410).[1] Both Gangadevi and Nayachandra were court poets, working with support from the Vijayanagara and Tomar dynasties, respectively, but both were atypical in certain ways. Gangadevi was a queen, certainly not without precedent among Sanskrit authors but far from the norm.[2] Nayachandra was a Jain monk, an identity that does not dictate how he wrote in Sanskrit but helps explain his social context. The producers of the inscriptions that I discuss below are harder to pin down, but at least one was sponsored by a Muslim merchant. We moderns sometimes forget that premodern Sanskrit intellectuals were a diverse lot, as were their patrons, in terms of religion, location within India, careers, and sex. The authors and sponsors that I discuss below were united by their attention to the subject of Indo-Persian rule and its implications for Sanskrit-based political commentary. I argue that Sanskrit thinkers who wrote during and about the first few centuries of Indo-Muslim political power expressed a wide range of possible cultural and royal identities for subcontinental political figures.

Becoming and Redefining Indian Kings

As Indo-Persian rule dawned, Sanskrit intellectuals invented two new terms, *hammīra* and *suratrāṇa* (or *suratāla*), to describe Muslim rulers. "Hammira," from the Persian and Arabic *amīr,* was coined in Sanskrit in the early twelfth century and "suratrana," from *sulṭān,* in the thirteenth century.[3] These new words were akin to *tājika* and *turuṣka,* invented in the late first millennium CE (see chapter 1), in that they were adaptations of foreign terms into Sanskrit. The description *sura-trāṇa* holds an additional meaning as a Sanskrit phrase, namely "the gods' protector."[4] Sanskrit suffers from no shortage of words for king. And so, the coinage of fresh terms, including one that reads as a Sanskrit compound, suggests that Sanskrit intellectuals glimpsed something distinctive about Indo-Muslim sovereignty that they wished to mark in Sanskrit discourse. What was the substance of that novelty? My interest here lies not in on-the-ground differences between Muslim and non-Muslim Indian rulers of the period. Rather, I want to know what differences were expressed by Sanskrit intellectuals, as part of understanding how they conceptualized and discussed political power exercised by Persian-speaking Muslims.

Premodern Hindu kings were also known as "hammira" and "suratrana," and this dual usage is crucial for recovering what the terms meant for the Sanskrit intellectuals (and their non-Muslim royal patrons) who used them. The curious expansion took place a century or so after the advent of each respective term, and was localized. Hindu kings began to use the title hammira in the thirteenth century, and several hammiras are known circa 1250–1350 in northern India, including Hammira Chauhan, Hammiravarman (a Chandella), Hammira of Mewar, and Hamiradeva of Bundelkhand.[5] Incidentally, no Hindu kings called themselves "Hindu" at this point in time. The earliest known use of "Hindu" in Sanskrit dates to 1347, when Marappa, one of the Vijayanagara founders, declared himself to be a suratrana above and against more lowly Hindu rulers, a *hindurāyasuratāla* (sultan among Hindu kings).[6] Five years later, in 1352, his brother Bukka similarly fashioned himself, using what became the more standard Sanskrit "suratrana," a *hindūrāyasuratrāṇa* (sultan among Hindu kings). Bukka is referred to with the title suratrana in several subsequent inscriptions, both with and without the prefix *hindūrāya-*.[7] Other non-Muslim rulers in southern India subsequently claimed the title "sultan among Hindu kings" as well as other types of suratrana titles, such as *andhra-suratrāṇa* (sultan of Andhra).[8] Throughout this period, Sanskrit authors also dubbed various Indo-Muslim kings hammira and suratrana.

Medieval Indian thinkers declined to expressly outline what it meant to be a hammira or a suratrana, but the defining features appear to have been largely cultural. Since Hindu and Muslim rulers both used the titles, being Muslim was not required. In this sense, the English word "sultan" and its presumption of referring to a Muslim does a disservice as a translation for *suratrāṇa*. Arguably, however, our sense of "sultan" today does not reflect its contours in premodernity. Richard Eaton points out that, beginning in the eleventh century, Persian thinkers redefined this Arabic term to have resonances with pre-Islamic styles of rule, such as that of the Sasanians, thereby making "sultan" transportable across religious lines.[9] Some non-Muslim hammiras and suratranas adopted cultural practices associated with Indo-Muslim or Indo-Persian sovereignty. For example, Hammira Chauhan included dates on his coins in imitation of Islamic customs.[10] Vijayanagara kings wore Islamic-style dress at court.[11] In this sense, some Indian kings seem to have opted into being a hammira or a suratrana as part of a larger set of cultural choices. In other cases, the title indicated a relationship with an Indo-Muslim king. In an inscription at a Jain temple in Rajasthan circa 1440, Rana Kumbha of Mewar is said to have been given the title (*biruda*) of *hiṃdusuratrāṇa*, "sultan of Hindus," by virtue of his association with the "sultan (*suratrāṇa*) of Gujarat and Delhi."[12]

Being a hammira or a suratrana did not imply a rejection of other, non-Muslim modes of kingship and cultural expression. We know about Hamiradevi of the Gehlot clan, the only woman known to have adopted the hammira title, because her name is engraved on a pillar commemorating her sati in 1287.[13] The Vijayanagara rulers donned traditional Indian garb in other contexts, such as during Hindu religious rituals, and expressed their sovereignty using a panoply of Hindu idioms.[14] At times Vijayanagara figures used culturally coded clothing and appearance to celebrate their seemingly symbiotic participation in two politico-cultural traditions. At the Varadaraja temple complex at Kanchipuram there is a hall, built circa 1550–1600, during Vijayanagara rule, that features horses whose riders are literally two-faced, appearing with a mustache and pants on one side and clean-shaven and wearing a dhoti on the other.[15] In the late Vijayanagara Empire (ca. sixteenth century–early seventeenth century), a series of four Sanskrit texts articulate a political foundation myth that links "the authority of the Vijayanagara state as deriving directly *from that of the [Delhi] Sultanate*."[16]

Being a suratrana could imply superiority over other types of Indian or "Hindu" kings. In the phrase *hindūrāya-suratrāṇa*, Bukka proclaimed himself a sultan (*suratrāṇa*) who stood out among Hindu kings (*hindūrāya*). In this context, "Hindu" did not denote a religious identity so much as a royal tradition, to which Bukka positioned himself as superior.[17] This reading is bolstered by Vidyatilaka's roughly contemporary use of "Hindu" as a political qualifier in Prakrit to refer to Hindu kings (*hiṃduarāyāṇo*) and Hindu rule (*hiṃduarajje*); he contrasts the latter to non-Aryan rule (*aṇajjarajje*).[18] "Hindu" was as new as "suratrana" in Sanskrit and so constituted part of the innovation in how to think about the changes that Indo-Muslim rule brought to the reality and imagination of Indian politics.

The cultural innovations embodied by the terms "hammira" and "suratrana" did not escape the notice of Muslim rulers. Some used the title hammira in limited cases where they expressed their political ambitions in Sanskrit. For instance, the coins of Muhammad Ghori (d. 1206) bear, in Devanagari script, the Sanskrit titles *śrīhammīra* and *śrīmad hammīra* (glorious hammira).[19] Iltutmish (r. 1210–36) issued coins heralding himself as *suratāna śrīsamsadīna* (glorious sultan Shamsuddin; "Shamsuddin" was Iltutmish's given name).[20] Such coins signal that Muslim rulers newly established on the subcontinent desired to communicate their sovereign claims in the language of Sanskrit kingship and that this idiom included, by early in the thirteenth century, adapted Perso-Arabic titles such as hammira.

In northern India, thirteenth-century and fourteenth-century Sanskrit intellectuals also integrated Indo-Muslim rulers into the tradition of Indian kingship by positioning them as successors to earlier, non-Muslim lineages. Three Sanskrit inscriptions near Delhi, dating between 1276 and 1328, list the Tomars, Chauhans, and early Delhi Sultanate rulers as successive kings of Delhi and surrounding areas.[21] The same chronology is found in a fourth

Figure 3.1 Two-faced rider, Kalyana Mandapa, Varadaraja temple, Kanchipuram, clean-shaven side
Photo by author, 2019

Figure 3.2 Two-faced rider, Kalyana Mandapa, Varadaraja temple, Kanchipuram, mustached side
Photo by author, 2019

inscription, in Jodhpur, that was sponsored in 1316 by a khatri who worked for the Delhi Sultanate.[22] Notably for my purposes here, these inscriptions do not elaborate any differences associated with the Delhi Sultanate. Neither do they mark the political transition to Ghurid rule as involving a cultural break. Take, for example, the 1276 Palam Baoli inscription:

> At first the land of Haryana was enjoyed by the Tomars,
> then by the Chauhans, and now it is ruled by the Sultanates
> [*śakendra*].[23]

Some of the inscriptions are a tad more verbose on the transition of power, but they use terms that roughly equate the dynasties. For example, the 1328 Sarban stone inscription lauds, in quite comparable terms, how the Chauhans rid their kingdom of thorns and how Shihabuddin Muhammad Ghori (*sahāvadīna*)—the first Delhi Sultanate ruler named in the inscription—scorched his enemies.[24] The Jodhpur inscription is the only one to bother to gloss the Delhi Sultanate (*śaka*), identifying their leaders as "lords of elephants, horses, and men," or, in simpler terms, kings.[25]

All four inscriptions focus on Delhi, and this is a major, if internally unacknowledged, innovation that reflects a change in political geography enacted by the Delhi Sultanate. The Chauhan kingdom was centered in Ajmer. Cynthia Talbot has traced how Delhi supplanted Ajmer in the popular memory of Prithviraj Chauhan, especially during the sixteenth and seventeenth centuries.[26] This shift appeared in Indo-Persian texts also, such as in an unpublished Persian work that, within its list of Delhi-based kings, from Yudhishthira to Humayun (d. 1556), places Prithviraj "on the throne of Indraprastha."[27] Even earlier, Barani's *Tārīkh-i Fīrūzshāhī*, completed in 1357, describes Prithviraj Raj as "of Delhi" (*pithūrā rāī-yi dihlī*).[28] The four Delhi-affiliated inscriptions offer an early glimpse of this turn to Delhi as the assumed epicenter of political power in northern India. In real-world terms, this shift was occasioned by the advent of Muslim-led dynasties centered in Delhi, beginning with the Ghurids. What strikes me here is how that reality was integrated, in a matter of decades, into Sanskrit representations of political authority in the present and the past. Sanskrit thinkers, indeed, integrated Delhi Sultanate rulers into the robust world of Indian kingship, and they moreover used changes introduced by the Sultanate as a springboard for recasting a much deeper political past.

Even beyond royalty, Muslim communities were viewed by Sanskrit authors as generally fitting within known Indian practices across religious groups. For example, Indian kings and merchants had long sponsored multiple religious communities.[29] In line with this practice, Jagadu, a thirteenth-century Gujarati trader and a Jain, bankrolled the construction or repair of a mosque used by Ismaili Muslims. Sarvananda mentions Jagadu's patronage in a favorable Sanskrit biography of the trader, the *Jagaḍūcarita* (Acts of Jagadu), likely composed in the fourteenth or early fifteenth century.[30] Sarvananda notes Jagadu sponsoring the mosque (*masīti*, in Sanskrit) in a section devoted to Jagadu's pious behaviour of financing religious buildings across multiple traditions, including numerous Jain shrines and a Hindu temple (*hariśaṅkaramandira*).[31] Likewise, writing in 1349, Rajashekhara says that the thirteenth-century Vaghela ministers Vastupala and Tejahpala gave money to support sixty-four mosques (*maśīti*).[32] Muslim communities slotted easily into preexisting transreligious patronage practices on the subcontinent and the tradition of praising such generosity in Sanskrit.

Muslims also sponsored the construction of mosques in thirteenth-century Gujarat, but even there Sanskrit thinkers expressed cultural continuity. Most notable here is the 1264 erection of a mosque in Veraval, near Somanatha on the Gujarat coastline. The mosque was patronized by Nuruddin Firuz (*noradīnapīroja*, in Sanskrit), a trader from Hormuz, and was accompanied by a Sanskrit inscription and a shorter Arabic summary dating two months later.[33] The very existence of this inscription, etched first in Sanskrit, expresses cultural consistency.[34] Indians had long lauded the establishment of places of worship with Sanskrit inscriptions, and, in this case, the addition of mosques to the religious landscape did not alter that practice. The Sanskrit inscription also attempts to adapt Islamic religious ideas, notably without comment. The Sanskrit inscription opens with praise of the "lord of the world" (*viśvanātha*), described as "omnipresent, formless, and both visible and invisible" (*viśvarūpa, śūnyarūpa, lakṣālakṣa*).[35] Vishvanatha, the "lord of the world," could be Shiva, but it could also be Allah, a reading that would make sense of the slightly unusual epithets.[36] That the reader cannot fully tell whether the opening lines refer to Shiva or to Allah signals the possibility of cultural similitude. Quite likely, the author of this Sanskrit inscription regarded broad Hindu ideas about divinity, expressed in Sanskrit praise poetry, as flexible enough to incorporate allusions to the Islamic God. Later Sanskrit and Arabic paired inscriptions in Gujarat offer analogous vagueness. For instance, a 1499 Sanskrit inscription at a stepwell near

Ahmedabad sponsored by Bai Harir, a woman and a courtier of the Gujarati sultan Mahmud Begada (r. 1459–1511), opens with praise to the Creator (*sṛṣṭikartṛ*), which could be equally construed as Allah or Brahma.[37]

By virtue of being in Sanskrit and Arabic, the 1264 Veraval inscription affords us an opportunity to ask what one could *not* say in Sanskrit in this period when discussing Islam and Muslims. The question is especially useful since the Sanskrit inscription is overall more verbose than the Arabic summary, and so omissions in the Sanskrit portion likely indicate agency rather than mere brevity. The Sanskrit inscription incorporates a number of Islamic cultural and religious ideas. In addition to likely praise of Allah, the Sanskrit inscription records the date in multiple calendrical systems, including the Hijri calendar (*rasūlamahammadasaṃvat*).[38] It mentions expenditures required for the mosque's upkeep and Muslim religious festivals to be celebrated at the site.[39] Incidentally, such details are absent from the Arabic summary. In one passage, the Sanskrit inscription employs several Persian terms, including *musulmān-jamā'at*, or the "Muslim community" (*muśalamāna-jamātha* in Sanskrit), and *shahr*, or "city" (*śahara* in Sanskrit).[40] However, the Sanskrit inscription omits a rhetorical wish for Somanatha to become an Islamic city, which is found in the Arabic summary. Perhaps an oblique allusion to this in the Sanskrit rests in the use of Persian *shahr* in lieu of a common Sanskrit word for city, such as *nagara*. Still, the Sanskrit inscription also elides some eulogistic titles for the patron Nuruddin Firuz and his father, such as "sun of Islam and Muslims" and "protector of Islam and Muslims," respectively, that are found in the Arabic portion.[41] Even such slight differences attest that the language in which one wrote mattered in premodern India. That aspects of Muslim peoples and cultures could not be easily expressed in Sanskrit poetry arguably makes it all the more remarkable that Sanskrit intellectuals repeatedly returned to the subject of Indo-Persian rule, both to document particular events and to find new inspirations and foils for their own identities.

Praising Political Violence at Madurai

Indo-Muslim rulers used force to achieve their aims, and thereby they perpetuated a core aspect of kingship in India and elsewhere: political violence. As Upinder Singh states bluntly in her recent tome, *Political Violence in Ancient India*, "Violence lies at the heart of the state."[42] There was light variation in the forms and targets of state-sponsored violence across dynasties, but all Indian rulers participated in this bloody world. Additionally, Sanskrit poets had long seized upon the reality of political violence as fodder for crafting poetry that reveled in the gore of battle. As Indo-Muslim kings entrenched themselves on the subcontinent and expanded their control through warfare, Sanskrit authors produced large-scale poems that feature violent encounters with these polities and thereby integrated their rulers into the intertwined realms, as articulated in Sanskrit literature, of kingship and poetry. An earlier generation of scholars misread, rather gravely, the significance of this literary development. Sanskrit poetic portrayals of violence involving Muslims did not mark Muslims as abnormally bloodthirsty, nor did they constitute some sort of mass literary resistance.[43] Rather, in a world where warring was an integral part of kingship and literature, Sanskrit authors signaled a willingness to investigate the literary possibilities of Muslim-led rule by pitching Muslims as worthy foes and, in some cases, as heros on the battlefield. In other words, writing about the violence enacted by Indo-Muslim political leaders likened them to, rather than distinguished them from, other Indian rulers.

Exemplifying this phenomenon in her *Madhurāvijaya* (Victory at Madurai), Gangadevi measures a Muslim military opponent using Sanskrit-based cultural and aesthetic values. The poem narrates the circa 1371 overthrow of the Sultanate of Madurai, known in Persian and Arabic sources as the Sultanate of Maʿbar.[44] Khalji and Tughluq troops had laid the groundwork for this polity roughly half a century earlier when they penetrated deep into Tamil Nadu, making it as far south as Madurai, in 1311 and 1323, respectively.[45] They left behind Muslim governors in Madurai who then broke away from the Delhi Sultanate in 1333.[46] Several successive rulers administered the independent Sultanate of Madurai for the next forty years, until the devastating assault of the Vijayanagara king Kampan around 1371.[47] Gangadevi, one of Kampan's wives, penned the nine-chapter *Madhurāvijaya* in the following few decades and may have been an eyewitness to Kampan's victory.[48]

From the beginning Gangadevi situates her work in the historical contexts of Khalji and Tughluq military campaigns in southern India, often enveloped within literary conventions. In the poem's first chapter, Gangadevi offers twelves verses that each praise a prior poet. The first nine poets are mainly classical authors, including Valmiki, Bharavi, Dandin, and Bhavabhuti.[49] The last three poets praised by Gangadevi—Agastya,

Gangadhara, and Vishvanatha—were all associated with the court of the last Kakatiya ruler, Pratap Rudra (r. 1289–1323), in Warangal, in the eastern Deccan.[50] Even while ruling nearly 1,000 kilometers north of Madurai, Pratap Rudra had been involved in the same Khalji and Tughluq campaigns, in 1311 and 1323, respectively, that affected Madurai. In 1311, Pratap Rudra joined Alauddin Khalji's troops and participated in the assault on the Pandyas at Kanchipuram. In 1323, Ulugh Khan sacked Warangal, thus ending the Kakatiya dynasty. Ulugh Khan tried to drag Pratap Rudra back to Delhi, but the dethroned king committed suicide en route.[51] Some modern commentators have taken Gangadevi's reference to three of Pratap Rudra's court poets as evidence for her projecting continuity between the defunct Kakatiya dynasty and Vijayanagara.[52] Some even see in these references evidence that Gangadevi was a Kakatiya princess.[53] I think that she alludes to Pratap Rudra's court in order to invoke the wider history of Delhi Sultanate military activities in southern India that, ultimately, resulted in the establishment of the Sultanate of Madurai.

In her mention of three of Pratap Rudra's poets, Gangadevi uses a Sanskrit convention to invoke political history, and this strategy, which recurs throughout her poem, provides insight into a key question: Why did she write in Sanskrit? Gangadevi is the earliest poet discussed in this book who faced a real choice between writing in Sanskrit versus vernacular languages. The Vijayanagara court sponsored Tamil and Telugu writers, and Gangadevi includes a thirteenth-century Telugu writer, Tikkana, in her list of twelve poets.[54] But in electing to write in Sanskrit, Gangadevi ensured full access to the rich universe of Sanskrit conventions and tropes. Practically, this means that Gangadevi expected her readers to possess a strong grasp of both Sanskrit poetics and Indo-Persian political history in order to understand her layered work. It also attests that she saw the edifice of conventions within Sanskrit literature not as a hindrance, but rather as providing a useful framework for writing about historical events. Indeed, throughout her poem, Gangadevi describes Madurai's Muslim rulers in conventional and historically specific ways, sometimes simultaneously.

Gangadevi portrays the Sultanate of Madurai as a strong political foe, most often describing it no differently than any other southern Indian polity. The Sultanate of Madurai was surrounded by "Hindu" powers, including the Sambuvarayas, Pandyas, and Vijayanagara. In her poem, Gangadevi describes large parts of Kampan's conflict with the Sultanate in a fashion similar to how she depicts an earlier Vijayanagara battle with the

Sambuvarayas, vassals that emerged in the late Chola period. Early on, Gangadevi pairs these two major enemies of Kampan in the voice of his father, Bukka, who exhorts his son:

Spare no effort in reaching Tundira
and laying waste to the battle-ready troops of Champa.
Then rule Kanchi as per the will of the people,
as Kubera rules Alaka.

After you have overpowered all the forest rulers,
then breaking the sultan [turushka] should not be difficult.
After engulfing the cover provided by hundreds of branches,
how can a forest fire fail to consume the tree trunk?

The sultan rules over the southern lands
with the evil designs of Ravana, lord of demons.
You should perform the pure action of Rama,
and rid the three worlds of this menace.[55]

In Bukka's words, as imagined by Gangadevi, the Sambuvarayas and the Sultanate of Madurai are tightly linked as enemies of Vijayanagara, with no difference noted between them on religious grounds. In the middle verse quoted above, she even describes the Sultanate as the tree trunk (*prakāṇḍa*) and the Sambuvarayas as the branches (*śākhā*).[56] In her account of the final battle between Kampan and the sultan of Madurai, Gangadevi returns to this association, declaring that Kampan shot at the sultan with arrows that had previously killed the Sambuvaraya king Champa.[57] Still, Gangadevi reserves her harshest and most protracted language for the sultan of Madurai, thus marking him as Kampan's most formidable enemy. Above he is imagined as the demon king Ravana, to be defeated by Rama-like Kampan. Elsewhere in the work, Gangadevi compares Kampan confronting the sultan to Krishna slaying the demon Kamsa.[58]

Gangadevi devotes more attention to describing the Sultanate of Madurai as compared to the Sambuvarayas, and her disparate attention marks Kampan's clash with Sultanate forces as the poem's narrative climax. Kampan's battle with the Sambuvarayas is narrated in the *Madhurāvijaya*'s fourth chapter, and the battle for Madurai occupies chapters 8 and 9, the poem's final surviving chapters. Historically, roughly a decade passed between these two events, a period during which Kampan ruled from Kanchi (Kanchipuram). Poetically this gap is represented by chapters 5 through 7, which depict Kampan's activities as a king, especially his amorous pursuits. For instance, chapter 6 is devoted to his water play with women. In the lead-up to the Vijayanagara-Sambuvaraya battle in chapter 4, Gangadevi keeps her focus, for roughly fifty verses, on Kampan's forces marching to battle, and makes little mention of the Sambuvarayas.[59] In contrast, the destruction brought by the Sultanate occupies much of the thirty-six surviving verses of the *Madhurāvijaya*'s eighth chapter.

Gangadevi devotes chapter 8 to a maligning description of the Sultanate of Madurai, put in the voice of a goddess who encourages Kampan to attack. The first verse of chapter 8 is largely lost, so we lack a clear identification of the goddess. Guessing from context, she is Durga.[60] In terms of the poem's plot, the goddess catalogues the Sultanate's sins in order to motivate Kampan to return to the battlefield after ten years spent pursuing the finer pleasures of royal life at Kanchi. While Gangadevi packs numerous historical references into this section (as I discuss below), her overarching framework is provided by Sanskrit conventions. A literary precedent for this part of the *Madhurāvijaya* is found in the description of Ayodhya in chapter 16 of Kalidasa's *Raghuvaṃśa* (Raghu's lineage; ca. fifth century CE) where a goddess also describes a ruined landscape. The *Madhurāvijaya* even repeats some of Kalidasa's imagery, such as mourning the loss of women's tinkling anklets on the royal highway and noting that sculptures are obscured by animals who have occupied a depopulated city.[61] In her own twist, Gangadevi adds an additional layer to the female voice in this section of her poem to underscore the virility of the Sultanate threat. She ends chapter 7 with a scene in which she, the queen, charms Kampan with a beguiling description of night. Coming immediately after this melodious female voice, which is Gangadevi's voice twice over as lover and author, the goddess's harsh words appear all the more jarring and damning.

Several verses in the first half of chapter 8 invoke the historical memory of Muslim-led campaigns that laid the groundwork for the Sultanate of Madurai. For example, verse 2 mentions the 1311 sacking of the Srirangam temple by Khalji forces led by Malik Kafur:

> Shesha, lord of snakes, fearful that Vishnu
> will awake from his deep meditative sleep at Srirangam,
> fans his hood to block the cascades of falling bricks.[62]

The 1311 assault on the Srirangam temple was an important precursor to establishing the Sultanate of Madurai. It also held a powerful place in historical memory, inspiring Sanskrit poetry that dwells on an aestheticized emotion of fear.[63] The immediately preding verse in chapter 8 mentions Chidambaram, where Malik Kafur damaged a Shiva temple before striking Srirangam.[64] In addition to their names evoking historical events, Chidambaram and Srirangam are on the road, in that order, from Kanchi to Madurai, and so these verses chronicle the geography of Kampan's marching forces. A few verses later, Gangadevi mentions the Kaveri River, which flows by Srirangam. For Gangadevi, there was no conflict between geographical references and her literary ambitions. Accordingly, she laments that the Kaveri River had overflowed its shore and now "flows crookedly in imitation of the Sultanate [*tuluṣka*]."[65]

Gangadevi's opening verses in chapter 8 also sketch out a sacred landscape inhabited by the gods who, her narrative goes, Kampan will save. After noting Vishnu's besieged position in verse 2, verse 3 bemoans that Shiva also suffered. Verse 4 offers a sweeping view of the Sultanate as having compromised the veneration of many Hindu gods:

> I am anguished to see many temples of the various other gods—
> their doors eaten away by woodworms,
> their halls overgrown with wild weeds,
> their inner sanctums in disarray.[66]

Gangadevi's approach here echoes that of Jayanaka in the initial chapter of his *Pṛthvīrājavijaya*, penned two hundred years earlier, in that both articulate a political threat in grounded religious terms. Some of the imagery is even similar. For example, both poets mention the tears of imprisoned Brahmins.[67] There is no evidence that Gangadevi knew of Jayanaka's poem, and so their similarities are best taken as part of a wider trend in Sanskrit literature to articulate kingship across a sacred landscape.

In the next twelve verses, Gangadevi, in the voice of the goddess, proclaims that the Sultanate has turned the proper state of affairs on its head in and around Madurai. She mourns that temple drums have been replaced by howling jackals, women's tinkling anklets by Brahmins' clanking chains, and so forth.[68] In a particularly evocative verse, she plays on both smell and sound:

Before Brahmin villages were scented with thick smoke from sacrifices
and resounded with the chanting of the Vedas.
Now they reek of raw meat
and are pierced by the jeering of drunken Sultanate men [tulushka].[69]

Not all of the inversions rely upon religious imagery, and Gangadevi also invokes more general destruction as a way to defame the Sultanate and thus spur Kampan into military action. For instance, in one verse the goddess anguishes that lush bunches of coconuts in Madurai's groves have been replaced by spears bearing necklaces of human skulls.[70] In another verse, Gangadevi draws upon the rich (and largely generic) Sanskrit tradition of describing bathing women to write, regarding the Tamraparni River south of Madurai:

The water of the Tamraparni River used to be whitened
by sandalwood paste washed off the breasts of young women.
Now it is reddened by the blood of cows
slain on her banks by evil men.[71]

The literary appeal is heightened by the play on the river's name, Tamraparni, which literally means "red-leaved" in Sanskrit. Gangadevi's inversions are poetically compelling, and they make the impending defeat of the Sultanate of Madurai at Kampan's hands a potent victory that can be celebrated in political and poetic terms.

The goddess concludes her initial speech to Kampan by underscoring what has been lost during Sultanate rule and thus what can be regained by Kampan's triumph. The final verse of the speech, verse 16, is best read with the crescendo of the prior two verses, which invoke regional identities and human suffering:

The earth no longer produces wealth as it used to.
Indra does not make it rain as he once did.
Even Yama drags people away before their time,
if they have not yet been massacred by the Sultanate [yavana].

I am anguished to see the faces of southerners [*dramiḍa*],
lips withered by heavy sighs,

curly hair droopy and disheveled,
eyes flooded with tears.

The Veda has sunk.
The rule of law has fled.
All talk of dharma has disappeared.
Good conduct has vanished.
Merit has perished.
Noble birth has ebbed.
What else is there to say?
The Era of Darkness alone flourishes.[72]

After this speech (translated more fully in appendix A.3), the goddess gifts Kampan a sword fashioned by Vishvakarman from the weapons of all the gods, which Kampan is to use to defeat the sultan.[73] The goddess then returns to her earlier theme of the harsh consequences of Sultanate rule, except that she focuses more on Kampan's ability to uproot this "thorn in the side of the three worlds."[74] The chapter breaks off after a verse proclaiming that the Kaveri River will resume its proper course upon Kampan's victory; the next ten leaves of the manuscript are lost.[75] While Gangadevi's intention to malign the Sultanate is clear, the terms in which she imagines this enemy require further parsing to appreciate their mix of specificity and tropes.

Gangadevi, in the goddess's voice, offers some commentary about what sets the Sultanate of Madurai apart from others Indian polities, but the markers are, in large part, generic markers for outsiders. She describes the Sultanate and associated people as "yavana" and "turushka" (using the southern variant *tuluṣka*), both, by this period, standard Sanskrit terms for Muslims of various ethnic backgrounds as well as for Greeks and Turks (including non-Muslims), respectively. Gangadevi says, in separate verses, that Sultanate men and women both drink alcohol.[76] She describes the Sultanate people as meat eaters and cow killers.[77] A similar lineup of features—including boozing, harming Brahmins, and beef eating—also appear in other contemporary Sanskrit sources that portray Muslim political enemies, such as a circa 1340 land grant in Andhra Pradesh that describes Tughluq forces.[78] As Cynthia Talbot has pointed out, many of these conventions repurposed older Sanskrit anxieties about non-Aryans who threatened to undermine Brahmin privileges.[79] Indeed, Gangadevi draws on Sanskrit poetic precedents for describing outsiders to the Hindu class system. For instance, her verse calling out drunken Sultanate women (*yavanī*) plays in both its language and imagery on a verse penned nearly a millennium earlier by Kalidasa, in his *Raghuvaṃśa*, on drunken Greek women (*yavanī*).[80]

Gangadevi comments on the appearance and speech of those affiliated with the Sultanate of Madurai, which adds some cultural and political specificity. In one verse, she describes the bushy beards, broad foreheads, and prominent eyebrows of Sultanate men.[81] The goddess also condemns the Sultanate's language choice of Persian:

> The screeching of owls in the old groves
> does not grate on me as much as
> the chatter of Persian words
> from parrots who live in Sultanate [yavana] homes.[82]

Both the physical appearance and speech of Muslims are subjects that also arose in Jayanaka's *Pṛthvīrājavijaya*. As I quoted in chapter 2, Jayanaka similarly compared Persian to animal sounds (in his case, "the cry of wild birds").[83] Gangadevi takes the likening of Persian to animal noises a step further by putting the language in the voices, not of men, but of pet birds. So far as we know, Gangadevi did not read Jayanaka. Nonetheless, these similarities indicate that these two poet-historians were working with a shared tool kit of thinking about Persian-speaking political figures. In terms of understanding whom Gangadevi is criticizing as Other, it is important that she does not appear to include all Muslims in Tamil Nadu. Muslim traders, attracted by commerce along India's southern coasts, spoke about a region they termed Maʿbar in and around Madurai as early as 1200–10.[84] But Gangadevi does not appear to link the Sultanate with earlier waves of Muslim merchants. Instead, she relies upon well-established ways of talking about sovereignty in Sanskrit literary culture, such as through discussing language, to describe the Sultanate of Madurai.[85] For Gangadevi, that the leaders of the Sultanate of Madurai were rulers seems to have been more crucial than their religious identity.

At times, Gangadevi's language suggests that region more than religion qualified the Sultanate of Madurai as different. In verses 14 and 15 (quoted above), Gangadevi's goddess contrasts yavanas, or Sultanate people, to dramidas, or southerners. Here the Sultanate of Madurai's origins in northern India seem to be at issue. Relatedly, Sanskrit thinkers used the term "yavana" for both Greeks and Muslims because of the commonality that both came from the north. A similar concern with place of origin arises in Indo-Persian texts from the same period. For example, writing in the Deccan around 1350, Isami assails the oppression of outsiders, pitting Mongols (*mughal*) against Indians (*hindiyān, hindūī*), the latter group including Indian Muslims.[86] Isami also explains the context of his writing, in his view, as pious Deccani Muslims rising up against the northern tyrant Muhammad bin Tughluq.[87]

Gangadevi also indicates sensitivity to a dynasty's region of origin in her attempts to pitch Vijayanagara kings as inheritors of the Pandyas, the pre-Sultanate rulers of Madurai. For example, the goddess gave Kampan a sword that Shiva had previously presented to the Pandyan kings.[88] Using this sword that embodied Pandyan power, Kampan later severed the head of the sultan who, Gangadevi notes, had failed to bow to the gods (*divaukasām apyakṛtapraṇāmaṃ*).[89] Gangadevi also connects the two dynasties by noting that the Pandyas marched with Kampan against the Sambuvarayas and in her repeated references to how Madurai and surrounding areas used to flourish under Pandyan rule and could again prosper under Vijayanagara control.[90] As Richard Davis has argued, Kampan was a Telugu in Tamil land and, as an outsider, benefited from this projected continuity.[91] Even today some Tamils perceive Vijayanagara's non-Tamil origins as worthy of comment. In January 2019, a resident of Madurai told me that the Vijayanagara kingdom constituted "foreign rule" over Tamil Nadu owing to the dynasty's origins farther north.

Religion comes up in various ways in Gangadevi's narrative that undermine any modern tendency to read rigid Hindu-Muslim conflict into this premodern work. For instance, Gangadevi lauds Kampan's seizure of Kanchi from the Sambuvarayas by proclaiming that Vijayanagara rule brought an end to intermingling in the caste system and confusion in life stages (*varṇāśrama*).[92] In other words, restoring varna-based dharma followed what was, in modern terms, a Hindu-on-Hindu battle. The Sultanate of Madurai appears to have shared the Sambuvarayas' lack of commitment to dharma, in Gangadevi's view. In the final verses of chapter eight, Gangadevi criticizes the Sultanate for spreading "a corrupt dharma [*adharmadharma*]."[93] Given the idioms of kingship in premodern Sanskrit, Gangadevi had every incentive to invoke religiously tinged language as part and parcel of discussing clashes with various political foes, whether Hindu or Muslim.

In the battle between Vijayanagara troops and the Sultanate of Madurai, narrated in the ninth and final chapter of the *Madhurāvijaya*, Gangadevi treats the Sultanate no differently than any other political opponent or, indeed, even the to-be-victor. The first hundred verses are missing in chapter nine, and so modern readers are thrown into the story during the heat of battle.[94] Notably, the surviving verses do not distinguish Vijayanagara and Sultanate warriors from one another. For example:

Blood-stained pearls tumbled down
as heroes' swords split open the temples of rutting elephants.
They seemed to spread out like showers of sparks
that arose from the frenzy of the moment.[95]

A few verses later:

After being locked in battle for a seeming eternity,
two warriors cut off each other's heads with swords.
A moment later, they abandoned their bodies
and went to heaven as friends.[96]

Such poetry trades on the appetite of premodern Sanskrit readers for butchery on the battlefield. Notably, Gangadevi does not distinguish Sultanate forces in any way in this section. In fact, she uses similar tropes to describe Kampan's battles with the Sambuvarayas and the Sultanate. In both clashes, she imagines warriors were dispatched to heaven as the battlefields were crisscrossed by rivers of blood.[97] In the Sambuvaraya clash, demon women drank blood from human trunks, and in the Sultanate clash, they wore detached heads as ornaments.[98] Both conflicts featured severed limbs. In the Sambuvaraya battle, eagles snatched arms, mistaking them for snakes, whereas in the Sultanate battle, hands fell into pools of blood like snakes at Janamejaya's sacrifice.[99]

Chapter 9 and the *Madhurāvijaya* as a whole climax with a duel between Kampan and the sultan of Madurai. The Kampan-sultan contest occupies twenty verses, in comparison to the seven verses that describe Kampan's one-on-one battle with Champa, the Sambuvaraya king.[100] Other aspects of the work also mark the battle between Kampan and the sultan as the key event, the *vijaya* of the title. For instance, at the moment of Kampan's birth in chapter 2, Gangadevi describes Bukka, Kampan's father, as emptying out his prisons in order to make room "for the imminent arrival of scores of Sultanate [tulushka] prisoners."[101] Narratively, this event does not come to pass. Instead, Gangadevi says that Kampan shows mercy to beaten Sultanate troops.[102] Historically things are murkier. Shams Siraj Afif, who wrote his *Tārīkh-i Fīrūzshāhī* in the late fourteenth century, reports that Vijayanagara forces demolished Madurai and the Muslims within, but there are good reasons to doubt his account.[103] In any case, some Muslim communities survived in and around Madurai. A 1387 inscription in Kayalpatnam, more than 150 kilometers south of Madurai, attests that Muslims participated in trade and maintained an active judiciary.[104] Even today you can visit graves of three of the sultans of Madurai that survive in two Sufi dargahs: the Goripalayam Dargah, in the northern part of Madurai, and the Thiruparankundram Dargah, just outside the city on the summit of Thiruparankundram.[105]

Gangadevi portrays the final duel as a fierce clash between worthy adversaries and thereby underscores the virulence of Kampan's triumph. She refers to the sultan as "suratrana," a complimentary term among Vijayanagara royalty, including Kampan's father (see discussion above).[106] Gangadevi upholds the sultan as a robust rival, in large part because of his prior conquests:

> The sultan valorously decimated the Cholas and Pandyas.
> He cut down the prosperity of the Hoysala king Ballala.
> The powerful hero King Kampan delighted
> to face the sultan [suratrana] in battle.[107]

After Kampan slices off the sultan's head, flowers rained down from the sky in a signal of divine approval, and the entire southern region (*digdakṣiṇā*) gleamed.[108] Such fancies are well grounded in Sanskrit poetics. But they offer little detail on the sultan beyond him being a serious regional threat and thus his overthrow constituting a serious regional victory.

In summary, Gangadevi's goal of commemorating a royal military triumph was well worn in her literary tradition, and, accordingly, she drew on a deep well of available tropes. Kampan's adversary, an Indian sultan, was still relatively new on the subcontinent and even more so in Sanskrit poetry. But arguably Gangadevi judged his religious novelty less important than the Sultanate's northern Indian origins. In any case, Muslim-led rule was a phenomenon that extended deep into southern areas of the

Figure 3.3 Goripalayam Dargah, Madurai, site of two graves of the sultans of Madurai
Photo by author, 2019

Figure 3.4 Thiruparankundram Dargah, outside of Madurai, site of grave of Sultan Alauddin Sikandar Shah, the last sultan of Madurai, external view
Photo by author, 2019

Figure 3.5 Thiruparankundram Dargah, outside of Madurai, site of grave of Sultan Alauddin Sikandar Shah, the last sultan of Madurai, internal view
Photo by author, 2019

subcontinent by the late fourteenth century, and Gangadevi integrated the sultan into Sanskrit poetry as a respected rival ruler. In a sense, we are left with what, absent our own bad assumptions in modern times, might be a bland observation: namely, the interests of Sanskrit intellectuals expanded apace with changes in their political environment. Others soon followed Gangadevi in discussing Indo-Muslim military events in Sanskrit, albeit often in pursuit of different goals and with a different relationship to their cultural inheritance. I next turn to Nayachandra, who worked only a few decades after Gangadevi. Nayachandra also wrote about a military takeover and the end of a dynasty, but he articulated more startling ideas regarding how Muslim political actors were changing the nature of Kshatriya heroism.

A Vaideshika Exemplifies Kshatriya Loyalty at Ranthambhor

Nayachandra's *Hammīramahākāvya* (Great poem on Hammira Chauhan) narrates the history of the Chauhan dynasty, including conflicts with Muslim and Indo-Muslim rulers over several centuries. The fourteen-chapter poem, written between 1402 and 1423, culminates with Alauddin Khalji's 1301 assault on Ranthambhor Fort, in Rajasthan, and the death of the last Chauhan king, Hammira, in battle.[109] Nayachandra does not reveal his sources for this history, although his narration of the 1301 battle accords with Indo-Persian accounts in many details. Like Gangadevi, Nayachandra expressed aesthetic motivations for his work:

> Those assembled at the court of the Tomar King Virama taunted:
> *These days nobody can craft a poem like the poems of poets of old.*
> In response, poet Nayachandra, who plays across the earth, crafted this new poem
> about King Hammira, complete with erotic love, heroism [*vīra*], and wonders.[110]

A few verses earlier, Nayachandra also cited a pseudohistorical motivation, writing that Hammira Chauhan appeared to him in a dream and inspired a heroic poem about his life.[111] In reality, Nayachandra's work is far more than a royal ballad. Nayachandra used Chauhan conflict with the

Delhi Sultanate as a backdrop against which to unfold an ethics of heroism, which he defined by actions that prove loyalty and did not restrict in terms of religion, social status, or place of origin.

The *Hammīramahākāvya* chronicles a dynasty that ended more than a century before Nayachandra's own time, but the work hinges on themes crucial to the Tomar context. Nayachandra reports that he wrote at the court of King Virama Tomar (r. 1402–23).[112] The fifteenth-century Tomar court was at Gwalior and was populated by, among others, Jains who had left Delhi in the aftermath of Firuz Shah's death, in 1388, and Timur's sack of the city, in 1398.[113] Gwalior was not a safe haven from political disruption, however, and experienced at least three assaults led by Delhi Sultanate forces between 1401 and 1421.[114] Nayachandra does not explicitly discuss any of these events, but his *Hammīramahākāvya* is shot through from start to finish with military conflicts involving Muslim rulers. From Vasudeva, the second king of the Chauhan dynasty, who "came to earth in order to conquer Muslim demons [*śakāsurān*]," to Hammira, who died at the hands of Alauddin Khalji, the Chauhans are depicted as repeatedly fighting Muslim-led polities.[115] The Tomars and the Chauhans had been linked as successive rulers for at least 150 years prior to Nayachandra's time, which perhaps further explains why a Tomar court poet focused on Hammira Chauhan's last stand.[116] Also, a temporal and dynastic distance from his own time perhaps contributed to Nayachandra's project to articulate a warrior ethos that was not confined to a single dynasty.

Nayachandra used Chauhan history as a canvas for sketching out a vision of valour articulated in the language of Sanskrit aesthetics, especially Kshatriya heroism. Nayachandra does not bring his personal religious identity into this ambition, so far as I can see, but rather participates in the robust trend of Jains authoring *mahākāvya*s complete with battle scenes and the like.[117] That I feel compelled to state this—that Nayachandra did not write as a Jain first and foremost—signals how overdetermined we often consider religious identity today. Rather than pursue some Jain-specific ambition of promoting nonviolence, Nayachandra saturates his poem in a Sanskrit aesthetic language of warrior heroism. Nayachandra uses the term *vīra* (hero) a number of times in the poem. He describes the *Hammīramahākāvya* in its final chapter as "delightful with the mark of heroism" (*vīrāṅkaramya*) and repeats in colophons at the end of each chapter that his work is "marked by heroism" (*vīrāṅka*).[118] The persistent mention of *vīra* arguably mars the poem's aesthetic appeal, according to Mammata, a Sanskrit poetic theorist whom Nayachandra cites approvingly in the poem.[119] But the strong overlay of *vīra* also leaves little doubt that Nayachandra was invested in redefining a Sanskrit-based heroism within, as I argue below, a political world increasingly shaped by Indo-Muslim military might.[120]

Nayachandra's vision of heroism comes out in descriptions not only of the battlefield, an expected setting, but also of more wily aspects of politics, especially defections. Defections provide the key narrative movement of the second half of the poem as people switch sides between the Chauhans and the Khaljis. Indeed, Hammira's final duel with Alauddin is so brief in the *Hammīramahākāvya*, narrated in two verses, that one could almost miss it (honestly, I did the first time I skimmed through the poem).[121] Instead, Nayachandra devotes the bulk of his attention to Hammira's kingship, defined largely in traditional terms. The poem's five middle chapters (chapters 5–9) begin with Hammira enjoying recreational aspects of rule and end with his ritual conquest of surrounding areas (*digvijaya*). In the final five chapters, loyalty is a pivotal consideration, and it is through a series of defections and demonstrations of steadfastness that Nayachandra defines the valor that he wishes to elevate.[122]

Nayachandra portrays the climactic Chauhan-Khalji clash as fated since before Hammira's birth, but, aside from the lead protagonists, individuals could and did change sides. Queen Hiradevi, while pregnant with Hammira, craves to douse the earth in Sultanate blood (*śakāsṛgbāṣpūraiḥ*), a specific application of the standard Sanskrit trope that violent inclinations while pregnant augur the birth of a heroic son.[123] However, when the moment comes for Hammira to spill Sultanate blood, both sides' identities are muddled. Khalji troops are supported by several former ministers of Hammira who had defected to Alauddin, including Bhoja, Ratipala, and Ranamalla. Hammira, too, boasts diverse leadership. According to Nayachandra, Hammira had eight major commanders, four Hindus and four Muslim Mongols.[124] Half of the Hindu commanders betray Hammira in the course of the poem, and only his brother, Virama, fights in the final battle.[125] The four Mongols all remain faithful to the death, including Mahimasahi, whose loyalty is singled out by Nayachandra as emblematic of Kshatriya heroism. Hammira is the formal hero of Nayachandra's poem, a position indicated by the work's title. But the lack of any choice on Hammira's part also strictly limited the narrative possibilities of his saga, whereas the agency of a defector offered an opportunity to affirmatively endorse a fresh incarnation of warrior ethics.

Mahimasahi, known as Muhammad Shah in Persian texts, was a Mongol convert to Islam who joined Hammira Chauhan in 1299 and, according to Nayachandra, showed exceptional loyalty to the Chauhans. The *Hammīramahākāvya* does not dwell on how Mahimasahi entered Hammira's court in the aftermath of a botched mutiny attempt, as narrated in Indo-Persian chronicles.[126] Rather, Nayachandra emphasizes the staunch devotion of Mahimasahi and other Mongols, including their penchant for punishing disloyalty to the Chauhans. For instance, in one episode, the Mongols initiate an attack on Bhoja, a Chauhan defector to the Khaljis, in retribution for Bhoja's duplicity.[127] Later Mahimasahi kills Uddanasimha, a captured Chauhan soldier who shot Radha Devi, Hammira's dancing girl, as she danced on Ranthambhor's ramparts.[128] When discussing with Alauddin Khalji the possibility of war with the Chauhans, the defector Bhoja names the Mongols as one of Hammira's strengths, saying, "Mahimasahi and the other northerners serve Hammira, and so how can that glorious hero Hammira be easily defeated in battle?"[129] A Khalji emissary even offers Hammira peace in exchange for turning over the four Mongols (*mudgala*) along with some treasure and a daughter, requests that Hammira denies.[130]

Mahimasahi's loyalty was unusual in Hammira's court, which seemed to overflow with defectors and cheats. Nayachandra often criticizes these traitors, such as Ratipala, who went over to Alauddin's camp, convinced Ranamalla to also defect, and spread rumors that undermined Hammira. Nayachandra reproaches Ratipala's treachery by describing how he adopted unsavory aspects of Delhi Sultanate court culture, such as drinking wine and womanizing. The poet even accuses Ratipala of sleeping with Alauddin's sister.[131] Such behaviors played upon established Sanskrit tropes about drunken, lascivious enemies. Notably, Nayachandra condemns a defector, rather than a lifelong supporter of Alauddin or even Alauddin himself, for bad behavior. This choice perhaps reflects that the poet was more concerned with loyalty than with outlining a general set of contrasts between the Khaljis and the Chauhans. It also suggests that being Muslim was not especially critical in this context; after all, Ratipala was, in modern terms, a "Hindu." Nayachandra even built Ratipala's moral weakness into his name, which means "protector of sex" and is a defaming variant of a more suitable name, given in one source as Rayapala (protector of the king) and in another source as Ramapala (Rama's protector).[132] Ratipala is bluntly condemned in the poem's final chapter with the words: "Damn you Ratipala,

Figure 3.6 Wall of Ranthambhor Fort, Rajasthan
Photo by author, 2019

Damn you! May you die! You are the worst of the sun lineage."[133] In the narrative of the *Hammīramahākāvya*, Ratipala's wave of damaging behaviors seems to introduce doubt into Hammira's mind about the fidelity of his men more broadly, including of Mahimasahi.

On the eve of the final battle, Hammira questions Mahimasahi's allegiance, which sets the stage for the Mongol to act out Nayachandra's vision of Kshatriya heroism. The saga began when Hammira attempted to send Mahimasahi away, saying to his Mongol general:

> We want to liberate our souls for the sake of our land.
> This is the dharma of Kshatriyas. It cannot be changed even when the end is nigh.
> Only he who roars even at the end of life is a Kshatriya.
> Is not King Duryodhana [*suyodhana*] a well-known example of this?
> You are an outsider [*vaideśika*]. Therefore, they are not coming for you.
> Tell us where you wish to go, and we will take you there.[134]

Here Hammira makes no mention of Mahimasahi's previous loyalty or his amply demonstrated battle skills. Rather, Hammira presents an identity crisis. He dismisses Mahimasahi as not a Kshatriya and thus unable to follow the example of Duryodhana, the defeated Kaurava ruler from the Mahabharata who is here mentioned by his more laudatory name Suyodhana (good warrior). Hammira brands Mahimasahi a "vaideshika," literally somebody from another place. Accordingly, the Mongol is invited, even expected, to leave at the eleventh hour and save his own skin. This passage constitutes what Sanskrit philosophers call the *pūrvapakṣa*, a losing position elaborated precisely so it can be defeated by the winning argument. In what remains of his poem, Nayachandra rejects this warrior-outsider dichotomy and provides three overlapping answers that affirm Mahimasahi as the exemplar of what Hammira dubs here "the dharma of Kshatriyas."

Nayachandra's first argument that Mahimasahi is, indeed, a paragon of heroism comes in a series of actions undertaken by the Mongol. Mahimasahi says nothing in response to Hammira's questioning of his devotion (quoted above) and goes home angry. Then, as the Sanskrit tells it in a half line, "Mahimasahi cut down his family with the sword."[135] Mahimasahi returns to Hammira and tells a lie, saying that his wife wished to see the king.[136] Hammira arrives at Mahimasahi's house expecting to see a living woman and instead walks into a homicidal mess. As Nayachandra put it: "Hammira saw that it was like Kurukshetra with all the severed limbs. There, the heads of children and even women were awash in blood."[137] Hammira faints at the gruesome sight. Upon recovering he proclaims that Mahimasahi was one "whose house is singularly devoted to the Kshatriya vow" (*kṣatraikavratāgāra*).[138] Trying to parse what about Mahimasahi murdering his family demonstrated Kshatriya valor, Michael Bednar has suggested that this was a Muslim equivalent of a Hindu *jauhar*, where a king's wives immolated themselves rather than be captured by an enemy.[139] Hammira's wives indeed commit jauhar in the *Hammīramahākāvya*, shortly after Mahimasahi's slaying of his family.[140] Nayachandra also tells his readers that, in the final duel, Hammira slit his own throat rather than letting Alauddin kill him, a detail not preserved in later versions of the story and that suggests a similar sort of honor in self-initiated death.[141]

Nayachandra further answers the challenge to Mahimasahi's loyalty by identifying him as a Kamboja, which places the Mongol on the frontier of the conventional Sanskrit possibilities of heroism. Nayachandra calls

Mahimasahi a Kamboja a few times, including in the immediate aftermath of his slaughtering his family and in the poem's final chapter while praising the fallen hero.[142] Kambojas are mentioned in Sanskrit texts dating back to the Mahabharata as from the subcontinent's liminal regions, roughly from northern Afghanistan.[143] In one sense, this identification places Mahimasahi within an accepted Sanskrit framework. Particularly relevant to Nayachandra's poem is that Duryodhana's mother, Gandhari, was from Gandhara, a region adjacent to the Kambojas' homeland. When Hammira acclaims Mahimasahi as "head of the Kamboja family," he is directly answering his own doubt a handful of lines earlier that Mahimasahi could not live up to Duryodhana's example.[144] Nonetheless, Sanskrit texts often describe Kambojas as having different customs, and so the label perhaps also reflected Mahimasahi's non-Indian origins.[145] Nayachandra seems to want his readers to view Mahimasahi as part of the Sanskrit-based cultural world, even if at its very edges, and yet also see somebody with the agency to adopt and thereby affirmatively endorse this tradition's heroic standards.

The end of Mahimasahi's story confirms the Mongol's position as one of the poem's heroes. In the *Hammīramahākāvya*, after Mahimasahi slays his wife and children, Hammira rewelcomes him into the army for the final Chauhan battle against Alauddin Khalji. Mahimasahi fights until the bitter end. He falls second to last, after Virama—Hammira's brother and the only of Hammira's original four Hindu commanders to remain loyal—and succeeded only by Hammira himself, whose death closes the poem's thirteenth chapter. Mahimasahi does not die on the battlefield, however, but is merely knocked unconscious (*mūrcchitaṃ mahimāsāhiṃ*).[146] Nayachandra picks up this loose thread in the poem's fourteenth chapter, which is not narrative but rather extols the poem's heros, criticizes its villains, and provides some poetic context for Nayachandra's work. Here Nayachandra devotes a pair of verses to praising Mahimasahi's martial valour, even on the brink of death. He narrates, somewhat cryptically, how Mahimasahi declines to commit suicide (as Hammira had) because it goes against his family code (*kulacarita*). Instead, after the battle, Mahimasahi is hauled into the Khalji court, where the Mongol brushes off Alauddin's offer of mercy and instead reiterates his commitment to Hammira.[147] Nayachandra does not narrate Mahimasahi's death, which we know about from other sources, perhaps because that would overshadow Hammira's climactic fall. Still, Nayachandra's narrative of the 1301 battle for Ranthambhor concludes, even if buried in a somewhat terse verse, with Mahimasahi's loyalty as a paradigm for Kshatriya valour. Nayachandra's final comment on Mahimasahi is that the hero (*vīra*) has no equal on earth.[148]

At the beginning of Nayachandra's take on Mahimasahi's story, a Mongol's support for a Chauhan king did not need to be explained and was simply another act of defection in a world of fluid military loyalties. It proved no hindrance to a political alliance that the two men came from distinct regions, practiced different religions, and had learned different social norms. But at the climax of the *Hammīramahākāvya*, Nayachandra underscores points of difference in order to elevate Mahimasahi's devotion to Hammira, which embodies a certain type of Kshatriya heroism. Hammira Chauhan lost both Ranthambhor Fort and his life in 1301, and so, narratively, the *Hammīramahākāvya* ends on a tragic rather than a triumphant note. But perhaps Nayachandra wants us to think that Hammira and, more provocatively, Mahimasahi, despite losing the battle, won the war. Nayachandra concedes the historical fact that Hammira Chauhan perished during the Khalji assault on Ranthambhor and Mahimasahi died shortly thereafter. But perhaps together they signaled the vitality of a newly reordered warrior culture enabled by a changing world.

Many Narratives of Indo-Muslim Rule

Sanskrit intellectuals who wrote during and about the first few centuries of Indo-Muslim rule opened up an astounding range of possibilities within the world of Indian kingship, an already heterogeneous and elastic tradition. Sanskrit authors adapted some of the terminology of Muslim-led rule with titles such as "suratrana" and "hammira" and by emphasizing Delhi as a political center. They also described how Muslims appropriated longstanding Indian practices, such as recording patronage of religious buildings in Sanskrit inscriptions. In lengthy Sanskrit poems, authors expounded upon military conflicts, although the configurations varied. Gangadevi narrated, in crude modern terms, a "Hindu" power toppling a "Muslim" one; Nayachandra narrated the opposite, namely a "Muslim" kingdom vanquishing a "Hindu" one. Both authors elaborated a vision of kingship, one of which unfolded on a battlefield delineated by classic tropes and the other of which was defined by a Muslim Mongol's loyalty-soaked heroism. The wide range of materials discussed above do not culminate in a grand narrative, and that is a crucial point. For Sanskrit intellectuals circa 1200 to 1450, thinking about specific moments and instantiations where Muslims exercised political power prompted multiple creative possibilities for reimagining themselves but did not lead to a shared project of either absolute othering or total assimilation.

Sanskrit approaches to Indo-Muslim rule in this period reflected reality to a great degree, although they tell us about so much more than political history. Between the thirteenth and fifteenth centuries, Indo-Muslim rule became manifest, in different pockets and configurations, across the subcontinent. Alongside this political change, by the fourteenth century Persian was the most widely used language for governance across India.[149] Both Hindu-led and Muslim-led empires often featured significant diversity in this period, with people of various religious and cultural backgrounds fighting on all sides. Much of this is reflected in the Sanskrit texts and inscriptions I discuss here, but the works also explore what it meant to discuss such matters in Sanskrit. In this sense, the cases of Persian and Mahimasahi stand out to me. Several Sanskrit works I discuss above give attention to the Persian language, both by adapting certain words into Sanskrit and by commenting on the spread of Persian. Such comments, made by Sanskrit intellectuals, embodied a recognition of the Persian-medium world and its growing political importance in India. Mahimasahi, as depicted by Nayachandra, constitutes an example of cross-cultural behavior that runs so deep that it is hard to neatly distinguish between two separate cultures anymore.

We have no evidence that the authors of the various inscriptions and texts I discuss in this chapter knew of one another's works, and this tells us something important about the disjointed nature of the tradition that I seek to define in this book. For example, the *Madhurāvijaya* and the *Hammīramahākāvya* have both come down to us in a small number of regional manuscripts. The *Madhurāvijaya* survives in four known manuscripts today: three are in Trivandrum, in southern India, and one is at the Punjab University Library, in Lahore.[150] All four are in Grantha script, which suggests, despite its far-flung location in Lahore, that in premodernity the poem was mainly, perhaps exclusively, read by southern Indians invested in local history. The *Hammīramahākāvya* exists in two known manuscripts, both dated to the fifteenth century; the work has a single commentary, which breaks off in chapter 5.[151] Sparse manuscript evidence does not prove limited circulation, since current archives preserve only a fraction of the handwritten copies that existed in premodernity. In fact, arguably we ought to be surprised that the *Madhurāvijaya* survived at all, given that literary energy was more concentrated in vernacular languages, rather than in Sanskrit, in the Vijayanagara Empire.[152] Still, it is hard to ignore the surmise, apparent by now in this book, that many Sanskrit texts on Indo-Persian rule survive in limited copies that circulated regionally. Even while perhaps unaware of similar projects, premodern thinkers across the Indian subcontinent shared the impulse to write about aspects of Indo-Muslim rule in Sanskrit. They repeatedly turned to local instantiations of this wave of political and cultural changes and tried to make sense of them using their inherited literary and intellectual resources.

Between 1200 and 1450, Sanskrit intellectuals wrote a variety of other poetry, plays, and creative works that were inspired by historical events involving Indo-Muslim rulers. Many of these works extend deeper into the realm of fiction than those I discuss above, but a number also contain historical references. For example, between 1227 and 1230 CE Jayasimhasuri wrote his *Hammīramadamardana*, a play about the Vaghelas repelling Iltutmish's army in Gujarat.[153] Among other historical references is the play's reference to the caliph (*khalīpa*, from *khalīfah*) of Baghdad, which signals some awareness of Islamic political structures beyond India.[154] Nayachandra's other major work, a play titled *Rambhāmañjarī*, models its protagonist, Jaitrachandra, on King Jayachandra of the Gahadavala dynasty, who was killed in battle by Muhammad Ghori, in 1194. The play contains several references to Muslim kings, and Jaitrachandra is described as a "new incarnation of Rama" and "destroyer of all foreign Muslims [*nikhila-yavana*]."[155] Nayachandra's contemporary Vidyapati mentions several Indo-Muslim figures, including Muhammad Ghori and Alauddin Khalji, in his didactic collection of tales intended to instruct upper-class Hindu men titled *Puruṣaparīkṣā* (Test of man; ca. 1412–1416).[156] Further comment on these works is beyond my purview here, but future attention to plays and story works promises to elucidate how the Sanskrit literary imagination expanded to incorporate new social and political circumstances into its rich landscape. My focus here remains more squarely on Sanskrit literary histories of Indo-Persian rule, which expanded apace with the growth of Muslim-led kingdoms on the subcontinent. Accordingly, I turn in the next chapter to two locally based minitraditions of such materials: Gujarati prabandhas and Kashmiri rajataranginis.

CHAPTER IV

Local Stories in Fourteenth-Century Gujarat and Fifteenth-Century Kashmir

Different perspectives, different storytellers, always complicate the narrative; that's good because what we are trying to make sense of is complex.

—GITHA HARIHARAN, 2016 INTERVIEW

As Indo-Muslim rulers made further inroads into parts of the Indian subcontinent from the fourteenth century onward, authors developed locally based traditions of Sanskrit historical writing that detailed this political trend. In this chapter, I investigate and compare two regional traditions that took off in the fourteenth and fifteenth centuries, respectively: Gujarati prabandhas and Kashmiri rajataranginis. Gujarat and Kashmir had both witnessed Muslim-led military activities and, at least in parts, Muslim-led rule for centuries prior to the inauguration of these respective bodies of Sanskrit texts. Both sets of materials narrate some of that history as relevant to their region. Additionally, because each set comprises multiple texts of the same type, each allows me to compare authorial choices and see trends and exceptions within a deepening interest in Indo-Muslim history among premodern Sanskrit intellectuals.

The Gujarati and Kashmiri materials that I discuss here differ from each other in numerous ways. The four Gujarati texts were composed within a tight time frame, between 1301 and 1349. The three Kashmiri works stretch across more than three centuries, with Kalhana penning his *Rājataraṅgiṇī* (River of kings) in 1149 and two successors writing in 1459 and 1486, respectively. The two series of texts were authored by men belonging to different religious communities: Shvetambara Jains (prabandhas) and Kashmiri Brahmins (rajataranginis). They exhibit distinct styles and foci. Nonetheless, both constitute regionally based Sanskrit traditions of history writing in areas shaped, relatively early on, by Muslim-led political activities. I consider Gujarati prabandhas and Kashmiri rajataranginis together here, not as two sides of the same coin, but rather as two distinct local traditions. When read against each other, these series of texts enable us to sketch out the increasingly complex contours of Sanskrit historical writing on Muslim-led incursions and rule in the fourteenth and fifteenth centuries.

Pairing Difference in Gujarati and Kashmiri Materials

The Gujarati and Kashmiri works both addressed local audiences, although delineated in rather different ways. Jain monks envisioned the four prabandhas I discuss below as being inspirational to the Jain faithful. Two authors, Merutunga and Rajashekhara,[1] penned collections of stories about Jain ascetics and laymen. The other authors—Kakka, Jinaprabha, and Vidyatilaka (Jinaprabha's continuer)—structured their narratives around Jain pilgrimage destinations. Extant manuscript evidence indicates that the four prabandhas were often read in and around Gujarat.[2] In contrast, Kashmiri Brahmins penned the first three rajataranginis for a more politically defined audience. Kalhana, who completed the inaugural *Rājataraṅgiṇī* in 1149, claimed to write for others who lived through the vicissitudes of sovereignty.[3] For Kalhana this was a personal subject, since his father had been ousted from the court of King Harsha (r. 1089–1101), leaving Kalhana unemployed.[4] Kalhana's chronicle found a reception, a bit ironically, among those who enjoyed royal patronage, and Jonaraja and Shrivara, the authors of the next two rajataranginis—who imitated Kalhana in style and focus—were court poets of the Shah Miri dynasty.[5] The *Rājataraṅgiṇī*s of Jonaraja and Shrivara doubled as extensions of Kalhana's text and as official court chronicles for an Indo-Persian polity.

Despite the distinct origins of these two bodies of historical materials, the founding authors of both local traditions envisioned the same key antecedent: the Sanskrit epic Mahabharata. Kalhana alludes to the Mahabharata throughout his work and also assigns his chronicle the same unusual aesthetic goal attributed to the epic in Kashmiri thought of his time, namely inducing quiescence (*śāntarasa*) in the reader, who would shun the world after perusing the monstrous cycle of politics.[6] Merutunga, who penned the earliest prabandha work I discuss here, was more direct. In an opening verse, he billed his *Prabandhacintāmaṇi* (Wishing-stone of narratives; 1305) as "pleasing like the Mahabharata."[7] Neither Kalhana nor Merutunga refer to any of the historical materials that I have dealt with earlier in this book, which accords with the generally fractious nature of Sanskrit historical writing on Indo-Muslim political events. But neither did these authors posit their works as clean breaks with the Sanskrit literary tradition. Rather, the authors imagined themselves as updating established ways of writing about past events in Sanskrit, modernizing (or early-modernizing?) them for new times and in response to new occurrences. Analyzing the prabandhas and rajataranginis together here underscores the self-proclaimed continuity of both sets of authors as well as their differences in interpreting what it meant to write political history in Sanskrit.

Kalhana and Merutunga focus on the present as a crux of their innovation. Again, Merutunga is more forthcoming. In an opening verse, he claims that his work narrates recent history (*vṛttaistadāsannasatāṃ*), which sets it apart from old stories (*kathāḥ purāṇāḥ*).[8] Kalhana indicates his emphasis on recent history by becoming more precise and verbose as he comes closer to his present day, such that his later chapters, on events increasingly close to his own time, are far longer and denser than his earlier ones.[9] More than half of Kalhana's *Rājataraṅgiṇī* concerns the sixty years prior to the text's composition. In this emphasis on recent history, Kalhana's *Rājataraṅgiṇī* is a far cry from the Mahabharata, which presents itself as about times and people that were long gone. More generally, the prabandhas and rajataranginis I discuss here concentrate on the lives of real, historical people and sometimes include specific dates and citations of sources. Their authors coupled these historiographical innovations with an incorporation of stories about how Indo-Muslim political actors were shaping the contemporary political and social realities of Gujarat and Kashmir, respectively. By reading these two bodies of works side by side, we can see both their similarities and their substantial divergences, both adding texture and depth to the growing tradition of Sanskrit historical writing.

Prabandha Style: Writing About the Past and the Present

In both their topic matter and narrative features, Jain prabandhas expressed a vision of historicity with little precedent in Sanskrit literature. Prabandhas defy strict definition, but they are typically nonsectarian collections of prose stories about Jain monks and kings.[10] As noted above, the clearest internal recognition of their historical novelty comes from Merutunga, who, in 1305, completed an early and defining text of the genre: *Prabandhacintāmaṇi* (Wishing-stone of narratives).[11] In an oft-cited opening verse, Merutunga proclaims:

> Because they have been heard ad nauseum,
> old stories no longer gratify the minds of the wise.
> Therefore, I compose this book, titled *Wishing-Stone of Narratives*,
> drawing on the lives of men close to my own time.[12]

Merutunga tells his readers that he relied on both oral and written testimonies, specifically noting that he critically read numerous works (*gumphān vidhūya vividhān*).[13] His text also bears additional markers of his emphasis on relatively recent events. For instance, he cites specific dates, a practice that has caught the eye of more than one modern scholar and sets his work apart from earlier texts focused more strongly on what we might now term legends or prehistory.[14] Building on Merutunga's innovations, Rajashekhara, who wrote nearly fifty years later, distinguished myth from recorded human history on the basis of dates. He categorized stories about legendary people said to have lived before the first century CE as charitas, a genre of Sanskrit narrative texts that he distinguishes from prabandhas, like his *Prabandhakośa* (Collection of narratives), which narrate lives that have unfolded in the last 1,300 years.[15]

Jain-authored prabandhas also claimed to advance goals beyond recording human history, such as spiritual pursuits. For instance, Jinaprabha's *Vividhatīrthakalpa* (Many places of pilgrimage), written in a mix of Sanskrit and Prakrit, opens with a discussion of the Jain pilgrimage site of Shatrunjaya as edifying for those who "wish to destroy sin."[16] Daud Ali has suggested that Jain prabandha writers took inspiration from the didactic dimension of earlier story (*kathā*) literature.[17] More generally, history often doubled as ethical guidance in premodernity, such as in premodern Persian *tārīkh*, usually translated as "history."[18] And so whereas we moderns might perceive a conflict between recording the past and moralizing, fourteenth-century Jain prabandha authors, like many of their contemporaries across literary traditions, saw a dovetailing of interests.[19]

Additionally, Jain prabandhas often invoke supernatural causality as an unquestioned part of human life and of their literary frameworks. If we

TABLE 4.1
Jain prabandhas 1305–49 that refer to Muslim political figures

Author	Date	Title (Sanskrit)	Title (English)
Merutunga	1305	*Prabandhacintāmaṇi*	Wishing-stone of narratives
Jinaprabha / Vidyatilaka	1333	*Vividhatīrthakalpa*	Many places of pilgrimage
Kakka	1336	*Nābhinandanajinoddhāra*	Jina Rishabha's restoration
Rajashekhara	1349	*Prabandhakośa*	Collection of narratives

relied upon modern genre divisions, such "fairy-tale elements" might place prabandhas beyond the limits of history, at least for some modern thinkers.[20] But to boorishly impose the limits of our modern historical imagination would constitute a roadblock to recovering the range and natures of writing that we might understand as historical in premodern Sanskrit texts, complete with possible differences—including possible extreme differences—from modern practices of history. Rather than condemn prabandhas as not-history in twenty-first-century terms, we are better served exploring the presuppositions of these texts and how they narrate the past.

In recounting events in Indo-Muslim political history, especially incursions and battles, Jain prabandha authors investigated forces that were reshaping the world around them. Before 1300, Gujarat had experienced Muslim-led incursions dating back more than half a millennium. For instance, several texts mention the eighth-century Arab raid on Valabhi, a wealthy city in Saurashtra.[21] More immediately, prabandha authors lived in regions actively delineated by Delhi Sultanate military activities and rule. Merutunga wrote in the midst of Khalji attempts to annihilate the Vaghelas en route to taking over Gujarat. In 1299, the Khaljis led an army that unseated the Vaghela king Karna, but Karna, assisted by a few Mongol defectors, reestablished himself in Baroda in 1304.[22] A year later, Merutunga completed his *Prabandhacintāmaṇi*—which focuses, with only a few exceptions, on Gujarati rulers—in Wadhwan, near modern-day Surendranagar and about 180 kilometers from Baroda.[23] The core story of Kakka's *Nābhinandanajinoddhāra* (Jina Rishabha's restoration) is how Samara Shah, a lay Jain, repaired damage inflicted by a 1313 Khalji-led assault at a

Rishabha temple on Shatrunjaya.[24] Jinaprabha, Vidyatilaka, and Rajashekhara all wrote, at least in part, from within Delhi Sultanate domains. Both Vidyatilaka and Rajashekhara worked from the Tughluq capital of Delhi.[25] Jinaprabha spent time at the Tughluq court between 1328 and 1334, during the zenith of Tughluq power, when Muhammad Shah (r. 1325–1351) controlled more territory than any Indian emperor since Ashoka.[26] Jinaprabha composed a portion of his *Vividhatīrthakalpa* in Daulatabad (i.e., Devagiri), where he resided for nearly three years on Muhammad bin Tughluq's orders.[27] While political reality explains, to a great extent, why Gujarati Jains in the first half of the fourteenth century wrote about Muslim-led incursions and rule, it is how they did so that invites further analysis.

Writing and Not Writing About Muslims in Fourteenth-Century Jain Prabandhas

A certain factual and narrative casualness marks how some prabandha authors wove stories involving Muslims into broader, meandering tales of Jain figures. For instance, moving up Indo-Muslim rule in the region by several centuries, Kakka says that a Muslim sultan (*yavanajātīyaḥ suratrāṇo*) was involved in Javari's mid-eighth-century restoration of Shatrunjaya.[28] Historically, this date is off by several centuries, although that seemed not to have bothered Kakka. In some cases, it is hard to discern whether a given mention is about Muslims or not, in part because of the utter lack of interest that prabandha authors demonstrate in discerning when Muslims came to India. A representative case is the third chapter of Rajashekhara's 1349 *Prabandhakośa* on the life of the monk Jivadeva.[29] In the middle of the chapter, Rajashekhara describes how a goddess stopped Lalla, a merchant follower of Jivadeva, from tearing down a temple that Lalla had built on Jivadeva's instructions. Speaking to Lalla, the goddess says that she became deified after jumping down a well and dying in an attempt to escape a barbarian army (*mlecchasainya*). Rajashekhara offers no further commentary or reflection on the goddess's earlier mortal death as the narrative swiftly moves on to her request to become the temple's guardian (*adhiṣṭhātrī*). Thereafter, the larger story of Lalla continues as some jealous Brahmins pollute his temple by placing a dying cow therein and so forth. Fourteenth-century readers would likely have read "mleccha" as "Muslim," and indeed it has been translated as such by one modern scholar.[30] That said, Rajashekhara dates Jivadeva—and thus, by extension, the mleccha-led army that traipsed through part of Gujarat—to the reign of Vikramaditya in the first century BCE, centuries before there were Muslims.[31] What is a temporal problem for us moderns, however, indicates the degree to which some prabandha authors accepted Muslims as part of the Indian cultural world, with no more need of explanation or temporal restriction than Brahmins or Jains.

Fourteenth-century Jain prabandhas reflect cultural familiarity with Muslims, but they do not dwell on Islamic religious or theological concerns. All use the known vocabulary of "suratrana" (Sanskrit for "sultan") and other common Sanskrit terms for Muslims, such as "mleccha," "yavana," and "turushka."[32] Several repeat standard tropes that perhaps also reflected reality, such as the association between Muslim kings and horses. For instance, Kakka notes Alauddin Khalji's strong cavalry.[33] There are also signs of more broad-based awareness of Islamic culture. Merutunga mentions "pilgrimage to Mecca" (*makhatīrthayātrā*), i.e., the hajj.[34] One of the more striking stories in the *Prabandhacintāmaṇi* regarding knowledge of Islam concerns Prithviraj Chauhan's 1192 defeat at Tarain. According to Merutunga, Prithviraj survived the Ghurid onslaught and was to be pardoned until Muhammad Ghori entered the Chauhan picture gallery and saw a painting of Muslims being slain by hordes of hogs. Incensed, he executed Prithviraj.[35] The narrative does not explain Muhammad Ghori's anger, which trades on knowledge that the pig is an unclean animal in Islam. What strikes me is the fluency this tale displays with basic Muslim social and cultural realities that, seemingly, required no special explication for Jain readers.

Prabandha authors often narrated true events involving Muslim political figures, but the degree of detail they used varied. Merutunga, for example, furnishes fewer historical details for events involving Muslims as compared with surrounding information. For example, he chronicled a late twelfth-century battle with Ghurid troops as follows:

> Beginning in 1230 Samvat [a premodern Indian calendar], Ajayadeva ruled for three years. Beginning in 1233 Samvat, his son, Mularaja, ruled for two years. His mother was named Queen Naiki, daughter of King Paramarddi. Holding her infant son close, she fought at Gadararaghatta Ghat and, assisted by masses of unseasonable rain

clouds drawn by her virtue, defeated the King of Mlecchas. Beginning in 1235 Samvat, Glorious Bhimadeva ruled for sixty-three years.[36]

Merutunga sandwiches the defeat of a Muslim ruler by Queen Naiki and her babe in arms between a heavy use of dates for non-Muslim rulers. He offers little historical information about Queen Naiki's battle or the vanquished Muslim sovereign. Nonetheless, the subject seems to have interested later readers, and one manuscript of the *Prabandhacintāmaṇi* adds the following vivid verses after mentioning the defeat of the King of Mlecchas:

> The army of the King of the Turushkas was scattered by that youngster,
> as if the baby had slipped away and crawled onto the battlefield.
> Looking at the ground piled high with splintered skeletons of mlecchas,
> Mount Abu did not remember its father, the snowy mountain.[37]

These verses are borrowed, verbatim, from Someshvaradeva's *Kīrtikaumudī* (Moonlight of fame), a circa 1250 text that is primarily a biography of the Vaghela minister Vastupala and has itself been acclaimed in modern times for its historical value.[38] A Sanskrit inscription written between 1179 and 1243 at Veraval, Gujarat, also reports the conquest of a Glorious Hammira by a woman during the reign of Mularaja, and so this story is likely true.[39] Scholars have guessed, probably correctly, that it refers to the 1178 Gujarati Chaulukya routing of Muhammad Ghori's army.[40] But, notably, Merutunga does not identify the Ghurid opponent beyond calling him a mleccha.

Indeed, so far as I can tell, Merutunga does not name any Muslim figures in his *Prabandhacintāmaṇi*. At different points, he mentions sultans (*suratāṇa*), mleccha rulers (*mleccharājā*; *mlecchapati*), and an alim (learned man, Sanskrit *mālima*), but no proper names.[41] Merutunga's generality regarding Muslim political actors stands out in a text devoted to chronicling named individuals' lives. This gap suggests that, while Merutunga narrates what we now identify as key moments in the establishment of Indo-Muslim rule, such as Prithviraj Chauhan's defeat in 1192, the subject remained subordinate within his broader textual project.

Some later prabandha authors were more verbose on the subject of Muslims in general and Indo-Muslim rule specifically. For instance, regarding the former, Rajashekhara repeats a passage from Merutunga about the largesse of the brothers Vastupala and Tejahpala, who served as Vaghela ministers, but adds a reference to Islam. According to both Jain authors, the pair of brothers supported Jain and Hindu temples, but only Rajashekhara mentions their support for sixty-four mosques (*catuḥṣaṣṭirmaśītayaḥ*).[42] Such adjustments can be an effective strategy for "reorder[ing] the past," also used by authors in other historiographical traditions, such as those working in premodern Chinese.[43]

Other Jain prabandha authors offered dazzlingly detailed accounts of Muslim-led military activities that suggest a sustained interest in thinking about the implications of establishing Indo-Muslim rule in parts of northern India. A compelling passage in this regard is the whirlwind tour of Alauddin Khalji's military assaults in the opening of chapter 3 of Kakka's 1336 *Nābhinandanajinoddhāra* (Jina Rishabha's restoration).

Then Sultan Alauddin, who pounds land with galloping horses,
like the ocean does with churning waves, became king.

He went to Devagiri and, having captured its ruler,
reinstalled him there like a victory tower to himself.

Having slain King Hammira, a proud hero and Chauhan ruler,
[Alauddin] gained all of his territory.

Having captured the lord of Chittor Fort and having looted his
wealth,
he sent him wandering about from city to city like a monkey
chained by the neck.

Karna, ruler of Gujarat, was destroyed quickly by his might.
Karna went wandering to foreign lands and then died like a beggar.

Likewise, the fort-based ruler of Malwa was led out like a slave
over many days and died, sapped of all strength.

[Alauddin], shining with Indra's strength, conquered many kings,
including the rulers of Karnataka, Pandya territories, and
Telangana.

He grasped towns such as Siwana and Jalor.
Who can count the many difficult places that he dominated?

He reacted to armies of the Mongol ruler that wandered into his land
such that those armies did not come again.[44]

In this passage, Kakka describes, in chronological order, Alauddin Khalji's attacks on Devagiri (1296), Ranthambhor (1301), Chittor (1303), Gujarat (1304), and Malwa (1305). Alauddin's troops traveled south, hitting Andhra, Karnataka, and other places between 1309 and 1311. Moreover, Kakka offers accurate details here of what happened to the conquered rulers. For instance, he reports that Alauddin reinstalled the defeated ruler of Devagiri (the Yadava king Ramachandra), whereas Karna, a Vaghela ruler, was forced to flee. Especially since he mentions Khalji-Mongol conflicts, Kakka does not seem exclusively interested in detailing Alauddin's assaults on "Hindu" kings. Rather, Khalji military might is perhaps the best way to encapsulate the unifying theme of these nine verses. In the text, this passage leads into the introduction of Alp Khan, the Khalji-appointed governor of Gujarat who helps Samara Shah restore temples at Shatrunjaya (I translate some of this in appendix A.4). Later in chapter 3, Kakka enumerates five earlier restorations of Shatrunjaya, thus situating the Khalji-assisted renovation as part of a longer, largely legendary tradition.[45] Kakka's early attention to Khalji military might suggests that he held a coexisting interest in explaining the immediate political context that enabled Samara Shah's repair of Shatrunjaya.

Kakka's work notwithstanding, most early fourteenth-century Jain prabandha authors attributed Muslim actors, including those engaged in military assaults, limited agency in bringing large-scale changes to Indian politics and society. To emphasize this point it helps to state the obvious: Muslim-led attacks and rule, over several centuries, altered the political landscape of Gujarat and surrounding areas. But fourteenth-century Jain writers often did not hold Muslims responsible for their military actions and, instead, proposed other types of agency. For instance, Merutunga narrates that the eighth-century Arab sack of Valabhi was engineered by a merchant named Ranka who sought revenge against the (non-Muslim) ruler of Valabhi and so invited the Arabs to invade.[46] Merutunga's last line in the episode blames Ranka, not the Arabs, for Valabhi's fall.[47] Another dramatic event is the end of an independent Gahadavala dynasty in 1194, when Muhammad Ghori killed the last king, Jayachandra, stormed Benares, and subsequently made Jayachandra's descendants vassal rulers. Merutunga narrates that the Ghurids (mleccha) came at the invitation of the Gahadavala queen, who was angered when Jayachandra overlooked her son for succession.[48] The same story is repeated in other fourteenth-century prabandhas with a similar displacement of agency. Rajashekhara adds that King Jayachandra acted callously toward a minister and that those bad actions precipitated the Ghurid incursion.[49] Thus, both Merutunga and Rajashekhara subsumed the Gahadavalas' fall within a human drama about a (non-Muslim) royal family and (non-Muslim) kingly faults. In short, fourteenth-century Jain prabandha authors seemed to see the Ghurids as the instruments, not the instigators, of political change.

Jain prabandha authors often invoked a degenerative theory of time to explain violent aspects of Indo-Muslim rule. In traditional Indian thought, time is imagined as a series of declining ages, and we currently live in the worst or one of the worst periods (Kali Yuga or, in Jain terminology, Duhshama Kala).[50] In his *Vividhatīrthakalpa*, Jinaprabha frequently cites the current corrupt age as a reason that bad things happen, including (although hardly limited to) Muslim-led desecrations of Jain icons and assaults on temples.[51] Jinaprabha includes eleven stories involving Muslim rulers sacking temples stretching across six centuries, a notably long time frame.[52] He also blames non-Muslims for harming temples, including the kiratas (a forest-dwelling people) and the king of Malwa, around 1210 CE.[53] The subject of larger causality comes up frequently in these stories. For instance, one narrative concerns an image of Parshvanatha, located at Suddhanti, whose head was smashed by Muslims (*turukka*, Prakrit for "turushka"). As the text explains, it was the Unhappy Age (*dūsamasamae*).[54] Likewise, Kakka names the power of the Duhshama Era (*duḥṣamākālānubhāvāt*) as one reason for the 1313 Khalji-led assault on Shatrunjaya.[55] Sometimes the logic contains an extra step. For instance, Jinaprabha explains at one point that "by the force of the Kali Yuga" (*kalikālamāhappeṇaṃ*), superintending deities have become lax, thus allowing Muhammad Ghori to smash a temple's main icon.[56] One upshot of the prabandhas' tendency to cite larger temporal and divine causalities was a partial stripping away of agency from Muslim political actors.

Glimpsing Indo-Muslim Rule in Jain-Authored Prabandhas

While the prabandhas typically narrate Muslim military assaults independently of one another, sometimes they are set apart or even thematized as part of an overarching plotline. For example, in part of his *Prabandhakośa*, Rajashekhara strung together several Muslim-led incursions. In the thirteenth-century Vaghela court, Rajashekhara wrote, various officials discussed ways to fend off an impending Muslim-led attack. A court official highlighted the gravity of the situation by listing four prior kings whose dynasties were eliminated by a military force from the northwest.[57] The first ruler, Gardabhilla, is usually said to have ruled Ujjain in the first century CE and to have been overthrown by Scythians (called "mleccha" by Rajashekhara).[58] Readers may well have understood these mlecchas as Muslim, despite the anachronism that Muslims did not exist in the first century, a view evidenced by illustrations of Gardabhilla's defeat in *Kalakācārya* texts that depict his overthrowers as Central Asian Turks in dress and facial features.[59] Muslim rulers unseated the remaining three kings: Shiladitya (last ruler of Valabhi), Jayachandra (last Gahadavala ruler), and Prithviraj Chauhan.[60] Rajashekhara specifically notes that Muhammad Ghori (*sahāvadīna-suratrāṇa*, "Sultan Shihabuddin") vanquished Prithviraj. In a parallel if less detailed passage, Jinaprabha connects his own rescue of a Jain icon from Muslim would-be desecrators with Prithviraj Chauhan, who, Jinaprabha says, advised the Jain community in the late twelfth century to bury the same icon.[61] In such stories, Jain thinkers indicate that they thought about Muslim raiders and rulers, from different backgrounds and time periods, as acting in similar ways.

In the *Vividhatīrthakalpa*, we find a few fleeting indications of a possible larger recognition of what we now term Indo-Muslim rule. For instance, Jinaprabha says that "Turkish rule" (*turukkarajjam*) began in 1248 Vikrama Samvat (1192 CE) after the victory of Shihabuddin over Prithviraj.[62] We say nearly the same thing today, often dating the start of Indo-Muslim rule from the 1192 victory of Shihabuddin Muhammad Ghori over Prithviraj Chauhan. Vidyatilaka, who authored an addendum to Jinaprabha's *Vividhatīrthakalpa*, also recognized the shift to Muslim-led rule. He says that Jain monks traveled around freely during both the prior era, "when Aryans ruled" (*hiṃduarajje*), and the current era, "when non-Aryans rule" (*aṇajjarajje*).[63] While Jinaprabha and Vidyatilaka concur that Muslim-led rule constituted a historical break, they submit different value assessments of India's newest kind of ruler. Jinaprabha mentions the advent of "Turkish rule" within a story about how Jains were compelled to bury an image of Mahavira in the sand in order to avoid Ghurid iconoclasm or, in Jinaprabha's words, the "violence of the Turks" (*turukkauvaddavāo*).[64] In contrast, Vidyatilaka names the shift to Indo-Muslim rule as devoid of negative associations, specifically underscoring that Aryan and non-Aryan kings respected Jain ascetic needs. Some modern people might be tempted to make something out of Jinaprabha's citation of Muslim political violence, whose iconoclasm followed on earlier examples of "Hindu" kings desecrating the icons and temples of rival rulers.[65] This is fair so long as we give equal consideration to Vidyatilaka's assurance that Muslims continued premodern India's political tradition of supporting multiple religious communities. There was not agreement, it seems, even among teacher and student writing in a single text, about how to characterize Indo-Muslim rule.

The prabandha authors discussed here allot some agency to Indo-Muslim rulers to exercise power over certain individual Shvetambara Jains, but they overall decline to probe social changes associated with those relationships. Jinaprabha and Vidyatilaka are the best examples. Jinaprabha tells his readers about how he entered the court of Muhammad bin Tughluq, received political concessions, and, within reason, acquiesced to royal demands. Jinaprabha says that he traveled from Delhi to Devagiri, in Maharashtra, on Muhammad bin Tughluq's orders.[66] Vidyatilaka relates that Muhammad bin Tughluq later wanted Jinaprabha to return to Delhi, and so the monk did.[67] In short, Jinaprabha and Vidyatilaka made no attempt to deny or mitigate the king's authority over Jain monks, including over Jinaprabha, who spent several years at Tughluq courts, including twice making the arduous journey between Delhi and Daulatabad along which many perished.[68] But the authors do not narrate how this exposure to Indo-Muslim political culture may have changed Jinaprabha's textual production and thus the larger Jain literary tradition. Most notably, Jinaprabha authored three Persian-language praise poems of the Jinas, ranging in length from one to twenty-five verses.[69] It is impossible to understand the creation of such texts without appreciating Jinaprabha's place within the Tughluq cultural milieu, and yet we hear nothing about these works in the *Vividhatīrthakalpa*. Even faced with the undeniable reality that Indo-Muslim rulers were altering not just the political but also the cultural and literary worlds inhabited by

Shvetambara Jains, prabandha authors were not yet interested in thinking through such changes in Sanskrit texts.

Rajatarangini Style: Bad and Better Paradigms

In the mid-twelfth century, Kalhana authored the first *Rājataraṅgiṇī* (River of kings), which purports to record royal rule in Kashmir stretching back thousands of years, furnishing increasing detail as Kalhana approaches events nearer his own time. Kalhana's *Rājataraṅgiṇī* features in my analysis here for its few tidbits on Muslim political figures and also as a model for later contributors to the Kashmiri tradition of Sanskrit royal chronicles. I devote more attention to Kalhana's successors, Jonaraja and Shrivara, who both wrote in the second half of the fifteenth century.[70] Writing in the mid-fifteenth century, Jonaraja covers the three hundred years from Kalhana to 1459, with a focus on the Shah Miri dynasty. Jonaraja's student, Shrivara, wrote about the next twenty-seven years of Kashmiri royal history, through 1486. The majority of Jonaraja's text and all of Shrivara's chronicle address Indo-Muslim rule; both wrote under the patronage of Shah Miri kings. Twenty-five years after Shrivara, Prajyabhatta penned another work updating Kashmiri royal history that, to our knowledge, does not survive.[71] Another seventy-odd years passed before two additional Sanskrit works were written that rounded out the premodern tradition of rajataranginis: 350 verses interspersed throughout Jonaraja's text (the work of the so-called Pseudo-Jonaraja) and Shuka's *Rājataraṅgiṇī* (on events between 1513 and 1589), neither of which I discuss further here.[72] Kalhana, Jonaraja, and Shrivara share a textured approach to discussing groups of Muslims and often emphasize the accompanying regional and political identities of specific communities rather than categorizing Muslims as a unitary whole.

The Kashmiri rajataranginis have long suffered from bad analytical paradigms, several of which are worth discussing briefly, because they have defined scholarship on these texts, and because working through them allows me to build the theoretical scaffolding required for a more fruitful analysis. First, many scholars have queried whether the rajataranginis, especially Kalhana's work, are history or poetry.[73] Some thinkers come down on one side or the other, whereas others answer that Kalhana mixes aspects of history and poetry, which are presupposed to be discrete genres. Scholars who have taken the binary history-or-poetry question most seriously

TABLE 4.2
Kashmiri rajataranginis in premodernity

Author	Composition date	Time period covered
Kalhana	1149	ca. 625–1149 CE
Jonaraja	1459	1150–1459
Shrivara	1486	1459–1486
Prajyabhatta (lost)	1513	1486–1513
Shuka	1586	1513–1589
Pseudo-Jonaraja	ca. 1575–1600	Added 350 verses to Jonaraja's work

have twisted themselves, and Kalhana, into knots by trying to separate out the text's historical and nonhistorical elements, but to no desirable end.[74] I agree here with Yigal Bronner, who pegged the history-or-poetry debate regarding Kalhana as "largely tedious and dull."[75] Crucially for my purposes in this book, this alleged distinction of history versus poetry did not interest or even make sense to the authors of the rajataranginis, and so it cannot help us recover how these thinkers imagined their own projects.

Kalhana, Jonaraja, and Shrivara present their works as history and poetry, not as a mixture but as fully both. All three presented their respective works as literature (e.g., *kāvya*) and fashioned themselves poets (*kavi*).[76] These authors also stated that they were narrating past events (e.g., *bhūtārthavarṇane* in Kalhana) and specifically royal history (e.g., *teṣām udyato vṛttavarṇane*, where *teṣām* = *nṛpāṇām* in Jonaraja and *bhūtaṃ yad rājyavṛttāntaṃ* in Shrivara).[77] All three expressed a perceived harmony, rather than a conflict, in producing literature-cum-history. To give one example, Shrivara wrote: "That poet uses the right words to bring royal history alive as if it were happening right now. Therefore, let Shiva be praised!"[78] In other words, you need poetry, perhaps Sanskrit poetry specifically, to write compelling history. Shrivara's formulation empowers us to bypass the history-or-poetry dichotomy as nonsensical and instead pursue the interesting question of what kind of literary language brought history alive for premodern Sanskrit intellectuals.

Another popular paradigm for trying to make sense of Kalhana's *Rājataraṅgiṇī* in particular is a nonparadigm; namely, to declare the text sui generis. Many scholars, even in the twentieth and twenty-first centuries, have clung to the belief that Kalhana penned a unique work.[79] There are indeed striking aspects of Kalhana's chronicle, such as his metanarrative, breadth, and citations of sources.[80] Kalhana himself recognized that he wrote an innovative work.[81] But, modern thinkers have long mobilized the sui generis theory to label Kalhana's *Rājataraṅgiṇī* as a unicorn, the sole book of proper history within the vast morass of Sanskrit literature and poetry. It is the exception that proves the rule—a rule that few living scholars verbally espouse but most live by all the same—that Sanskrit is devoid of written history. Damningly, the sui generis thesis guts the analytical possibilities for making sense of Kalhana's work. A major upshot of proclaiming a text to be anomalous is to deny the explanatory value of trying to contextualize it. Rather than isolating the text as peerless, we would do better to see Kalhana as he saw himself and was seen by later interpreters: as part of a Kashmiri tradition of Sanskrit literary histories.

As a side effect of labeling Kalhana's work as special and unparalleled, modern scholars have largely ignored Kalhana's successors—Jonaraja, Shrivara, Prajyabhatta, Shuka, and Pseudo-Jonaraja. When other scholars bother to mention Jonaraja or, even more infrequently, Shrivara and the rest, they often condemn these later authors as having produced inferior rajataranginis that pale in comparison to Kalhana's masterpiece. For instance, writing in 2001, one Sanskritist blasted Jonaraja for penning a "bland chronicle" in which "for once the self-deprecation with which Sanskrit literary works conventionally begin, from Kālidāsa to Bāṇa and onward, finds some purchase."[82] In 2013, another scholar proclaimed that the works of Jonaraja and Shrivara "were not of the quality of Kalhaṇa's work, neither in their writing nor in their understanding of the past."[83] I am not interested in adjudicating each man's literary and historiographical skills in some sort of talent contest decided more than half a millennium too late, and so such value judgments find no space in my project.[84] For me, Kalhana matters not as the bar of poetic or narrative excellence but rather as the inaugural text in a regional tradition of Sanskrit writing on Kashmiri politics that was fleshed out by Jonaraja and Shrivara.

Kalhana's Muslim and Non-Muslim Turks

Kalhana's *Rājataraṅgiṇī* contains numerous references to Muslim political figures, most of which do not strongly set Muslims apart. Even Kalhana's vocabulary for Muslims is fluid. He calls some Muslims "mleccha," but he may also use the term for non-Muslims (this is not entirely clear).[85] He applies "turushka" to Muslims, ethnic Turks, and those from the northwest who lived centuries before the time of Muhammad.[86] He employs "shaka," a term we saw used for Muslims in slightly later Sanskrit texts and inscriptions in chapter 3, in its old sense of Scythians.[87] He uses "yavana," "chandala," and "hammira" to refer to Muslims.[88] Kalhana mentions Muslims as military foes, but he also names Muslims ("turushka" and "mleccha") as military allies.[89] He refers to a few Muslims in nonpolitical roles, such as concubines and, in one case, a shifty craftsman.[90] Kalhana supplies few specifics on what set Muslims apart, beyond their place of origin being outside of Kashmir. In a rare case of elaboration on the topic, he describes a Muslim homeland (*mlecchabhūmi*) where some people eat cows while others labor with water wheels and hand mills.[91] Here Kalhana mixes a form of labor, which was perhaps specific to the Muslims and region he describes, and beef eating, which was an old Brahminical trope for those operating outside the fourfold class (varna) system.

Within the story of Harsha (r. 1089–1101), part of the Lohara dynasty with origins near Kashmir and a "Hindu" in modern terms, Kalhana alludes to negative associations with Muslim political figures. Kalhana discusses Harsha at greater length than any other ruler save Jayasimha, the king during Kalhana's life.[92] Kalhana was no fan of Harsha, and the poet catalogues a variety of bad royal behaviors, including incest, ill-advised alliances with Turks, and consuming pork.[93] In his many criticisms of Harsha, Kalhana calls him, for instance, a "Turk King" (*rājaturuṣka*), as a maligning epithet meant to encapsulate Harsha's penchant for desecrating temples. Kalhana precedes the insult with several verses that describe how Harsha ordered the plunder of temple treasuries and the desecration of divine images by dragging them on roads while people spat on them. As Harsha watched, disfigured naked mendicants threw piss and shit on divine icons.[94] The identity of the malformed naked mendicants (*nagnāṭaiḥ śīrṇaghrāṇāṅghripāṇibhiḥ*) is not entirely clear.[95] But for my purposes what is most striking is that this series of fiscal and physical assaults on temples and the icons therein culminates in Kalhana maligning Harsha as a "turushka." The key verse reads: "There was no temple in any village, town, or city that was not stripped of its icons by Harsha, the Turk King (*rājaturuṣka*)."[96]

Kalhana's insult of Harsha, who was neither Muslim nor Turkish, indicates a link between Muslim political figures and temple desecration in the

Sanskrit imagination of mid-twelfth-century Kashmir. Moreover, this criticism packed a punch among premodern Kashmiri Brahmins, who echoed it even centuries later. Three hundred years after Kalhana, Jonaraja adapted Kalhana's verse to criticize Suha Bhatta, a Brahmin convert to Islam and courtier of Zayn al-Abidin, writing: "There is no city, town, village, or forest where temples were spared by Suha, the Turk [turushka]."[97] The general idea of applying a Sanskrit term commonly used for Muslims, such as "turushka," to non-Muslims is quite normal. Such a transference also occurred with "hammira" in the thirteenth century and with "suratrana" in the fourteenth century (see chapter 3). Also expected is Kalhana's focus on political figures, indicated here by the pairing of "turushka" with "raja." The rhetoric of Kalhana and Jonaraja stands apart, however, in being a criticism tied to temple desecration. Still, this is only one part of the story for Jonaraja, an author who offers us more substance than Kalhana regarding how premodern Kashmiri intellectuals thought and wrote about Indo-Muslim political history in Sanskrit.

Jonaraja's Sultanate of Kashmir

Jonaraja began where Kalhana left off, with the rule of Jayasimha (r. 1128–55), but he devotes more than two-thirds of his work to Indo-Muslim kings of the Shah Miri dynasty. The Shah Miris established themselves in Kashmir in 1339, and Jonaraja traces their line to his patron, Sultan Zayn al-Abidin (r. 1418–1419, 1420–1470), who was on the throne when Jonaraja died suddenly in 1459.[98] Overall, Jonaraja wrote about political intrigue and both good and bad governance, following Kalhana. He also aimed to extol Zayn.[99] Zayn al-Abidin, a Persian speaker, is unlikely to have been well versed enough in Sanskrit to fluently understand Jonaraja's chronicle (although Shrivara attests that Zayn enjoyed hearing Jayadeva's melodious *Gītagovinda* recited by none other than Shrivara himself, so the king was perhaps accustomed to hearing Sanskrit).[100] Still, it remains unclear if, much less how, Jonaraja's patron read his chronicle. It was not unusual for a premodern king to sponsor texts in a language incomprehensible to himself; after all, "Hindu" sovereigns had varying levels of Sanskrit ability. In any case, the Shah Miris fell on hard times a few decades after Jonaraja's untimely death, and so the broader reception of his court chronicle remains murky. Jonaraja mentions Muslims throughout his *Rājataraṅgiṇī*, from the reign of the first king he describes (Jayasimha) until the last (Zayn al-Abidin).[101] But, at the outset, Muslim political figures are not at the forefront of Jonaraja's narrative.

Early in Jonaraja's chronicle, Muslims flit in and out of the picture without leaving much of a trace and generally without any emphasis on their religious identity. At times, Jonaraja seems to avoid identifying Muslims as such. For example, in several dozen verses devoted to the Ladakhi king Rinchen, Jonaraja notes that Rinchen, originally a Buddhist, asked for a Shaiva initiation and was declined.[102] But Jonaraja elects not to mention Rinchen's successful conversion to Islam, about which we know from other sources.[103] When Jonaraja narrates the establishment of the Sultanate of Kashmir, in 1339, with the ascension of Shamsuddin Shah Mir, he marks the moment with a new benedictory verse that is most noteworthy perhaps in its absence of anything drawn from Muslim or Persian traditions. The verse reads:

> It reveals its nature all around by the sentient and insentient forms
> it creates.
> Its luster surges through producing space and time.
> Whether it be the Self, Shiva, Vishnu, Brahma, Buddha, Jina, or
> Action itself,
> Praise to that Divine One![104]

This verse mentions numerous Hindu gods, the Gautama Buddha, and a Jain arhat, and it refers to aspects of Sanskrit philosophy. In so doing, the verse places the Shah Miri lineage in a broad Sanskrit-based cultural context, but it gives no indication of the Shah Miri affiliation with Islam.

When Jonaraja criticizes political figures, he typically underscores foreign origins and behavior, rather than religious practices or beliefs. Jonaraja employs what were, by the mid-fifteenth century, standard Sanskrit terms for Muslims, mainly "yavana," "mleccha," and "turushka."[105] But, as others have noticed, he rarely applies these labels to people from Kashmir, instead reserving them largely for those from West and Central Asia.[106] Jonaraja sometimes calls attention to this emphasis, including when it is unclear whether he is speaking about Muslims. For example, writing about a Mongol named Khajlak who, en route to Delhi, slew the Kashmiri ruler Lakshmadeva, in 1286, Jonaraja explicitly states that Khajlak hailed from outside the region (*bahir etyātha maṇḍale*).[107] He further depicts Khajlak as an impure outsider by giving his name as Kajjala (collyrium) and describing him as dirty (*malina*).[108] Jonaraja openly maligns another Mongol invader whom he names as Dalca and whose attack left Kashmir depopulated. Jonaraja terms Dalca a "demon" (*rākṣasa*) and "king of the foreign Muslims" (*mleccharāja*) and links him with Harsha the Turk.[109] Dalca's Mongol origins and his ransacking in Kashmir, rather than whom he worshipped, seem to have merited the label of "mleccha." In fact, the religious identity of both Khajlak and Dalca is not entirely clear, either historically or in Jonaraja's chronicle. A passage on Sultan Sikandar Shah criticizes the sultan for following bad Muslim ideas (*yavanadarśana*), meaning that he welcomed more foreign Muslims into Kashmir and put an end to local Kashmiri practices (*kaśmīradeśācāra*).[110] The same passage refers to Sultan Sikandar Shah destroying religious icons in accordance with bad Muslim impulses (*mlecchapreraṇayā*), a rare application of "mleccha" to describe the behavior of a Kashmiri in Jonaraja's work.[111]

Jonaraja does not generally include Kashmiri Muslims in his negative category of "mleccha," with the clearest example being his patron, Sultan Zayn al-Abidin. Jonaraja crafted his *Rājataraṅgiṇī* as a praise poem of Zayn al-Abidin, in large part, and one of his laudatory strategies is to extol Zayn as separate from and superior to earlier mleccha rulers of Kashmir. Jonaraja says that Zayn ascended the throne in a land ruined by mlecchas, meaning Zayn's ancestors and brother (*deśe 'smin mlecchanāśite*).[112] A bit later in his section on Zayn, Jonaraja wrote more explicitly:

> King Zayn felt immense sorrow
> that the region had been oppressed by mleccha rulers.
> And so, step by step, he rescued the region,
> as Vishnu had done for the earth when it was oppressed by
> demons.[113]

Here Zayn is, definitionally, declared not a mleccha and, moreover, is likened to Vishnu.[114] In brief, Jonaraja used "mleccha" to distinguish, not Muslims from Hindus, but rather tyrannical kings from virtuous kings.

Even while criticizing some prior Shah Miri rulers, Jonaraja incorporated Zayn and his ancestors into Sanskrit literary culture and Hindu religious ideas. For instance, he describes Kuru Shah, the grandfather of Shamsuddin, who founded the Shah Miri dynasty, as a descendent of Shiva who inherited the god's distinctive feature of having three eyes.[115]

He names Kuru Shah's ancestors as a second Arjuna, followed by his son Babruvahana (both characters in the Mahabharata).[116] Nearly a hundred years before Jonaraja, a 1369 inscription from Kotihar, in Kashmir, had identified the Shah Miris, specifically Sultan Shihabuddin (r. 1355–1373, Zayn's great-grandfather), as descendants of the Pandavas.[117] But Jonaraja elaborated beyond earlier thinkers regarding how Shah Miri kings demonstrated interest in and empathy with Indian religious traditions beyond Islam. A good example is a story about Shihabuddin.

Jonaraja narrates how, one time, Shihabuddin finds his treasury depleted and so considers melting down a Buddhist statue to use the metal for minting coins. Shihabuddin's Hindu minister, Udayashri, enthusiastically endorses the suggestion and lobbies to also melt down a larger Buddhist image.[118] After sleeping on the idea, however, Shihabuddin recants. Jonaraja relates Shihabuddin's impassioned speech where he admonishes Udayashri to consider the people who had done the good deeds of making, venerating, and maintaining such images. Shihabuddin also cites four examples of what is remembered about other Indian kings, namely Sagara, Bhagiratha, Dushyanta, and Rama (all well-known figures in Hindu mythology). Later Shihabuddin is seen, in a dream, to be ruler of the gandharvas, a class of heavenly beings that comes up frequently in Sanskrit literature.[119] In such passages there is little indication that Jonaraja viewed the Shah Miri kings as distinguishable, on religious grounds, from earlier "Hindu" rulers of Kashmir. Rather, in their lineage, personal inclinations, and cultural context, Shah Miri kings appear much like prior Kashmiri rulers in Jonaraja's *Rājataraṅgiṇī*. Jonaraja goes so far as to say, in the only two uses of the term *hinduka* in his text, that Sultan Shihabuddin protected high-caste Hindus (*hinduka*) and was king of high-caste Hindus (*bhūpālo hindukānāṃ*).[120]

For Zayn al-Abidin, his patron and chief topic, Jonaraja goes even further and portrays the king as more supportive of local Brahmins than prior Kashmiri kings. According to Jonaraja, Zayn privileged Brahmins repeatedly, giving them justice, establishing mathas and dharmashalas, feeding mendicants, and reducing the jizya tax.[121] Zayn punished foreign Muslims such as Sadaula, a yavana from Mecca (*makkadeśāgata*) who murdered a yogi and was subsequently grotesquely tortured on Zayn's orders.[122] Zayn al-Abidin also continued the old Indian practice of supporting multiple religious traditions. For instance, he protected Buddhist images and appointed Tilakacharya, a Buddhist, as a minister of the state, a position of political power.[123] Tilakacharya's elevation also advertised Zayn's support of

Brahmins because, according to Jonaraja, the Buddhist minister helped many Brahmins find positions at the Shah Miri court.[124] Jonaraja also reports that Zayn was a good ruler in nonreligious terms, doing virtuous acts such as reinforcing river banks. But his recurrent attention to Brahminical well-being and learning is noteworthy and also occurs in more general descriptions of Zayn. For instance, Jonaraja says that Zayn listened to the *Nīlamatapurāṇa* and other shastras and compares Zayn to a host of Hindu figures and gods.[125]

Jonaraja periodically refers to Muslim ideas and religious practices, but, even when collated, these mentions constitute a thin collection. Jonaraja notes that a military leader, named as both Lola and Lolaka, was buried upon his death in what the poet terms "Muslim burial rites" (*yavanapretasaṃskāra*).[126] Zayn al-Abidin came to power the first time in 1418, when King Ali Shah decided to go on a pilgrimage (*tīrthānusaraṇa*).[127] A reader can infer that this is the hajj, although Jonaraja furnishes no clarifying details.[128] In a single verse Jonaraja may refer to Allah (*alleśvara*), although the manuscript tradition is not altogether clear on the point.[129] There is no explicit mention of Lal Ded or Sheikh Nooruddin, mystics known for spreading Islam through Kashmir in the fourteenth and early fifteenth centuries.[130] This omission suggests that, at least when writing a royal chronicle in Sanskrit, Jonaraja was largely uninterested in the spread of Islam within Kashmir.

Jonaraja's most persistent invocation of Indo-Persian culture is his use of Perso-Arabic names, something imposed on him by the basic facts of history, but he harnesses the unavoidable linguistic contrast to argue for Shah Miri cultural assimilation. A poignant example is Jonaraja's narration of the births of Zayn al-Abidin and his elder and younger brothers, respectively. Jonaraja says that the three princes—Mir Khan, Shahi Khan, and Muhammad Khan (Merakhana, Shahikhana, and Mahmada Khana in Sanskrit)—adorned their names as the Ganges River does the three worlds. He further fancies the brothers as the three conventional aims of Hindu life (*dharma, artha, kāma*) personified.[131] Jonaraja could hardly be clearer in expressing the view that the Shah Miri princes, their Perso-Arabic names notwithstanding, participated fully in Sanskrit-based cultural norms.

While Jonaraja appears little interested in the spread of Islam in Kashmir, he was highly concerned with Brahminical practices and social status during Shah Miri rule. A key passage in this vein concerns the persecution of Kashmiri Brahmins (*dvijātipīḍana*) during the reign of Sikandar Shah

(r. 1389–1413) at the hands of his minister, the Muslim convert Suha Bhatta.[132] Jonaraja introduces Suha Bhatta as someone who "despises Brahmanical rituals" (*brāhmakriyādveṣī*) and "strives to abolish caste" (*jātividhvaṃse . . . kṛtodyamaḥ*).[133] At the height of the minister's power, Jonaraja reports, Suha Bhatta closed Kashmir's borders and then hunted down and tortured Kashmiri Brahmins, compelling many to commit suicide while others dressed like Muslims to escape detection.[134] Suha Bhatta also forbade Brahminical rituals, which, Jonaraja notes, deprived Brahmins of income and caused them to beg for food scraps like dogs.[135] Jonaraja specifically identifies "attachment to Muslim ideas" (*turuṣkadarśane bhaktyā*) as inciting Suha Bhatta's oppression of Brahmins.[136] Aspects of this passage echo Jayanaka's emphasis on the Ghurid harm to Brahmins in his *Pṛthvīrājavijaya* (Victory of Prithviraj Chauhan), a text that Jonaraja had read and commented upon. But there is also specificity in Jonaraja naming a convert to Islam (rather than his Muslim king, notably) as the chief enemy of Kashmiri Brahmins. I am less interested here in the historicity of these events than in what prompted Jonaraja to emphasize this tale of Brahminical oppression at the hands of the former Brahmin Suha Bhatta.

When Suha Bhatta converted to Islam he did not reject Hinduism, which arguably did not exist as a cohesive religious identity in fifteenth-century Kashmir, but rather a locally manifested Brahmin identity. As mentioned, Jonaraja writes about the position of Kashmiri Brahmins repeatedly throughout his *Rājataraṅgiṇī*, evincing anxiety when Brahmins suffered under certain rulers and praising kings who protected the interests of local Brahmins. In this wider context of Jonaraja's near obsession with the position of Brahmins in Kashmiri society, Suha Bhatta embodied a potent threat to undermine this group's privilege and authority. As Jonaraja puts it:

> The hawk kills other birds.
> The lion hunts other animals.
> A diamond scratches other gems.
> The earth is dug by earth-digging tools.
> Planets, like flowers, fade in the sun.
> The rule is this: horrific harm comes from one's own kind
> [*sajātiyataḥ*].[137]

Perhaps as a rhetorical response to the treachery of rejecting one's own kind, Jonaraja refers to Suha Bhatta as such throughout the *Rājataraṅgiṇī* and never by his name taken upon conversion: Malik Saifuddin. Using Suha Bhatta's discarded Brahmin name also keeps Jonaraja's emphasis on Brahmin normativity, which appears to have been far more important to Jonaraja than social changes, religious or otherwise, introduced by Shah Miri rule. In short, for Jonaraja, writing about Suha Bhatta was, by and large, a way to talk about Brahmins and Brahminical privilege.

Shrivara's Robust Sanskrit Commentary on Muslims

Shrivara began where Jonaraja left off temporally, but Shrivara's *Rājataraṅgiṇī* differs substantially in focus and style from its predecessor. Shrivara details the full or partial reigns of four Shah Miri kings in four books: the last decade of Zayn al-Abidin's reign (d. 1470), the reigns of Haydar Shah (r. 1470–1472) and Hasan Shah (r. 1472–1484), and the first two years of Muhammad Shah's rule.[138] Shrivara closes his chronicle in 1486, when Muhammad Shah was deposed (for the first time) by Kashmiri nobles who placed Muhammad Shah's uncle Fath Shah on the throne.[139] Shrivara's four books are arranged chronologically in relation to each other but by topic internally.[140] Certain broad similarities link how Jonaraja and Shrivara talk about Muslims and Muslim-led rule. For instance, like his teacher, Shrivara identifies Zayn al-Abidin as related to Shiva and thereby places the Shah Miris in a Hindu lineage.[141] He also describes Zayn al-Abidin as in tune with a broad range of Hindu ascetic practices. For instance, he claims that Zayn is able to recognize a sage who had been accomplished in siddhis and tapas (meditative and ascetic practices) by merely seeing his bones.[142] In addition, Shrivara repeats older Sanskrit ideas about Muslims, when, for instance, he associates Muslim political figures with horses or names specific foreign places linked with Muslims, such as Khurasan and Mecca.[143] But the most immediately striking thing about Muslims in Shrivara's *Rājataraṅgiṇī* is their robust presence. As compared to Jonaraja's, Shrivara's work is characterized by a huge uptick in mentions of Muslims, especially groups involved in politics. Whereas Jonaraja rarely commented on Muslims as such and instead focused on Brahminical life, Shrivara tendered detailed commentary on cultural and religious implications of Muslim-led rule in Kashmir.

Shrivara uses two new Sanskrit terms, *saida* and *mausula*, to describe groups of Muslims in Kashmiri society. Sanskrit *saida* is adapted from the

Perso-Arabic *sayyid*. Whereas Jonaraja had invoked the term as part of an individual's name, Shrivara mainly uses it to refer to the Baihaqi Sayyids who exerted significant political influence in late fifteenth-century Kashmir (in this sense, I capitalize the term Saida).[144] In Arabic and Persian, a "sayyid" is a descendent of the Prophet Muhammad. Shrivara shows awareness of this connotation, writing that Saida Nasira and his family were descended from *paigambara*, a Sanskrit adaptation of the Persian *paighambar* (prophet).[145] But he is primarily concerned with the Baihaqi Sayyids' political machinations, a subject that also arises in other sources on Kashmiri politics, such as the early seventeenth-century *Bahāristān-i Shāhī*.[146] Shrivara devotes significant chunks of his chronicle to narrating Saida conflicts with Kashmiri Muslims, often emphasizing in such passages that the Baihaqi Sayyids were foreign to Kashmir (*paradeśajāḥ*).[147] Moreover, in certain passages, Shrivara refers to the Saida and mausula as discrete groups.[148] He also names the Saida and turushkas separately.[149] Shrivara is not consistent on these divisions,[150] but that he makes a stab at setting the Saida apart suggests an interest in distinguishing between discrete groups of Muslims.

Shrivara narrates the tale of the Baihaqi Sayyids in Kashmir as their political capital rose and fell during the last half of the fifteenth century. Shrivara says that Sultan Zayn al-Abidin had welcomed the Saida, giving them Kashmiri estates and even Shah Miri princesses as wives (both points are confirmed by other historical sources).[151] But the Saida caused some consternation among local Muslims, and so they were exiled from Kashmir first by Zayn al-Abidin and again by Hasan Shah.[152] A minister of Hasan Shah subsequently invited the Saida back to Kashmir as part of a bid to undercut another intimate of the king. The Saida quickly went about consolidating their own power.[153] By the time Hasan Shah died, in 1484, the Baihaqi Sayyids found themselves in a position to select the next ruler of Kashmir.[154] After the Saida placed the boy king Muhammad Shah on the throne, other Kashmiri groups felt challenged and fought back. In the final chapter of his *Rājataraṅgiṇī*, Shrivara narrates various conflicts between the Saida and Kashmiris.[155] Many Saida were killed in the clashes, which Shrivara describes complete with its bloodshed, severed limbs, and impact on the local population. The Saidas' political power had ebbed by the end of Shrivara's narrative after Muhammad Shah, their puppet king, was dethroned by Kashmiri political elites.

Shrivara mainly focuses on the political threat posed by the Saida. For instance, Shrivara issues some of his harshest rhetoric against the Saida after they crowned the young Muhammad Shah, at one point calling them cruel, haughty, ill-tempered, greedy, and envious.[156] In an adjacent verse, Shrivara draws on cultural differences to express the threat of the political coup engineered by the Saida:

> Mocking those learned in Sanskrit and vernacular knowledge systems,
> [The Saida] indulged in the vice of women inside their homes and hawks outside.[157]

Elsewhere in books 3 and 4 of his *Rājataraṅgiṇī*, Shrivara attributes cultural attributes to the Saida drawn from the larger playbook of standard Sanskrit discourse on outsiders, saying that the Saida liked to hunt, drink alcohol, and eat beef.[158] At times, Shrivara deploys these more general features in specific political situations. For instance, he notes that, after depopulating a mountain of its deer, the Saida convinced Hasan Shah to attack a cow-herder group.[159] Shrivara also specifically highlights Saida antipathy toward Kashmiri Brahmins. For instance, he writes in one verse that the Saida, having lost affection for Brahmins, instead directed their charity to the Muslims (mausula).[160] Shrivara's emphasis on Brahminical well-being, especially fiscal comfort, evoked an old anxiety for premodern Brahmin intellectuals and was a chief concern of Shrivara's teacher, Jonaraja.

Shrivara uses his second new term for Muslims—*mausula*, along with the related term *musula*—roughly a dozen times in his text, and here seems to indicate a larger outsiders identity that builds on prior Sanskrit knowledge and introduces new ideas. Perhaps the first indication that "mausula" mixes old and new information about Muslims is its etymology. "Mausula" is derived from the Persian *musalmān* (Muslim), and its adaptation into Sanskrit follows a time-honored model also seen with "tajika" and "turushka" (see chapter 1) as well as "suratrana" and "hammira" (see chapter 3). "Mausula" had also been used in Kashmiri Sanskrit since at least the eleventh century CE to refer to an obscure Pashupata sect.[161] It is unclear whether Shrivara intended readers to hear a faint echo of this older usage (he does not otherwise link Muslims and the Pashupatas so far as I can see). But perhaps using a recycled term, even without carryover content, tempered some of the novelty of Shrivara's robust Sanskrit commentary on Muslim communities.

Shrivara uses the word "mausula" mostly to express well-worn Sanskrit ways of writing about Muslims. Shrivara notes that some mausulas were foreigners, mentioning that an eminent Muslim (*musulavṛddha*) left Kashmir to return to his homeland (*svadeśa*).[162] He says that Muslims speak their own language (*mausulabhāṣā*), presumably Persian, something mentioned by Sanskrit authors going back to Jayanaka, in the late twelfth century.[163] Shrivara uses "mausula" to describe the oppressive tactics of Sultan Sikandar Shah, whom Jonaraja had earlier criticized.[164] Twice Shrivara says that non-Muslim merchants ate beef and thus earned the favor of Muslims (*mausulapriya*; *mausulavallabha*).[165] Eating beef was a well-worn trope that arose in Brahminical Sanskrit depictions of many groups, including but not limited to Muslims.

When writing about mausulas, Shrivara sometimes furnishes additional information on Muslim practices mentioned by earlier Sanskrit intellectuals. For instance, Shrivara describes a Perso-Arabic name, which had appeared in Sanskrit as long as Sanskrit intellectuals had written about Muslims but had more rarely been the subject of comment, as "fitting for a Muslim" (*mausulocita*).[166] Shrivara outlines the Muslim ritual of burial, to which Jayanaka and Jonaraja had alluded, in a more concrete and judgmental way. Jayanaka offered a poetic verse about how a whipping wind covered dead warriors who had fallen in the desert with sand, as if performing their death ritual out of kindness.[167] Shrivara derided the elite Muslim custom of building tombs, which he personally witnessed, as a demented practice (*durvyasanamātra*) and costly (*bahukāruṣu dattavittāḥ*).[168]

In a few uses of "mausula," Shrivara provides new information about Muslim social and religious life. For instance, in his passage about an eminent Muslim (*musulavṛddha*), Shrivara describes the individual in question, Mir Thakkur, as a judge (*prāḍviveka*[169]) and well-read. Shrivara does not specify, but presumably he meant that Mir Thakkur was well-read in Persian or, given his legal work, in Arabic. Elsewhere Shrivara describes the Quran with the cultural translation of "the Muslim Veda" (*mausulaveda*).[170] The phrase appears in a passage where Shrivara catalogs various rumors about what ill-fated actions prompted the death of Haydar Shah, in 1472, after less than two years on the throne. One accusation, according to Shrivara, was that Haydar Shah had sworn on "the Muslim Veda" to not attack some foreign lands and then had done so treacherously. This passage contains a basic recognition of Islam as a system of thought with a revered book, comparable to the Vedas. As Andrew Nicholson has noted, premodern Sanskrit intellectuals generally did not theorize Islam as a philosophical tradition.[171] The exceptions I have noted earlier in this book come from non-Brahmins, most notably Kalachakra Buddhists (see chapter 1). Shrivara refers to the Quran elsewhere as "the Saida's Veda," (*svaveda*, where *sva* = *saida*) and perhaps also indicates a wider set of Muslim religious texts (*yacchāstra*, where *yac* = *mleccha* and *mausula*).[172] Shrivara's mentions of Islamic scriptural texts are brief, but even without further elaboration they provide a striking contrast to the repeated elision of Islam by Brahmins in Sanskrit philosophical literature. It is also noteworthy that Shrivara seems to give ethical weight to Muslim theological ideas, by portraying breaking an oath made on the Quran as furnishing a moral justification for death.

Beyond the language of "mausula," Shrivara dapples his chronicle with details about Muslim social and religious practices that had become part of the Kashmiri cultural landscape. For instance, when discussing a fire that ravaged a town, Shrivara writes about activities at a community mosque (*bṛhanmasjeda*, where *masjeda* is Sanskrit for *masjīd*).[173] He mentions that such mosques housed Eid celebrations and other festivals (*edhāmahotsavādyeṣu*).[174] Shrivara recounts the occurrence of Friday congregational prayer, where "worshippers bow down and rise again like lines of lofty waves in a rippling lake."[175] Such a description works well as Sanskrit poetry and simultaneously constitutes an accurate depiction of Muslim prayer rituals. Shrivara delineates the architecture of large Kashmiri mosques, such as using four minarets (*catuḥstambha*), enclosures, and both wood and stone.[176] He indicates that Muslims fast for a month (presumably referring to Ramadan).[177] Shrivara uses the phrase *mlecchadarśana*, which is perhaps best translated here as "Islam," a few times when talking about some of these practices.[178] The identification of a *darśana* (view) attributable to Muslims was not without precedent (see, e.g., discussion of *yavanadarśana* in Jonaraja's text above), but Shrivara describes performative aspects of Islam with far greater specificity than his teacher. Shrivara shows limited interest, however, in Islamic theology. He evinces no concern with the social mechanisms by which Islam spread in Kashmir over several centuries, a topic that has interested modern historians and proven politically explosive in debates about Kashmiriyat, Kashmir's alleged noncommunal heritage.[179] Shrivara's primary interest remained how Muslim-led rule was changing the landscape of elite Kashmiri politics.

Shrivara contrasts Muslims with high-caste Hindus, often specifically Brahmins, at certain moments in his narrative. This contrast indicates that

Shrivara perceived and recorded religious difference, but modern readers are liable to misinterpret that difference in two respects. First, Shrivara's dichotomy of Muslims and high-caste Hindus does not define his *Rājataraṅgiṇī*. Thus, while I highlight this feature of Shrivara's chronicle within a discussion of how Sanskrit intellectuals wrote about Muslim-led rule, it remains a relatively minor characteristic of his text overall. Second, modern readers may be misled by Shrivara's terminology, especially his use of the Sanskrit term, quite new in Shrivara's time, "hinduka."[180] Shrivara employs the word "hinduka," not to mean "Hindu" as most understand the identity today, but, rather more narrowly, as a synonym for "Brahmin" or "high-caste Hindu," specifically in passages that concern ritual activity. Shrivara indicates this meaning in a relatively early use of the term "hinduka" in his text, where he employs "dvija" (high-caste Hindu) as a synonym in the next verse.[181]

Shrivara depicts Muslims and Brahmins as in conflict with each other mainly when discussing behavior that might compromise Brahminical ritual purity. For instance, in chapter 4, Shrivara says that calamities arose after merchants discarded Brahmin customs (*svācāraṃ hindukōcitam*) and killed cows, thereby earning the favor of Muslims (mausulas).[182] In a similar passage in book 3, Shrivara says that a fire wreaked havoc after some merchants who had followed Brahmin customs their whole lives (*ājanmahindukācārāś*) decided to eat beef and so became loved by the mausula.[183] Shrivara discusses the fire at some length and closes the passage by saying that such massive destruction followed from going against class customs (*varṇācāraviparyāsa*).[184] In a short anecdote, told in only a few verses, Shrivara says that an angered hinduka damaged the property of Saida Khan. In response, the yavanas (Muslims) grew angry and so the king (also a Muslim) ordered attacks on high-caste Hindus (dvija).[185] In a more general verse, Shrivara writes that the faces of Muslims (mlecchas) became blackened and downturned in the face of a newly constructed, gleaming white temple.[186] The imagery of contrasting light and darkness has a long lineage in Sanskrit poetry, and, in this case, the poetic trope is deployed to comment on an expression of power, presumably upper-class power, by those who financed and would run such a temple.

Shrivara's comparisons of Muslim and Brahmin actions do not always contain a negative value judgment against Islamic norms, but they do generally foreground ritual practice. For instance, in book 3, Shrivara laments the death of Haydar Shah's mother, Golkhatun (Gul Khatun), eulogizing, "Remembering that she nurtured high-caste Hindu customs [*hindukasamācāra*] like the sun nurtures lotuses, all men mourned and wept bitterly."[187] Rather than condemnation, an emphasis on praxis links the disparate mentions of high-class Hindu customs in Shrivara's chronicle. Certainly, Shrivara comes closer than any other Sanskrit intellectual we have encountered thus far to conceptualizing Islam as a set of religious practices that can be contrasted with at least the upper sliver of Kashmiri Hindu society. Although, based on the example of Golkhatun, Muslims could actively support both Brahmin and Muslim customs. As per Shrivara, Golkhatun also built a madrasa.[188] In this sense, Shrivara appears to describe potentially compatible, rather than necessarily exclusive, elite religious traditions.

Shrivara also underscores aspects of Indo-Muslim ruling culture that are not explicitly religious, especially the flourishing of Persian literary culture in Kashmir under Shah Miri patronage. These mentions are worth detailing for the nuance they provide within Shrivara's understanding of the relevant identity markers of the Shah Miris and Kashmiri Muslims. Shrivara mentions Persian as a language several times in his chronicle and uses several Perso-Arabic terms, including "paighambar," "masjid," "madrasa," and *khāngāh* (Sufi lodge).[189] He specifically refers to the Perso-Arabic script (*yavanākṣara sambaddhamiti lekhaṃ*) and Persian literature (*pārasībhāṣayā kāvya*).[190] Given that Sanskrit intellectuals typically considered kavya to be restricted to Sanskrit and related languages, the positing of Persian kavya is an arresting innovation. In a remarkable display of granular knowledge, Shrivara cites Firdawsi's epic *Shāhnāma* by name as the basis for a Sanskrit text titled *Jainavilāsa* (Zain's play) by Bhattavatara.[191]

Shrivara discusses Sanskrit and Persian in several places in his *Rājataraṅgiṇī* as part of a triad whose third member is local vernaculars. Most notably, he narrates that Zayn al-Abidin directed men who knew Sanskrit, Persian, and vernaculars (*saṃskṛtadeśādipārasīvāg*) to translate Sanskrit texts into Persian and vice-versa.[192] Attestations in other Shah Miri histories and surviving translations indicate that Zayn al-Abidin's court followed his orders.[193] Shrivara does not specify the role of vernaculars (presumably dialects of premodern Kashmiri) in these translations.[194] Perhaps a shared vernacular enabled communication between translators proficient in Sanskrit and Persian, respectively, as Hindi did for Mughal translations a century later.[195] Elsewhere, too, Shrivara emphasizes the multilingual nature of Shah Miri court culture. For instance, in one passage, he says that Hasan Shah listened to Persian songs translated into vernacular by none other than Shrivara himself and that the king was versed in Sanskrit poetry, especially that which praised music.[196] In another episode, Shrivara explained Kashmiri (*deśabhāṣā*) music to Hasan Shah by drawing upon Bharata's *Nāṭyaśāstra* (Treatise on drama) and other classic Sanskrit aesthetic treatises.[197] Music seems to have been a cross-cultural affair at the Shah Miri court; according to Shrivara, musicians from as far away as Karnataka performed for Hasan Shah.[198] In short, Shrivara did not see support of Persian and aspects of Islamic cultures through Shah Miri rule and patronage to be at odds with the ongoing flourishing of Kashmiri and Sanskrit traditions.

In summary, Shrivara goes further than either of his predecessors, Kalhana or Jonaraja, in exploring how Muslim-led rule was changing Kashmiri society, including in cultural, literary, and, to a limited degree, religious terms. The contrast between Jonaraja's meager comments on Muslims versus Shrivara's robust commentary on specific Muslim groups is especially striking since the two men's lives overlapped and less than thirty years separated the production of their respective *Rājataraṅgiṇīs*. Still, when seen holistically, none of the authors of the three rajataranginis discussed here viewed Indo-Muslim or Indo-Persian rule as such, and none depicted it as an abrupt shift from that of earlier Kashmiri kings. Rather, Jonaraja and Shrivara posited continuation and light synthesis as a key way that the Shah Miri kings cultivated their ruling culture. All three authors depict Muslim individuals or groups involved in conflict, but they calibrated these situations in precise terms and emphasized the bad behavior of certain political figures (e.g., Suha Bhatta) or specific groups (e.g., the Saida) rather than Hindu-Muslim conflict, or even Hindu and Muslim identities, writ large.

Some modern readers might see traces, especially in Jonaraja and Shrivara, of Kashmiriyat, the supposed indigenous syncretic nature of Kashmiri society that is sometimes invoked in modern-day political discussions. It is tempting to think that Kashmir's premodernity offers a magic key that could unlock or at least give hope regarding modern conflicts in and about Kashmir.[199] Indeed, at the time of going to press (September 2020), Kashmir is the subject and site of much discussion owing to the BJP government's abrogation of Article 370 in August 2019, the subsequent multimonth communications and media blackout, and ongoing oppression and restrictions in Kashmir. But I caution against reading a modern framework onto Kashmir's premodern past. The banal if bitter truth is that historical works from premodern Kashmir are not a ready-made antidote to the region's present political and cultural quagmires.[200] That said, when placed in a larger context and read alongside works such as Gujarati prabandhas, the Kashmiri rajatarangini tradition is an important piece of the larger subcontinental puzzle of Sanskrit historical writing and intellectual history.

Whither History?

The rajataranginis of Kalhana, Jonaraja, and Shrivara were treated as historical texts by a range of readers within and beyond the Kashmiri and Sanskrit cultural spheres. Other Kashmiris extended the tradition of composing royal chronicles in Sanskrit. Shuka completed the next extant *Rājataraṅgiṇī* in 1586 and wrote, in language mirroring that of Jonaraja and Shrivara, that he sought to pen royal history (*tadvṛttavarṇana*, where *tad* = *rāja*).[201] At the late sixteenth-century court of Akbar, the initial trio of rajataranginis were translated into Persian by Muhammad Shahabadi and subsequently revised by Abdul Qadir Badauni.[202] Abul Fazl, one of Akbar's official historians, described the rajataranginis as "tarikh" (history).[203] Authors of Persian-medium histories, both within and outside Kashmir, drew upon Persian translations of Kalhana, Jonaraja, and Shrivara, and perhaps, more rarely, upon their Sanskrit originals.[204] The rajataranginis were considered so authoritative and definitional to Kashmiri history that one author even billed his Persian history of Kashmir as a translation (*tarjuma*) of the rajataranginis when, in fact, he relied on Persian sources.[205] Manuscripts of the rajataranginis also crop up in some key early modern manuscript collections, such as in the library of Kavindracharya Sarasvati, a major Sanskrit intellectual of the seventeenth century who enjoyed links with the Mughal court.[206]

Likewise, premoderns understood the fourteenth-century Gujarati prabandhas as works about real people and real events. One indication of this is that the prabandha genre flourished going forward and subsequent authors continued to feature historical figures, including some of the same individuals and stories first popularized by the authors discussed here. For instance, the *Purātanaprabandhasaṅgraha* (Collection of old stories) contains prabandhas that begin with Padalipta, who dates to roughly the first century CE according to Jain tradition and is thus an appropriate starting point for historical works as per Rajashekhara (see above).[207] The *Purātanaprabandhasaṅgraha* includes narratives of events such as the eighth-century Arab raid of Valabhi abbreviated from Merutunga.[208] Additionally, some later prabandha authors wrote about contemporary political events in greater depth. In the next chapter, I discuss some of these works that date from the sixteenth and seventeenth centuries and feature Mughal elites.

For all their substantial differences, fourteenth-century Jain prabandhas and the first three Kashmiri rajataranginis share certain overarching features that help us reconstruct some common contours of the fragmented tradition of premodern Sanskrit historical writing. For instance, all the texts considered above exhibit significant interest in local events and only intermittently engage with broader trends of Indo-Muslim rule. One might characterize this as a deficiency. In this reading, we would say that the majority of texts discussed here are devoid of a large-scale conception of Indo-Persian rule.[209] We might suggest that some works, at least in parts, lack even a basic sense of historical change over time. But what would such formulations achieve except to further entrench the intellectually impoverished idea that India has no history? At best, this conclusion would tell us that we are looking for the wrong things. We might instead turn the query back on ourselves: Why do we keep searching for narratives about all of India or all Muslims, or at least our version of historical causality, as if those could be the only stories that matter? In the prabandhas and rajataranginis, local histories take center stage and were enlivened by Sanskrit poetry, to paraphrase Shrivara.

Even while writing in the cosmopolitan language of Sanskrit, many authors sought to speak quite specifically to localized concerns and narrow audiences. The authors discussed in this chapter told stories about the needs, ties, and conflicts between specific communities, such as the Khaljis and Gujarati Shvetambara Jains (Kakka) or the Baihaqi Sayyids and Kashmiri Muslims and Brahmins (Shrivara). These stories are no doubt hard for us moderns to grasp, since they feature groups about which some have never heard or that were defined differently in premodern India. But it is decisively a modern problem if our capacity for nuance and our willingness to try to understand difference prove inadequate to recovering the complexities expressed by premodern Sanskrit poet-historians.

We ought to understand the Kashmiri rajataranginis and the Gujarati prabandhas, as their premodern readers did, as captivating narratives about the political past. But that reading need not require that we write onto Kalhana and Kakka, Jonaraja and Jinaprabha, our own modern ideas about what is involved in analyzing historical events. In terms of finding other frameworks for conceptualizing historical writing, reading these two sets of materials in comparison proves fruitful. The Gujarati prabandhas and the Kashmiri rajataranginis have more differences than similarities regarding their patronage contexts, how they discuss Muslim political figures, and their frameworks for making sense of political conflict. That diversity served as neither a weakness nor an analytical problem for subsequent generations of Sanskrit intellectuals. Rather, many found their increasingly expansive, if regionally demarcated, tradition of how to write about the Indian past, and specifically aspects thereof related to Indo-Muslim political history, an invitation for further innovation. History appears to have become a more popular option in Sanskrit as time went forward, evidenced by the sheer number of people who wrote texts in rather different contexts and styles.

CHAPTER V

Meeting the Mughals and Reformulating Jain Identity

Black Panther isn't just a win for black people. Crazy Rich Asians isn't just a win for Asians. When we stretch culture we all have more room to be ourselves. When we see a wider range of stories, we stop seeing each other as OTHERS.

—RIZ AHMED, TWITTER, 2018

Dozens of Shvetambara Jains from western India spent time at the Mughal courts of Akbar and Jahangir over a roughly thirty-five-year period, between 1583 and 1618, and many Jains wrote Sanskrit texts about this set of cross-cultural experiences. The resulting works constitute one of the largest known bodies of Sanskrit literary histories that feature Indo-Persian political figures. In terms of social history, a Jain monk first arrived at Akbar's court in the early 1560s, when Mughal power was beginning to stretch across northern India, and died there a few years later. After a gap of more than a decade, Shvetambara Jains again entered Akbar's court, in 1583, and a rotating group of monks maintained a consistent presence at the court of Akbar and, later, Jahangir, until 1618. As I have written about elsewhere, Jain monks engaged in a plethora of activities at the Mughal court.[1] They debated religious questions, educated Mughal princes, explained Sanskrit texts to Mughal kings, dedicated Sanskrit praise poems to imperial elites, traveled with the royal entourage, performed astrological ceremonies, and secured *farmāns* (imperial orders) that benefited Jain and Gujarati interests. Jain monks penned chronicles, inscriptions, and biographies that discuss their imperial ties as early as 1589, with subsequent works dated to 1592, 1594, and so forth. But Jains did not stop writing about their Mughal links after they were broken in the real world. Well into the late seventeenth century, writing in a variety of genres and contexts, Jains produced texts and public inscriptions that outline their imperial experiences and invoke language inspired by their prior exposure to Mughal court culture. In other words, Jains penned live-action accounts of real-world events featuring Mughal political figures, and they also produced what were, for them, histories about imperial relations that had eroded decades ago. The resulting collection of Jain-authored materials, especially the expansive biographies, offers an extraordinary case study in how discussions of an Other can serve as fertile ground for rethinking one's own community identity.

In both reality and writing, Jain-Mughal connections built upon a history of Shvetambara monks visiting Indo-Persian rulers, especially in Delhi, dating back to the early fourteenth century. Most famously, in 1328, Jinaprabhasuri (also referred to here as Jinaprabha) entered the Delhi-based court of Muhammad bin Tughluq and subsequently passed several years in Delhi Sultanate domains. In chapter 4, I discussed some of the fourteenth-century historiography surrounding Jinaprabha's Tughluq connections. In the fifteenth century, Sanskrit authors continued to write about meetings between Jinaprabha and Muhammad bin Tughluq, or Firuz Shah (r. 1351–1388), as some later works named the king.[2] These fourteenth- and fifteenth-century works provide frameworks and tropes that guide, to some degree, Sanskrit narratives of Jain-Mughal links. As I have argued earlier in this book, narrative tropes do not block the production of history; if they did, no society, including our own, could generate written histories. Rather, literary models and narrative expectations add layers of interpretive complexity that make premodern Sanskrit historical works all the more textured and compelling to analyze. I explore below how Jain authors adapted specific tropes and story lines to explore their own community values, social and cultural anxieties, and objectives in narrating their Mughal connections for local audiences.

Jain monks from the Tapa Gaccha and the Kharatara Gaccha, two Shvetambara branches largely based in Gujarat, authored works on their Mughal ties. Authors from both lineages wrote about encounters with the Mughals at greatest length in Sanskrit biographies of individual monks, which I supplement here with briefer mentions found in monastic chronicles and inscriptions. The works were squarely aimed at Jain readers. No Jain biographies or chronicles were sponsored by Mughal patrons, despite robust imperial support for Sanskrit texts under Akbar and Jahangir, and none received a Mughal reception.[3] Indeed, most manuscripts of these works are found today in Gujarat, and many are housed in Jain libraries or temples.[4]

All but one work privilege the experiences of Jain monks, rather than Jain laity or merchants, who had their own parallel set of connections with the Mughal kings.[5] As such, these sources constitute attempts at local, often specifically monastic, stories. The biographies are arguably even more narrowly pitched than the Gujarati prabandhas and Kashmiri rajataranginis that occupied my attention in chapter 4. They signal an ongoing interest on the part of Sanskrit intellectuals in using a cosmopolitan language to communicate local history.

The various types of Jain-authored sources—chronicles, inscriptions, and biographies—present some differences important to how I analyze them below. In the chronicles, interactions with the Mughals appear relatively infrequently, typically as part of a synopsis of an individual monk's life. In addition to the chronicles' general brevity, another relevant factor is that usually only one or two monks, out of dozens, enjoyed Mughal imperial links. Here I draw on two chronicles, both focused on Tapa Gaccha monks and sharing the same title: Dharmasagara's *Tapāgacchapaṭṭāvalī* (Tapa Gaccha's monastic lineage, 1592) and Meghavijaya's *Tapāgacchapaṭṭāvalī* (ca. 1670–1700).[6] The inscriptions are equally or more succinct; they are also public in a way that monastic-focused texts were not. Many of the inscriptions I discuss here are found on Mount Shatrunjaya, a revered pilgrimage site in southern Gujarat; others are in Patan. Even today, anybody can walk up and see these words etched in stone. In sharp contrast to the concise chronicles and inscriptions, the Jain-authored individual biographies, of which I discuss seven in some depth below, are expansive, sometimes stretching to hundreds of pages of printed text. Most narrate the life of a single individual, and several spotlight time that their subject spent in royal Mughal environs. These individual biographies together constitute one of the most copious expressions of historical energy in the history of premodern Sanskrit, and they enable us to see how individual thinkers wrote about a Mughal Other, often as not other at all, to ultimately reformulate a sectarian Jain Self.

Deciding Not to Write in Gujarati

When Gujarati Jains sat down to write about interactions with Mughal political figures, they faced a choice of whether to write in Sanskrit or in Gujarati. Earlier generations of Jain monks based in Gujarat had chosen

TABLE 5.1

Individual biographies 1589–1652 featuring Jain activities at the Mughal court

Author	**Date**	**Title (Sanskrit)**	**Title (English)**	**Subject**
Padmasagara	1589	*Jagadgurukāvya*	Poem on the teacher of the world	Hiravijaya
Jayasoma	1594	*Mantrikarmacandra-vaṃśāvalīprabandha*	Account of Minister Karmachandra's genealogy	Karmachandra
Devavimala	ca. 1600	*Hīrasundaramahākāvya*	Lovely great poem on Hiravijaya	Hiravijaya
Devavimala	ca. 1590–1610	*Hīrasaubhāgya*	Hiravijaya's good fortune	Hiravijaya
Siddhichandra	ca. 1620s	*Bhānucandragaṇicarita*	Acts of Bhanuchandra	Bhanuchandra
Hemavijaya/Gunavijaya	1624–1632	*Vijayapraśastimahākāvya*	Great praise poem for Vijayasena	Vijayasena
Vallabha Pathaka	1652	*Vijayadevamāhātmya*	Vijayadeva's greatness	Vijayasena

between employing Sanskrit or a Prakrit, sometimes selecting both (e.g., Jinaprabha and Vidyatilaka in their *Vividhatīrthakalpa*, see chapter 4). Jain authors may have selected a Prakrit over Sanskrit for accessibility, to honor long-standing Jain customs, and for ease of reusing older materials.[7] But writing in the local vernacular was a slightly newer, although not altogether novel, option in early modern Gujarat. The Tapa Gaccha used Gujarati widely from at least the early fifteenth century onward, to communicate with the laity and conduct public business.[8] By the late sixteenth century, Tapa Gaccha affiliates considered writing a vernacular text to be a legitimate option across a notably large geographical area, exceeding the boundaries of the modern state of Gujarat.[9] Accordingly, Jain-authored Sanskrit works on the Mughals are complemented by a parallel body of Gujarati texts. An incomplete list of such texts is as follows: Dayakushala's *Lābhodayarāsa* (1593), Gunavinaya's *Karmacandravaṃsaprabandha* (1599, on Karmachandra), Darshanavijaya's *Vijayatilakasūrirāsa* (1622–1623), and Rishabhadas's *Hīravijayasūrirāsa* (1629, on Hiravijaya).[10]

Even a cursory review reveals that Gujarati and Sanskrit texts on Jain-Mughal connections share some key features. Certainly, their topics are similar and their biographical subjects sometimes one and the same. Hiravijaya and Karmachandra both feature as the main focus in Sanskrit and Gujarati works listed above.[11] At least one author worked in both languages. Gunavinaya wrote a Sanskrit commentary on Jayasoma's *Mantrikarmacandravaṃśāvalīprabandha* (Account of Minister Karmachandra's genealogy; 1594) and penned the Gujarati *Karmacandravaṃsaprabandha*. Whether the same people were reading texts in both languages remains an open question. In fact, beyond the surface-level observations hazarded in this paragraph, nearly everything remains unknown about the relationship between Gujarati and Sanskrit texts concerning ties between Jain monks and Mughal elites. I do not further attempt to advance this promising line of analysis in this book, which is, for practical and theoretical reasons, devoted specifically to Sanskrit texts. To recap (I discuss the issue at greater length in the introduction), if a scholar considers everything, then she loses depth. To avoid this predicament, I impose linguistic limitations on my project that also allow me to pursue certain questions about Sanskrit literary culture. For instance, Sanskrit literature involved a host of literary norms and a rhetorical lexicon whose nuanced use I unpack throughout this book. I also argue that the decision to write in Sanskrit mattered, and I prioritize recovering the meaning embedded in that choice for specific authors in specific times and places, including Shvetambara Jains writing in Gujarat during and about Mughal rule. No scholar can do it all, and I invite others to take up the sorely needed project of reconstructing the probable web of connections between vernacular and Sanskrit historical materials, in this case study and in others.[12]

For my purposes here, it suffices to emphasize that many Gujarati Jain authors chose to write in a cosmopolitan language over a literary vernacular. No prior authors that I have discussed faced a similar sort of decision, with the exception of Gangadevi, who might have written in Telugu. Some of Nayachandra's contemporaries, such as Vidyapati and Raidhu (a slightly later contemporary) wrote in Apabhramsha, but it is a far stretch to imagine that Nayachandra perceived his language selection as a relatively even choice. Crucial here is that I have largely focused on Sanskrit works authored in northern India, and, as compared to their southern counterparts, northern Indians were latecomers to producing vernacular literature.[13] I argue in chapter 3 that, writing in Tamil Nadu, Gangadevi chose Sanskrit over Telugu, at least in part, to ensure access to the vast array of Sanskrit literary conventions that she often skillfully deploys to comment on specific historical events. Going in a slightly different direction, some Jain authors used Sanskrit's robust literary styles and tropes to reimagine themselves and their local religious communities through their Mughal encounters.

Producing Local Histories

Jain-authored biographies, chronicles, and inscriptions that discuss the Mughals contain indications that their authors were engaged in a conscious attempt to produce written histories for their own communities. The works offer some basic markers of historical writing, such as using dates and featuring real people and events. Accordingly, scholars of Jainism have long used the chronicles and biographies to reconstruct lineages and the lives of specific monks, even if these efforts are often little appreciated in wider Sanskrit scholarship, which continues to sideline Jain texts.[14] From my perspective, the authors' investments in crafting coherent narratives are equally indicative of their intention to produce written histories. The Jain sources I discuss here are not lists of dry facts. The authors attempt to shape narratives about a set of largely real-life topics and to explain their relevance to a defined audience.

One way we can determine that the Jain-authored works are works of narrative history, rather than mere time lines, is by examining what they leave out. Written history is partly defined by the selective recording of facts as germane to a particular story line. As E. H. Carr put it, "The historian is necessarily selective."[15] One notable feature in this regard is that early modern Jain monks from the Tapa Gaccha and Kharatara Gaccha omitted any narrative of interactions between Akbar and Padmasundara, thus eliding the initial Mughal encounter with a Jain monk.[16] Padmasundara, a Nagapuriya ascetic, was the first Jain monk to enter Akbar's court; he arrived in the 1560s, and he died there around 1570.[17] But Tapa Gaccha and Kharatara Gaccha narratives generally champion Hiravijaya's arrival at Agra in 1583 as inaugurating the Jain-Mughal connections that they wish to explore. Padmasundara comes up in discussions of later monks, most notably in the story of Akbar offering Padmasundara's library, which had been absorbed into the imperial Mughal library upon the monk's death, to Hiravijaya (I discuss this story further below). But there is no Sanskrit narrative, of which I am aware, about Padmasundara's time at the Mughal court. Rather, our most concrete evidence regarding Padmasundara's engagements with Mughal elites is a Sanskrit text on aesthetic theory that he wrote for Akbar, in 1569, titled *Akbarasāhiśṛṅgāradarpaṇa* (Mirror of Shah Akbar's erotic passion). This intriguing treatise begins with praise of Allah (Arabic *raḥmān*, adapted into Sanskrit as *rahamān*) and features verses calling out to Akbar as the ultimate aesthete of erotic love (*śṛṅgāra*).[18]

From the perspective of a modern historian, Padmasundara's circa 1560s entry into Akbar's court is critical to reconstructing the social history of Jain-Mughal relations and the intellectual history of Sanskrit textual production for Mughal elites, but early modern Jains were narrating a different story. We might consider interlineage competition as a reason for the seemingly en masse decision to not recount Padmasundara's time at Akbar's court, but this explanation falls flat. Tapa Gaccha and Kharatara Gaccha monks were often rivals at court, but they wrote about each other's imperial experiences. For instance, Bhanuchandra, a Tapa Gaccha monk, recorded and likely embellished an approbatory story about the lay Kharatara Jain Karmachandra leading a ceremony to counteract a curse on Jahangir's infant daughter.[19] Vallabha Pathaka, a Kharatara Gaccha monk, authored an acclamatory biography of the Tapa Gaccha leader Vijayadeva.[20] Given that it was normal to repeat flattering stories about their immediate competitors, one might expect Tapa Gaccha authors to have also included an episode featuring a monk from an affinal lineage.[21] But Padmasundara's tale did not fit into the particular narratives that Shvetambara monks sought to craft when they wrote about the history of their Mughal links, and so they foregrounded a different story.

Tapa Gaccha authors identified Jain ties with regional Indo-Muslim political figures, especially in Gujarat, as relevant precedents for Hiravijaya's 1583 entry into the Mughal court. For instance, in 1592, Dharmasagara penned a chronological account of Tapa Gaccha leaders (*Tapāgacchapaṭṭāvalī*), in which he details a number of Hiravijaya's activities at Akbar's court.[22] Dharmasagara primes his readers for Hiravijaya's fairly extensive Mughal connections by first remarking that the prior two Tapa Gaccha leaders, Anandavimala (d. 1540) and Vijayadana (d. 1566), enjoyed relations with regional sultans. Dharmasagara is fairly brief in both of these early mentions, but he builds up to the multifaceted Hiravijaya-Akbar relationship by growing more verbose through each introduction of an Indo-Muslim ruler. He connects Anandavimala with a sultan (suratrana), Vijayadana with Sultan Mahmud (*sūratrāṇamahimūda*), and Hiravijaya with "Glorious Padshah King Akbar, emperor over all rulers" (*sakalarājādhirājapātisāhi-śrīakabbararāja*).[23] Several biographers present a more immediate context, of how Hiravijaya first arrived at the court of Sahib Khan, a Mughal-appointed governor of Gujarat, before heading to Fatehpur Sikri.[24]

Tapa Gaccha authors made a meaningful choice in citing a local history of links between regional Indo-Muslim rulers and Jain monks, a point further underscored by Nagapuriya and Kharatara materials. Writing about Padmasundara's entry into Akbar's court in the 1560s, Nagapuriya works allege earlier affiliations between monks from their lineage and Delhi-based Indo-Persian dynasties. A circa 1580–1600 note written at the end of a copy of Padmasundara's *Akbarasāhiśṛṅgāradarpaṇa* reports that Jayaraj was patronized by Babur, Anandaraya by Humayun, and Padmasundara by Akbar.[25] In the early seventeenth century, Harshakirti, a Nagapuriya monk, placed Padmasundara as the penultimate of eight monks who had enjoyed royal, generally Indo-Muslim sponsorship. Among the earlier six monks were men supposedly supported by rulers from the Khalji, Tughluq, and Lodi dynasties.[26] It is tempting to think that this difference—that Nagapuriya materials cite earlier Mughal and Delhi Sultanate links whereas Tapa Gaccha authors refer to ties with Gujarati Muslim political figures—is explained as accurate history. But the authors were not simply reporting the truth. The facticity of many of the projected prior Nagapuriya links is dubious, to put it lightly. And so, we are left wondering: If Nagapuriya monks could make up prior Mughal and Delhi Sultanate ties, why could not Tapa Gaccha monks do the same? The answer is that they could have, but the latter chose a local, Gujarat-based precedent instead.[27] Kharatara materials, too, point up the agency embedded in the Tapa Gaccha's preference for local history. A 1594 temple inscription at Patan lists Kharatara leaders through Jinachandra who, the inscription tells its readers, received numerous imperial concessions from Akbar. As precedent, the inscription links the prior two Kharatara leaders to a Delhi-based ruler and to Muslims more generally, respectively, reporting that Jinahamsa (d. 1526) convinced Sikander Lodi to release some prisoners and Jinamanikya (d. 1555) used meditation to shatter a Muslim-led attack (*yavanopadrava*).[28]

The chronicles, inscriptions, and biographies discussed here refer to one another, which indicates that at least some authors envisioned themselves as creating an archive of interlinked historical works. For instance, for more expansive (*vistarataḥ*) information on Hiravijaya's life, Dharmasagara refers readers to Devavimala's *Hīrasaubhāgya* (Hiravijaya's good fortune; ca. 1590–1610).[29] Similarly, writing nearly a century later, in the late seventeenth century, Meghavijaya directs readers seeking a more detailed (*vistarataḥ*) account of Vijayasena's life to Hemavijaya's *Vijayapraśastimahākāvya* (Great praise poem for Vijayasena; 1624–1632).[30] In another work, Meghavijaya refers to the *Hīrasaubhāgya* by name.[31] Sanskrit intellectuals in other times and places had been known to inventory their sources generally. For instance, in the introduction to his *Rājataraṅgiṇī*, Kalhana lists earlier chronicles, poems, and inscriptions (while pitching his work as superior).[32] In comparison, Dharmasagara and Meghavijaya are far more precise in naming sources for specific information in what read as early modern footnotes.

Jain sources on the Mughals also refer to one another by repeating certain bits of information. A good example is Hiravijaya's list of accomplishments during his initial stint at Akbar's court, from 1583 until 1585. Dharmasagara wrote in 1592 that, having been enlightened by Hiravijaya, Akbar "banned harming animals for six months, relinquished the jizya tax, and promoted the glorious Jain teaching as enlightening for all people."[33] These triumphs and similar feats pop up again and again in Tapa Gaccha sources. Several inscriptions and texts report that Hiravijaya convinced Akbar to ban animal slaughter for six months, often using the language that "animals were born for six months without fear," and to rescind the jizya tax.[34] Regarding nonviolence toward animals, some Jain works are more specific, noting concessions such as Akbar's outlawing of fishing in a lake near Fatehpur Sikri.[35] Inscriptions at Shatrunjaya publicized such feats, both on temple walls and near footprints representing Hiravijaya. Such repetition and overt advertising created a standard historical narrative that Jains beyond the Tapa Gaccha sought to emulate quite quickly. For example, Kharatara sources dating to the 1590s laud Jinachandra for inciting Akbar to ban animal slaughter and prohibit fishing in the Gulf of Cambay, acts that mirrored Hiravijaya's deeds.[36] In a short time frame, Mughal-issued imperial orders became part of the language of competition between the Tapa Gaccha and Kharatara Gaccha and shaped both groups' self-identities.

To be sure, there are other ways of understanding these Jain-authored biographies besides the framework of historical writing. For instance, Devavimala used the well-known Sanskrit poem *Naiṣadhīyacarita* (Nala of Nishada's deeds) as a literary model for his *Hīrasaubhāgya*.[37] It is not entirely clear whether the *Hīrasundaramahākāvya*, an abbreviated version of the *Hīrasaubhāgya*, was produced as an initial draft or a later summary, but either way the two works are closely related.[38] Padmasagara's *Jagadgurukāvya* (Poem on the teacher of the world; 1589) contains a creative history of the early Mughal Empire, and so I discuss parts of it in chapter 7. Nearly all the biographies discussed here cover aspects of the lives of their respective subjects that had nothing to do with the Mughals. The texts also span several genres, including kavya, charita, pattavali, and prabandha (poetry, story, lineage, and narrative, respectively). Some scholars have made more of those genre classifications than is prudent for my purposes here.[39] In short, I do not offer the only way of reading these Jain-authored monastic biographies. Rather, I offer one way that seeks to get at how and to what ends the authors of these materials shared an impulse to write about their historical encounters with Mughal elites and thereby write about themselves.

Placing the Narrative

Jains situated their narratives in both a Mughal imperial geography and a Jain religious geography, two maps that increasingly overlapped in early modern India. All the biographers discussed here mention the Mughal capital, which shifted several times during the reigns of Akbar and Jahangir between Delhi, Agra, Fatehpur Sikri, and Lahore (all come up in Jain sources). Jain monks often used their rich inherited tradition to integrate the peripatetic seat of Mughal power within traditional Sanskrit and specifically Jain ways of mapping the world. For instance, Siddhichandra locates Agra within standard Sanskrit cosmography:

> On the island called Jambudvipa and in the southern land of Bharata,
> the city of Ugrasena [Agra] shone like the moon in the middle of the land.[40]

Taking a slightly different and more verbose tack, Devavimala invokes a near avalanche of tropes over ten verses to present the region of Delhi (*dillīdeśa*), identifying it as the goddess Shri's playground, comparable to Kubera's Alaka, and unassailable by enemies, just like Indra's thunderbolt.[41] Jain monks also employed tropes to convey specific information about some locales. For instance, Hemavijaya and Devavimala both wrote about the wealth of Fatehpur Sikri, albeit in slightly different modes. Hemavijaya praises women in Fatehpur Sikri who donate lavishly during festivals and even use pearls to outline swastikas, an ancient Indian symbol of good luck and good fortune.[42] Devavimala describes Fatehpur Sikri's robust markets, which proffered jewels, cloth, sandalwood, gold, spices, and more.[43]

Some Jain authors display an interest in Mughal territorial expansion through conquests. For instance, a now fragmentary 1587 inscription at a Jain temple in Bairat, a village north of Jaipur in Rajasthan, says that Akbar's sovereignty extends across "Kashmir, Kamrup, Kabul, Badakhshan, Delhi, Marusthali [Marwar], Gurjaratra, and Malwa."[44] Mughal control of Badakhshan remained an aspiration rather than a reality in 1587, but the inclusion of Kabul, taken only a few years earlier, suggests an interest in up-to-date politics. Writing a few years later, Dharmasagara stuck even closer to Akbar's vision of political expansion, describing Akbar as "lord of the twelve subas [*sūba*] called Gujarat, Malwa, Bihar, Ayodhya, Prayag, Fatehpur, Delhi, Lahore, Multan, Kabul, Ajmer, and Bengal."[45] In this list, Dharmasagara matches Abul Fazl's list of twelve provinces given in the *Āʾīn-i Akbarī* (Akbar's institutes), a text also written in the 1590s.[46] Dharmasagara even uses official Mughal terminology, transliterating the Persian term *ṣūba* (province) rather than substituting a Sanskrit equivalent. At times, Dharmasagara adds a traditional twist, such as labeling the province of Allahabad using its older name of Prayag. Other times, he follows Mughal norms, such as naming Lahore as such (*lāhura*) rather than the Sanskritized *lābhapura* (city of wealth), favored by several of his Jain contemporaries.[47] In a nod to local interests, Dharmasagara opens his list with Gujarat, whereas Abul Fazl lists the same suba fifth and dubs it Ahmedabad. Other Jain authors preferred to depict Mughal conquests across an idealized landscape. For instance, around 1587, Shantichandra penned his *Kṛpārasakośa* (Treasury of compassion) for Akbar; in it he describes the Mughal Emperor completing a *digvijaya* (conquest of the four directions) across a timeless, trope-laden subcontinent that contains no overt references to sixteenth-century politics.[48] Such an example points up Dharmasagara's agency in emphasizing a realpolitik landscape as relevant to Tapa Gaccha monastic leaders.

For Tapa and Kharatara Gaccha Jains, their core religious geography was based in Gujarat, a region increasingly subject to imperial control during Mughal rule. Siddhichandra puts his cohorts' general fondness for the area succinctly in his *Bhānucandragaṇicarita* (Acts of Bhanuchandra), writing, "the unparalleled region of Gujarat is like a slice of heaven."[49] Even Jayasoma, who focuses on a lay Jain politician from Bikaner, talks about Gujarat in the context of discussing Kharatara monks.[50] Jain authors mention political locations in Gujarat, such as Ahmedabad, a regional focal point of Indo-Muslim power. But religious sites, such as Mount Shatrunjaya, arise more frequently. Both Tapa Gaccha and Kharatara Gaccha monks secured Mughal orders ensuring their lineage's control over Shatrunjaya at different points in time, and the subject comes up in multiple biographies. Sometimes the authors were quite blatant in identifying interlineage competition, adjudicated by the Mughals, as a motivating factor. For instance, Siddhichandra narrates how Bhanuchandra once convinced Akbar to rescind a Shatrunjaya-related tax against the background of Kharatara jealousy (*kharatarairīrṣyābharair*) of Tapa Gaccha imperial favor.[51] At Shatrunjaya, too, stone inscriptions herald Tapa Gaccha successes in securing concessions from the Mughal kings.[52] Both Tapa Gaccha and Kharatara Gaccha representatives also carved inscriptions at Shatrunjaya that otherwise have nothing to do with the Mughals but describe themselves as in "the kingdom of victorious Sultan Nuruddin Jahangir Sawai" or, for later dates, "in the kingdom of victorious glorious Padshah Shah Jahan."[53] Several inscriptions also refer to the Mughal princes Khusrau and Khurram and the local Mughal governor.[54] In these inscriptions,

Gujarati Jain monks evince almost hyperawareness of their location within an imperial geography and then project it across a sacred space.

Jain Agency in a Mughal World

Jain leaders who visited the Mughal courts contended with the considerable depth of Mughal power that manifested in social, religious, and political aspects of court life. This sometimes worked to the advantage of visiting Jain monks, such as when they received beneficial imperial orders. But it also threatened Jain ascetics' reputations, religious vows, and even lives at certain moments of conflict. Jain monks responded by finding different ways to express agency within the Mughal milieu, including by harnessing, outdoing, or even contradicting imperial power. The real-life challenges of negotiating with Mughal imperial authority also cropped up in Sanskrit texts on Jain experiences at the imperial court. Perhaps taking more liberties than they could in real life, Jain biographers carved out numerous ways for Jain monks to exercise agency within a realm circumscribed by multifaceted imperial authority.

Some biographers depicted Jain leaders as making decisions ethically superior to those of the Mughal emperor. A good example comes in the story of the initial 1583 meeting between Akbar and Hiravijaya. Both Sanskrit biographies of Hiravijaya (*Jagadgurukāvya* and *Hīrasaubhāgya*) narrate that, in the first meeting between the two, Hiravijaya outsmarted Akbar while simultaneously showing the virtues of Jain beliefs. The story goes that a hospitable Akbar invited Hiravijaya to step upon a luxurious carpet within the Mughal palace, but Hiravijaya refused, to avoid harming the worms and insects he knew were hidden therein.[55] Then, to quote Padmasagara, "Glorious Padshah Akbar removed the cloth with his own hand and saw small worms wiggling out."[56] Devavimala adds that Akbar initially contradicted Hiravijaya, proclaiming "there is no living creature whatsoever in this cloth, just as there is no mortal in heaven." Following the emperor's pompous claim, "a small worm came into Akbar's line of vision."[57] The story heralds Hiravijaya's clairvoyance that allowed him to demonstrate the Jain value of ahimsa (nonviolence) on a royal stage. The tale also portrays the Tapa Gaccha leader as wiser than Akbar. This narrative, centered around a king and his cloth, perhaps finds precedent in a story about Jinaprabha at the Tughluq court in the early fourteenth century, but, crucially, the ending differs. In the *Vividhatīrthakalpa* (Many places of pilgrimage), Jinaprabha says he refused blankets offered by Muhammad bin Tughluq, to avoid compromising his vow of mendicancy. But, upon further reflection, Jinaprabha accepted the blankets, to obviate the king's wrath.[58] Whereas Jinaprabha bowed to royal authority and Indo-Persian gifting norms, Hiravijaya showed up Akbar.

Mughal-period Jain authors dealt with the sticky subject of imperial gifts in another story, namely that of Akbar bequeathing Padmasundara's library to Hiravijaya, and here too forged Jain agency within the Mughal court. Devavimala unfolds this saga over a few dozen verses and underscores Hiravijaya's ability to challenge the Mughal king.[59] In short, Padmasundara had died at Akbar's court around 1570, and Akbar, finding the monk's disciples lacking, had assumed control of his library.[60] A little more than a decade later, Akbar deemed Hiravijaya a worthy recipient for this collection of manuscripts, presumably written in languages such as Sanskrit, Prakrit, and Gujarati that Akbar could not access directly.[61] Hiravijaya declined the library despite Akbar's persistent offers.[62] Akbar even called in Abul Fazl, his vizier, and Sthanasimha, a lay Jain leader in Agra, to persuade Hiravijaya to accept the manuscript collection. The high-profile involvement of Abul Fazl signals the imperial importance attached to gift giving and how Hiravijaya's refusal disrupted accepted norms.[63] Ultimately, Hiravijaya accepted Padmasundara's library, but he directed the collection to be managed by Sthanasimha, in Agra. By giving the library to a lay Jain, Hiravijaya followed a known Jain tradition of laymen managing bhandars and also avoided the risk that acquiring material objects might infringe upon his mendicant vows, a source of community angst so long as Jain monks had visited luxurious courts.[64] Also, Hiravijaya dictated the terms under which he acceded to a royal request. According to Devavimala, Hiravijaya's wisdom at the end of this episode supersedes Akbar's self-claimed wisdom at the tale's beginning. Akbar had judged Padmasundara's students unworthy of the library, but Hiravijaya, rather than Akbar, indicated the manuscripts' proper home.

Jain authors also mitigated the long reach of Mughal power by advertising how Jain figures solicited imperial orders (farmans) and thereby turned royal authority to their advantage. The Mughals issued some farmans that benefited specific Shvetambara lineages, such as one turning over control of Shatrunjaya, as mentioned above. Other orders advanced broader Jain ethical values, such as bans on animal slaughter during the Paryushan festival and permission to repair temples in Gujarat (an act that also sometimes had a sectarian edge).[65] Much of this history is attested in the surviving Persian-language farmans and, occasionally, in other material objects. For instance, a stupa commemorating Hiravijaya survives in Diu that, according to Siddhichandra, originally sat on land donated by Akbar.[66] Jain biographies also repeat numerous episodes where monks receive imperial orders.

Jain biographers integrated stories about their leaders procuring royal farmans into their larger narratives in a few different ways. At the level of language, Jain authors used the term *sphuramāna* (sometimes with alternative spellings), coined perhaps in the fourteenth century as a loose phonetic Sanskrit adaptation of the Persian *farmān*.[67] "Sphuramana" also means, appropriately, "something that goes forth." Such a meaning-laden vocabulary import follows the model seen with "suratrana" (Sanskrit for "sultan"; means "protector of the gods"), a word that also crops up in Mughal-era Jain biographies. Moreover, individual episodes often climax with a monk receiving an imperial order. A typical, succinct example is found in Jayasoma's *Mantrikarmacandravaṃśāvalīprabandha* (Account of Minister Karmachandra's genealogy):

> One time when Karmachandra heard about some temples being harmed in Dvaraka,
> he asked Glorious Jalaluddin Akbar to protect Jain temples.
> The king was so pleased that he gave all the Jain pilgrimage destinations,
> chief among them Mount Shatrunjaya, to Minister Karmachandra.
> The shah, his mind delighted, directed Azam Khan to give a sphuramana,
> stamped with his own royal seal, to Karmachandra.[68]

Gaining imperial concessions also increased the fame of specific individuals, a praiseworthy goal in these biographies. For instance, Vallabha Pathaka writes that Vijayasena received a farman from Akbar that pleased the Jain community at large.[69] Waxing more poetic, Siddhichandra celebrates that, after Bhanuchandra secured an imperial order that released prisoners in Saurashtra, his "fame shone like the autumn moon's light across all lands."[70]

Jains competed with Brahmins for imperial resources and attention at the Mughal court, a dynamic that shines through periodically in Jain sources as a way to underscore the position of Jain monks at the Mughal court. Jain works hardly scratch the surface of the full variety of roles filled by Brahmin Sanskrit intellectuals at the Mughal court, which we can piece together from other Sanskrit and Persian materials.[71] In Jain-authored texts, Brahmins serve as foils for Jain successes. For instance, Siddhichandra narrates how Bhanuchandra taught Akbar to recite the Sanskrit *Sūryasahasranāma* (Thousand names of the sun). Brahmins had given the work to the Mughal king but then failed to instruct Akbar in its proper recitation.[72] Akbar's sun worship finds confirmation in Persian and European texts.[73] But more important for Siddhichandra's narrative is that Bhanuchandra teaches the sun's Sanskrit names to Akbar after the Brahmins at court proved incapable of doing so. A subtler knock against Brahmins comes in Kharatara and Tapa Gaccha texts that report how Karmachandra performed a Jain astrological ceremony to remove a curse on Jahangir's newborn daughter.[74] The Mughals kept both Brahmin and Muslim astrologers on staff at court, but apparently neither was able to sway the ill-fated stars afflicting the young Mughal princess.[75]

Jain Theology in a Mughal World

Jain authors wrote little about theological aspects of the Mughal court, with one dazzling exception that compares Islamic and Jain religious ideas en route to declaring the latter superior. In his *Hīrasaubhāgya* (Hiravijaya's good fortune), Devavimala narrates a story where Abul Fazl asks Hiravijaya's opinion about Islamic theology and therein outlines basic Islamic beliefs. This extraordinary passage cuts against the general tendency to not discuss Islamic theology in Sanskrit texts, and it is worth quoting in full (Abul Fazl refers to Hiravijaya by his title of suri):

> Abul Fazl said, "O Suri, this was laid out by the ancient prophets in our scriptures—all Muslims [yavana] who are deposited on earth as guests of the god of death will rise at the end of the earth and come before the court of the Supreme Lord called *khudā*, just as they come to the court of an earthly king. He will cast good and bad qualities onto his own pure mind as if onto a mirror and bring about rightful

judgment there, having refuted the false construction of mine versus another's. Having reflected, he will bestow the appropriate result of [the yavanas'] virtues and vices, like the fertile soil generates plentiful grain from different seeds. Some will be brought to heaven by him, just as boats are led to the edge of the ocean by a favorable wind. Then they will find joy, nearly overwhelmed with floods of suitable, amazing enjoyments. Others will be sent to hell by him because of sin. Like birds being crushed by hawks and pots being fired by potters, they will suffer great agonies at the mercies of hell's guards. O Suri, what is the validity of this Quranic speech [*kurānavākyaṃ*]? Is it true, like the speech of great-souled people, or is it false like a flower sprouting in the sky?"[76]

Sanskrit texts had not offered such detail on Islamic beliefs in centuries, arguably not since the Kalachakra works written between 1025 and 1040 CE (see chapter 1). Given the subsequent decline of Buddhism in India, Mughal-era Jain authors almost certainly did not know about these works from more than half a millennium earlier. In other words, Devavimala was doing something entirely innovative, from his perspective, in elaborating basic Islamic theological precepts in Sanskrit.

Devavimala attempts to soften the searing newness of producing a Sanskrit description of Islamic beliefs in minor ways. For instance, he cites Sanskrit and Prakrit verses in his autocommentary as precedents for specific ideas outlined by Abul Fazl (e.g., see notes on the translation of this section in appendix A.6).[77] Earlier in his work Devavimala describes yavana as a jati, thus categorizing a new group within an older metacategory.[78] All of this is buried in the commentary. And, in any case, light contextualization only slightly mellows the startling novelty of the above passage. Especially given that other Jain authors discussed here do not offer a comparable discussion of Islamic beliefs, we must ask: What is this passage doing in the *Hīrasaubhāgya*?

Devavimala uses Abul Fazl's description of basic Muslim beliefs to set the stage for Hiravijaya's winning retort that is designed to demonstrate the superiority of Jain ideas. Again, this deserves a lengthy quote:

Having spoken, Abul Fazl fell silent in the hopes of gaining wisdom from Hiravijaya's response. Then, the lord of sages spoke sweetly: "He—who is free of dirt like a shell, devoid of defects like the sun,

> made of flames like fire, and without a body like the god of love—is the Supreme Lord. In what form does he attend court like a living being that adopts many appearances in his wanderings through existence? There he sets a person on the path to heaven or hell for what reason? A previous action, once ripened, has the power to grant both joys and sorrows. Thus, let action [karma] alone be recognized as the creator of the world, since otherwise [God] has no purpose." When Hiravijaya, the lord of ascetics, fell silent after speaking, Shaykh Abul Fazl replied: "So you recognize that book [commentary: Quran] as false just as inconsistency is recognized in the speech of a garrulous, vile person." Lord Hiravijaya spoke again: "If the creator first made this world and then later destroyed it as if he were fire, he would have unparalleled distress. There is no creator or destroyer of the world whose variety is brought into being by its own karma. Therefore, the existence of a creator, like the birth of a son to a barren woman, appears false to me." Having enlightened Shaykh Abul Fazl with correct speech and cured him of his prior false opinion, Hiravijaya planted the dharma of compassion in the Shaykh's mind like a farmer plants a seed in the earth.[79]

This story champions Hiravijaya and Jain thought as superior to Abul Fazl and Islam, respectively. Such a laudatory stance is a classic, even definitional goal, of Jain biographical literature, here climaxing in the historically unlikely claim that Abul Fazl essentially became Jain. Devavimala makes a similar rhetorical move of declaring the Mughals to be almost Jain in the final chapter of his work, where he portrays a newly deceased and deified Hiravijaya as visiting Akbar in a dream and inspiring the king to fund a stupa memorializing the Tapa Gaccha leader-turned-god.[80] Such accounts, even when beyond what we moderns might admit as hard fact, underscore that exerting influence over Mughal elites provided a key narrative element in Jain histories of their imperial relations. Moreover, Devavimala's willingness to elaborate Islamic theology, treated as off-limits by most intellectuals working in Sanskrit, marks this part of his text as highly unusual.

Other biographers similarly depict the Mughals as exhibiting Jain proclivities, but generally without first describing Muslim beliefs. For instance, Siddhichandra narrates an episode set at Gwalior Fort where

Akbar felt distressed (*khedabhṛt*) at seeing some large Jain icons mutilated (*jainabimbāni . . . vyaṅgāni*) and so ordered them repaired.[81] Siddhichandra also imbues Jahangir with Jain inclinations and insights in the *Bhānucandragaṇicarita*. For instance, he depicts Jahangir as discoursing eloquently on the Jain philosophical concept of relativism (*syādvāda*).[82] But only Devavimala situates the Mughals' supposed Jain-inclined sentiments against a backdrop of Islamic beliefs. That innovative framing enables Devavimala to underscore the power of Jain leaders to counter Mughal authority. Devavimala was not entirely alone in using aspects of Mughal court culture in innovative ways, and I discuss below Siddhichandra's quite different harnessing of Persian learning to elaborate Tapa Gaccha community identity. But, first, it is worth briefly dwelling on Devavimala's claim that Jains deny a creator God, articulated in Hiravijaya's response as quoted above. This theological stipulation laid the groundwork for later narratives of religious discussions between Mughal and Jain elites that would ensnare successive leaders of the Tapa Gaccha and become part of the lineage's internal identity narrative.

Tapa Gaccha monks were called upon to explain the Jain view of God several times at the Mughal court. Even today both practitioners and scholars debate whether Jains believe in God, sometimes answering both yes and no.[83] In the Mughal context, the question had a harsh political edge, since Mughal tolerance did not extend to atheism. Jains could lose imperial favor and be thrown out of court if they were judged atheists. Seeing this subject as an opportunity to eliminate their rivals, around 1593, Brahmins urged the Mughals to query Vijayasena, a Tapa Gaccha leader, about God. This was not the first time that the Mughals had discussed religious questions, including Jain positions on theism, with Jain leaders. Dharmasagara and Devavimala narrate an amicable conversation that began when Akbar asked Hiravijaya about Jain dharma, including what God (*parameśitā, parameśvara*) Jains worship.[84] Samayasundara, a member of the Kharatara Gaccha, penned an entire Sanskrit work for the Mughals, the *Artharatnāvalī* (String of jewels of meaning; 1592), to demonstrate interpretive practices that allowed for multiple readings, including theistic readings, of Jain religious texts.[85] But Akbar's questioning of Vijayasena was different in its overt and intentional political risk for Jain monks, although Jain Sanskrit retellings of the conversation came to serve rather different purposes.

Numerous Jain writers narrated Vijayasena's 1593 defense against the charge of atheism, including long after contact with the Mughals had ceased to be part of their lineage's regular activities, and their accounts vary wildly from one another. Perhaps the earliest Sanskrit record of this event is found in the circa 1595 Adishvara inscription at Shatrunjaya, which proclaims:

> [Vijayasena] established openly in the assembly of Shah Akbar
> that Arhat was be understood as God [parameshvara] using such lofty words
> that the Bhattas, lords of the Brahmins, whose babbling was sheer madness,
> became blinded by powerful proofs like thieves confronted by a great light.[86]

After this inscription, the next four Sanskrit sources that retell this episode all postdate the end of Mughal relations with Jain monks, in 1618. Accounts penned in the 1620s and 1630s follow the Adishvara inscription in underscoring the political angle that Brahmins failed to have Jains ousted from court and instead discredited themselves. The Adishvara inscription (quoted above) maligned Brahmins as mindless babblers, akin to thieves, and blindsided by Jain logic. Siddhichandra, writing in the 1620s, describes the Brahmin instigator, Bhattacharya, as "trounced and stunned by a powerful ocean of reasoning."[87] Hemavijaya (ca. 1630s) offers the colorful verse: "When the Brahmins were defeated by the Suri, they became so emasculated that it is amazing the townspeople did not lust after them as if they were women."[88] In contrast, Jains writing in the 1650s and later elided the immediate context of Jain-Brahmin competition. Both Vallabha Pathaka (ca. 1650s) and Meghavijaya (ca. 1670–1700) only name a vague instigator in passing.[89] Vallabha does not even specify that the troublemaker was a Brahmin, only noting that somebody tipped off Akbar (*kenacitpreritaḥ sāhir*).[90] It seems that, as time passed, the imperial context of Brahmin competition for Mughal favor faded in importance for Jain thinkers, who instead treated Vijayasena's theism arguments as a productive foil for elaborating, in other ways, the theological and social positioning of Jain thought in the early modern Indian religious landscape.

The last three writers to narrate this debate in Sanskrit—Hemavijaya, Vallabha, and Meghavijaya—all used Vijayasena's theism defense as an opportunity to proclaim that Jains worked with a similar set of religious ideas as other Indian religious communities. Meghavijaya and Hemavijaya narrate a rather similar story here, with the former drawing upon the latter explicitly. In both texts, Vijayasena's climactic response to Akbar's query about Jain theism is as follows:

> The Shaivas revere him as "Shiva" and the Vedantins as "Brahma."
> The Buddhists who are sharp in logic worship revere him as
> "Buddha" and the Mimamsakas as "Karma."
> Those who ascribe to Jain teachings worship him as "Arhat"
> and the Naiyayikas as "Creator."
> May that Hari, the Lord of the Three Worlds, give you whatever
> you desire.[91]

In other words, Jains worship God by a different name, like followers of other Indian religious and philosophical traditions. Notably, this verse was known in Sanskrit for several hundred years preceding these Jain authors and often appears in Hindu contexts, such as in praise poems and on a temple wall in Karnataka.[92] In quoting this verse, Meghavijaya and Hemavijaya articulate ideas that were neither exclusively Jain nor specific to the Mughal court. The authors' interests seem to have shifted to placing Shvetambara communities within a wider early modern Indian religious context.

Vallabha Pathaka offers a different story of this same discussion that foregrounds even more forcefully what we would now call Hindu deities. Vallabha reports that Akbar invoked the names of Hindu gods in his initial inquiry, asking: "O Suri! Why do you not believe in Rama and mother Ganga?"[93] Vijayasena answers that Jains, indeed, revere both Rama and Ganga, even if they define them differently.[94] Such a question seems unlikely to have arisen, in this exact form, from a Muslim, but the Mughal imperial context had faded in importance for Shvetambara monks by the time Vallabha was writing, in the 1650s. Indeed, shortly after this story, Vallabha narrates how Vijayasena was invited by a Christian padre to Diu and there enlightened the Portuguese governor.[95] For Vallabha, the backdrop of political power appears interchangeable, whereas his consistent goal remains to demonstrate the persuasive power of Jain views and Jain parity with what we might now call Hindu thought.

Becoming the Mughal Other

Jain biographers adapted aspects of Mughal imperial culture to praise Jain monks. In real life, Jain monastic and Mughal political leaders operated in distinct religious, linguistic, and cultural traditions, at least most of the time. But significant differences proved no barrier to Jain authors importing imperial and, in one case, specifically Persianate norms to extol renunciant leaders. In a sense, it is unsurprising that Tapa Gaccha authors found an imperial model useful for expressing their ascetic order's identities and ambitions. As Sarah Pierce Taylor has pointed out: "The mobilization of royal language and imagery is so superficially apparent in the world of South Asian religion that it almost seems too obvious to thematize."[96] Jains in particular often appropriated royal imagery "as a way to articulate an alternative sovereignty located within the true kingdom of asceticism."[97] Still, this move takes on a different hue when we consider how Jain works appropriated Mughal standards, cultural norms, and so forth within the larger tradition of Sanskrit narratives of Indo-Muslim rule. In the history of Sanskrit views of a Muslim Other, these works mark a moment when the "Muslim Other" became oneself.

From the very first Sanskrit accounts of Mughal relations with Jains monks, Jain biographers applied markers of Mughal sovereignty to ascetic leaders. Take, for example, Padmasagara's description of Hiravijaya processing from Akbar's court:

> Having been given an order by the king for the sake of purifying
> the earth and supporting the faithful,
> Hiravijaya processed from the royal courtyard.
> He exited the court, followed by groups of poets, kings, and
> logicians,
> and accompanied by heroes, ministers, and the best of the town.
>
> Emperor Akbar following on foot, bowed down at Hiravijaya's feet
> and stood again.
> From the door of his own home, he sent all his soldiers to
> Hiravijaya.
> He ordered musical instruments played energetically by
> men sitting on top of elephants and had his own splendor

[*svaśriyam*]—complete with chariots, horses, and elephants—go
before the great Suri.

Accompanied by resounding grandeur ordered by the king,
the lord of Suris made his way across town.
He left no doubt in anybody's heart that this was the arrival of a
Tirthankara.
Like a Tirthankara, he found favor with the wise because of his
pure virtues.

At every step, the faithful spread out gold-thread cloth.
Beggars grabbed at the well-spoken Suri.
Devout women scattered the best pearls and legions of jewels with
their own hands,
and thereby covered the ground, making it appears like the
ocean.[98]

Hiravijaya is called a Jain mendicant here, but he is honored with the trappings of a Mughal sovereign. Accoutrements provided by Akbar announce the monk's arrival, and his followers-cum-subjects respond with flashy displays of wealth, covering the earth with gold, cloth, and precious stones. Such imagery contrasts sharply with the story about Hiravijaya refusing to set foot on a Mughal carpet, found only twenty verses earlier in the same text. Here, a victorious Hiravijaya trods on golden threads rather than let his royal feet touch the earth. Padmasagara makes no attempt to square this disjuncture in his narrative. His use of such imagery, despite towering internal contradictions, attests that he found Mughal sovereignty a compelling model, akin to earlier sorts of Indian sovereignty.

Other Jain authors also invoked the model of Mughal sovereignty, sometimes expanding it from individual stories to capture an individual's entire life or even an entire religious group. Consider, for instance, the multivalence of *saubhāgya* (good fortune), which appears in the title of one of Hiravijaya's Sanskrit biographies. The term echoed the 1467 *Somasaubhāgya* (Somasundara's good fortune), a biography of the Tapa Gaccha leader Somasundara.[99] Mughal-period Jains also associated *saubhāgya* with royalty. For instance, in his 1630s commentary on the *Vijayapraśastimahākāvya*, Gunavijaya glosses *saubhāgya* as "being loved by a king" (*nṛpādipriyatvaṃ*).[100] Thus, Devavimala's contemporaries likely understood the title *Hīrasaubhāgya* as foregrounding monastic-Mughal connections in Hiravijaya's life story. The late seventeenth-century *Digvijayamahākāvya* (Great poem on conquering the directions) moves beyond a single person and employs royal sovereignty to encapsulate the workings of the entire Tapa Gaccha. The work's title refers explicitly to royal conquest (digvijaya), thus giving away its core edifice of imperial power. In the text, Meghavijaya describes the four Tapa Gaccha leaders after Hiravijaya as world conquerors who command armies of monks.[101] Such a framework suggests that one reason why Jain monks wrote about ties with the Mughals long after they had ceased was because Indo-Persian ruling culture furnished frameworks useful for the self-definition of some Jain lineages.

Siddhichandra also imports Mughal norms, but in a quite different and striking way as compared to other Jain authors. Siddhichandra's *Bhānucandragaṇicarita* (Acts of Bhanuchandra) stands apart from the rest of the Jain biographies that discuss Mughal figures for several reasons, chief among them its topic. The *Bhānucandragaṇicarita* claims, by its title, to be a biography of Bhanuchandra, but it is both more and less than that. Siddhichandra's opening story concerns Hiravijaya's 1583 meeting with Akbar, which inaugurated thirty-five years of Tapa Gaccha monks enjoying Mughal connections. Siddhichandra ends his work, more than thirty years later, with his own triumphant return to the imperial court, in 1616 (following a brief period of exile after an argument with Jahangir), which was the final flourishing of consistent ties between Jain monks and Mughal kings. With the exception of only a few brief passages, all of the intervening stories in the *Bhānucandragaṇicarita* take place at the Mughal court and feature Mughal political figures, although not all concern Bhanuchandra.[102] In other words, Jain-Mughals links furnish the narrative arc that binds together the otherwise disparate stories in the *Bhānucandragaṇicarita.*

Throughout his account of imperial relations with Jain monks, Siddhichandra depicts the Mughals as fully steeped in Sanskrit culture and traditional Indian kingship. For instance, in his initial description of Akbar, Siddhichandra compares the Mughal emperor to several model Indian sovereigns, including the chief royal model: Rama.

> Glorious Shah Akbar ruled the city of Agra with such righteous conduct
> that nobody remembered Rama anymore.[103]

In subsequent verses, Siddhichandra equates Akbar with Krishna, Indra, and other deities. He uses a range of Sanskrit tropes, such as lauding Akbar's gleaming white fame (for a translation, see appendix A.7). In a similar vein, after Akbar's death, Siddhichandra likens the newly crowned Jahangir's leisure activities to those of "Indra in heaven" (*svarge hariryathā*).[104] Siddhichandra includes culturally specific images in this passage, such as Jahangir enjoying "the wonder of hearing the clear singing of kinnaris [celestial musicians]."[105] Siddhichandra compares Jahangir's wife, Nur Jahan, to Lakshmi and describes the Mughal queen's beauty in a classical head-to-toe description favored by many Sanskrit poets.[106] Perhaps the most conspicuous passage concerns Abul Fazl, whom Siddhichandra holds up as a paradigm of Sanskrit learning. The passage is worth quoting in full (also translated in appendix A.7):

> Shaykh Abul Fazl's wisdom extended to all the shastras, including Jainism, Mimamsa, Buddhism, Sankhya, Vaisheshika, Charvaka, Jaiminiya, Sanskrit literature [kavya], yoga, Vedanta, lexicography, music, drama, aesthetic tropes, mythology [purana], metrical works, the science of omens, astrology, mathematics, physiognomy, political science, erotics, veterinary sciences, and guardianship. In terms of Sanskrit writing [*vāñmaya*], there is nothing that he has not seen or heard.[107]

Siddhichandra's vision of Abul Fazl as embodying the entirety of Sanskrit learning stands in sharp contrast to how Devavimala depicts the Mughal vizier as voicing Islamic theology in the *Hīrasaubhāgya* (quoted above; also see appendix A.6).[108] Siddhichandra drew more narrowly on Sanskrit norms for elaborating the culture milieu of Mughal political elites, a decision that sets a contrastive framework for his own partaking of Persian court culture.

When Siddhichandra refers to the Persian-medium culture that flourished at the Mughal court, he generally associates it with himself. Siddhichandra tells his readers that Akbar gave him the Persian title *khūshfahm* (wise man).[109] Siddhichandra mentions twice that he learned Persian and even read Persian texts (*pārasīgrantha*) to the Mughal princes and king.[110] In the midst of an argument with Jahangir about the merits of asceticism, spurred when Siddhichandra rebuffed Jahangir's order to take a wife, Siddhichandra narrates his (not Jahangir's) citation of Ibrahim ibn Adham, the king of Balkh known for renunciation in the Perso-Arabic tradition.[111]

Siddhichandra's reference to Ibrahim ibn Adham also constitutes the single Hindavi verse in the *Bhānucandragaṇicarita*. In contrast, Siddhichandra depicts Jahangir as responding with an argument about the Jain philosophy of relativism (syadvada). Much about Siddhichandra's participation in Indo-Persian culture is corroborated by other sources. For instance, Siddhichandra's title of "khushfahm" appears in a 1599 nastaliq seal, found on at least two Sanskrit manuscripts.[112] His teacher, Bhanuchandra, confirms Siddhichandra's knowledge of Persian.[113] One remarkable aspect of the *Bhānucandragaṇicarita* is the contrast between Siddhichandra's portrayal of himself as engaging in Persian culture versus his depiction of the Mughals as more narrowly remaining within Sanskrit conventions. For Siddhichandra, Jains could become the Mughal Other, even as the Mughals became indistinguishable from traditional Indian kings.

Innovative Writing

Jains made an important decision in writing at all about their links with the Mughal court. That is perhaps hard to see in this book, where I analyze these Jain works within a larger trend of Sanskrit historical writing on Indo-Muslim political figures that by the dawn of Mughal rule already dated back several hundred years. But a more immediate context for Jain biographies, chronicles, and inscriptions about their Mughal connections is a screaming silence from their Brahmin counterparts at court. As I mention above in passing, Sanskrit-literate Brahmins also maintained ties with the Mughals. In fact, Brahmin-Mughal ties lasted about one hundred years, from 1560 until 1660, nearly three times as long as long as Tapa Gaccha and Kharatara Gaccha monastic links with Mughal elites.[114] But Brahmins refer to their Mughal links only intermittently in Sanskrit texts and never produced Sanskrit narratives of their time at court.[115] Brahmins had proved taciturn in the past regarding Muslim political activities as compared to their Jain counterparts, such as when Dhanapala wrote about Ghaznavid raids while Brahmins appear to have remained mute (see chapter 1). But here we are not dealing with a sole, brief, Jain-authored poem but rather with thousands of pages of Jain narrations of their activities at the Mughal court. The Brahminical choice to not write produced a pointed, resonant silence with which we as historians must contend in our analysis of this period.[116] One upshot is that the Brahminical silence underscores Jain agency in producing such a prolific, varied archive of historical materials that explore what it might mean to write about Mughal power in Sanskrit.

In some regards, Jains appear to have become more interested in narrating their Mughal relations after those relations had ceased to exist, and this tells us a great deal about the purposes and presuppositions of Jain-authored Sanskrit histories. The *Bhānucandragaṇicarita*, for instance, postdates the cessation of Mughal relations with Tapa Gaccha monks but represents a stunning moment in Sanskrit historiography. It is arguably the first Sanskrit text to treat cross-cultural relations with Indo-Persian political elites as its main subject. Another poignant example of depicting Tapa Gaccha ascetic leaders using the language of Mughal sovereignty comes from Meghavijaya, who wrote decades after the end of cross-cultural relations between the two groups. Perhaps the clash between Mughal elites and Jain monks that effectively ended relations between them indicates at least a partial explanation for why Jain thinkers remained interested in using the template of Mughal power to serve their own community interests after their monks had exited the imperial court.

Siddhichandra narrates the explosive argument between himself and Jahangir that marked the beginning of the end of Mughal connections with Jain monks. The circa 1616 debate, which I have analyzed and translated in full elsewhere, revolved around Jain asceticism, but the underlying issue was the extent of Mughal authority.[117] In brief, Jahangir ordered Siddhichandra to marry, and the monk refused. Despite numerous arguments, a cameo appearance by Nur Jahan, and the threat of being crushed to death by a mad elephant, Siddhichandra remained firm in his repudiation of Jahangir's command to marry. In the end, Jahangir exiled an insubordinate Siddhichandra, along with all other Jain monks, save for Bhanuchandra. Jahangir soon relented, and Siddhichandra closes the *Bhānucandragaṇicarita* with his jubilant return to the Mughal court. But, in reality, things did not remain patched up for long. In 1618, Jahangir again exiled Jain ascetics from populated centers across the Mughal kingdom.[118] Like with the first order, Jahangir soon rescinded this ban, but Tapa Gaccha monks never regained their esteem in Mughal eyes. By the 1620s, Jahangir referred to his relationship with Bhanuchandra in the past tense, describing the monk as someone "whom I used to know" (*bhānuchand . . . kih mā ū rā shinākhtīm*).[119] Siddhichandra wrote his *Bhānucandragaṇicarita* within a decade or so after the dramatic end of relations between Mughal political figures and Jain ascetic leaders. Thus, Siddhichandra does not record the world around him so much as a world he recently lost. Perhaps creating a narrative about these cross-cultural connections memorialized a vanished reality as a way to open up possibilities for reworking local Jain identities.

CHAPTER VI

Rajput and Maratha Kingships in an Indo-Persian Political Order

I know two things that are sources of pleasure and joy:
one is union with the beloved, and the other is praising a prince.

—MASUD SAAD SALMAN (D. 1121)

By the late sixteenth century, Indian rulership was a complicated, diverse, crowded scene, and Sanskrit histories of Indo-Persian rule followed suit. The Mughals were the largest political and military force in northern India and, under the leadership of Akbar (r. 1556–1605), actively endeavored to expand south. Several successor states to the Bahmani Sultanate—including the Nizam Shahis of Ahmadnagar, the Adil Shahis of Bijapur, and the Qutb Shahis of Golconda—presided over kingdoms covering parts of central and southern India.[1] Across the subcontinent, Rajputs and Marathas exercised power over smaller areas. Crucially, Rajputs and Marathas were full participants in an early modern political world dominated by Indo-Persian dynasties. They fought against specific Muslim-led polities at times, but, perhaps more commonly, they warred on behalf of the Mughals, the Adil Shahis, and so forth. Sanskrit histories written for Rajput and Maratha courts discuss these shifting alliances and frequent conflicts, both of which usually involved Indo-Persian polities but never fell squarely along religious lines. Some readers may find it hard to swallow that there was no mass Hindu resistance against Muslim rulers, either in hard fact or in the Sanskrit literary imagination. In fact, most of the "Hindus" I talk about in this chapter did not commonly, if ever, refer to themselves as such in Sanskrit. Rather, if there was a shared concern among the Sanskrit histories I discuss below, it was Kshatriya kingship, a much more narrow, political, and (usually) class-based identity. But, even there, the texts converge on no single vision of an ideal ruler. Rajput- and Maratha-sponsored Sanskrit histories express a rich plurality of Kshatriya kingships that individual rulers might enact and relate, in different ways, to Indo-Persian rule, often diverging wildly from one another even within the same court.

We have an embarrassment of riches when it comes to Sanskrit historical texts produced under Rajput patronage. Between 1590 and 1690, in Amer, Baglan, Bundi, Mewar, and elsewhere, Rajput patrons sponsored Sanskrit histories of their own lineages.[2] In a notably bold move, in 1687, the rana of Mewar, Jai Singh, ordered Ranachoda Bhatta's *Rājapraśasti* (Royal praise), sponsored by the prior Mewar ruler Raj Singh, inscribed on twenty-four stone slabs (one canto per slab). These slabs line a ghat on the bank of the artificially constructed Rajsamand Lake. They are preceded by an inscription about the construction of the lake, for a total of twenty-five slabs in all.[3] Other scholars have analyzed individual Rajput-sponsored Sanskrit histories, often pairing them with vernacular works or material objects produced in the same court. For instance, Cynthia Talbot and Ramya Sreenivasan have compared Sanskrit and vernacular writings (texts and inscriptions) patronized by the Sisodiyas of Mewar and the Kachhwahas of Amer, respectively.[4] Elsewhere Talbot has read the *Śatruśalyacarita* (Shatrushalya's deeds), a circa 1635 Sanskrit account of the Hada Bundi leader Shatrushalya (r. 1631–1658), alongside murals completed during the reign of his grandfather, Rao Ratan (r. 1607–1631).[5] Jennifer Joffee has analyzed the *Rājapraśasti* in its material context at Rajsamand Lake and argued that the rulers of Mewar emulated Shah Jahan in some of the contents of the introductory inscription and by patronizing the construction of the lake.[6] These analyses offer strong models for in-depth studies of similar materials, especially in the inclusion of vernacular works and material culture. In this chapter, I foreground a different context for Rajput and Maratha Sanskrit histories, asking how they fit into the larger tradition of Sanskrit literary accounts of Indo-Muslim rule.

I pair histories patronized by Rajput and Maratha courts because both Rajputs and Marathas were actively forging political identities within an environment shaped by Indo-Persian kings. Neither "Rajput" nor "Maratha" is a timeless category. As pointed out by other scholars, both groups were figuring out who they were and who they wanted to be during the sixteenth and seventeenth centuries, settling on specific instantiations of martial identities.[7] The projects of defining such communities hardly ended with the dawn of the eighteenth century, and readers should note that "Maratha," in particular, came to have a different sense after 1700.[8] Of the myriad of early modern Rajput communities, two small kingdoms located in central India and Rajasthan, respectively, and the Sanskrit histories penned in their respective services, are my focuses in this chapter: the Rathods of Baglan and the Hada Chauhans of Bundi.[9] I also analyze historical works written for aspiring Rajputs, namely the Maratha Bhonsle clan that tried more than one method of claiming Kshatriya status, including inventing a Sisodiya Rajput heritage.[10] In the hopes of clarifying a complicated scene with some historical background, at the outset I briefly consider an earlier text: Gangadhara's *Maṇḍalīkacarita* (Mandalik's deeds; ca. 1460), written for a sort of pre-Rajput Chudasama ruler of Junagadh in fifteenth-century Gujarat.

In addition to expressing comparable types of Kshatriya-based authority, Rajputs and Marathas navigated the politics of early modern India in similar ways. In brief, they fought on all sides. Shivaji Bhonsle offers a typical example. At different moments, Shivaji fought for and against the Adil Shahis and both rebuked and submitted to Mughal authority. Likewise, Shivaji both struck against and allied with other Maratha and Rajput lineages.[11] In shifting alliances in pursuit of political power, Shivaji was not exceptional. Many Rajputs also changed their allegiances, sometimes frequently, within the convoluted politics of early modern India.[12] One thing that I investigate in this chapter is how Sanskrit thinkers expressed or, alternatively, glossed over this reality of fluid alliances.

In early modern Rajput and Maratha courts, the vernacular was vividly present as a literary medium that influenced intellectuals who crafted Sanskrit histories. Many of the Rajput and Maratha courts I mention in this chapter patronized vernacular literature, sometimes about political events and often around the same time as they also sponsored Sanskrit historical works.[13] Occasionally, we glimpse something of the thought process behind why a given poet chose Sanskrit over vernaculars. For instance, in his *Rājapraśasti* (1676), written for the Mewar kings, Ranachoda Bhatta writes in his opening chapter:

> Vernacular texts are as short-lived as mortals.
> But Sanskrit works such as the Mahabharata are as immortal as the gods.
> Therefore, O king! I write this work
> in the language of the gods.[14]

While, in the eyes of some authors, Sanskrit offered a longevity exceeding that of vernaculars (*bhāṣā*), the two literary realms increasingly overlapped in this period. At least one poet, Jayarama Pindye, who worked for both Shahji (Shivaji's father) and Shahji's youngest son, Ekoji (Shivaji's half-brother), wrote in both Sanskrit and vernaculars. In Jayarama's case, he used multiple languages in the same text, the *Rādhāmādhavavilāsacampū* (Radha and Krishna's love play; ca. 1655).[15] Even in his Sanskrit works, such as the *Parṇālaparvatagrahaṇākhyāna* (Saga of seizing Panhal Fort; 1673), Jayarama boasts about his mastery of twelve languages and refers explicitly to the languages of Maharashtra and Hindustan, Marathi and Hindi, respectively.[16] In contrast, he describes his current task of writing a text in Sanskrit alone as difficult (*atidurghaṭa*).[17] Vocabulary and stories crossed between languages. For instance, the *Surjanacarita* (Surjan's deeds; ca. 1590s) narrates Prithviraj Chauhan's tale with details borrowed from a version of the Hindi *Pṛthvīrāj Rāso*.[18] The *Rājapraśasti* refers readers to the "vernacular Rāso text" (*bhāṣārāsāpustaka*), meaning the *Pṛthvīrāj Rāso*, for a more elaborate discussion of the Mewar ruler Samar Singh's conflict with Muhammad Ghori.[19]

Alongside high literature, more popular genres of vernacular writing also emerged in this period and sometimes featured political events. Marathi authors coined the genres of ballads (*povāḍa*s) and histories (*bakhar*s) in the late seventeenth century or earlier. At roughly the same time, their northwestern counterparts penned Dingal *bāt*s (biographical tales), *khyāt*s (lineage narratives), and *vigat*s (clan chronicles).[20] Authors of the period faced a plethora of options, including high Sanskrit and a wide range of vernacular languages, styles, genres, and registers in which they might write. Such a world is a far cry from that occupied by Jayanaka, who, writing about Prithviraj Chauhan's conflict with the Ghurids in the late twelfth century, had no real option to write in a vernacular. By the mid-seventeenth century, intellectuals faced a layered decision about whether to write in Sanskrit or in one of numerous vernacular registers, and some chose both.[21]

In terms of both literary and political orders, the world occupied by early modern Rajputs and Marathas found limited parallels earlier in Indian history. One important precursor, where Sanskrit and vernacular literatures both thrived and Indo-Muslim rulers expanded their control while contending with a medley of non-Muslim local rulers, was fifteenth-century Gujarat. Accordingly, I begin with this regional example, focusing on Gangadhara's vision of the unexceptional nature of Indo-Muslim rule at Junagadh in Saurashtra.

A Regional Prelude in Fifteenth-Century Gujarat

In 1407, the Tughluq-appointed governor of Gujarat, Zafar Khan, exploited the chaos that followed Timur's 1398 sack of Delhi to declare independence from the Delhi Sultanate. Thus, under his new name of Muzaffar Shah (r. 1407–11), he established the Sultanate of Gujarat, also known as the Muzaffarid Sultanate and the Ahmadshahi Sultanate, and ruled from Ahmedabad. The Muzaffarid Sultanate expanded over the coming decades, negotiating through diplomacy and battle with Muslim and Hindu local rulers. In her book, *In Praise of Kings*, Aparna Kapadia has examined Sanskrit and vernacular texts produced in fifteenth-century Gujarat for warrior elites who wanted to claim Kshatriya status. In terms of historical works that feature Indo-Muslim political figures, one Sanskrit text stands out: Gangadhara's *Maṇḍalīkacarita*, written around 1460.[22] The work narrates some of the martial and marital history of the Chudasama ruler Mandalik (r. 1451–1472, sometimes called Ra Mandalik) who governed Saurashtra from Junagadh. Gangadhara treats Muslim political figures as unremarkable and shows almost no interest in religious distinctions, so much so that we cannot even discern all rulers' religious identities in the text.

Muslim political figures are an integral part of the Chudasamas' story as told by Gangadhara. They appear sometimes as military foes but more prominently as key allies. Early in the text, Gangadhara outlines Mandalik's lineage, a preoccupation among fifteenth-century rulers in western India.[23] He includes brief mentions that some of Mandalik's ancestors warred against numerous enemies, including Gohilas, Jhallas, and otherwise unspecified yavanas.[24] In the stories of the main characters, however, the text narrates that the Chudasama family fought on behalf of yavanas, a switch that Gangadhara did not see a need to explain. Mandalik even goes to some extraordinary lengths to do the Muzaffarid Sultanate's bidding. Most notably, in the poem's third chapter, an envoy of Muhammad Shah II (r. 1442–1451) visits Junagadh and asks the Chudasamas to attack Duda, a Gohil chieftain who was causing chaos in Sultanate domains. Mandalik was married to Duda's daughter, and their wedding is described in the prior chapter of the *Maṇḍalīkacarita*. Nonetheless, in service of the sultan, Mandalik kills his own father-in-law. Gangadhara frames the assassination as a good decision, using the voice of a Chudasama minister to make the argument, which convinces the prince Mandalik and his father, King Mahipala:

> The yavana who conquered the world on the battlefield
> with an army of elephants and thousands of horses wants your friendship.
> King Mahipala—What more favorable development could there be?[25]

In other words, there is nothing better, politically speaking, than being the sultan of Gujarat's ally.

The *Maṇḍalīkacarita* offers precious little in terms of rhetoric against Muslim rulers, and where it does criticize a political enemy, the work is vague about his religious identity. Most notably, Mandalik fights a ruler named as Sangan (*saṅgaṇa*) twice in the work. Gangadhara does not tell us much about Sangan, identifying him as a king (*nṛpa*) and "ruler of the far ocean" (*parasaritpatipa*).[26] By digging into colonial-era gazetteers, we can reasonably guess that Sangan belonged to the Vadhel clan that operated along the Saurashtra coast.[27] What we cannot tell for sure is his religion. Gangadhara praises Mandalik, shortly after he defeats the coastal chief Sangan for the second time, as Kalki, Vishnu's final incarnation, born to destroy the mlecchas (*mlecchānhantuṃ . . . jātaḥ kalkiḥ*).[28] The term "mleccha" often meant Muslim in fifteenth-century Sanskrit, but not always, and so this small hint is far from conclusive. Maybe Sangan was Muslim, as at least one modern scholar has suggested.[29] But the bigger point given my concerns here is that Gangadhara does not give his readers enough information to decisively discern Sangan's religion. This inattention suggests that the poet considered the religious identity of Mandalik's major opponent as relatively inconsequential to his historical narrative.

Gangadhara's literary production and that of his contemporaries in western India further buttress the argument that fifteenth-century Gujarat-based Sanskrit intellectuals often cared little, or not at all, about Muslim religious identity. In another work, Gangadhara reports that he stayed for six months at the court of Sultan Muhammad Shah II, where he silenced all the court favorites (*sabhākovidān mūkīkṛtya*).[30] It seems that Jonaraja, whom we met in chapter 4, was not the only Sanskrit intellectual working for an Indo-Persian patron in the 1450s. So far as we know, Gangadhara wrote nothing for Muhammad Shah II. But another author, Udayaraja, wrote the

Sanskrit eulogy *Rājavinoda* (King's play; 1462–1467) for Sultan Mahmud Begada (r. 1459–1511), about how the sultan was an ideal Kshatriya warrior.[31] In the sixteenth and seventeenth centuries, too, Sanskrit thinkers often worked for Muslim, Persian-speaking political elites and wrote praise poems for them, in addition to producing historical works about them.

Historical energy found other creative outlets in fifteenth-century Gujarat, in Sanskrit and vernaculars. For instance, in 1455, Padmanabha, a Brahmin, crafted the *Kānhaḍade Prabandha* (Kanhadade's narrative), a Gujarati account of Alauddin Khalji's successful circa 1310 assault on Jalor.[32] Like Nayachandra (see chapter 3), Padmanabha narrated Khalji-related events that occurred more than a century before his own time, although Padmanabha wrote under the umbrella of Indo-Persian power, since his patron, Akheraj, had accepted the sovereignty of the Muzaffarid Sultanate.[33] Around 400 kilometers south at around the same time, Gangadhara wrote the *Gaṅgadāsapratāpavilāsa* (Play on Gangadasa's brilliance), a Sanskrit drama about Gangadasa of Champaner's 1449 victory over Sultan Muhammad II.[34] Historical interest had long spilled over into Sanskrit plays, dating back to Somadeva's circa 1150s *Lalitavigraharāja* (see chapter 2) and Jayasimhasuri's circa 1230 *Hammīramadamardana* (see chapter 3). But, the terms of engagement had changed by the mid-fifteenth century. In these earlier two dramas, Muslims were not always portrayed negatively, but they generally spoke Prakrit, a sign of exclusion from the Sanskrit-inscribed world of Indian sovereignty as imagined in theater (in chapter 2, I note the amir's ambassador in Somadeva's play as an exception). In the *Gaṅgadāsapratāpavilāsa*, Muhammad II of Ahmedabad speaks Sanskrit as a proper Indian ruler should in the Sanskrit imagination.

Like Gangadhara, slightly later Rajput- and Maratha-sponsored poets also integrated Muslim political figures into traditional models of Indian sovereignty. In fact, by the late sixteenth century, such inclusion had become normal, even standard. Accordingly, below I focus on an aspect of Rajput and Maratha Sanskrit histories that proved far more varied, namely how to define Kshatriya kingship in a political world dominated by Indo-Persian kingdoms.

Divergent Rajput Visions of Kshatriya Kings

Of the many Rajput texts that narrate events involving Indo-Persian rule, the two I pair here furnish distinct visions of Kshatriya rulership in what was increasingly a Mughal world. Chandrashekhara wrote his *Surjanacarita* (Surjan's deeds) in the 1590s, in Benares, and Rudrakavi wrote his *Rāṣṭrauḍhavaṃśamahākāvya* (Great poem on the Rashtraudha dynasty) in 1596, in Baglan. Despite being composed in locations more than 1,200 kilometers apart, the two works bear some remarkable contextual and structural similarities. Both poet-historians worked in the 1590s, a decade that also witnessed the creation of several major Indo-Persian histories, including *Tārīkh-i Alfī* (History of the millennium), Nizamuddin Ahmad's *Ṭabaqāt-i Akbarī* (Generations of Akbar), and Abul Fazl's *Akbarnāma* (Akbar's book).[35] Both Sanskrit texts feature Rajput collaboration, of the Baglan Rathods and the Bundi Chauhans, respectively, with the Mughals. Structurally, the texts each contain twenty chapters, the nineteenth of which sees the main hero's plotline peak, while the twentieth chapter concerns his son.[36] The two works repeat some of the features we saw in the *Maṇḍalīkacarita*, such as brief citations in their early chapters to ancestors fighting Muslim political foes, citations that are then woven seamlessly into larger family histories of military aggression. For instance, Rudrakavi says in a single verse that Gajamalladeva, a Rathod forefather, conquered the Gurjaras, Malavas, and Allaudin the yavana king.[37] In a nice bit of poetry, Rudrakavi celebrates that Virasena, another ancestor, burnt a yavana-controlled city in a blaze that was like a Holi celebration gone wild.[38] Reading these texts in tandem, what is most striking to me is not their similarities but their differences. The *Rāṣṭrauḍhavaṃśamahākāvya* and the *Surjanacarita* articulate rather divergent, even conflicting, views on what it meant to act as a subsidiary Kshatriya ruler in Mughal India. The *Surjanacarita* climaxes with pilgrimage as the major achievement of a militarily emasculated king, whereas Rudrakavi underscores how his Baglan patrons helped Indo-Persian rulers, both Burhan Shah of the Nizam Shahi dynasty of Ahmednagar and the Mughals, to conquer parts of the Deccan.

Rao Surjan of Hada (r. 1554–1585), a Chauhan Rajput based in Bundi, is the main hero of Chandrashekhara's *Surjanacarita* (Surjan's deeds). Most likely, Surjan's son Bhoj (r. 1585–1607) sponsored the text, which narrates Surjan's death at the beginning of chapter 20.[39] The early chapters cover the exploits of Chauhan ancestors, including familiar faces such as Prithviraj and Hammira. Surjan appears on the scene in chapter 13, where his birth is introduced as follows:

He is a sun [*śūra*] among the lotuses of his family, a lion [*śūra*] of
battle and dharma.
Thus, the teachers called that child Shurajana, lion-man.[40]

It is standard enough for a Sanskrit poet to praise a king as a hero of battle (*raṇa*) and dharma, but these two strands play out in somewhat unexpected ways in the rest of the text. In short, Surjan's glory days on the battlefield are short-lived, and instead he carves out a way of being a Kshatriya king outside claims to political power.

Even at first blush, Surjan is an unlikely candidate to be praised for his martial prowess, since Hada military weakness had made the dynasty subservient, twice over, to other rulers. The Hadas of Bundi had formally recognized the political supremacy of the Sisodiyas of Mewar in the fourteenth century. In subsequent clashes between the two lineages, the Hadas failed to fully break from their subordinate status.[41] Additionally, faced with a Mughal siege in 1569, Surjan handed over Ranthambhor Fort to Akbar and acknowledged Mughal authority. In so doing, the Hadas became one of the first Rajput lineages to accept Mughal political supremacy, helping to initiate a wave of Rajput submissions during the coming years.[42] The *Surjanacarita* embraces the superior political position of the Mughals without further comment. The work refers to Surjan as a king (e.g., *nṛpa*, *bhūpati*) but introduces Akbar as an emperor (*cakrivān*), who enjoys total sovereignty (*sāmrājya*).[43] The poet tries his hand at praising Surjan's battle skills, especially in a series of verses that mix some real achievements, such as recovering nearby Kota, with nonsense boasts, such as pressing into southern India.[44] Surjan's big opportunity for military glory came in the 1569 Mughal assault on Ranthambhor. Indeed, the poet praises Surjan's performance during the one-month fight over the fort, even depicting Akbar as impressed.[45] But Surjan surrenders to Mughal forces pretty quickly, and so there was no glorious battle to serve as the climax of Chandrashekhara's history.

Chandrashekhara narrates Surjan turning over Ranthambhor to Mughal control as a positive development. The story goes that after a brief period of military clash, Akbar sends an emissary to offer Surjan peace terms. The *Surjanacarita* does not name the go-between, but Nainsi, writing in Rajasthani in the mid-seventeenth century, indicates that it was Bhagvant Das Kachhwaha.[46] The proposed deal was that Surjan relinquish Ranthambhor in exchange for control, under Mughal authority, over three places: a region along the Narmada River, Benares, and Mathura. In the *Surjanacarita*, Akbar's envoy makes the offer to Surjan as follows:

> Agree to take the rich region purified by the Narmada River,
> Shiva's city gleaming with the Ganges River,
> and the entire circle of Mathura shining with the Yamuna.
> You have desired this paramount sovereignty for a long time.
> O King, if you only relinquish Ranthambhor Fort to Akbar,
> that alone will give this emperor great affection for you.[47]

In Chandrashekhara's Sanskrit narrative and in real life, Surjan accepted these terms. The *Surjanacarita* tries to put a positive gloss on this capitulation, arguing in the above verses, for instance, that Surjan gains paramount sovereignty (*paraṃ surājyaṃ*) over three places in exchange for a single fort. A few lines later the Mughal messenger argues explicitly that trading three cities for a lone fort will be "a great gain for you."[48] But would any premodern reader believe this arithmetic? After all, the fall of Ranthambhor was a moment celebrated in Mughal court texts precisely because it demonstrated that Mughal military dominance could compel Rajput submission.[49] Certainly, later generations were discomforted by Surjan's easy capitulation. For instance, writing in Braj Bhasha seventy years later, for another ruler of Bundi, Matiram omitted altogether Surjan's ceding of Ranthambhor to Akbar.[50] Sanskrit literary conventions stipulate that a mahakavya (great poem) praising a king should climax with a victory, and it is perhaps in response to that expectation that Chandrashekhara charts another path for Surjan's heroism, namely the dharma of a pious pilgrimage.

After surrendering Ranthambhor to Akbar in chapter 18 of the *Surjanacarita*, Surjan embarks on a tour of holy sites (*tīrtha*s) and, in Chandrashekhara's narrative, never returns to political life. As part of a Kshatriya king's story, a pilgrimage is often a virtuous activity, and so, at first, Surjan's travels seem exceptional only because they follow a military defeat.[51] But then, in chapter 19, a Brahmin priest implores Surjan to stay in Benares for the remainder of his days, and the king agrees.[52] Modern readers might not blink at this plot twist, but most premodern Sanskrit readers would find this decision surprising, even shocking. For a king in the prime of his life to remain forever on pilgrimage, without appointing a political successor, goes against the fundamental duty of a sovereign to rule.

Reluctant kings had featured earlier in Sanskrit literature. Most prominently, Yudhishthira longs to retire to the forest rather than ascend the throne at Hastinapur in the wake of the cataclysmic Mahabharata War. But, in the end, Yudhishthira agrees to govern, as a good Kshatriya ruler ought to do. In contrast, Surjan's decision to shun political life is final in the *Surjanacarita*. Narratively, it serves as the climax of the entire text, a role typically filled by a major battle. As Cynthia Talbot has noted, in real life Surjan served the Mughals as a high-ranking officer for about fifteen years, battling on Akbar's behalf in numerous military campaigns.[53] But warring for another king was not a story, apparently, that Chandrashekhara wished to tell.

Chandrashekhara praises Surjan's decision to prioritize pilgrimage as the best decision that the king could have made, extolling pilgrimage's fruits (moksha) above those of the more typical Kshatriya path of combat (heaven). For instance, describing Surjan's pilgrimage years, Chandrashekhara writes:

> Rambha and the other celestial women lay around with nothing to do.
> Indra sat on his throne without fear.
> Since by Shiva's compassion, King Surjan, whose crown used to be Ranthambhor,
> brushed heaven aside, as if it were a mere blade of grass,
> and instead took refuge in God.[54]

In other words, because he was a religious pilgrim, Surjan would achieve liberation upon his death, rather than the lesser prize of going to heaven to enjoy carnal pleasures, the usual fate of Kshatriya warriors. Chandrashekhara also compares Surjan's decision, favorably, with that of his ancestor Ham mmorder to die failing to protect Ranthambhor from Khalji advances, in 1301. In the initial narration of these events, Chandrashekhara praises Hammira as a Chauhan hero (*vīra*) who won fame (*kīrti*).[55] Indeed, the *Surjanacarita* attests to Hammira's renown by devoting two chapters to his story.[56] Later in the work, the Mughal envoy to Surjan condemns what happened to Hammira, its notoriety notwithstanding, as a calamity (*vipāka*).[57] The Mughal messenger almost certainly refers here to Hammira's death at Ranthambhor, which was a military loss but also meant that Hammira never completed his interrupted pilgrimage. The climax of Surjan's life, visiting tirthas, contrasts with this unfinished aspect of Hammira's tale, and, moreover, it earns Surjan a fate better than heaven. This is an admirable attempt to proclaim that Surjan's model of pilgrimage leading to moksha might supplant Hammira's model of defeat resulting in fame.[58] Overhauling the nature of Kshatriya dharma was no easy task, and plenty of traces linger in the poem of an older military-focused model. Still, Chandrashekhara's attempt to articulate a nonmartial way to be a Kshatriya king is noteworthy, and a project that contrasts considerably with the vision of Rudrakavi, who was writing in the Deccan around the same time.

Rudrakavi composed his *Rāṣṭrauḍhavaṃśamahākāvya* as an acclamatory history of the Rathods of Baglan. He begins with the dynasty's namesake, Rashtraudha, and covers many rulers, along the way shoring up the dynasty's descent from the Rathods of Kanauj.[59] But Rudrakavi devotes the majority of his work to the exploits of Narayan Shah, the Baglan king in 1596 and Rudrakavi's patron.[60] He concludes with the military prowess of Pratap Shah, the Baglan prince and heir. Rudrakavi claims a verbal source for his tale, namely a pandit called Lakshmana, who had been at the Baglan court at least since Shah Narayan's consecration, some years earlier.[61] We do not know when Rudrakavi entered the Baglan court, but we do know he was still there fifteen to twenty-five years after finishing the *Rāṣṭrauḍhavaṃśamahākāvya*. In the first few decades of the 1600s, Rudrakavi crafted four additional Sanskrit works on the then king Pratap Shah's orders, all of them praise poems for Mughal political elites.[62] Rudrakavi also wrote about Muslim political figures in the *Rāṣṭrauḍhavaṃśamahākāvya*, especially how Narayan Shah and Pratap Shah fought on behalf of Indo-Persian polities, including the Nizam Shahis (also known as the Ahmadnagar Sultanate) and, following military pressure, the Mughals. Politically, Narayan and Pratap followed a known strategy, also used by Surjan of Bundi and many other Rajput contemporaries, of warring on behalf of Indo-Persian dynasties as a way to retain some degree of power. Baglan also maintained some autonomy from Mughal control until the 1630s, likely, in part, due to the dynasty's willingness to fight for imperial causes. But the court poets of Baglan and Bundi had rather different takes on their patrons providing military assistance to more powerful kings. Rudrakavi hails as definitional to Kshatriya kingship the assistance that the Rathods of Baglan rendered to the Nizam Shahis and the Mughals in their bids to conquer parts of the Deccan.

Eschewing religion, anything resembling ethnicity, and many other identity markers, Rudrakavi uses region, specifically access to the Deccan or the south, to frame the military prowess of the Baglan kings. In his early chapters, on prior rulers in the dynasty, Rudrakavi mentions conquering the Deccan (*dakṣiṇa, dakṣiṇadik, dakṣiṇadeśa*) several times. This geographical emphasis is also underscored in a verse that the poet repeats at the end of each of the work's twenty chapters, in which he identifies himself as a southerner (*dakṣiṇadigbhava*).[63] Rudrakavi's geographical framework comes to the fore most strongly in the three battles that punctuate his narration of Narayan Shah's rule. The first major clash begins when an otherwise unnamed "king of the south" (*dakṣiṇamahīpāla*) attacks Narayan Shah, who successfully defends his territory.[64] The next two battles feature the Rathods of Baglan advancing the expansion campaigns of the Nizam Shahis and the Mughals, respectively. We might collectively describe these two dynasties as "Indo-Persian" or "Indo-Muslim" today, but Rudrakavi seems to have been far more interested in regional ambitions. The opening narrative framework is consistent in both conflicts, namely a royal figure requests Narayan Shah's assistance to "conquer the South," and the ruler of Baglan readily agrees.[65]

Perhaps Narayan Shah's greatest victory in Rudrakavi's history is when the Baglan ruler helps Burhan Shah (r. 1591–1595) of the Nizam Shahi dynasty of Ahmadnagar to become "king of the south." Rudrakavi narrates the actual military conflict in only a few verses:

> Then, one day, King Burhan Shah wanted to seize the south.
> So, he asked Narayan Shah to go to the village of Vata, near Mount Galan.
>
> Narayan Shah quickly sent half of his own army to assist Burhan Shah's cause.
> He himself remained in the village, besieging much of the enemy army.
>
> When King Narayan Shah's honorable army had killed many heroes there,
> then, without delay, he consecrated Burhan Shah ruler over the southern lands.

The sun's greatness is that the first red rays of dawn destroy the night.
Such was Narayan Shah's brilliance, achieved by these heroic deeds.[66]

This brief narrative does not name Burhan Shah's target, which was likely the Adil Shahis of Bijapur, immediately south of Nizam Shahi territory. The poet is far more verbose on Narayan Shah's rewards for his crucial assistance to Burhan Shah. In subsequent verses, Rudrakavi says that Narayan Shah earned the freedom to loot nearby towns, which led to the Baglan ruler's universal sovereignty (*sāṃrājya*).[67] These verses close out chapter 13, and the following four chapters constitute a literary consecration of Narayan Shah's kingship, earned through helping the Nizam Shahi sultan. The text's modern translator, J. L. de Bruyne, declined to translate chapters 14–17 of the *Rāṣṭrauḍhavaṃśamahākāvya*, describing them as concerning "only very conventional matters: descriptions of the seasons, noontime, setting sun, sexual pleasures etc."[68] What de Bruyne dismissed as mere conventions, however, are Rudrakavi's celebration of "stories about glorious Shah Narayan's glittering fame," as the poet put it in his repeated closing verse.[69] The text's narrative arc clarifies that such fame was earned by ensuring the military successes of Indo-Persian rulers or, closer to the work's own terminology, would-be rulers of the south.

The *Rāṣṭrauḍhavaṃśamahākāvya* climaxes with Narayan Shah and his son, Pratap Shah, aiding the 1595 Mughal assault on Ahmadnagar led by Prince Murad. In this final battle, Rudrakavi declares equivalence, often using region-focused language, between the rulers of Baglan and the rulers of Delhi. Rudrakavi refers to Akbar using various epithets, among them "king of the north," "conqueror of the north," and "leader of the north."[70] Even more commonly, he dubs Akbar "King of Delhi."[71] But, according to Rudrakavi, the Baglan rulers held the keys to the south. As a Mughal envoy put it when speaking to Narayan Shah, at the beginning of chapter 20:

Prince Shah Murad waited for the time you named
and has now set out with his army to the land of the Nizam Shah king.
To be victorious in this monumental task, the prince needs your help, diadem of kings!
The southern region cannot be conquered without your brilliance and your son.[72]

At Narayan Shah's request, Pratap Shah fights alongside Murad against the Nizam Shahis. Upon the first meeting of the two, the poet says that the princes of Delhi and of Shalagiri (site of one of the key forts held by the Rathods of Baglan) shine like the twin Ashvins.[73] The subsequent verse records that the two exchange gifts before Murad once again reiterates that Pratap Shah is the linchpin in the Mughal plan to take the south (*dakṣiṇadig*).[74] In battle, too, the two princes are presented as a pair that fight, pillage, and conquer side by side.[75] After ensuring Mughal victory, Pratap Shah goes on a brief pilgrimage before returning to his father, Narayan Shah, and basking in his hard-earned glory.[76] According to Rudrakavi, the Rathods of Baglan shone as illustrious Kshatriya kings precisely through battling on behalf of Indo-Persian rulers. It seems to be a nonissue for Rudrakavi that Narayan Shah fought against the Nizam Shahis just a few years after he had fought on their behalf. There is no preoccupation here with loyalty, a value we saw on display in Nayachandra's *Hammīramahākāvya* (see chapter 3). Rather, Rudrakavi takes a more mercenary view of the military services that Kshatriya rulers might provide to more powerful, Indo-Persian kings.

The *Surjanacarita* and the *Rāṣṭrauḍhavaṃśamahākāvya* present starkly different visions of Kshatriya kingship, even while working with the same narrative building blocks. Both works mention pilgrimages, for instance, but as an alternative to battle-based identity for one poet (Chandrashekhara) and as a brief activity after military victories for the other (Rudrakavi).[77] Both poets, too, crafted selective narratives. For instance, Rudrakavi omitted the role of Chand Bibi in defending Ahmadnagar in the 1590s, a historical episode that has captured modern imaginations since it features a relatively rare instance of a woman in both combat and a political leadership role.[78] Rudrakavi only mentions Suhayl Khan, a male Bijapuri commander who assisted Chand Bibi.[79] When women appear in Rudrakavi's account of this battle, it is a far more conventional mention of beautiful women on balconies observing the carnage below.[80]

Perhaps more notable for thinking about ways to perform Kshatriya kingship, Chandrashekhara elides Surjan's life as a Mughal imperial servant. Chandrashekhara's omission exercises the prerogative and necessity of every historian to be selective, but the contrast with the Indo-Persian tradition is striking. Surjan's life as a Mughal imperial officer is fairly well documented in Indo-Persian texts such as the *Ma'āsir al-Umarā*, which, incidentally, omits all mention of his pilgrimages.[81] Might we chalk up this disparity to language differences? Certainly, other contemporaries of

Figure 6.1 Surjan of Hada submitting to Akbar, *Akbarnāma*, ca. 1590–95
Victoria and Albert Museum, London, IS.2:75–1896

Rudrakavi perceived a divide between what one might say in Persian versus in Sanskrit. For instance, in the 1590s, Akbar's general Man Singh Kachhwaha sponsored three inscriptions, two in Persian and one in Sanskrit, to commemorate a newly constructed palace at Rohtas Fort in Bihar. The Persian inscription focuses on Akbar, who is missing entirely within the Sanskrit epigraph's elaborate praise of Man Singh's authority and kingship.[82] But Chandrashekhara's vision of Surjan as a religious pilgrim, without the standard accoutrements of political power, also clashes with Rudrakavi's vision of the Baglan rulers proving themselves as strong Kshatriya kings precisely by warring for Indo-Persian sovereigns. Moreover, Chandrashekhara's attempt to rewrite the standards of Kshatriya rule did not seem to speak to later Hadas. The *Śatruśalyacarita*, written a few decades later, for one of Surjan's successors, proffers detailed accounts of Hada Chauhan collaboration with the Mughals.[83] Even seemingly failed arguments, like Chandrashekhara's image of a king sans political power, attest to the many possibilities for political identity envisioned by Rajput-sponsored poets in early modern India. We find even more diversity in terms of royal identities and gain fresh insight into Sanskrit terminology for Indo-Persian political figures by looking to a line that made a contested claim to Kshatriya status: the Bhonsle family in Maharashtra.

Political Histories for the Bhonsle Family

In less than twenty years, Sanskrit poets wrote at least five historical works for members of the Maratha Bhonsle clan. Three successive Bhonsle rulers—Shivaji (d. 1680), Sambhaji (r. 1680–1689), and Rajaram (r. 1689–1700)—patronized accounts of their own exploits: respectively, *Sūryavaṃśa* (Dynasty of the sun; better known as *Śivabhārata* [Shivaji's epic], ca. 1675), *Śambhurājacarita* (Sambhaji's deeds; 1685), and *Rājārāmacarita* (Rajaram's deeds; 1690).[84] Two additional texts on Shivaji and Sambhaji, respectively, were authored for other Bhonsle patrons.[85] In 1673, Ekoji, Shivaji's younger brother who ruled in Thanjavur, sponsored Jayarama's *Parṇālaparvatagrahaṇākhyāna*, on the taking of Panhal Fort, and appears in the text asking what his elder brother did next.[86] Likely working for Sambhaji, Paramananda (or somebody using his name[87]) wrote an additional thirteen chapters of the *Sūryavaṃśa* that were never integrated into the larger work and so survive today as a separate text, dubbed the *Paramānandakāvya*

(Paramananda's poem).[88] The five texts diverge starkly from one another in structure, length, approach, and topic. An entire book could be written on this intense concentration of historical energy in the early days of Maratha rule, and I hope that another scholar writes that book. My efforts here are more modest. In the following two sections, I focus, respectively, on the Sanskrit terminology that these texts employ for Muslims and on the *Sūryavaṃśa*'s commentary on Shivaji's kingship.

The Maratha-sponsored Sanskrit histories largely concentrate on true events, with a strong political focus. For instance, in his five-chapter *Parṇālaparvatagrahaṇākhyāna*, Jayarama narrates numerous military actions undertaken by Shivaji's forces against Bijapur and the Mughals, chief among them the seizure of Panhal Fort, a Bijapuri stronghold, in March 1673.[89] The *Rājārāmacarita* of Keshava (also referred to as Keshava Pandit) focuses on Rajaram's 1689 flight to Jinji Fort as he was pursued by Mughal troops, with a positive spin on how Rajaram "warded off the Lord of Delhi's pride" (by various skirmishes en route, I guess).[90] Keshava wrote within a few months of these events, in January 1690, and hypes his work, also five chapters, as a "prabandha of fame" (*yaśaḥprabandhaṃ*).[91] Even in the expansive *Sūryavaṃśa*, a work of thousands of verses that remains unfinished at thirty-two chapters (the final one incomplete), Paramananda maintains a relentless emphasis on political moments. In the text, the poet narrates the exploits of Shahji and Shivaji to a group of Benares Brahmins, a community who

TABLE 6.1
Sanskrit histories sponsored by the Maratha Bhonsle family, 1673–1690

Author	Date	Title (Sanskrit)	Title (English)
Jayarama	1673	*Parṇālaparvatagrahaṇākhyāna*	Saga of seizing Panhal Fort
Paramananda	1673–1680	*Sūryavaṃśa* (modern title: *Śivabhārata*)	Dynasty of the sun (Shivaji's epic)
Harikavi	1685	*Śambhurājacarita*	Sambhaji's deeds
Attributed to Paramananda	ca. 1685	*Paramānandakāvya*	Paramananda's poem
Keshava Pandit	1690	*Rājārāmacarita*	Rajaram's deeds

had come to wield intellectual and political influence across much of India in the sixteenth and seventeenth centuries.[92] In the *Sūryavaṃśa*, the Benares Brahmins serve, among other functions, to keep Paramananda's attention on political developments. For instance, Paramananda segues into speaking of Shivaji's childhood play (*bālalīlā*) at the end of chapter 7, and then chapter 8 opens with the pandits asking how Shahji captured Shivneri Fort.[93] Chapter 9 concludes with some nice verses on Shivaji learning his first letters, and chapter 10 begins with the pandits requesting more information on how twelve-year-old Shivaji reached Pune on Shahji's orders.[94] By my count, the Benares pandits speak around two dozen times in the *Sūryavaṃśa*, and they invariably ask about politics, sometimes snapping the poet out of digressions on other subjects.

Like earlier Sanskrit historians, the Maratha-sponsored historians also wrote their histories through and as poetry, drawing liberally on Sanskrit literary conventions and echoing early works. For instance, the *Rājārāmacarita* opens with a conversation between Shiva and Narada.[95] The *Paramānandakāvya* contains a fairly elaborate story about Kali, the current age, taking birth as Shivaji's wife Soyarabai, to lead the king astray.[96] The *Śambhurājacarita*, which survives in fragments, has been described as notably heavy on poetry.[97] The *Sūryavaṃśa* imitates Kalidasa's *Raghuvaṃśa*, in both its title and in specific verses.[98] The *Sūryavaṃśa* also bills itself in colophons to each chapter as an *anupurāṇa*, a "new purana."[99] "Anupurana" is an anomalous genre in the collection of texts I discuss in this book, and it likely was meant to highlight Shivaji's claim to be part of the solar lineage, one of the five appropriate topics (*pañcalakṣaṇa*) of a purana.[100] Additionally, the *Sūryavaṃśa* cites verses from the Mahabharata and adopts the epic's metaframework of a story being told to Brahmins.[101] Notably, as described above, Paramananda deployed even the trope of a Brahmin audience in pursuit of, not in spite of, Maratha political history.

Bhonsle Definitions of the Other

The Maratha-sponsored Sanskrit histories often invoke a framework of opposition, Us versus Them, with the identifies of both sides defined in military and political terms. For example, Jayarama starts off with a strong othering stance against the Adil Shahis of Bijapur, writing about Shivaji, whom he names as Shiva (this is common in Sanskrit texts):

The great lord of the earth, Shiva,
uplifts that very Panala from amidst an ocean of yavanas,
as if he were Indra who compassionately uplifted Himalaya's son
Mainaka,
who feared drowning for a time.[102]

Jayarama plays a little loose with the facts here, since Shivaji remained in Raigad, some 250 kilometers north of Panhal, during the 1673 assault. Still, he clearly identifies the Adil Shahis as a military enemy. Speaking of the Mughals, Keshava Pandit ponders early in his *Rājārāmacarita* (Rajaram's deeds):

How will men find peace in this ghastly Kali Yuga
that is bringing on the victory of the great Mughals [*mleñcchas*]?
Everywhere the Mughal king destroys class boundaries
[*varṇadharmavighātin*].
Every field of dharma has been destroyed by that bad-souled
man.[103]

These two authors use known Sanskrit terms for Muslims, but they are both more specific in referring, in context, to particular political dynasties, rather than to all Muslims.

In the *Sūryavaṃśa*, Paramananda further complicates the identity of the Other by including as yavanas Rajputs and Marathas who fought on behalf of Indo-Persian rulers. This is a different sort of imprecision than we saw in Gangadhara's *Maṇḍalīkacarita*, where there were few to no markers of the enemy king Sangan's religious identity. It is perhaps closer to Nainsi's *Khyāt* (ca. mid-seventeenth-century, in Rajasthani), which includes Muslims within a Rajput jati.[104] In the *Sūryavaṃśa*, the names indicate who is (Hindu) Rajput or Maratha. As discussed below, the text is equally clear that members of both fight as yavanas, an identity overlap that is presented as unproblematic. "Yavana" had a capacious sense across much of the subcontinent by the late seventeenth century, and even earlier. For example, more than 150 years earlier, the Vijayanagara ruler Krishna Raya (r. 1509–1529) had captured the Bahmani capital of Gulbarga and then fashioned himself "the establisher of yavana rule" (*yavanarājyasthāpanācārya*).[105] Apparently, venerating Hindu deities was no handicap to Krishna Raya's ability to bring about yavanarajya (yavana rule). Paramananda expresses a similar nonchalance concerning any religious restrictions on one's ability to enact different types of rule, and he also extends this tendency in the other direction. Shahji's service to the Adil Shahis, which occupies much of the *Sūryavaṃśa*'s initial chapters, culminates with these lines:

> Having conquered Kerala and Karnataka with cruel actions,
> Shahji made the Adil Shahis ecstatic by filling their treasury.
> Having overpowered other fierce kings of his own accord,
> he made Ibrahim's kingdom like Rama's kingdom [*rāmarājya*].[106]

According to Paramananda, there was indeed ramrajya in premodern India: an Adil Shahi ramrajya brought into being by Shahji's military conquests.

The Maratha-sponsored histories contain a rich tapestry of vocabulary for Muslim political figures and groups, perhaps the most varied since Jayanaka wrote in the late twelfth century. The Sanskrit term "yavana" is by far the most common across the five texts, especially in the *Sūryavaṃśa*, but it cannot always be accurately translated as "Muslim."[107] Sometimes the term seems to denote only Muslims, such as when the Adil Shahi general Afzal Khan accuses Shivaji of razing the holy places of yavanas (presumably meaning mosques) in the towns of Kalyan and Bhivandi.[108] But Paramananda's repeated inclusion of Rajputs and Marathas among yavana troops cuts against his own rhetoric of clash that surfaces periodically in the poem. A good example of such rhetoric is found in chapter 17, when Ali Adil Shah speaks to his general, Afzal Khan, about the threat posed by Shivaji. Among other accusations, Ali Adil Shah says: "Alas, Shivaji, that proud, powerful hero, is so fixated on his own dharma that he is destroying Islam [*mlecchadharma*]."[109] This language of clash, however, is tempered later in the chapter when Paramananda lists the Adil Shahi allies that accompanied Afzal Khan, including two Nayaks, a Jadhav (Shivaji's lineage through his mother), and Shivaji's uncle Mambaji.[110] The authors also use the standby Sanskrit terms "turushka" and "mleccha," although Keshava Pandit sometimes uses *mleñccha* (is this slight variation meant to indicate the Mughals specifically, an identity clear from context?).[111]

The Bhonsle-patronized works also offer some lesser known terms for Indo-Persian polities and Muslim communities, some likely inspired by Marathi and Persian. For instance, Muslims are called *aviddha*, meaning "unpierced" and referring to the ears (Marathi *avindha*).[112] Borrowing from Persian, Paramananda refers to both Pathans and Uzbeks in a show of ethnic specificity.[113] It is striking that none of the authors seemed to feel any need to explain this varied vocabulary, some of it adapted from other languages. This lack of comment indicates the complicated world that early modern readers were expected to understand, including well-worn Sanskrit terms and more recent vernacular and Persian categories.

Two words for Muslims used by the Maratha-sponsored Sanskrit authors require further discussion: *tāmra* and *tāmrānana*, meaning "reddish" and "red-faced," respectively, and referring to skin tone. Several authors use these terms.[114] In both Sanskrit and Marathi, "tamra" can also describe Europeans and generally carried a negative connotation. However, the authors of the Bhonsle Sanskrit histories often use "tamra" alongside positive descriptors of the Mughals. In the *Parṇālaparvatagrahaṇākhyāna* (Saga of seizing Panhal Fort), for instance, Jayarama calls the Mughals, in a single verse, "strong," "numerous," "red," and "fierce" (*atyanta, vipula, tāmra, ugra*).[115] Paramananda designates Jahangir as "lord of the tamra" and "intensely heroic."[116] Perhaps "tamra" had simply lost its negative connotation and was a neutral term for some of these authors, similar to "mleccha" for many of the poet-historians I discuss in this book. It is also possible that Sanskrit intellectuals were thinking of the Persian equivalent that is attested in contemporary Mughal sources: *surkh-rū*, meaning honorable (literally, red-faced).[117] Elsewhere in their poems, the authors use both neutral and positive language for Muslim political figures. For instance, Paramananda calls the Siddis "black-faced" when Shahji is fighting as their ally, so the reference is presumably not maligning.[118] Even more unambiguously, the first yavana named in the *Sūryavaṃśa*, Nizam Shah, is introduced as "full of dharma" (*dharmātma*).[119] Such a description has thrown off some modern interpreters, who seem to assume that Maratha-sponsored Sanskrit intellectuals must have had a negative view of all Muslims, especially those with political authority.[120] But repeated textual evidence indicates a far more varied set of views.

Whether we are analyzing moments of criticism or praise, our modern religious categories cannot capture these texts' textured vocabulary for Indo-Persian political actors and their allies. Frankly, that is one of the more uninteresting points to make regarding this mesmerizing trove of textual treasures, but it remains important as a corrective to earlier scholarship. Those not able to read Sanskrit texts for themselves should be wary of

English translations of these materials that interpolate "Muslim" inappropriately.[121] Likewise, some modern translators like the word "Hindu," although it appears only sparingly in this body of materials and not at all in some works.[122] In the *Rājārāmacarita*'s verses quoted several paragraphs above, protecting upper-caste privileges (*varṇadharma*) appears to be the defining issue. Likewise, in the *Sūryavaṃśa*, Paramananda criticizes Afzal Khan, using Shivaji's voice, as "hell-bent on obstructing the path of caste dharma [*varṇadharma*]."[123] Both works are invested in preserving difference, not unity, within what we can only anachronistically call Hinduism. Even once we move beyond the realm of religious-based delineations, other works further complicate how we understand the Us in an Us vs. Them dichotomy. The *Paramānandakāvya*, for instance, portrays a Bhonsle family battle between supporters of Rajaram and Sambhaji, respectively, in the aftermath of Shivaji's death. In other words, the text names both the Us and the Them as half-brother, would-be Maratha rulers. The Bhonsles, especially Shivaji, expressed more broad-based identities at times. However, as I discuss below, Shivaji's big-picture view centered around a type of kingship more than a religion. In short, at the risk of sounding like a broken record, it is a modern desire to see Hindu-Muslim conflict in these texts, and so I leave that program where it originated: in modernity.

Shivaji as a Kshatriya King in an Indo-Persian World

In his *Sūryavaṃśa*, Paramananda presents Shivaji as a Kshatriya king who skillfully operates in a political order largely dominated by Indo-Persian dynasties. Paramananda advanced multiple arguments about how Shivaji was a good Kshatriya ruler, probably because many people thought then, as many people think now, that Shivaji was low caste.[124] Certain actions undertaken by Shivaji indicate that he wanted to be perceived as a Kshatriya in the eyes of at least some of his contemporaries. Perhaps the strongest indication was Shivaji's successful bid to convince a Benares Brahmin, Gagabhatta, to sanction a fabricated link between the Sisodiya Rajputs of Mewar and the Bhonsle family.[125] This was perhaps not a hard sell to Gagabhatta, who had deemed Bhonsle claims to kingship legitimate since at least 1664.[126] Also, as Jadunath Sarkar and others have noted, Gagabhatta happily accepted Shivaji's lavish financial remuneration for his troubles.[127] Gagabhatta's reputation as a legal expert made him well suited to this role of certifying Shivaji as a Kshatriya. As Ananya Vajpeyi put it, "If anyone could tell high-born kṣatriyas from lowly śūdras, it was Gāgābhaṭṭa."[128] Gagabhatta traveled to Raigad in 1674 and performed an elaborate ceremony at the Bhonsle court that involved Shivaji doing penance for having lived as a Maratha, rather than as a Kshatriya, and had the king don the sacred thread for the first time.[129] Gagabhatta next performed a coronation ceremony that proclaimed the newly minted Kshatriya an emperor (*chatrapati*).[130] Not everybody was convinced that this intricate ritual was done properly, however, and so three months later Shivaji underwent a second coronation-cum-varna-recovery ceremony overseen by one Nishchala Puri.[131] This second ceremony is discussed more infrequently in secondary literature, although the Sanskrit manual for the do-over survives today.[132] Perhaps trying to provide Shivaji with further cover, Paramananda offers several other ways that Shivaji acts as a Kshatriya, many of which foreground his treatment of Brahmins and some of which make sense specifically in a political environment increasingly shaped by Indo-Persian military might.

In his *Sūryavaṃśa*, written between 1673 and 1680,[133] Paramananda ignored Gagabhatta's theory of Shivaji's Rajput descent and instead used some of the favorite techniques of Sanskrit poets to represent Shivaji as a Kshatriya. The very act of writing the poem advanced this argument, since, as Vishvanatha put it in his *Sāhityadarpaṇa* (Mirror of literary art; ca. 1350), "The hero in a great poem should be a god or a brave, virtuous Kshatriya from a good family."[134] Paramananda indicates his view that Shivaji is an incarnation of Vishnu in the work's title, *Sūryavaṃśa*, which refers to the solar lineage commonly associated with Rama, the archetype royal Vishnu incarnation. Being Vishnu-in-the-flesh was a claim commonly made by premodern Indian kings and their panegyrists. We have seen several examples, most recently in the *Maṇḍalīkacarita*, from fifteenth-century Gujarat. Some in the Bhonsle court made a double claim, that Shivaji was descended from both Vishnu and the Sisodiyas. This was the case with Bhushan, who wrote about both lines of descent in his Braj Bhasha *Śivrājbhūṣaṇ* (Ornament of King Shivaji; 1673).[135] By the seventeenth century, the royal assertion to be Vishnu incarnate was so popular it was even repeated by Muslim kings, most notably Akbar, whose claim to be Vishnu's avatar is attested in Persian and Sanskrit sources.[136] Still, there is agency in Paramananda's decision. Some contemporary works, such as the *Parṇālaparvatagrahaṇākhyāna*, frame Shivaji as merely "like Vishnu" (*viṣṇoriva*), rather than pitching him as Vishnu's avatar on the model of Rama.[137] Going a different direction, the Sanskrit manual for Shivaji's second coronation hails him as an avatar of Shiva.[138]

According to Paramananda, Shivaji revered and protected Brahmins, thus fulfilling one of the foundational duties of a Kshatriya king in Sanskrit thought. Impressing Brahmins is a driving force behind the poem's metanarrative of Paramananda narrating Shivaji's political exploits to Benares pandits. More generally, Paramananda repeatedly testifies that Shivaji protected Brahmins and gave them money. At one point, Afzal Khan tries to force Shivaji to fight a Brahmin, and Shivaji refuses in order to avoid the possible sin of Brahminicide (although, as Paramananda tells us elsewhere in the text, Shivaji had no issue hosting Brahmin commanders within his army).[139] Soon after refusing to take up arms against a Brahmin, Shivaji slays Afzal Khan. This key moment in the *Sūryavaṃśa* is marked by the only specific date in the entire work, precise to the hour:

In 1581, a Vikari year,
in the bright half of the month of Marga,
on the seventh day, a Thursday,
in the middle of the day,
that demon Afzal was slain by Shiva.[140]

At times, Paramananda tries other ways of defining Shivaji's leadership. For instance, he frames Shivaji, in separate passages, as the protector of Maharashtra and a mountain king (*śailādhipati*).[141] But these references are fleeting, often singular, and they pale in comparison to the recurrent rhetoric of Shivaji being Vishnu incarnate, a protector of Brahmins, and the subject of a mahakavya that delights a Brahmin audience.

Paramananda's ways of declaring Shivaji a good Kshatriya are generic and action-based. In a situation where doubts lingered concerning Shivaji's varna, his actions as a classic Kshatriya king could perhaps demonstrate his fitness to rule. Such claims make sense against the backdrop of his low reputation among Rajputs, especially following Shivaji's breach of joint Rajput-Mughal protocol at Aurangzeb Alamgir's court in 1666. As Richard Eaton has put it, after witnessing Shivaji's "egregious breach of courtly etiquette" by falling to the floor, moaning, and speaking out of turn, "Rajputs standing in his midst perceived him as distinctly alien."[142] Speaking to the Mughal king afterward, Jaswant Singh, leader of the Rathod Rajputs of Marwar, called Shivaji "a mere bhumia [petty landholder]."[143]

Arguing against such entrenched views, Paramananda outlines how Shivaji acted according to a time-honored model as a Kshatriya king.

Paramananda depicts Shivaji as a fierce warrior, specifically by measuring his battle skills against yavanas'. For this comparison to flatter Shivaji, yavanas must be strong foes on the battlefield. Indeed, throughout the poem, Paramananda extols the considerable martial skills of both the Adil Shahi and Mughal armies.[144] Even his earliest mention of yavanas, in verse 15 of the poem's first chapter, describes them as untamable (*durdānta*). This poetic fancy is arguably historically accurate, especially for the Mughals who expanded their territory considerably during Aurangzeb Alamgir's reign (1658–1707).[145] But more important for my argument here is that Paramananda names, in Sanskrit literature, Indo-Persian military might as the bar for Kshatriya battle prowess. For instance, in chapter 10, the Hindu god Shiva proclaims to Shahji in a dream that "your son will conquer the earth and slay all yavanas."[146] Paramananda also praises Shivaji's military skills in more general terms, such as by giving a long list at Shivaji's birth of the peoples and places that he is fated to conquer.[147] Later in the work, he praises Shivaji as "crueler than the god of death."[148] But, sometimes, Paramananda prefers the early modern update to such classical praise, namely acclaiming Shivaji as the "ender of yavanas."[149] This terminology posits a martial, not a religious, clash between those fighting for the Bhonsles and those fighting for the Mughals. Further cutting against any modern tendency to let religion creep into our understanding of this divide, as I discuss above, a sizable chunk of yavana warriors were Rajputs and Marathas, according to Paramananda. In such moments, Paramananda envisioned Shivaji's Kshatriya kingship, rooted in varna divisions that were projected as ancient, as uniquely suited for the Indo-Persian political world of late seventeenth-century India.

Unpopular Narratives

Rajput- and Maratha-sponsored Sanskrit histories do not furnish the narrative that many people want today. Shivaji, especially, is a politically explosive figure, so much so that in recent decades scholars have been subjected to book bans and violence for writing about him.[150] When I published a book in 2017 on Aurangzeb, another lightning rod for controversy, I was legally advised to censor some historical information in the Indian edition, not about Aurangzeb but about Shivaji.[151] There is a gulf of difference between the dominant modern-day Shivaji, a nationalist symbol of Maharashtrian and Hindu pride, and Paramananda's Shivaji, a Kshatriya king who flourished in an Indo-Persian political order. Our modern Shivaji is much remembered, if contested, today.[152] Most recently, there are plans for him to be commemorated in a towering 212-meter statue off the coast of Mumbai.[153] Paramananda's Shivaji, however, is in danger of being forgotten. It is hard enough to stretch our imaginations to conceptualize the ideas, categories, and languages of early modern Sanskrit intellectuals. This difficulty is compounded by modern pressures to see certain types of identities, even in nascent forms, and certain kinds of conflict in India's early modernity. But Maratha-sponsored Sanskrit histories do not exist to teleologically justify our present. Moreover, they shy away from a single conclusion altogether. Instead, they and their Rajput counterparts present a wealth of nuance and plurality grounded in decisively premodern and early modern ways of seeing the world.

One type of multiplicity attested in these works, which I have not discussed much above, is the geographical origins of the texts and their authors. All five of the Maratha-sponsored works discussed in this chapter were written south of the Vindhyas, in the Deccan and southern India. The *Parṇālaparvatagrahaṇākhyāna* and the *Rājārāmacarita* were penned in Tamil Nadu, in the latter decades of the seventeenth century, and copies of both survive today in Thanjavur.[154] They were perhaps the first Sanskrit histories of Muslim-led rule written so far south since Gangadevi's *Madhurāvijaya*, from around 1380. The Maratha court at Thanjavur sustained a strong interest in history for the first few decades of the eighteenth century, producing at least three further Sanskrit royal histories of Bhonsle kings.[155] The Rajput-sponsored histories were written further north, although their authors, or at least the authors' families, came from all over the subcontinent. Ranachoda Bhatta, author of the Mewari *Rājapraśasti*, was from Telangana.[156] More unusually, Chandrashekhara, who penned the *Surjanacarita*, hailed from Bengal.[157] Indeed, the only premodern manuscript of the *Surjanacarita* survives today in Kolkata.[158] Chandrashekhara's ties with Bengal constitute a bit of evidence, admittedly wafer thin, that eastern India was not entirely left out of the tradition of Sanskrit historical writing on Indo-Persian history.

The major type of plurality that I have written about in this chapter are the many views expressed by Rajput- and Maratha-sponsored Sanskrit intellectuals on how to act and be seen as a Kshatriya ruler. Moreover, this was also a concern in other Sanskrit histories of Indo-Persian rule. I discuss above Gangadhara's vision of Kshatriya kinship, imagined in fifteenth-century Gujarat. Nayachandra's *Hammīramahākāvya*, analyzed in chapter 3, is also worth mentioning again, even if more robust comparative work awaits the efforts of another scholar. There is far more to say about the texts that I have referenced in this chapter, including those that find mention in the footnotes but no treatment in the main text. But, rather than continue to drive home the bare fact of multiplicity, perhaps it is worth underscoring in closing what the Rajput and Maratha texts analyzed here shared: a desire to express royal claims in both classical and contextual ways. In part, the works present a reified vision of a ruling Kshatriya class, especially when drawing on the deep well of Sanskrit poetry, mythology, and tropes. But they also envisioned kings who were dynamic within an early modern world increasingly dominated by Indo-Persian dynasties, above all by the Mughals. For Rudrakavi, a Kshatriya fought for Indo-Persian kings. For Paramananda, he both fought for and bested them, at different moments. For Chandrashekhara, the best Kshatriya was one with the freedom to not rule and instead aim for moksha under Akbar's benevolent protection. Moreover, these men were not the last to comment on Mughal rule in Sanskrit. In the next chapter, I turn to another batch of Sanskrit intellectuals who chose to write more explicitly and exclusively about Mughal power as a defining political development of early modern India.

CHAPTER VII

Mughal Political Histories

You say there are no words to describe this time, you say it does not exist. But remember. Make an effort to remember. Or, failing that, invent.

—MONIQUE WITTIG, *LES GUÉRILLÈRES*, 1969

Between 1589 and 1721, several Sanskrit intellectuals crafted political histories of the Mughal Empire. Writing about the Mughals may sound old hat by this point, since Mughal figures feature prominently in texts I discuss in the prior two chapters. But the works I analyze here stand apart in being explicitly focused on Mughal politics. I consider four texts: Padmasagara's creative account of the Mughal Empire's early days, a Sanskrit translation of part of Abul Fazl's *Akbarnāma* (Akbar's book), and Lakshmipati's pair of texts about power struggles between the Mughal kings and their advisors in the early eighteenth century. These narratives vary greatly from one another, but they all take as their chief topic the establishment or the fragmentation of Mughal authority. At times, it seems to me that these histories might have been written in Persian rather than Sanskrit, and, indeed, the *Akbarnāma* was, before it was translated. But a more thorough examination reveals that the works cultivate ways of constructing the recent past that are contingent on access to the fully cultivated set of Sanskrit literary conventions, poetic tropes, and writing styles. In modern times, many people go in for a story of decline, in which the quality of Sanskrit literary production reached its glorious apex sometime in the first millennium CE and thereafter tumbled down to its abysmal nadir in early modernity. But it seems to me that we might reverse that logic. By being late in the history of Sanskrit literature, the writers I discuss in this chapter participated in the richest, most well-developed incarnation of Sanskrit aesthetic and narrative traditions. In this sense, Sanskrit Mughal histories offer a rich opportunity to focus on the poetry of history and glimpse how writers used their inherited literary tradition in order to bring the past alive to their readers.

The Mughals commanded robust attention within Sanskrit historical literature, appearing more frequently than any other Indo-Persian dynasty. In chapter 5, I analyze Jain-authored records of their imperial encounters that used Mughal power as a template for reimagining the identities of certain Jain lineages. In chapter 6, I discuss how authors treated the Mughals as political allies and foes of specific Rajput and Maratha dynasties, often using the Mughals as foils for Kshatriya kingship. There are further Sanskrit texts that I have not yet managed to work into this book. One worth mentioning briefly is Madhava's *Vīrabhānūdayakāvya* (Poem on Virabhanu's rise; ca. 1555). This work outlines the political history of Rewa's Vaghela dynasty through the birth of Virabhadra, Virabhanu's grandson. Madhava mentions several Indo-Muslim political figures in his narrative, including Babur, Humayun, and Sur Adali (Saidali in Sanskrit), the brother-in-law and cousin of Islam Shah of the Sur dynasty.[1] The works I consider in this chapter join these and others in thinking about the largest, most influential—in political, cultural, and social terms—empire, Indo-Persian or otherwise, in Indian history up until that point in time. But the texts I consider here stand apart in concentrating historical attention specifically, sometimes exclusively, on Mughal power. This Mughal-centric approach broke the mold of the already notably diverse tradition of Sanskrit historical narratives.

None of the Sanskrit-medium Mughal histories indicate an imperial audience or readership, although the real and purported authors generally enjoyed links with the Mughals or with patrons who relied upon the Mughals. Padmasagara, who wrote a quasi-fictional account of the origin of the Mughal kingdom, was part of the Tapa Gaccha lineage of Shvetambara Jainism that benefited from robust relations with Akbar and Jahangir. The Sanskrit rendering of the *Akbarnāma* is attributed to Mahesh Thakur, a Brahmin pandit who, via a grant from Akbar, became the founder of the Khandavala dynasty (also known as the Darbhanga Raj), based in Mithila in the sixteenth century.[2] As I discuss below, this attribution is probably false, but it indicates that a later reader wished to project a close link between this abnormal Sanskrit text and the Mughal court. Lakshmipati authored two works about Mughal political intrigues that unfolded in the aftermath

TABLE 7.1
Sanskrit-language Mughal political histories

Author	Date	Title (Sanskrit)	Title (English)
Padmasagara	1589	*Jagadgurukāvya* (vv. 40–121)	Poem on the world's teacher
Attributed (falsely) to Mahesh Thakur	ca. 1600s	*Sarvadeśavṛttāntasaṅgraha*	Collection of events across the land
Lakshmipati	ca. 1720	*Nṛpatinītigarbhitavṛtta*	A political history
Lakshmipati	1721	*Ābdullacarita*	Abdulla's deeds

of Aurangzeb Alamgir's death, in 1707. Lakshmipati worked under Jagacchandra of Kumaon, who operated under the umbrella of Mughal authority. The three authors were likely ignorant of one another's works, but all explore key political events that established and, eventually, undermined the Mughal imperial project. In other words, they sought to explain, in Sanskrit literature, major changes in their Mughal-delineated political world.

Reimagining Mughal Politics

In 1589, Padmasagara wrote the earliest Sanskrit history of the Mughal Empire, playing a little fast and loose with the facts. Padmasagara sandwiched his creative narrative within the *Jagadgurukāvya* (Poem on the world's teacher), the majority of the which concerns the Jain Tapa Gaccha leader Hiravijaya. Accordingly, I discuss parts of this text in chapter 5. After narrating Hiravijaya's early life, Padmasagara departs from his named subject and narrates the establishment of Mughal rule in eighty-two verses. This digression into early Mughal history constitutes a full one-third of the 233-verse text,[3] and it is perhaps usefully considered alongside contemporary Persian chronicles on the same subject. After all, 1589 was a banner year for Mughal history. That year Akbar commissioned the *Akbarnāma*, a Persian history that took nearly a decade for Abul Fazl, his royal vizier and chief ideologue, to complete, and that became, for better or worse, the defining chronicle of Akbar's reign.[4] Also in 1589, Akbar asked three members of his court—Gulbadan Begum, Bayazid Bayat, and Jawhar Aftabachi—to write Persian-medium histories about his father, Humayun.[5] Writing at the same time in Sanskrit, Padmasagara significantly reworked the Mughal Empire time line for its early days. In so doing, Padmasagara created a quasi-fictional history, a sort of premodern version of what Hayden White once dubbed a non-non-history.[6] Padmasagara used the building blocks of historical narrative—including real people, events, and dates—but he rejiggered the details to offer a streamlined narrative of the establishment of Mughal power.

Padmasagara condensed and reordered key political events in order to present the establishment of the Mughal Empire as a swift, smooth process. In reality, the Mughal imperial project had a bumpy rollout, featuring Babur's 1526 victory at Panipat; Humayun being driven out of northern India by the Surs, in the 1540s; and a 1555 reconquest of Delhi, with Safavid assistance. Padmasagara mentions none of these events. Instead, Padmasagara expunges Babur from the record and presents Humayun as the first Mughal king. As a point of contrast, contemporary Jain Sanskrit thinkers, writing around 1569 and 1590, included Babur in the lineup of Mughal rulers.[7] Padmasagara relays three stories involving Humayun: his seizing of Delhi from Sher Shah Suri, his capture of Gujarat and Malwa from Bahadur Shah, and his untimely death.[8] In real life, the first event never happened and the latter two unfolded in 1535–1536 and 1556,

TABLE 7.2
Time lines of the establishment of Mughal power

Hard history	**Padmasagara's history**
1526: Babur takes Delhi	
1530: Humayun ascends the throne	
1535–1536: Humayun conquers Gujarat	
1540–1555: Sur Interregnum	1552: Humayun conquers Delhi
1555: Humayun retakes Delhi	ca. 1554: Humayun conquers Gujarat
1556: Humayun dies; Akbar ascends the throne	1556: Humayun dies; Akbar ascends the throne
1556–1560: Bairam Khan's regency	

respectively, with Humayun's fifteen-year exile from Hindustan separating the two. But Padmasagara portrays these three events as following in quick succession, dating the Mughals' one and only seizure of Delhi to when Akbar was eight years old and dating Humayun's death to when Akbar was twelve.[9] In this way, Padmasagara erases entirely the embarrassing episode of the Sur Interregnum (1540–1555), when Humayun lost control of his northern Indian kingdom, and proclaims that only four years (as opposed to the actual thirty) separated the Mughals' first and only conquest of Delhi and Akbar's enthronement.

Throughout his streamlined version of Humayun's establishment of the Mughal Empire, Padmasagara argues that forceful Mughal expansion led to broad cultural flourishing. For example, following his account of the Humayun-Sur clash, he praises Humayun for fostering freedom and wealth across the empire:

> When the Sur king was defeated, Humayun made the Sur warriors his own servants, who, free from punishment and happy, inhabited that land.
>
> Then he established a kingdom without fear, where elephants, horses, oxen, camels, and men traveled on the road between Kabul and Delhi and millions of houses on tall mountains were adorned with heaps of pearls, gems, and gold.[10]

The Gujarati Jain community included traders, monks, and lay pilgrims, all of whom benefited from security on the Kabul–Delhi road.[11] In a later verse, Padmasagara celebrates that the Mughal conquest brought prosperity more generally to Gujarat and Malwa.[12] For Padmasagara, the Mughal Empire extended tangible benefits, and it is this truth that he sought to explain through crafting his creative narrative.[13] Padmasagara's acclamatory view of a strong Mughal Empire is also on display in his lament of Humayun's untimely death as a great loss.

> *Damn, damn, damn fate that kills mortals.*
> *Fate makes a man king and then, whether he is good or bad, throws him in a dusty hole.*
> Thinking this, the people produced a tumult of noise. Then, when the sun was setting in Humayun's city, there was nobody who was not insensible and blinded with grief.[14]

Padmasagara next turned to Emperor Akbar in his *Jagadgurukāvya* and continued to massage the recent past to present Akbar, like his father, as a laudable king. Padmasagara narrates three major events in Akbar's reign: the young king warding off Sur warriors who sought to take advantage of the power vacuum created by Humayun's death, the establishment of Fatehpur Sikri, and the siege of Chittor. In reality, Bairam Khan, a seasoned general and Akbar's regent for the first four years of his reign (1556–1560), deserves credit for nullifying the Sur threat. But Padmasagara preferred a virile Akbar from the start, so he omitted Bairam Khan's role.[15] In his accounts of both the siege of Mewar-controlled Chittor (1567/1568) and the founding of Fatehpur Sikri (1571), Padmasagara praises Emperor Akbar using time-honored standards of good kingship in Sanskrit literature. The poet likens Akbar's Fatehpur Sikri to Krishna's Dvaraka and celebrates that a wide range of people live there, including traders, all four Hindu classes (*cāturvarṇya*), Jains, followers of the six philosophies (*saḍdarśana*), Sufis, dervishes, and Mughals (*śophi*, *daraveśa*, and *mudgala*).[16] The last three categories are more recent updates, but praise of a flourishing city goes back to the beginning of Sanskrit literature, most notably to descriptions of Ayodhya in Valmiki's Ramayana.

In his account of the battle for Mewar-controlled Chittor, Padmasagara emphasizes Akbar's virtues as a strong warrior and a compassionate ruler, two ideals slightly at odds with each other. In terms of the first, at times he draws on the long-standing tradition in Sanskrit poetry of brandishing extreme political violence as proof of a powerful sovereign, praising Akbar for his skill in battle at the head a victorious army.[17] Padmasagara was hardly unusual in glorifying Akbar's victory at Chittor. For instance, the 1568 *Fatḥnāma* (Book of victory) celebrates how the Mughal army slaughtered the Mewar general Jaimal's men by the hundreds.[18] An illuminated *Akbarnāma*, created circa 1590–1595, illustrated the mass burning (jauhar) of Rajput women at Chittor as a victorious moment.[19] But Padmasagara also expresses some hesitation at endorsing Akbar's tactics. For instance, at the moment when Akbar assassinates Jaimal, the Mughal king is characterized as both cruelhearted and righteous-hearted.[20] Moreover, unlike his Persian-medium counterparts, Padmasagara breaks from his largely triumphalist narrative of conquest at the end of the siege. He says that Akbar—upon seeing the carnage at Chittor (exacerbated by his order to massacre civilians) or the mass burning (jauhar) of Rajput women, or both—is filled with compassion (*kāruṇya*).[21] Fearing being the cause of further loss of life, Akbar, as Padmasagara has it, releases Uday Singh, the Mewar ruler who had controlled Chittor. In reality, Uday Singh turned tail and ran before Akbar even got to Chittor, but Padmasagara's twist accomplishes two distinct objectives. First, the story of Akbar's compassionate release of Uday Singh quashes the potentially uneasy question of how a conqueror—and, for Padmasagara, Akbar is a conqueror—let his enemy escape. Also, Padmasagara uses this moment to imbue Akbar with a Jain-friendly trait, namely aversion to killing, which segues into the poet's return to Hiravijaya's story in subsequent verses.[22]

In his creative reworking of Mughal history, Padmasagara defines the Mughals in political, geographical, and cultural terms. He uses the term "Mughal" ("mudgala" in Sanskrit) as well as more common Sanskrit identifiers for Muslim political figures, like "mleccha." "Mudgala" and "mleccha" appear to be synonymous for Padmasagara at times, such as when he dubs Humayun "Lord of mlecchas" and then, a few verses later, "Lord of Mughals" (*mlecchānāmadhipa* and *mudgalapati*, respectively).[23] He also names Humayun as Lord of Delhi (*dillīśa*) and Lord of Kabul (*kābilanāyaka*), both of which meant, for Padmasagara, that Humayun was located in northern India from the beginning.[24] Padmasagara foregrounds this geography in his initial verses introducing the Mughals.

> In the glorious land of India [*bhārata*], where there are more than twenty-five regions that have been graced by incarnations of the best of men, such as the great, illustrious Jina and Vishnu, the wonderful northern region [*madhyadeśa*] contains shining palaces, idols, and great libraries and is inhabited by worthy people. Here, near the good land of Khurasan, lies a great city called Kabul that is filled with good men and renowned as the dwelling place of heroes. In Kabul, a hundred thousand Mughals, their power unbroken and a terror to demonic Hindus, feast with great pleasure upon hundreds of delicacies at will.[25]

Writers contemporary to Padmasagara, working in both Sanskrit and Persian, typically depict Kabul and northern India, sometimes called Hindustan, as geographically and culturally distinct places.[26] Padmasagara erases this sense of difference and any history of Mughal migration to the subcontinent by portraying the Mughals as situated from the beginning in northern India.

Figure 7.1 Burning of the Rajput women during the siege of Chittor, *Akbarnāma*, ca. 1590–95
Victoria and Albert Museum, London, IS.2:69–1896

Padmasagara offers a few indications of cultural features that might set the Mughals apart from non-Muslim Indian rulers, although his descriptions of the Mughals are generally positive. For instance, in one verse, Padmasagara employs the word "chandala," a term used by the twelfth-century authors Kalhana and Jayanaka for Muslims. But Padmasagara invokes it as a contrast to the practices of Mughal kings. After Akbar sees the carnage at Chittor, he laments, "Alas, are my actions worse than those of a chandala?" The question is seemingly answered in the negative when Akbar decides to free rather than kill Uday Singh of Mewar.[27] Elsewhere in the *Jagadgurukāvya*, Padmasagara explains the name of Fatehpur Sikri (*phattepura* in Sanskrit) as "comprising the best syllables of Persian" (*yāvanabhāṣayākṣaravara*).[28] Padmasagara's praise of Persian syllables signals how much the views of Sanskrit intellectuals had changed in the four hundred years since Jayanaka lamented the pallid phonemes of Persian speakers.

Padmasagara writes about the Mughals warring against "Hindu" kings, using that term, and thereby sets up a contrast of political identities. Padmasagara uses *hindu* more than half a dozen times in his creative history, mainly in a cluster of verses in the middle of the text and primarily as a political category (see appendix A.5 for a translation).[29] He refers explicitly to "Hindu kings" (*hindunṛpā*) and observes that Uday Singh of Mewar held a revered position among all Hindus (*samastahindukalaśa*), which likely reflected the Sisodiyas of Mewar's perceived status as the premier Rajput lineage (see chapter 6).[30] Indeed, just as Padmasagara's "mleccha" might be translated as "Mughal," his "Hindu" is perhaps best translated as "Rajput." Padmasagara expresses an unkind view of Rajput rulers at times, labeling them twice as "demonic Hindus" (*hindvāsura* and *hindvāsurakṣmāpa*), against which the Mughal rulers, Humayun and Akbar, exert control and thereby prove their superior strength.[31]

Padmasagara further considers Mughal power over Rajput rulers in his discussion of the military consequences following Uday Singh's refusal to marry his daughter into the royal Mughal family. According to Padmasagara, Akbar was accustomed to marrying "the daughters of mlecchas and Hindus."[32] Indeed, Akbar had married Rajput princesses since 1562.[33] But, the Rajput ruler Uday Singh, overconfident in his own military prowess (*uddhatabala*), proclaims: "My ancestors did not give their daughters to a mleccha, and so neither will I." A Mughal emissary tries to reason with the Rajput king, arguing that "other Hindus had given their daughters without being asked, in order to protect their wealth and sovereignty."[34]

But Uday Singh flatly refuses and even backs up his position by citing a verse on adhering to family customs, from Bhartrhari's much-celebrated *Nītiśataka* (Hundred verses on politics).

> Following the example of virtuous, noble mothers,
> brave men who have pure hearts and are devoted to good customs
> happily abandon their lives,
> but never break a promise.[35]

The Mewar-Mughal disagreement is settled militarily, when Akbar seizes Uday Singh's Chittor. While Padmasagara narrates the battle for Chittor at some length, he does not specify the Mughal concession: to exempt the Sisodiyas, alone among Rajput lineages, from giving their daughters in marriage to the Mughals.[36] For Padmasagara, the conquest of Chittor seems to speak for itself, as a positive development that shows the Mughals to be a formidable political force that conquers Rajput kingdoms and creates a prosperous empire.

Translating Akbar's Book

Whereas Padmasagara wrote his own version of early Mughal history, a later Sanskrit text offered a Mughal-approved version of similar events by translating a portion of the *Akbarnāma*. Abul Fazl completed the original, Persian-medium *Akbarnāma* in 1598. Sometime later, likely in the seventeenth century, a Sanskrit translation was penned under the title *Sarvadeśavṛttāntasaṅgraha* (Collection of events across the land). The translation as it has come down to us narrates the early days of Mughal power, covering the Persian original's first thirty-five chapters and then breaking off mid-sentence in the account of Humayun's Sur-imposed exile from northern India.[37] A lot remains unclear about the *Sarvadeśavṛttāntasaṅgraha*, including its author, its date, and whether it was ever completed. A later colophon ascribed the partial translation, falsely, to Mahesh Thakur, a sixteenth-century Brahmin pandit and ruler of Mithila who died three decades before Abul Fazl finished the *Akbarnāma*. This misattribution perhaps communicates some of the anxiety surrounding the production of such an atypical Sanskrit text. To put it bluntly, it was unprecedented to translate a Persian court chronicle into Sanskrit. There are few Sanskrit renderings of Persian literature of any sort, and sporadic earlier translations retold popular mythological and religious stories. For instance, in the late fifteenth century, Kalyanamalla penned his *Sulaimaccaritra* (Sulayman's life), drawing on the Bible, Arabic accounts of the Prophets, and the *Arabian Nights*.[38] In 1505, Shrivara wrote his *Kathākautuka* (Strange story), based on the Persian poet Jami's premodern best seller *Yūsuf va Zulaykhā* (Joseph and Potiphar's wife).[39] Both poets worked for Indo-Persian patrons (respectively, Lal Khan Lodhi of Awadh and Muhammad Shah of Kashmir).[40] Perhaps, then, by dating the Sanskrit *Akbarnāma* as roughly contemporary with the original Persian chronicle and situating it within a dynasty that owed its birth to Akbar, one reader attempted to ease the novelty embodied by this startling translation of a Persian imperial history. Since we lack information about its production context, I focus here on analyzing the text itself. I argue that while the *Sarvadeśavṛttāntasaṅgraha* largely reproduces the content of the original *Akbarnāma*, the work also sets itself apart as a distinctively Sanskrit text.

The *Sarvadeśavṛttāntasaṅgraha* opens with several dozen verses on the virtues and limits of speech; the verses replicate the substance of the Persian chronicle to a great degree, in a style appropriate for a Sanskrit text. Abul Fazl wrote the *Akbarnāma* in a mixture of poetry and prose, never choosing one word when he could use a hundred and drawing on a vast range of Persianate and Islamic learned traditions. In the original Persian, the chronicle's opening section constitutes a prime example of Abul Fazl's notoriously impenetrable writing style, as he meditates on how to describe incredible things like God and the Mughal Empire using mere words. The Sanskrit *Akbarnāma* renders many of Abul Fazl's ideas and phrases in this introductory section quite literally. For instance, Abul Fazl wrote:

> What is this utterance that appeared
> and unveiled the eighteen thousand?
> There is no feast more intoxicating,
> nor any stronger rival.[41]

The Sanskrit translates these lines as:

> What is this speech that unveils all universes?
> Since when the world was visible,
> there was no one more intoxicated.
> Even though strong, there was no equal.[42]

It is not clear to me whether the translator grasped all the nuances of Abul Fazl's words, although he seems to have understood that "eighteen thousand" refers to the totality of God's creation. More generally in the opening section, the Sanskrit translation follows Abul Fazl in speaking about God (parameshvara) repeatedly. At times, it reproduces specific turns of phrase, such as saying that speech "originates in the fire-temple of the heart" (*agnimandirarūpāntaḥkaraṇastham* in Sanskrit; *manbaʿash-i ātashkadah-yi dil* in Persian).[43] But the Sanskrit text differs from the Persian original in form. In Sanskrit, the initial section constitutes seventy-odd verses, following which the entire rest of the work is prose. The effect is reminiscent of Sanskrit *gadyakāvya*s such as Bana's seventh-century *Harṣacarita* and *Kādambarī*, where introductory poetic verses proceed a prose work. In other words, the *Sarvadeśavṛttāntasaṅgraha*'s content comes from the Persian tradition, but its form follows Sanskrit expectations.

In the main body of text, the Sanskrit *Akbarnāma* abridges and updates parts of the Persian original, all the while doggedly reproducing many details. The translator shortens Abul Fazl's unwieldy prose at times and cuts entirely a few sections of the work. For instance, the Sanskrit work omits most of Akbar's horoscope, given for him at birth.[44] Later, the translator elides Shah Tahmasp's edict to the governor of Khurasan.[45] Between the occasional, seemingly deliberate lacunae, the translator closely follows the Persian chronicle, something perhaps best evidenced in the small details. The Sanskrit rendering maintains the post-death names for royal Mughal figures, such as, for Humayun, Jannat Ashyani (Heaven dweller; *jannat-āshyānī* in Persian and *jannatāśayānī* in Sanskrit). The Sanskrit reproduces, exactly, many of the lists from the Persian chronicle, naming Akbar's wet nurses, Mughal ancestors, those who accompanied Humayun into exile, and so forth.[46] The *Sarvadeśavṛttāntasaṅgraha* retains many of the dates given by Abul Fazl, using the Hijri calendar, complete with transliterated names of the months. For instance, the Sanskrit text reports Babur's death, closely following the Persian, as follows: "In the year 937, in the month of Jumada al-Avval [*jamādula-avval*], on the sixth day, on the bank of the Yamuna in Agra, in the garden that he had made known as Char Bagh [*cyāribāga*], Firdaus-Makani [*phiradausamakānī*] went to the next world."[47] The translation reproduces even brief events from the Persian chronicle, such as the death of a half-sister of Babur in infancy (*bālya eva mṛtā*), and fine details, such as the name of an Afghan war elephant.[48]

The Sanskrit translation maintains specific cultural information from the Persian *Akbarnāma*, if somewhat inconsistently. The translation retains hundreds of Perso-Arabic names and Persian words, which are listed by the modern editor in two appendixes to the Sanskrit text. The translator even used Persian adaptations when he might have chosen Sanskrit equivalents, such as naming Lahore as *lāhura* rather than the Sanskrit *lābhapura*. At other times, however, the work falls back on older Sanskrit forms, referring to Kanauj (*qanūj* in Persian) as *kānyakubja* and to Chunnar as *caraṇādri*.[49] The translation often transliterates the Persian *hindūstān* (north India; Sanskrit *hindustāna*), but it also sometimes translates it as *madhyadeśa* (north India).[50] At times, both are used, in a seeming slip of the pen.[51]

The translation reproduces references to specific Persian texts at times and elides such references at other points. For instance, at a certain point the *Sarvadeśavṛttāntasaṅgraha* omits a mention of the *Ẓafarnāma* (Book of conquest).[52] But, later, the translation mentions by name "a text called Zafarnama" (*japharanāmākhyapustakaṃ*).[53] Elsewhere, the translation declines to give the title of Shahrazuri's *Tārīkh al-Ḥukamā*, instead referring vaguely to "yavana books" (*yavanapustakeṣu*) for information about the Prophet Noah (*nūha-paigambara*, from Persian *paighambar*) at the time of the flood (Sanskrit *tuphāna*, translating Persian *ṭūfān*).[54] But, in separate passages, the translation names the *Shāhnāma*, *Vāqiʿāt-i Bāburī* (Babur's memoirs), and *Tārīkh-i Rāshīdī*.[55]

At times, the translator responsible for the *Sarvadeśavṛttāntasaṅgraha* seems to retain cultural and political features of Mughal kingship while distancing the translation from Islamic theological views. For instance, in separate passages the Sanskrit text mentions Sikander and Feraydun, kings from the Persian classical tradition, Mughal librarians (*kitābadār*, from Persian *kitābdār*), and reading the Friday *khuṭba* in the ruling king's name.[56] In such ways, the translation accurately communicates features of Mughal sovereignty. In contrast, the translator sometimes disowns Muslim theological perspectives. For instance, he labels the belief that the world is only seven thousand years old as prevalent among yavanas, whereas Abul Fazl does not specify who holds this, in his view, idiotic opinion.[57] The translation's disparate treatment of more political versus more theological views comes to the forefront in a passage on Humayun that deals with both. Here, the translation refers to Humayun wearing red clothing (*raktavāsāṃsi*) on Tuesdays to honor Mars, part of Humayun's claims to be a sacred ruler. But, a few lines later, the same section omits a story about a dullard Imam who bumbled a Quranic reading.[58]

The translation lightly acculturates certain aspects of the *Akbarnāma*, which makes for both interesting passages and confusing ones. In an instance of the former, in a nice bit of cultural approximation, the Sanskrit text says that the Prophet Enoch inscribed architectural manuals (*śilpaśāstras*) on the Egyptian pyramids.[59] Similarly, the translation identifies the light said to be manifest in Akbar, inherited from his ancestor Alanquwa, in Abul Fazl's mythology, as *tejas* (radiance).[60] Alongside such productive descriptions, the translation contains occasional misfires. For instance, it translates a "river excursion" (*sayr-i daryā*) taken by Humayun as *jalakrīḍā*, a Sanskrit phrase that usually refers to erotic water play.[61]

Strikingly, the translator recognizes Turkish and Persian literature as such, calling writers in these languages poets (kavis). He describes their poetry collections using the Persian *dīvān* (*dībāna* in Sanskrit) and translates Persian *ma̱snavī* as "versified prabandha" (*padyamayaḥ prabandhaḥ*).[62] This acknowledgment of Persian and Turkish literature took no heed of the long-held preference of some Sanskrit thinkers to restrict the number of languages in which one could produce kavya. Indeed, the existence of this translation, a piece of Persian literature turned into a Sanskrit gadyakavya, embodies this view of comparable and compatible Sanskrit and Persian literary traditions.

The *Sarvadeśavṛttāntasaṅgraha* introduces some additional information, beyond what is found in the Persian chronicle, regarding Sanskrit philosophy and Hindu religious traditions. For example, an opening verse refers to those who make their living glossing shastras (*śāstravṛttyupajīvinām*).[63] Another verse praises the wisdom found in the Mahatmyas and Vedas, two genres of Hindu religious texts (*māhātmyāvedakagranthoddeśasyātyuttamaṃ vacaḥ*).[64] At one point, the Persian chronicle details Jain and Brahminical views of time. The Sanskrit translator reworked this section, referring to the written texts of specific Indian philosophical traditions and naming the Naiyayikas, philosophers of a specific branch of Sanskrit knowledge, of northern India specifically.[65] Such references, even if limited, distinguish the *Sarvadeśavṛttāntasaṅgraha* from the Persian *Akbarnāma*, although it is difficult to know what to make of these differences without more knowledge of the translation's production context. We know equally little about its reception, or if it even had a reception. The *Sarvadeśavṛttāntasaṅgraha* survives in a single premodern manuscript today.[66] The work stands apart as highly unusual in being a Sanskrit translation, but not in focusing on Mughal history. In fact, by selecting Indo-Persian rule as a relevant topic about which one might write in Sanskrit, the translator of the *Akbarnāma* made a decision similar to that of a few dozen premodern intellectuals before him—and at least one after him: Lakshmipati.

Defending Kingmakers and Moralizing Mughal History

In the early 1720s, Lakshmipati wrote two Mughal political histories in rapid succession. Both works focus on the Sayyid brothers of Baraha, Hasan Ali Khan (commonly known as Abdulla or Abdulla Khan) and Husain Ali Khan, who wielded unprecedented power over Mughal kings.[67] First Lakshmipati penned the *Nṛpatinītigarbhitavṛtta* (A political history; ca. 1720), which details, in more than 1,600 verses, the growing influence of the two Sayyid brothers during the reign of Farrukh Siyar (r. 1713–1719).[68] In many ways, the work is a glory story about Abdulla Khan and prominently features his sage advice. Next, Lakshmipati wrote the *Ābdullacarita* (Abdulla's deeds), a champu of prose and roughly 1,800 verses on how the Sayyid brothers fell from grace during the initial year or so of Muhammad Shah Rangila's rule (r. 1719–1748).[69] The *Ābdullacarita* narrates the death of Husain, the younger brother, and ends with the, in Lakshmipati's view, lamentable imprisonment of Abdulla on Muhammad Shah's orders. Lakshmipati does not mention Abdulla Khan's execution, which Persian-medium histories report as occurring shortly thereafter.

In focusing on the Sayyid brothers, first their rise and then their fall, Lakshmipati wrote about the major shift in Mughal politics of his day, namely how ministers and regents wrested power away from the Mughal royal family. It was a watershed moment when the Sayyid brothers assassinated Farrukh Siyar, in 1719, and appointed two short-lived puppet kings in his place: Rafi-ud-Darjat and Rafi-ud-Daulat.[70] As one modern historian of the period put it: "The year 1719 marked the final collapse of the Mughals as an effective ruling dynasty."[71] Whereas some moderns view the Sayyid brothers as heralding the end of the Mughal political experiment, Lakshmipati took a more pro-minister view. Sympathy to the Sayyid brothers runs throughout both of Lakshmipati's Mughal histories, which together make for a compelling, multilayered culmination of the long tradition of Sanskrit histories on Indo-Persian rule.

Lakshmipati describes his works' audience as kings who should temper their anger toward their ministers, with overtones of speaking directly to his patron. Lakshmipati enjoyed the support of Jagacchandra of Kumaon, in modern-day Uttarakhand. He mentions Jagacchandra in both texts, and opens his *Nṛpatinītigarbhitavṛtta* with praise of the Kumaon king.[72] In addition to his twinned works on late Mughal history, Lakshmipati also wrote, for Jagacchandra, the *Yāgīśvaramāhātmya*, on the Yagishvara linga, dedicated to the Hindu god Shiva and famed for its link with Kusha, one of Rama's sons.[73] Lakshmipati served as both a scholar and a political advisor at the Kumaon court.[74] He speaks in this latter role at the end of the *Ābdullacarita*, after Muhammad Shah arrests Abdulla Khan, in a passage that is shot through with personal reflection:

> Kings truly believe that killing a minister based on rumors
> is one of the aims of life. But it is never virtuous.
> Just as the king arrested Abdulla based on gossip,
> so too may my lord order my arrest based on what people say.
> That is why I wrote this.
> This work should be read affectionately by powerful people,
> whether they are Hindu or Muslim (*hindūkaiścāpi yavanair*),
> to solidify their own position.
> Hatred that would destroy me should not arise based on rumors.[75]

According to Lakshmipati, Mughal political intrigues should serve as a cautionary example for a Hindu king, such as his patron, and for a Brahmin minister, such as himself. In the *Nṛpatinītigarbhitavṛtta*, Lakshmipati says, more generally, that he aims "to instruct all kings."[76] The content of his *Nṛpatinītigarbhitavṛtta*, which is bookended by advice given by Abdulla Khan to Farrukh Siyar and his successor, Rafi-ud-Darjat, respectively, leaves little ambiguity that one of the poet's main arguments is that kings ought to listen to their ministers.

Lakshmipati expected his readers to be fluent in both Sanskrit literature and contemporary Mughal politics, and he often intertwines the two. He seems to assume that readers will know the relevant political actors and so only cursorily introduces them. For instance, in the *Nṛpatinītigarbhitavṛtta*, he presents the key characters, the Sayyid brothers and Farrukh Siyar, as follows:

When the son in Emperor Aurangzeb's line,
a king called Muizuddin [*maujadīna*][77]—
who was wise in statecraft, skilled in warfare,
and pounded corrupt ministers—went to heaven,
the Sayyids [*śayada*], who quaked with fear,
went quickly to Patna to see and become advisors to the king's nephew.
When they saw that the son of Azimuddin [*ajamadīna*], called Farrukh Siyar [*pharkasāha*],
bore the marks of royalty, they paid him homage and stood without fear.[78]

Just as he expects his audience to be up-to-date on the major players and have an outline of Mughal politics, and so declines to provide much in the way of backstories, Lakshmipati also presumes that readers and Mughal figures alike possess deep knowledge of Sanskrit learning. In the *Ābdullacarita*, he quotes from the Bhagavadgita, puranas, and other works.[79] His *Nṛpatinītigarbhitavṛtta* overflows with mythological references to specific gods, sages, and stories. Lakshmipati sometimes mixes contemporary and classical Sanskrit-based references. For instance, in both works, he discusses sons who overthrew their fathers, mentioning, in close proximity, the examples of Kamsa dethroning Ugrasena and Aurangzeb imprisoning Shah Jahan.[80] It is hard to find people in the twenty-first century who are versed in both Mughal history and classical Sanskrit learning. But Lakshmipati seems to have lived in a world where it was possible to hold such expectations.

Lakshmipati compares Hindus and yavanas, citing both political and religious practices, in a sort of difference without othering. For instance, early in the *Nṛpatinītigarbhitavṛtta*, Abdulla Khan is described as citing the examples of Ashvatthama killing Dhrishtadyumna and Parashara slaughtering the rakshasas—each avenging his father's murder—in order to persuade Farrukh Siyar to kill Jahandar Shah, who had gained the throne by slaying Farrukh Siyar's father, Azimusshan (Azimuddin).[81] Abdulla Khan then summarizes: "Just as Hindus [*hinduka*] please their ancestors by doing them homage, / Yavanas do likewise by killing their father's murderer."[82] In other words, the Mughal king Farrukh Siyar ought to follow Hindu examples. Lakshmipati also uses the term "yavana" for Muslims more broadly. For instance, in the *Ābdullacarita*, he offers fifteen or so verses on Mecca (*makka*), a Muslim pilgrimage destination (*yavanānāṃ . . . tīrthaṃ*) that he likens to a range of Hindu pilgrimage sites such as Kashi, Gaya, and Pushkar.[83] He even identifies Mecca as containing Vishnu's footprints to worship, similar to Gaya (see appendix A.9 for translation).[84] For Lakshmipati, Muslim and Hindu practices were comparable and even mirrored each other at times, in both political and religious realms.

Lakshmipati's narration of Mughal history is factually solid and quite detailed in certain sections. For instance, he gives the standard lineup of charges against Jahandar Shah, including gambling, drinking, and womanizing.[85] Jahandar Shah's penchant for wine also finds mention in Braj Bhasha texts of the period, such as Shridhar's *Jangnāmā*.[86] Other times, Lakshmipati offers more unusual details, such as when he says that Farrukh Siyar had Jahandar Shah's food poisoned, which led to the latter's death.[87] He perhaps even obliquely refers to Lal Kunwar, Jahandar Shah's favorite wife and a popular subject in Persian-medium historiography, in an alliterative reference to the king "overindulging in women's caresses" (*lalanālālana*).[88] This example also indicates Lakshmipati's penchant for adding a moral edge to his stories, a prominent feature throughout his history.

One eye-catching example of how Lakshmipati wove together moralizing and facticity comes in a grisly passage about a medical procedure undergone by Farrukh Siyar. According to Lakshmipati, Farrukh Siyar could neither sleep nor eat due to piles (*arśas*), and so became sickly and emaciated.[89] At the outset, Lakshmipati identifies a moral cause for this physical ailment, namely the sin of killing his uncle Jahandar Shah (*maujadīnavidhvaṃsanodbhavāt pātakād*). Farrukh Siyar's health problems caused a great disturbance among the people, who wished to see their king, and so Abdulla found the best doctor, who had come from Europe (*phiranga*) and was called Makara.[90] Makara, known in Persian and English sources as William Hamilton, told Farrukh Siyar that he could be cured, but the treatment would render the king impotent (*bhavitā ṣaṇḍatā tava*). Lakshmipati does not specify why this procedure would affect the king's virility, but likely it was because Hamilton planned to use mercury or arsenic to cauterize the wound (both were common in early eighteenth-century English medicine and can cause impotence).[91] In any case, according to Lakshmipati, Farrukh Siyar replied, "impotency is better than death," at which point Hamilton freed Farrukh Siyar from pain by cutting the protrusion from the king's anus (*vaidyena tatkāle sañchinnaṃ gudakīlakam*) (see appendix A.8 for translation).[92] This story is known, typically in vaguer terms, from both Mughal Persian sources and early East India Company records.[93] But Lakshmipati's narration is more detailed and suggests some of the potential value, for reconstructing the finer points of political history, of taking seriously Sanskrit narratives of Indo-Persian rule.

Why did Lakshmipati not write in Persian? At least three authors—Muhammad Qasim Lahori, Mirza Muhammad, and Kam Raj—wrote Persian works around the same time as Lakshmipati that cover similar events.[94] Lakshmipati, too, wrote a work exclusively about Mughal history, and so I think it is reasonable to ask: Why did he not craft it in Persian, a well-established Indian language by the early eighteenth century and a more standard medium for discussing Mughal politics? One answer is that Lakshmipati did write in Persian, to some degree, anyways. J. B. Chaudhuri cataloged hundreds of non-Sanskrit words in the *Nṛpatinītigarbhitavṛtta*, many of them adapted from Persian.[95] The *Ābdullacarita* is similar. Lakshmipati even uses bits of Persian grammar at times, such as the accusative marker *rā* and the locative preposition *dar* (in).[96] At times, Lakshmipati fuses Sanskrit and Persian, producing lovely compounds such as *rājajāda* (prince, with Sanskrit *-jāda* for Persian *-zāda*).[97] He also plays on the effect of combining the two languages, such as a series of verses that each begin with a Persian word.[98] In the *Ābdullacarita*, he uses in the same line the near homonyms *gostanī* (grapes, in Sanskrit) and *gosta* (for Persian *gosht*, meat).[99] In Lakshmipati's robust mixing of Persian and Sanskrit, we glimpse an approach more commonly seen in vernacular texts. To take one example, Braj Bhasha works often incorporated significant amounts of Persian vocabulary.[100] But Lakshmipati made the more unusual decision to infuse Sanskrit with Persian, sometimes to stunning aesthetic effect.

Lakshmipati acknowledged his linguistic innovation in dynamically mixing Sanskrit and Persian. He wrote in some of the opening verses of the *Nṛpatinītigarbhitavṛtta*:

> Although speaking in Persian [*yavanānāṃ bhāṣāyāḥ*] is forbidden,
> Nonetheless I write in this language at times
> in this book I have written myself.[101]

Chaudhuri calls these verses an "apology," whereas V. Mohan suggests an attempt on Lakshmipati's part to make his work widely accessible.[102] I see a skilled poet making a tongue-in-cheek claim, since these lines contain, themselves, two non-Sanskrit terms, including the word for "forbidden."[103] To put Lakshmipati's point in Sanskrit aesthetic terms, the *dhvani* (suggested meaning) of this verse overrides its literal meaning. A classic example of this literary strategy is found in a much-discussed verse, cited in Anandavardhana's *Dhvanyāloka* (Light on suggestion), where a young woman says:

> Mother-in-law sleeps here, I there:
> look traveler, while it is light.
> For at night when you cannot see
> you must not fall into my bed.[104]

The verse is an invitation for the traveler to slip into the young woman's bed in the middle of the night, and its poetic appeal is enhanced by the contrast that its literal meaning is the opposite. Similarly, Lakshmipati highlights his decision to write using Persian vocabulary by issuing what amounts to a nonwarning against doing just that. By the early eighteenth century, some Sanskrit intellectuals viewed Persian as a legitimate source for literary innovation within Sanskrit literature.

It remains unclear if anybody in premodern India appreciated, or even read, Lakshmipati's striking Sanskrit histories. In what has become a common refrain in this book, both texts survive in single manuscript copies (in London and Calcutta, respectively). Perhaps we should make little of such documentary evidence, however, especially since premodern Sanskrit literary culture was to come to a close in Indian history soon after Lakshmipati wrote. Lakshmipati's fascinating works remain largely unknown today, which is to our detriment. The twinned texts examined in this chapter offer insightful information about a critical and understudied period of Mughal history. They also constitute a challenge to the death-of-Sanskrit thesis.[105] Other scholars have failed to see newness and vitality in Sanskrit texts produced after the seventeenth century, but perhaps they looked in the wrong places. In Lakshmipati, I see a dynamic treatment of Mughal political history as Sanskrit literature, using the fully ripened aesthetic tools of the Sanskrit tradition. A rich project awaits the scholar willing to look past our modern bias of favoring earlier Sanskrit materials and further analyze Lakshmipati's literary histories.

Other No More

The works of Padmasagara, of the *Akbarnāma*'s translator, and of Lakshmipati mark the culmination, or at least one major culmination, of narrative historical energy focused on Indo-Persian rule in Sanskrit. At this late moment, a few key changes are visible in the rich tradition of Sanskrit Indo-Muslim historiography. First, Sanskrit authors focused specifically, even exclusively, on the Mughals. At earlier points, most Sanskrit authors had written about Muslim political figures when they came into contact with non-Muslim figures, as part of Chauhan history (e.g., Jayanaka, Nayachandra) or Shivaji's story (e.g., Paramananda, Jayarama). The main exceptions were Jonaraja and Shrivara, who wrote official court histories for Shah Miri patrons. But, at the twilight of written Sanskrit histories, we witness a precise focus on Indo-Muslim historiography, specifically of the Mughal Empire, over and against other options. For instance, Lakshmipati could have written an account of Jagacchandra of Kumaon's relations with Farrukh Siyar and subsequent Mughal kings, but he did not. Instead, he wrote about Mughal politics, only noting Jagacchandra's role as his patron or mentioning him in an aside amid broader narratives of Mughal affairs. Mughal history was now a proper subject in its own right for Sanskrit intellectuals. One individual took that development as an opportunity to do something nearly unthinkable, namely transcreate the Persian *Akbarnāma* as a piece of Sanskrit literature.

By the late sixteenth century, Sanskrit historians seemed to have got past some of their intellectual predecessors' hang-ups with respect to writing about a Muslim Other, perhaps because Muslims and Indo-Persian ruling culture had ceased to be Other. All three authors I discuss in the present chapter admit Persian as a language of politics and literature. Long gone are the harsh dismissals penned by Jayanaka and Gangadevi, whose ears ached from the offense of hearing, as they perceived it, Persian nonspeech. In contrast, Lakshmipati plays with Persian, making it part of Sanskrit aesthetics and his narrative style. The *Sarvadeśavṛttāntasaṅgraha* took a Persian work as its starting point to produce Sanskrit literature. In general, the authors I discuss here have no sense that they are writing about people irreconcilably different, Muslim or otherwise. Sudipta Kaviraj reminds us that there are "very different conditions of difference," ranging from differences that all involved deem insignificant to those that prompt violent conflict.[106] For the Sanskrit intellectuals examined in this chapter, Indo-Muslim political figures were marked by differences in certain ways, but those differences were comparable and dynamic vis-à-vis a politically defined community of upper-class Hindus.

All three authors refer to "Hindus," most commonly contrasting them with Indo-Persian rulers (and, less frequently, with Muslims in general) and sometimes equating the two communities. Sanskrit intellectuals writing in other places in early modernity, too, paired Hindus and Muslims as political categories defined by cultural differences. For instance, a 1614 grant from Balabhadra of Chamba, in the western Himalayas, refers to Hindu and Muslim kings (*nṛpatayo hindavo vā turuṣkā*) who consider it a sin to eat cows and pigs, respectively.[107] Here difference is posited between two types of rulers, and it generally falls along religiously demarcated habits. But it privileges comparability rather than engaging in harsh othering. Such usages are more specific than what we saw in the fourteenth century (see chapter 3), when "Hindu" appears to have been first used in Sanskrit. A larger history of the slow Indian adoption of the Perso-Arabic term "Hindu" is yet to be told. But, when it is written, what we have seen in Sanskrit historiography—namely, the tendency to use "Hindu" to mark certain kinds of kings, rather than members of a broad religious tradition—will be a critical part of that story. At times, our authors speak of larger Hindu and Muslim communities, such as when Lakshmipati likens Mecca to Kashi. Another part of the unwritten narrative of the term "Hindu" will be premodern proclamations of cultural and religious similitude.

Lakshmipati's two works on Mughal history seem to conclude the long tradition of Sanskrit narratives on Indo-Persian rule. Further archival discoveries may well oblige us to revise this end point, but it is unlikely to shift forward more than a few decades, due to larger political and literary trends that changed India in the eighteenth century. In terms of literature, many people stopped writing in Sanskrit and instead chose to produce vernacular literature, which thrived across the early modern subcontinent. Vernacular texts sometimes covered the same topics as later Sanskrit histories of Indo-Persian rule. For instance, in the late eighteenth century, Gumani Ram Kayasth translated the *Āʾīn-i Akbarī*, the final volume of Abul Fazl's *Akbarnāma*, into Hindi. Three copies of the work survive in Jaipur's Pothikhana. India's political world also shifted dramatically during the eighteenth century as the Mughal Empire became a shell of its former self. Above I note how the Sayyid brothers, minister kingmakers, grabbed power away from the Mughal royalty during the 1710s. The Mughal Empire fragmented relatively quickly thereafter, as many areas broke away from imperial control. In 1739, Nadir Shah came from Iran, took Emperor Muhammad Shah Rangila hostage, and sacked Delhi in a spectacular display of how the Mughals had lost authority even over their capital city. Indo-Persian rule never manifested in India again beyond regional instances. Writers still mentioned the Mughals and other Indo-Persian rulers in the occasional Sanskrit text, but more as historical or cultural figureheads than as part of a vibrant political present.[108] Just as Indo-Persian rule and Sanskrit histories thereof began at about the same time, in the 1190s, they ended relatively in sync as well, in the early eighteenth century.

Epilogue

Starting Points

Tell all the truth but tell it slant.

—EMILY DICKINSON, D. 1886

Sanskrit histories of Indo-Muslim rule were written all over the subcontinent, with the exception of Bengal, in eastern India. This exception is striking, in part, because both Sanskrit literary culture and Muslim-led rule flourished in medieval Bengal. Premodern Bengal hosted a robust regional Sanskrit tradition, especially in puranas penned between the eighth and thirteenth centuries that fused Brahminical and local cultures.[1] In twelfth-century Bengal, Jayadeva wrote his *Gītagovinda* (Krishna in song), a stunning piece of Sanskrit literature that arguably created a new genre.[2] Politically, Muslim-led rule began in Bengal in 1204. First, the region was a province of the Delhi Sultanate, and, in 1342, an independent Bengal Sultanate dawned.[3] When Muslim rulers first arrived in eastern India, they found Sanskrit to be useful for expressing their political ambitions. For instance, after he overthrew the Sena dynasty, in 1204, Muhammad bin Bakhtiyar Khalji struck gold coins that boasted "on the victory of Bengal" (*gauḍavijaye*) in Sanskrit, written in Devanagari script.[4] By the fifteenth century, the cultural norms of Muslim-led rule were so entrenched in Bengal that when a Hindu, Jadu, ascended the throne thanks to the shrewd calculations of his father, Raja Ganesh, Jadu converted and ruled as Sultan Jalaluddin Muhammad (r. 1415–1432).[5]

Despite such fertile literary and political conditions, intellectuals do not appear to have used Sanskrit to discuss Indo-Muslim political power in Bengal. This apparent absence remains to be fully investigated. But I hazard a preliminary explanation here that also helps to crystalize one of my core arguments throughout this book; namely, that Sanskrit poet-historians who wrote on Indo-Persian polities were specifically interested in explaining new forms of political power. This brief meditation on absence also helps elucidate one promise of further studying Sanskrit literary histories and other, history-adjacent materials.

Premodern Bengalis wrote many Sanskrit texts, including the sixteenth-century *Sekaśubhodayā* (Shaykh's auspicious appearance). *The Sekaśubhodayā* narrates tales about Shaykh Jalaluddin Tabrizi (d. 1225 or 1244), one of the earliest known Sufis in Bengal, who is credited with helping disseminate Islam throughout the region.[6] The work's emphasis on religious changes perhaps indicates why Bengal-based Sanskrit intellectuals did not write about Indo-Muslim political history. In making this suggestion I build on the assessment of Richard Eaton, who sees the *Sekaśubhodayā* as attempting to explain religious changes, specifically the spread of Islam, across Bengal.[7] I would add that widespread religious conversion did not accompany most expansions of premodern Muslim-led polities in other parts of the subcontinent. In seeing broad Islamic-conversion trends, Bengal was an exception among regions of the Indian subcontinent. This is explainable in historical terms; one may note, among other things, that areas of Bengal dominated by forest dwellers experienced conversion to Islam at a faster rate and to a greater extent than those integrated into Hindu caste and class systems.[8] But I am more interested in the literary repercussions. Whereas most Sanskrit intellectuals sought to explain the rise of Muslim-led political power, a phenomenon across much of India, Bengalis had a different, more religiously focused story to tell.

Trace links remain between Sanskrit historical literature and Bengal, but they are faint. Chandrashekhara, author of the *Surjanacarita* (see chapter 6), was a Bengali, although he worked at the Bundi court.[9] Premodern Bengalis may have read some Sanskrit histories, even if they did not write them. Both the *Surjanacarita* and Lakshmipati's *Ābdullacarita* (see chapter 7) survive in single manuscript copies in Kolkata.[10] Still, as suggested above, premodern Bengal-based Sanskrit thinkers seem to have focused on explaining religious changes.

The Bengal exception helps to underscore that premodern Sanskrit intellectuals wrote about Indo-Muslim rule, in large part, in order to explain political changes. Some authors also comment on religious practices, but this is fairly sporadic as compared to the persistent attention to issues associated with rulership and sovereignty. Military might is the most robust, recurrent topic among the Sanskrit histories that I have surveyed here. Also, many authors, from Jayanaka to Shrivara to Lakshmipati, remarked on the Persian language. In the context of Sanskrit literary culture, political violence and language are two key topics in expressing sovereignty. In other words, Sanskrit intellectuals not only wrote about Indo-Persian rule but also explored how this new type of ruling culture was changing how one might think about claims of political authority in Sanskrit. Perhaps it is not especially insightful to reiterate at the end of this book that Sanskrit intellectuals were interested in political developments, but consider a related query, concerning a possible connection between Indo-Muslim rule and Sanskrit historiography.

Was there a causal link between the rise of Indo-Persian power and history writing in Sanskrit? It is a tempting idea. If there was a link, one might think about whether Sanskrit thinkers had connections with, or at least gained critical awareness of, the Persian tarikh tradition. For example, there seem to be a high number of both Persian and Sanskrit histories written in northern India during the 1580s and 1590s (see chapters 6 and 7). Is this concurrence mere coincidence? Or perhaps both historiographical trends were spurred by the same political changes? Or maybe Sanskrit-medium and Persian-medium thinkers conducted intellectual exchanges more widely than we have appreciated to date? How might such exchanges, if they occurred, change how we understand broader trends in Sanskrit literature during the second millennium CE, which has been dubbed the "vernacular millennium"?[11] To return to Bengal, perhaps there is a connection between the region's lack of early modern Sanskrit histories (noted above) and its lack of early modern Persian chronicles (noted by Sumit Guha).[12] Answers to these questions await future scholarship, but my work here has laid some essential groundwork for meaningfully, rather than whimsically, posing such queries.

It is striking that Jayanaka wrote within a few years of the Ghurid conquest of the Chauhans. Something about the advent of rulers in Delhi who happen to be Muslim prompted a response of Sanskrit writing about their political activities, but how new was this sort of reaction? Did this mode of literary history, inaugurated by Jayanaka in my story, differ from prior Sanskrit styles of writing about the past? If so, how? To pursue this line of inquiry, we need further research on Sanskrit works of political history written before the late twelfth century CE, which I do not offer here. Many of the premodern works I have discussed evince continuity in form and style with earlier Sanskrit literature, even while their content reflected more current political affairs. I have noted some links in my analysis of specific texts, such as how Jayanaka's *Pṛthvīrājavijaya* stylistically echoed Bilhana's eleventh-century *Vikramāṅkadevacarita* (see chapter 2). In form, the *Sarvadeśavṛttāntasaṅgraha* evokes Bana's seventh-century *Harṣacarita* (see chapter 7). Several authors played on verses from Kalidasa's fifth-century *Raghuvaṃśa*. But I largely leave it to other scholars to work out whether and how to integrate these texts and other, less discussed pre-1200 works into a longer lineage of Sanskrit histories.[13] Still, I raise these important sets of questions about political and literary developments in premodern India, which I cannot answer in this book, as a demonstration of what we stand to learn if we further develop Sanskrit histories as an area of study.

Resilient History

Histories of Muslim-led and, later, Indo-Muslim or Indo-Persian rule had a spectacular run in premodern Sanskrit literature. In the pages of this book I have discussed nearly three dozen such texts and referred in passing to numerous other historical works as well as many inscriptions. Some authors produced records of political and military episodes involving Muslims as they unfolded in real time or shortly thereafter. Others chronicled events that had occurred decades or even more than a century earlier. By and large, individual authors were not aware of one another's histories, at least outside local traditions such as the Kashmiri rajataranginis and Mughal-era Jain materials, respectively. The disjointed nature of Sanskrit histories of Muslim-led rule makes this tradition all the more astounding for the sheer number of texts encompassed therein. Again and again, premodern Indian intellectuals decided that Sanskrit literature was an apt medium for thinking through their political pasts and presents. In other words, the subject of Indo-Muslim rule was not of casual or imitative interest for premodern Sanskrit intellectuals. Rather, it was a pressing topic that numerous premodern authors, patrons, and communities judged important to explore in Sanskrit.

The robust nature of these Sanskrit historical materials is further underscored by a feature that I have mentioned repeatedly but hardly analyzed: much of it nearly did not survive. I have written what feels like a dozen times in this book that such-and-such a text comes down to us in a single copy. Some of those lone copies remain unfinished, whereas others are fragmentary. This is true for works penned more than eight hundred years ago, such as Jayanaka's *Pṛthvīrājavijaya*, and also for works composed three hundred years ago, such as Lakshmipati's twinned Mughal histories. What do we make of such a precarious archive? In some cases, arbitrary preservation restricts our certainty about aspects of the past, as I discuss regarding pre-1000 inscriptions at the end of chapter 1. Perhaps, in other cases, limited material evidence indicates a limited circulation. For instance, the late seventeenth-century *Śambhurājacarita* (mentioned in chapter 6) was quite possibly never read beyond Surat, where it was written and where Georg Bühler found a sole fragmentary copy in the late nineteenth century.[14] But it would be an error to read too much about circulation into modern manuscript preservation since only a fraction of the manuscripts that were penned in premodernity survive in the twenty-first century.[15] Of extant premodern Indian manuscripts, many remain unknown and uncatalogued. Many are lost every day.[16] When faced with such fragile circumstances, I find myself astonished that dozens of Sanskrit narratives of Indo-Persian rule do still exist, such that I can present them as a usable archive of historical materials.

Many of the Sanskrit histories I have discussed in this book circulated only regionally and were, from the get-go, aimed at local audiences. This means that, in the practice of history, Sanskrit narratives often operated as highly localized commentaries on power and historicity. For those accustomed to thinking of Sanskrit as timeless, endless, and boundless, as the evocative "language of the gods," perhaps this is surprising. But it should not be. More than a decade ago, Yigal Bronner and David Shulman argued that second-millennium Sanskrit poetry was regional in the sense of participating in localized mediums and traditions.[17] What remains to be more fully worked out is how Sanskrit intellectuals related the regional and transregional to each other in specific texts. My analysis of tropes and emerging identities offers some thoughts on potential links. I leave for other scholars to query whether the local turn in Sanskrit was really, well, a turn. Was being regional a new phenomenon in second-millennium Sanskrit texts, or have we not asked the right questions to foreground the recovery of social production and reception contexts for earlier periods?

The rich archive that I have examined in this book leaves little doubt that narrative history on Muslim-led rule was a formidable branch of premodern Sanskrit learning in practice, even as it was and remains unaccounted for in theory. I think we should change that and account for it. Specifically, I think we ought to adjust the intellectual frameworks through which we order Sanskrit literature so that we see historical writing as a serious branch of learning that attracted the attention of premodern thinkers and so deserves our modern attention. Throughout this book, I have drawn out the implications of conceptualizing this archive as such for how we understand premodern India in intellectual, literary, cultural, and political terms. In closing, I focus on today and try to tease out some of the problems and promises of my arguments for modern thinkers in modern times. At the core of both sets of arguments, about the past and about the present, stands an embrace of multiplicity when thinking about how to define historical narratives and historical consciousness.

Challenging History

Throughout this book, we have been touring aspects of India's past from the vantage point of our present. This posture is normal, but it benefits from being named and then subjected to scrutiny. As Eric Hobsbawm wrote: "We swim in the past as do fish in water, and cannot escape from it. But our modes of living and moving in this medium require analysis and discussion."[18] Redirecting our gaze from past societies and intellectual traditions to instead rest squarely on our present, I ask here: How can Sanskrit histories of Indo-Persian rule inform and enrich what we do as historians? What analytical insights do my arguments hold for how we exist more broadly, as scholars in the present day? This body of materials offers substantial promise of intellectual gains, both specific to the study of South Asia and for historians more broadly. But my analysis of this archive and this archive's very existence also pose challenges, both big and small, that may well cause some of my colleagues to bristle. Typically, the upsides and downsides go together, and so I consider them in tandem below as I work through some of the potentials of these materials in modern academic contexts.

I have opened up a fresh archive, previously untheorized as such, of Sanskrit-medium materials pertinent for the study of Muslim-led polities in second-millennium South Asia. Historians of Indo-Muslim rule and Sanskritists may find these new materials uncomfortable, for different reasons. Historians of South Asia who focus on the period of Indo-Persian rule (roughly the late twelfth century through the early to mid-eighteenth century) rarely read Sanskrit. For them, it is unclear how to even attempt to use a largely untranslated and thus, to them, largely inaccessible archive. Linguistic limitations are a real, if perennial, issue in the study of premodern India. Archives are sometimes excluded from modern historical consciousness simply because people cannot read them. I offer some excerpted translations in the appendix as a small gesture to opening up this Sanskrit archive for further study. I also discuss in the introduction the possibilities of adapting some of my methodologies and insights to more fruitfully interrogate literary aspects of Indo-Persian historical texts.

My fellow Sanskritists can read premodern Sanskrit histories, of course, but I wonder if the beleaguered field of Indology has the intellectual framework and bandwidth required to accommodate such works as anything other than exceptions or curiosities. Western-based Sanskrit studies is having a hard go of things. Externally, the field faces significant withdrawals of institutional support. Internally, some Indologists are proving susceptible to academically compromising influences from the saffron wave of hateful Hindutva ideology. Additionally, the field's faculty have become notably homogenous, due to unchecked gender biases that have produced an atmosphere suffocating for most women and, relatedly, much innovative research (see the introduction). The field as a whole has yet to meaningfully confront any of these problems.

The current circumstances within the field of Indology—especially its unapologetic embrace of male dominance in the professoriate—seem ripe for a scenario analogous, in some ways, to how Mary Beth Norton experienced the sidelining of women's history and women historians in the field of history in the early 1980s. Professor Norton wrote that she saw three main groups of historians. The first dismissed women's history as a fad; the second group relegated it to a subfield. The third were the most promising, in that they seemed keen to integrate women's history into their teaching repertoire, but, she lamented, "They have not yet fully assimilated women's history scholarship or recognized its significance. . . . [They] isolate the insights of women's history, placing them in a separate category that does not affect the core of their work."[19] Today historians do a good deal better integrating both women's history and women historians than they did in the 1980s.[20] Modern Sanskritists might do well to follow the critical self-reflection, confronting of prejudice, and concrete plans of action that facilitated these changes.

Undefining History

Adopting a wider academic lens, Sanskrit narratives of Indo-Muslim rule allow us to crack open, just a bit, the modern definition of written history. The discipline of history as constituted in modern academic settings is Western in its origins, but I know of no respected historian today who wishes it to remain exclusively so in terms of its practitioners, areas of study, and methodologies. Shouldn't the desire for insights arising from greater diversity apply to the past also? I certainly think so. As I mention in the introduction, I have no intention of offering a decisive, final definition of written history, because that would undermine the flexibility that is central to my project. Rather, I want to underscore multiplicity as a key aspect of how I understand historical narratives and historical consciousness. In a thought-provoking article, Ashis Nandy once wrote: "It is my suspicion that, broadly speaking, cultures tend to be historical in only one way."[21] I disagree, and instead join those who have identified "rich historiographical diversity" in premodern India as well as in other times and places.[22] I think that a key value of understanding that premodern Sanskrit thinkers wrote history is precisely that what they produced is so different than what we call written history today, and that acknowledging this can help the modern discipline of history grow in particular ways.

Some might mistakenly think that, in trying to broaden the scope of history, I am calling for a de-emphasis on facts and accuracy in modern interpretations of the past. I am actually arguing for the opposite. To me, as a modern historian, facts and historical causality matter a great deal. In fact, historical truth is more crucial than ever in India's burgeoning Hindu Rashtra (Hindu nation), where rabid myths are prompting the slaughter of both knowledge about the past and Indian minorities.[23] There are intellectual and human casualties of the abandonment of historicity in the present day. But there is also far more to writing history than figuring out what actually happened, such as tropes, story lines, and literary expectations that inform how we narrate the past. I have no wish to "dissolve the historical fact into narration."[24] In fact, I agree that the historian's craft "demands more than delightful storytelling," including careful attention to facts, precision, and causality.[25] One reason I insist on calling Sanskrit works on Indo-Muslim rule "histories" is precisely so that they can inform our methods of writing history today, not to undermine the commitment to accuracy as an ethical bedrock for modern historians but to enhance our attention to other crucial aspects of writing history.

Also, recognizing that historians are storytellers empowers us, as modern historians, to tell better—more compelling and more accurate—stories, by seeing where we rely on tropes and conventions in lieu of historical analysis. Sometimes, tropes cover up modern prejudices. For instance, in my corner of the academy, Islamophobia remains a pernicious problem, often manifested in the story line that Muslims destroyed something, such as Indian Buddhism, Sanskrit literature, or massive numbers of Hindu temples (all three claims are false).[26] Other common tropes among some Indologists include the assumption that Sanskrit is coterminous with Indian civilization, that Indian civilization can be imagined in the singular, and the persistent privileging of Brahminical voices and interpretations. Once we see these rhetorical devices as such in our own historiography, we can interrogate what analytical work they do for us (or prevent us from doing), then direct our energies to developing better ideas.

Focusing on literary aspects of the historian's craft also allows us to identify as conventions things that we often imagine to be almost natural to writing history. Dates are a good example. Dates occur relatively infrequently in the materials I analyze here, but they are required for modern history writing. I like dates as much as the next historian, but do we ever casually rely on temporal proximity in lieu of meticulously establishing historical causality? Probably, because dates can be a rhetorical crutch for modern historians. The answer to this problem is not to abandon dates. Rather, we ought to more carefully analyze the literary value of dates for us, both generally and in specific instances, to help ourselves more precisely discern their proper historical explanatory value. In short, historians ought to think more critically and more often about the centrality of narrative and literary conventions to our work so that we might produce more accurate, insightful analyses of the past.

Yet another virtue of embracing a bit more flexibility in our definition of historical writing is that flexibility allows us to read premodern Sanskrit narratives as histories. The force of this admittedly circular argument it perhaps best seen if we consider the alternative—namely, a more rigid, exclusive definition of history. If we say that Sanskrit intellectuals did not produce written histories but only hagiographies or some other sort of not-quite-histories, then we limit the production of history to the modern West. As Hayden White put it, "In short, it is possible to view historical consciousness as a specifically Western prejudice by which the presumed superiority of modern, industrial society can be retroactively substantiated."[27] I am not interested in that agenda. We would lose too much in terms of how we understand Sanskrit intellectual culture, our own historical contingency today, and what it can mean to write history. I prefer the path less traveled, where the other is not projected as irremediably Other and so has the potential to change how we understand ourselves. To me, diversifying how we think about the historian's craft is a promise, more than a threat, one that may yet make us better historians.

APPENDIX

Select Translations from Sanskrit Histories

A.1. Chaulukya King Pulakeshiraja's Defeat of a Tajika Army (738 CE Navsari Plate)

The [tajika army] vomited forth arrows, maces, and other weapons. With glittering swords, they shredded the lofty kings of Sindh, Kacchella, Saurashtra, the Chavotakas, the Mauryas, Gurjaras, and others. They wanted to enter into southern India in order to conquer all southern rulers, and first they approached Navasarika. They darkened the sky with dust thrown up by the pounding hooves of their galloping horses. Their bodies were disfigured and their armor reddened by gushing blood from their entrails that spilled out of holes in their large stomachs as they rushed into battle and were ripped apart by spears.

[In trying to defeat the tajikas], the best of scores of kings had offered their own heads in order to gain favor and gifts from their master [*svāmī*]. The kings' lips were filled with holes where they had been mercilessly pierced by their own teeth. Those great warriors had sharp sword blades reddened by reams of thick blood oozing from injured trunks, sides, and hips of enemy elephants snagged by traps across countless battlefields, and still they did not gain supremacy. They sliced off the heads of their enemies as if their necks were delicate lotus stalks by striking them with sharp arrows that were released to annihilate foes. Many bodies were covered with an armor of bristling hair, electrified by the violence of the battlefield. But the tajikas had never before been defeated.

When the tajika army was vanquished in battle [by Pulakeshiraja], their headless trunks began to dance in a circle while loud drums were struck repeatedly, seeming to rejoice at the thought that [the tajikas] had finally repaid their debt to their master [svami] at the price of their own heads.[1]

A.2. Description of Pushkar

(Jayanaka's ca. 1191–1200 Pṛthvīrājavijaya, *1.36–56)*

One time, long ago, Brahma,
whose throne is the thousand-petaled navel lotus,
folded his hands and respectfully beseeched
Vishnu, who was absorbed in meditation—

Just as I have not experienced even a trace of discomfort
while dwelling in your lotus [*puṣkara*],[2]
likewise, protected by you, I dwell happily
in the earthly pilgrimage site of Pushkara.

You are known as lotus-eyed.
You also bear a lotus in your navel.
Those three lotuses together reside in Pushkar.
Therefore, people call that auspicious place Three-Lotused
[*tripuṣkara*].

The three-eyed god Shiva also resides in Pushkar,
under the name of Ajagandha,
as if dispelling the conceit of the Ganges
that she purifies the three worlds.

Before this place was full of sacrifices to me.
Where once there were three pits full of fire,
with the passage of time,
those very pits are full of water. 1.40

People seek liberation in Pushkar
because of the presence of us three.
Now they take no pleasure
in the worlds of you, me, or Shiva.

Pushkar is also known as "Three-Lotused"
because of the pure waters that flow from Mount Kailasa,
the nectar of immortality that flows from the milk ocean,
and the sweet fragrant lotus from the navel lotus.

O Unrivaled Lord! The three Vedas dwell happily
in the homes of Brahmin sages as the eyes of Sarasvati.
From them flow three streams of tears of joy
that, naturally cool, become heated.

Since it is the Age of Darkness, Shiva's bull
has been reduced to standing on one leg with support from the
  Pashupata weapon.
Due to the precariousness of his mount,
three-eyed Shiva has turned away from traversing the three worlds.

Even you, as you were dropping off to sleep
on the night of the Age of Darkness,
as if you feared its thunder, you left behind thick hair
and found peace by reincarnating at the Buddha. 1.45

In this Age of Darkness, when Brahmins
have ceased to perform sacrifices
and sacrificial offerings are not received,
Indra finds his strength sapped.

Fearing that, without sacrifices,
the earth has been ruined
by terrible droughts in this Age of Darkness,
Karttikeya's peacock refuses to take him to the earth.[3]

Having seen his lineage as distressed
by your incarnation as the Buddha

as it was invigorated by your birth as Rama,
Surya shines less brightly now, as if he doubts his own family.

O Vishnu, while you adopted asceticism as the Buddha incarnation
and took to being friendly with deer,
my homeland, Pushkar, has been overrun by the terror of the Ghurids [matanga]
as if being trampled by elephants.

That place where I sprinkled water at the end
of the great sacrifice that created the world,
the Ghurid [mleccha] army now uses it to refresh themselves
from their violent assaults on temples and Brahmin lands. 1.50

Your tears of joy that comprise the Narmada
and Yamuna rivers used to enter Pushkar.
But now only the waste of the Ghurids [janangama]
who live nearby enters again and again.

Pushkar's shores used to be warmed by fire from Shiva's third eye
when the eleven Rudras bowed low to bathe in the waters.
Now those shores are warmed by the tears of Brahmins
imprisoned by the Ghurids [matanga].

In the past, heavenly courtesans smiled to themselves
that Shachi had forbidden them from bathing in Pushkar
so that she alone—Indra's beloved—could bathe there.
Now, the menstruating wives of these vile men plunge in.

During the arduous trek across the desert, those evil men
slit their own horses' throats and drank their blood.
Their thirst still not slaked, they now drink
from the waters that only the purest ought to touch.

The seven sages used to prepare rice in milk and sugar
with the milk of the divine wishing cow there.
Now savages [pulinda] snatch fish
and cook them while alive on those pure banks. 1.55

Uttanapada's son used to perform austerities there
and thus became the polestar, known as Dhruva.
Now in Pushkar a special hell has been created by those sinners,
singularly devoted to sin.

A.3. Goddess's Description of Madurai

(Gangadevi's ca. 1380 Madhurāvijaya, *8.1–17)*

[mainly missing] . . . that is called "City of Tigers."[4]

Shesha, lord of snakes, fearful that Vishnu
will awake from his deep meditative sleep at Srirangam,
fans his hood to block the cascades of falling bricks.

Hell! Shiva lost the broad covering of elephant skin
and resorted to crushing forest elephants . . . [5]

I am anguished to see many temples of the various other gods—
their doors eaten away by woodworms,
their halls overgrown with wild weeds,
their inner sanctums in disarray.

Those temples used to resound with unceasing drumming.
Now they echo with the terrifying shrieks of jackals. 8.5

The Kaveri River has transgressed its ancient shores
and flows in all the wrong places.
Now it flows crookedly in imitation of the Sultanate [tulushka].

Before Brahmin villages were scented with thick smoke from sacrifices
and resounded with the chanting of the Vedas.
Now they reek of raw meat
and are pierced by the jeering of drunken Sultanate men [tulushka].

I am anguished to see Madurai's groves
stripped of their lush bunches of coconuts,

enclosed by a line of spears trembling from bearing
a necklace of human skulls.

Madurai's royal highway used to be charming,
filled with the tinkle of anklets of charming women.
Now it is filled with the ear-splitting sounds
of Brahmins being dragged away in chains.

Spiderwebs whose threads stretch in all directions
shroud the carvings that adorn the city's gates.
They have taken the place
of Chinese silk coverings. 8.10

It strikes terror in my heart that royal courts,
which used to be cooled
by sprinkling cool sandalwood water,
are now wet by the tears of Brahmin chain gangs.

The screeching of owls in the old groves
does not grate on me as much as
the chatter of Persian words
from parrots who live in Sultanate [yavana] homes.

The water of the Tamraparni River used to be whitened
by sandalwood paste washed off the breasts of young women.
Now it is reddened by the blood of cows
slain on her banks by evil men.

The earth no longer produces wealth as it used to.
Indra does not make it rain as he once did.
Even Yama drags people away before their time,
if they have not yet been massacred by the Sultanate [yavana].

I am anguished to see the faces of southerners [dramida],
lips withered by heavy sighs,
curly hair droopy and disheveled,
eyes flooded with tears. 8.15

The Veda has sunk.
The rule of law has fled.
All talk of dharma has disappeared.
Good conduct has vanished.
Merit has perished.
Noble birth has ebbed.
What else is there to say?
The Era of Darkness alone flourishes.

Having thus catalogued before the king
the universally-condemned crimes of the Sultanate [yavana],
[the goddess] used her terrifying powers
to conjure up a sword.

A.4. Description of Alauddin Khalji and the 1313 Assault on Shatrunjaya

(Kakka's 1336 Nābhinandanajinoddhāra *3.1–29)*

Then Sultan Alauddin, who pounds land with galloping
horses,
like the ocean does with churning waves, became king.

He went to Devagiri and, having captured its ruler,
reinstalled him there like a victory tower to himself.

Having slain King Hammira, a proud hero and Chauhan ruler,
[Alauddin] gained all of his territory.

Having captured the lord of Chittor Fort and having looted his
wealth,
he sent him wandering about from city to city like a monkey
chained by the neck.

Karna,[6] ruler of Gujarat, was destroyed quickly by his might.
Karna went wandering to foreign lands and then died like a beggar. 3.5

Likewise, the fort-based ruler of Malwa was led out like a slave
over many days and died, sapped of all strength.

[Alauddin], shining with Indra's strength, conquered many kings,
including the rulers of Karnataka, Pandya territories, and Telangana.

He grasped towns such as Siwana and Jalor.
Who can count the many difficult places that he dominated?

He reacted to armies of the Mongol ruler that wandered into his land
such that those armies did not come again.

A servant called Alp Khan, leader of men in the town,
became an object of favor of the suratrana king in that conquest. 3.10

Because of [Alp Khan], enemy women, whose husbands had been sent away,
did not sleep a wink since their eyes were flowing with incessant tears.

Because of him, the wives of kings became slaves,
as if announcing their importance with the noise of their tinkling bracelets.

Samarasimha, son of Sadhu Deshala,[7]
always served him in all kinds of ways.

Also, the king, pleased by his virtues, loved that sadhu as if he were a brother.
Indeed the virtues of men cause their good standing.

Some people, having obtained even a taste of friendship, become intolerable, like dust.
But, even having secured royal favor, [Samarasimha] is cool like the moonstone. 3.15

Having obtained royal favor, he accomplished tasks
also, on behalf of the rulers of the lands, like a rain cloud that has
become saturated.

Like the ocean shines with the moon, Desala gleamed with his son,
who brought joy to people, had righteous conduct, and displayed
virtuous splendor.

For him, who has complete sovereignty like Kubera and is
straight-minded,
how much time can be passed happily?

One time, by the power of the Awful Age for those who live on
earth,
because of the fickleness of existence, because of the errors of good
people,
because of fate, the mleccha army destroyed Rishabha's Temple
at Shatrunjaya, the king of all pilgrimage sites. 3.19–20

Having heard that, which was almost painful to the ears,
the minds of good people were overpowered, as if they did not
remember themselves.

Some, their minds distressed with sorrow, resorted to not
eating.
Others cried without ceasing, their eyes submerged in flowing
tears.

There was no child, no youth, and no elder who was not thus.
Lay Jain men and women were likewise. No one drank water.

Desala too, having heard of this, fell as if struck by a thunderbolt.
Having lost his usual calmness, he said:

> Damn you evil Age of Darkness, the leader of the obstacles to
> dharma,
> destroyer of a pilgrimage site, corrupter of truth, purity, and
> good people. 3.25

The great pilgrimage site of Shatrunjaya, able to deliver people
to the far side of the ocean of existence, was destroyed by you,
vile one!

The Age of Darkness afflicts a man even if he is wise and
contented,
just like a demon afflicts the evil-minded.

The Age of Darkness is a clever corruptor. It throws into
chaos
virtue-filled existence, like a potter who fires pots filled with
water.

Having grieved thus, the sadhu went before Lord Siddhasuri
and reported all the actions done by the mlecchas at the pilgrimage
site.

A.5. Description of Fatehpur Sikri and Mughal-Rajput Relations

(Padmasagara's 1589 Jagadgurukāvya*, vv. 84–96)*

When the king achieved total victory over that land,
he established Fatehpur [*phattepura*], a beautiful name in the
Mughals' language,
just as Krishna established the wonderful city of Dvaraka, full of
large, beautiful buildings.
The establishment of a city in the place of victory is a royal
prerogative.

Victorious Padshah Akbar rules in Fatehpur, the best of cities,
which is
inhabited by the community of traders and shines with houses of
the four classes,
Jain temples, the schools of those engaged in the six philosophies,
and with the best palaces, which are inhabited by Sufis, virtuous
dervishes, and Mughals.

400,000 horses and 10,000 of the best elephants are found there in pairs.
Countless cows, skilled in obtaining the food they desire, play.
There are also camels and herds of buffalos. Many heroic foot soldiers stand at the palace door,
their bodies shining with elegance and reflecting the king's generosity.

Having lifted up a metal chain weighing far more than any ordinary man could lift,[8]
the king whirls it around in the sky with a single hand, as if it were a small bell.
That Glorious Akbar inspires wonder in the heart.
He shows no weakness to any Hindu demon kings [*hindvāsurakṣmāpa*] on earth.

Upon hearing about his strength, some Hindu kings [*hindunṛpa*] think it prudent
to give him their daughters in the hopes that it would protect their kingdoms.
Others give him presents, such as arrangements of moonstones, and fall before his feet.
Others act like his followers. But all are devoted to serving him.

It is said that because of lustrous good fortune he has lovers numbering in the thousands,
the daughters of both Hindus and mlecchas [*hindumlecchasūtāḥ*], who exceed even goddesses in beauty.
The fruits of his pleasures with those women are three sons, shining with virtue.
Even the smallest beings, on account of possessing a son, become lords of the earth.

One time, King Akbar, incomparable ruler of the earth, heard that Glorious Rana Uday Singh,
the King of Mewar, who was revered by all Hindus [*samastahindukalaśa*]
and overconfident in his army, announced with pride:
"My ancestors did not give their daughters to a mleccha, and so neither will I."

Glorious King Akbar, wise in the ways of sovereignty and knowing that
the rana was distinguished, sent his own minister to that king.
Having arrived, the minister spoke well in the rana's assembly with pure speech:

Since good people are never the first to transgress a command or a custom,
you must give your daughter to King Akbar,
just as other Hindus, unasked, gave their daughters to protect their own sovereignty.
The appointed time is now here. Since you are wise, then be sensible!
Otherwise, how will it be clear that you know the proper time?

Still, the rana said:

The family custom protected by my ancestors was that daughters ought not
be given to a mleccha, so I do not transgress that for my own daughter.
Let lands go. Let elephants go. Let my own power be destroyed on the mountain.
Let even my home go. Let only the family custom set by my forefathers remain.

Thus, it is said—
Following the example of virtuous, noble mothers,
brave men who have pure hearts and are devoted to good customs
happily abandon their lives
but never break a promise.[9]

Akbar's minister said, "King Rana! If you do not give your daughter, there will be violence.
I have been told to communicate that you will soon experience this.

Whatever happens, he should order it directly."
Having spoken thus, the chief counselor went before Akbar.

The minister relayed the rana's speech just as it had occurred.
Good people tell the truth, whether desired or not, regarding speech.
Immediately after hearing those words, Akbar departed from Fatehpur,
surrounded by his powerful army, which was intent on breaking down lofty hill forts.

A.6. Theological Discussion Between Hiravijaya and Abul Fazl

(Devavimala's ca. 1590–1610 Hīrasaubhāgya, *13.137–51)*

Abul Fazl said,

O Suri, this was laid out by the ancient prophets in our scriptures—all Muslims [yavana] who are deposited on earth as guests of the god of death will rise at the end of the earth and come before the court of the Supreme Lord called *khudā*, just as they come to the court of an earthly king. He will cast good and bad qualities onto his own pure mind as if onto a mirror and bring about rightful judgment there, having refuted the false construction of mine versus another's.[10] Having reflected, he will bestow the appropriate result of [the yavanas'] virtues and vices, like the fertile soil generates plentiful grain from different seeds. Some will be brought to heaven by him, just as boats are led to the edge of the ocean by a favorable wind. Then they will find joy, nearly overwhelmed with floods of suitable, amazing enjoyments. Others will be sent to hell by him because of sin. Like birds being crushed by hawks and pots being fired by potters, they will suffer great agonies at the mercies of hell's guards.[11] O Suri, what is the validity of this Quranic speech [*kurānavākyaṃ*]? Is it true, like the speech of great-souled people, or is it false like a flower sprouting in the sky?

Having spoken, Abul Fazl fell silent in the hopes of gaining wisdom from Hiravijaya's response. Then, the lord of sages spoke sweetly:

> He—who is free of dirt like a shell, devoid of defects like the sun, made of flames like fire, and without a body like the god of love—is the Supreme Lord. In what form does he attend court like a living being that adopts many appearances in his wanderings through existence? There he sets a person on the path to heaven or hell for what reason? A previous action, once ripened, has the power to grant both joys and sorrows. Thus, let action [karma] alone be recognized as the creator of the world, since otherwise [God] has no purpose.

When Hiravijaya, the lord of ascetics, fell silent after speaking, Shaykh Abul Fazl replied: "So you recognize that book [commentary: Quran] as false just as inconsistency is recognized in the speech of a garrulous, vile person." Lord Hiravijaya spoke again: "If the creator first made this world and then later destroyed it as if he were fire, he would have unparalleled distress. There is no creator or destroyer of the world whose variety is brought into being by its own karma. Therefore, the existence of a creator, like the birth of a son to a barren woman, appears false to me." Having enlightened Shaykh Abul Fazl with correct speech and cured him of his prior false opinion, Hiravijaya planted the dharma of compassion in the Shaykh's mind like a farmer plants a seed in the earth.[12]

A.7. Description of Akbar and Abul Fazl

(Siddhichandra's ca. 1620s Bhānucandragaṇicarita, *1.39–77)*

Description of Akbar

Glorious Shah Akbar ruled the city of Agra with such righteous conduct
that nobody remembered Rama anymore.

Bad people are scorched by the light of his majesty, like locusts singed by the sun's fire.
He skillfully separates them from among the town's elders. 1.40

Even though he is awash with the collyrium-tinted floods of tears
from enemy women,
his fame shines white as the moon. How amazing![13]

Although he is amazingly cool and pure white, the moon of his
fame
inflames the hearts and blackens the face of enemies.

His brilliance emaciates the valor of enemies as if they were mere
weeds.
He scatters broken swords across the battlefield, as if filling a forest
with fallen leaves.

Always the offerings of his dharma, which extends everywhere,
are stretched out with divine charity by the edge of his flags.

Enemy women, their eyes clouded with tears, see his sword in
battle,
upraised like a pillar of smoke arising from the fire of his rising
brilliance.

His fame shone as bright as camphor in the milk ocean,
despite having come up time and again against the black infamy of
his enemies.

Men, their faces darkened by the dust thrown up by his moving army,
quickly conquered the lands of those who could not see, along with
enemies.

Even the underworld of snakes was deafened by the thundering
noises of his marching army.
Therefore, the world cried out to Shesha.

Afraid that his army, kettle drums, and elephants would split apart
the very universe,
how can Brahma restrain the world-elephants that support every
direction? 1.50

Fearful of the ever-rising waves of dust thrown up by his army,
the ocean advances and retreats through the daily tides.

Thinking, "Let him not leave Meru at the mercy of beggars!"
Brahma appointed the sun and moon both as watchmen.

Seeing him rain down streams of gold, a cloud turns dark,
suddenly proud to rain down its own streams.

Like Krishna, [Akbar] protects the six philosophies, animals, and
villages.
That king of the earth radiates on this lovely earth.

The hooves of his galloping cavalry pound the dust of the earth.
They darkened the sky, such that day seemed to become night. 1.55

There is no art, no knowledge, no act of boldness or strength,
that was not attempted by the young shah [*śāhi*].

How did Krishna, afflicted with the burning fire of his brilliance,
lie on the primordial ocean?
Even Shambhu, who resides in the Himalayas, retreated to a lotus.

Even the earth, whose parameters are set,
desires to expand, because of his generosity.

His fame is world-renowned. It is amazing
that he vanquishes all his enemies in battle.[14]

Having seen that king ready to fight, the gods become fearful,
lest he should grasp even heaven. 1.60

Akbar has three sons, called Shaykhu ji, Pahari, and Danyal Shah,[15]
Who are endowed with virtues and known across the three worlds.

He has 270,000 military horses
and 12,000 for his personal use.

He owns 14,000 handsome elephants.
His army is known to be fourfold; his infantry is numbered at 100,000.

Having conquered hostile groups with his own, staff-like arm,
he took Gujarat, an unparalleled land that is like a slice of heaven.

He shone intensely as he was served, like Indra,
by wise men from across the earth who have no equals in intellect. 1.65

Description of Shaykh Abul Fazl
Endowed with eightfold mental qualities[16], devoted to his lord, luminous,
displaying virtuous behavior, devoid of sinful actions,
Shaykh Abul Fazl[17] became Akbar's wise minister,
insightful about the entire range of speech and the best of wise men.

Shaykh Abul Fazl's wisdom extended to all the shastras,
including Jainism, Mimamsa, Buddhism,
Sankhya, Vaisheshika, Charvaka, Jaiminiya,
Sanskrit literature [kavya], yoga, Vedanta,
lexicography, music, drama, aesthetic tropes,
mythology [purana], metrical works, the science of omens,
astrology, mathematics, physiognomy, political science,
erotics, veterinary sciences, and guardianship.
In terms of Sanskrit writing [*vāñmaya*], there is nothing that he has not seen or heard. 1.68–71

Having seen that bull of shaykhs, endowed with all traits, the foremost of which is intellect, the creator doubted whether he was his own creation.

Shesha bore the world on his back and was almost unable to breath.
But the shaykh stood upright, even after placing the world on his heart. Amazing!

Having seen his ocean-like vastness of virtues, the ocean left.
And having seen his mind, the seven sages vanished.

Having heard that his own son, Shah Murad, was overcome by sickness,
the king sent his vizier south. 1.75

When the shah's son [Murad] died, the powerful enemy army rose up
and was broken by Abul Fazl. He protected the Mughal army.

Having heard that news, the king's eyes gleamed with joy,
and he called [Abul Fazl] *Dalathambana*, Pillar of the Army.

A.8. William Hamilton Cures Farrukh Siyar of Hemorrhoids

(Lakshmipati's ca. 1720 Nṛpatinītigarbhitavṛtta, *31–32)*

One time, due to the sin that arose from killing
Muizuddin [*maujadīna*], Farrukh Siyar [*pharkasāha*] was taken very ill
with piles, which torment the bodies of men.
He who had been filled with vigor became devoid of energy.
Overpowered by infirmity, he was unable
to appear in court. Then, in the city,
the people made a mighty uproar about not seeing the king.
Witnessing the people so agitated, Abdulla asked the king:

> Your highness, might it be possible for you to go outside the palace?
> Because men cannot come before you, they are agitated.
> They are wilting like flowers in winter.

Having heard that report from Abdulla,
the king responded correctly and affectionately:

> I have been attacked by piles, a sickness arising from sinful action.

Day after day, I am not able to go out.
I can neither sleep at night nor eat during the day.
I do not have the ability to act, so you should.
Quickly, find the best doctor, whoever he may be, and bring him to me.

Having heard the king's order to seek out a physician,
Abdulla went out from the palace
to seek someone with the unparalleled skill to cure the malady.
A wise, eloquent, well-dressed priest [*udgātṛ*] who knew about Ayurvedic medicine
and was an accomplished physician had come from Europe [*firaṅga*].
Abdulla introduced the doctor to the emperor.

O Lord, on your orders, I went in search of Makara,[18]
and I found this wise man.
Examine him and ask him to treat you as you wish.

Having heard that speech, the king spoke affectionately to the doctor:

If it is possible for you to give the requested cure,
which will eliminate the hemorrhoids and cure my illness,
then I will reward you in a thousand ways.
A king who obtains a good doctor but does not eliminate the disease—
How will he destroy his enemies in battle?
A physician who does not make healthy a king attacked by a fierce illness—
What is to be done with him on earth?

The physician accepted the king's proposal.
Then he approached the king and gave his best response:

My treatment can completely cure your illness, your highness,
but it will certainly render you impotent [*ṣaṇḍatā*].
If, having agreed to impotency, you wish your illness cured,
then let my treatment proceed.

Having heard this speech of Makara, the king replied:

They say that impotency is preferable to death.
And nobody ought to live like this on earth.
Since my death will not come about from this illness,
let me not shy away from what you must do.

Then, on the command of the emperor of all kings,
the doctor cut his piles [*sañchinnaṃ gudakīlakam*] at that time.
After the cutting, the king lived free from pain.

A.9. Tirtha of Mecca

(Lakshmipati's 1721 Ābdullacarita*, 54, vv. 411–27)*

The Sayyid brother Abdulla is speaking to Muhammad Ibrahim, a Mughal prince whom Abdulla wanted to place on the Mughal throne. Ibrahim lost the throne to Muhammad Shah Rangila.

Abdulla said:

If you do not desire victory,
then I ought to go see the long beloved land of Mecca.
Just as Kashi is a special pilgrimage site for Hindus
[*hindūka*],
so too is the pilgrimage destination called Mecca [*makka*] pure
for Muslims [yavana].

Just as Gaya is the best pilgrimage site for Hindus, surely,
the pilgrimage destination of Mecca is likewise for us Muslims,
Lord!

Just as Pushkar is the most distinguished pilgrimage site for
Hindus, always,
so is Mecca for us, Lord!

My compassionate ancestors honored the Lord of the World

and established this special pilgrimage place that can ensure one's liberation,
having given compassionately. Everyone knows this.

Prayag is the king of pilgrimage sites, giving all people release.
Prayag's wife is Kashi, which grants enlightenment.

Kashi also breaks the bonds of sin for all people.
So, you might ask—Why are you asking now about another land?

Having heard that speech, [the prince] replied:
But what about God, who is wise and all-knowing?

Having heard such talk of God, [Abdulla] folded his two hands and then spoke as appropriate to the moment:
O omniscient One, O giver of all blessings, one praised as immortal,
Kashi and so forth are universal pilgrimage sites.
But surely you know that there is one special pure place for Muslims.

Having heard that request, the ruler said:
You should tell me about it with wisdom and compassion.

[Abdulla said:]
There is a place called Mecca [*makka*] in the land of Muslims.
There is a special set of Lord Vishnu's lotus footprints.
Just as Lord Vishnu's lotus footprints are found in Gaya,
so too are Vishnu's pure lotus footprints found in Mecca.
Just as charity, sacrifice, vows, studying the Vedas, asceticism, and recitation
are present in Kashi without ceasing, so too it should be for me.
The truth found in Mecca is not in doubt for Muslims.
Just as dying in Kashi brings about liberation for all social classes [*sarvavarṇa*],

it is likewise for Muslims in Mecca.
Surely a Muslim who remembers Mecca at the time of death,
even not leaving his house, will not despair.
Mecca is to be served by the son of a Muslim who thinks:
"May the most enlightened Muslims not find fault in me."[19]

Glossary

AHIMSA (*ahiṃsā*): Sanskrit [Skt.], nonviolence; a core Jain value.

AMIR (*amīr*): Persian [Pers.], Arabic [Ar.], lit. "lord"; a common title among Muslim nobles; transformed into Sanskrit as "hammira."

ANUPURANA (*anupurāṇa*): Skt., lit. "new purana" or "following purana"; self-description of Paramananda's *Sūryavaṃśa*.

ARHAT: Skt., an enlightened Jain; Jain texts stipulate that there are twenty-four main Arhats, also known as Jinas and Tirthankaras.

ASURA: Skt., lit. "demon"; often applied to enemy kings, regardless of religious identity, in Sanskrit literature.

AVATAR (*avatāra*): Skt., incarnation of a god, most commonly of Vishnu.

BHATTARAKA (*bhaṭṭāraka*): Skt., head of a Digambara order; in premodernity usually a monk and today often a layman.

BHAGAVADGITA (*bhagavadgītā*): Skt., part of the Mahabharata and also circulated as a stand-alone text; sometimes known as the Gita; often considered a key Hindu religious text.

BRAHMIN (*brāhmaṇa*): Skt., uppermost class of the four varnas and the class that supplies priests.

CHAMPU (*campū*): Skt., a literary genre in which texts mix poetry and prose.

CHANDALA (*caṇḍāla*, *cāṇḍāla*): Skt., low caste group; sometimes used to refer to Muslims.

CHARITA (*carita*): Skt., lit. "deed"; category of Sanskrit narrative texts; often the final word in the title of such works.

DHARMA: Skt., a notoriously difficult term to translate that can mean righteous conduct, duty, law, justice, and religion.

DHARMASHALA (*dharmaśāla*): Skt., a physical space that provides for pilgrims; associated with Hinduism and Jainism.

DIGAMBARA: Skt., lit. "sky-clad"; one of the two major branches of Jainism.

DIGVIJAYA: Skt., lit. "conquest of the four directions"; often alleged to have been performed by premodern Indian kings.

DIVAN (*dīvān*): Pers., collection of poetry.

DRAMIDA (*dramiḍa*): Skt., southerner.

DVIJA: Skt., lit. "twice-born"; can refer to Brahmins or to the three upper varnas (Brahmins, Kshatriyas, and Vaishyas) collectively.

DUHSHAMA KALA: (*duḥṣamākāla, dūsamasama*): Prakrit [Prkt.], Skt., in Jain thought, the fifth of six declining eras, and our current age; cognate with the Kali Yuga.

FARMAN (*farmān*): Pers., imperial order.

GADYAKAVYA (*gadyakāvya*): Skt., lit. "prose literature"; prose genre in which only the introductory section is versified.

HAJJ: Ar., pilgrimage to Mecca undertaken by Muslims (in theory, at least once during their lifetime).

HAMMIRA (*hammīra, haṃvīra, hambīra*): Skt., Sanskrit adaptation of the Perso-Arabic term "amir"; used by and for both Hindu and Muslim kings in premodern India.

HINDAVI: Hindi [Hin.], premodern Hindi.

HINDU (*hindu, hindū, hiṃdu*): Ar., Pers., Prkt., Skt., originally an Arabic term, used subsequently in Persian and, several centuries later, in Sanskrit and Prakrit; in premodern usages, it can be a geographical, protoethnic, political, or religious category; accordingly, I translate it, at different points, as "Hindu," "Indian," "Aryan," "Indian kings," and so forth.

HINDUKA (*hinduka, hindūka*): Skt., first used by Jonaraja and Shrivara in their *Rājataraṅgiṇī*s to refer to upper-class Hindus; can also refer to Rajputs, in later Sanskrit texts.

HINDUSTAN (*hindūstān*): Pers., lit. "land of the Indians"; often refers to what we now call northern India.

HINDUTVA: English [Eng.], Hin., a modern political ideology that endorses Hindu supremacy; it projects a connection with Hinduism, but many modern Hindus find this offensive; a synonym is "Hindu nationalism."

ITIHASA (*itihāsa*): Skt., literally "thus it was"; lore.

JANANGAMA (*janaṅgama*): Skt., low caste group; sometimes used to refer to Muslims.

JATI (*jāti*): Skt., caste; overlaps with varna.

JAUHAR: Hin., practice of royal women burning themselves rather than being captured by an enemy; usually associated with Hindus.

JIZYA: Ar., Pers., tax levied on non-Muslims.

KALACHAKRA (*kālacakra*): Skt., a late Vajrayana Buddhist tradition that began in the early eleventh century and survives today in Tibet.

KALI YUGA: Skt., in Hindu thought, the fourth, final, and worst era, and also the one in which we currently live; said to be when dharma is the weakest; cognate with the Duhshama Kala.

KHARATARA GACCHA: Skt., branch of Shvetambara Jainism; their monks enjoyed relations with Delhi Sultanate and Mughal kings.

KARMA: Skt., the results of one's actions, often manifested in a future lifetime.

KAVI: Skt., poet.

KAVYA (*kāvya*): Skt., literature or poetry; sometimes restricted in classical Indian thought to texts written in Sanskrit or Prakrits.

KHUSHFAHM (*khūshfahm*): Pers., lit. "wise man"; title given by Akbar to some Jain Sanskrit intellectuals.

KHUTBA (*khuṭba*), Ar., Pers., Islamic sermon typically given as part of Friday noon prayers; in many premodern Muslim kingdoms, reading the khutba in the name of the reigning king was an affirmation of sovereignty.

KINNARI (*kinnarī*): Skt., a group of celestial musicians.

KIRATA (*kirāta*): Skt., a forest-dwelling people; typically outcastes from the fourfold class system; sometimes listed along with pulinda.

KSHATRIYA (*kṣatriya*): Skt., second of four Hindu classes (varna); considered the ideal class for kings.

KURUKSHETRA (*kurukṣetra*): Skt., location of the great battle in the Mahabharata.

MADRASA: Ar., Pers., school.

MAHABHARATA (*mahābhārata*): Skt., one of the two great Sanskrit epics.

MAHAKAVYA (*mahākāvya*): Skt., great poem.

MAHATMYA (*māhātmya*): Skt., genre of Hindu religious texts.

MASJID (*masjīd*): Pers., mosque.

MASNAVI (*ma̱snavī*): Pers., versified poem.

MATANGA (*mātaṅga*): Skt., low caste group; sometimes used to refer to Muslims.

MATHA (*maṭha*): Skt., Brahmin monastery.

MAUSULA: Skt., adaptation of Perso-Arabic *musulmān* into Sanskrit that meant Muslim; can also refer to an obscure Pashupata sect.

MLECCHA (*mleccha*, *mleñccha*): Skt., barbarian; can refer to Muslims.

MOKSHA (*mokṣa*): Skt., lit. "liberation."

MUDGALA: Skt., adaptation of "Mughal."

MUSALAMANA (*musalamāna*): Skt., adaptation of Perso-Arabic *musalmān* that first appeared in a circa 700 CE Buddhist text.

MUSULA: Skt., synonym of "mausula" (Muslim).

PAIGHAMBAR: Pers., prophet.

PANDIT (*paṇḍita*): Skt., teacher or learned man.

PARAMESHVARA (*parameśvara*): Skt., god or God.

PARASI (*pārasī*): Skt., lit. "Persian"; can refer to either the language or people from Persia.

PARASIKA (*pārasīka*): Skt., lit. "Persian."

PARYUSHAN (*paryuṣaṇ*, *paryuṣaṇa*): Gujarati, Skt., a Shvetambara Jain festival that occurs in late summer.

PATTAVALI (*paṭṭāvalī*): Skt., lit. "lineage"; genre of Sanskrit and Prakrit texts.

PERSIANATE: Eng., indicates things that are part of Persian culture but not necessarily connected, geographically, to Persia.

PRABANDHA: Skt., narratives genre of Sanskrit and Prakrit texts.

PRAKRIT (*prākṛta*): a set of languages related to Sanskrit; some Jain communities preferred to write in a Prakrit as opposed to Sanskrit; in Sanskrit plays, some characters speak Prakrits as a sign of a lower social status.

PULINDA: Skt., an outcaste tribe; sometimes listed along with the kirata; sometimes used as a synonym for "mleccha."

PURANA (*purāṇa*): Skt., a genre of texts that purport to record the ancient past; mythology.

RAHMAN (*raḥmān*): Ar., Pers., God.

RAJA (*rāja*): Skt., king.

RAJATARANGINI (*rājataraṅgiṇī*): Skt., genre or type of Sanskrit historical chronicles produced in Kashmir.

RAJAVALI (*rājāvalī*): Skt., lit. "line of kings"; a type of text found in Sanskrit, Persian, and vernaculars.

RAMA (*rāma*): Pers., hero of the Ramayana; archetype Kshatriya king.

RAMARAJYA (*rāmrājya*): Skt., lit. "Rama's rule"; an ideal political system in traditional Indian thought that is often invoked in political contexts today.

RAMAYANA (*rāmāyaṇa*): Skt., one of the two great Sanskrit epics.

RASA: Skt., aesthetic emotion.

SAIDA: Skt., adaptation of Perso-Arabic "sayyid," meaning a descendent of the Prophet Muhammad; used by Shrivara to refer to the Baihaqi Sayyids in fifteenth-century Kashmir.

SATI: (*satī*): Skt., lit. "virtuous woman"; refers to a woman who self-immolates on her husband's funeral pyre.

SAYYID (*sayyīd*): Ar., Pers., descendent of the Prophet Muhammad; sayyids mentioned in this book include the Baihaqi Sayyids, a group that exercised political power in fifteenth-century Kashmir, and the Sayyid brothers of Baraha, Mughal ministers who became kingmakers in the early eighteenth century.

SHAH (*shāh*): Pers., king; transliterated into Sanskrit as *śāha* and *śāhi*.

SHAKA (*śaka*): Skt., a group of people who originated northwest of the subcontinent; in later centuries, used for Muslims.

SHAKENDRA (*śakendra*): Skt., lit. "lord of Shakas"; used for Delhi Sultanate leaders in some thirteenth- and fourteenth-century inscriptions in northern India.

SHASTRA (*śāstra*): Skt., technical treatise that delineates a domain of knowledge.

SHLESHA (*śleṣa*): Skt., double-entendre; a set of phonemes, verses, or even an entire text that can be read as having two different meanings.

SHVETAMBARA (*śvetāṃbara*): Skt., lit. "white-clad"; one of the two major branches of Jainism.

SPHURAMANA (*phuramāna, phuramāṇa, sphuramāna, sphuranmāna*): Prkt., Skt., lit. "a thing that goes forth"; adaptation of Persian "farman."

SUBA (*ṣūba*): Pers., province; used in Akbar-period literature for divisions of the Mughal Empire; transliterated into Sanskrit as *sūba*.

SUFI (*ṣūfī*): Pers., Muslim ascetic or saint.

SURATRANA (*suratrāṇa, suratāṇa, surattāṇa*): Prkt., Skt., adaptation of Perso-Arabic "sultan"; used for premodern Hindu and Muslim rulers.

SVAMI (*svāmi*): Skt., lit. "lord" or "master."

SYADVADA (*syādvāda*): Skt., the Jain philosophical concept of relativism or many-sidedness.

TAJIKA (*tajika, tājika, tājiya, tāyika*): Skt., adapted from Pahlavi *tāzīg* in the eighth century CE; originally referred to Arabs and later meant Muslims generally; post–eleventh century usages usually refer to a branch of Sanskrit astrology that borrows heavily from Persian and Arabic traditions.

TAMRA (*tāmra*): Skt. and Marathi [Mar.], lit. "reddish"; usually meant "European" but used for "Muslims" in Sanskrit texts patronized by the Bhonsle family.

TAMRANANA (*tāmrānana*): Skt. and Mar., red-faced; same meaning as "tamra."

TAPA GACCHA (*tapāgaccha*): Skt., branch of Shvetambara Jainism; their monks enjoyed relations with Akbar and Jahangir and wrote several narrative accounts about these imperial connections.

TARIKH (*tārīkh*): Pers., genre of history writing.

TIRTHA (*tīrtha*): Skt., pilgrimage destination.

TURUSHKA (*tuluṣka, turukka, turuṣka*): Prkt., Skt., adapted from Altaic *turuk* in the seventh century CE; originally referred to ethnic Turks but soon came to also refer to Muslims generally.

VARNA (*varṇa*): Skt., a class within the fourfold division of society into Brahmins, Kshatriyas, Vaishyas, and Shudras; many premodern Sanskrit thinkers, especially Brahmins, endorsed the varna system as a social ideal, sometimes using the phrase *varṇāśramadharma* (dharma according to class and life stage); it overlaps with "jati."

VAIDESHIKA (*vaideśika*): Skt., outsider; a person from another place.

VIJAYA: Skt., lit. "victory"; category of Sanskrit narrative texts; often the final word in the title of such works.

YAVANA: Skt., originally denoted Greeks and later came to also refer to Muslims.

YAVANARAJYA (*yavanarājya*): Skt., lit. "yavana rule"; an expression used self-referentially by the Vijayanagara ruler Krishna Raya

VEDA: Skt., lit. "knowledge"; can refer to the four Vedas and also to the larger collection of Vedas and associated texts.

Notes

Introduction

1. In 2018, I had armed protection when I lectured in New York (April) and in Delhi (August). In January 2019, following a heckling incident, I had armed security when I spoke in Chennai.
2. Truschke, "Silencing Scholarly Voices."
3. For recent discussions of saffron (Hindu right-wing) rewritings of textbooks in India, see, e.g., Chowdhury, "Inspired by the RSS"; Jain and Lasseter, "Rewriting History"; Shalini Sharma, "How Some Hindu Nationalists are Rewriting Caste History"; Thapar, "They Peddle Myths"; Traub, "India's Dangerous New Curriculum." For a recent discussion of saffron pressure to rewrite textbooks in the United States, see Thaker, "Latest Skirmish in California's Textbooks War."
4. Said, *Orientalism*. For a recent discussion of defining the Self vis-à-vis an Other in premodern India, see Thapar, "Presence of the Other."
5. Cf. Warder, *Introduction to Indian Historiography*, ix; Asthana, *Indian View of History*, iii–iv.
6. Many of the texts I cite here were first printed in the late nineteenth or early twentieth century, and so they have long been available to any professor with access to library-resource sharing. Library-resource sharing, culminating in modern-day interlibrary loan, dates back just over a century (Stabler, "Brief History of Interlibrary Loan," 42–53). The title of this subsection echoes Pollock, "We Need to Find What We Are Not Looking For."
7. On Sanskrit views of the Muslim Other, see, e.g., Avasthy and Ghosh, "References to Muhammadans" (1936) and "References to Muhammadans" (1937); Chattopadhyaya, *Representing the Other?* For an overview of scholarship on "Hindu" history

writing in premodern and colonial India, see Bowles, "Historical Traditions in Hindu Texts."

8. Quoted in Tawney, introduction to *Wishing-Stone of Narratives*, v; for the German original of the letter, see Georg Bühler's 1899 obituary, written by Jolly (*Georg Bühler*, 13–14). Also note: "The recovery of [the *Prithivîrâjavijaya*] is a proof for the assertion which I made in the introduction to the *Vikramânkacharita* that the Hindus did, and do still, possess many historical poems, and that with a little patience they will come out" (Bühler, *Tour in Search of Sanskrit Mss* [1877], 64).
9. Tawney, introduction to *Wishing-Stone of Narratives*, v.
10. E.g., Asthana, *Indian View of History* (on an Indian "approach to historiography" while denying "proper writing of history," 22); Pathak, *Ancient Historians of India* (on four texts, of which the latest is *Pṛthvīrājavijaya*); Raje, *Biography and History* (my favorite chapter title is "India has no Regular History!," 5–10); Warder, *Introduction to Indian Historiography* (including vernacular texts). For a more positive assessment of the field's progress on recognizing Sanskrit histories, see Ali, "Temporality, Narration, and the Problem of History," 237–41.
11. E.g., see citations in Cort, "Genres," 469–70.
12. MacDonell, *History of Sanskrit Literature*, 11.
13. Stein, introduction to *Rājataraṅgiṇī* of Kalhana, 31–32. On al-Biruni's views on Indian history and their influence on later commentators, see Thapar, *Past Before Us*, 16–17.
14. Thapar, *Past Before Us*, 19–24.
15. Quoted by Lohuizen-de Leeuw as "incontestable" ("India and Its Cultural Empire," 35).
16. For 1980s proclamations of India's lack of written history, see Larson, "Karma," 305; de Certeau, *Writing of History*, 4; and Veyne, *Writing History*, 80 (de Certeau and Veyne cited in Pollock, "Pretextures of Time," 365n3; for de Certeau and Veyne, the original publication date was in the 1970s and the translations came out in the 1980s). For 1990s claims, see Asthana, *Indian View of History*, 20–31; Perrett, "History, Time, and Knowledge" (Perrett says there was history in ancient India, but it was not considered important). For a 2003 claim, see Lal, *History of History*, 14–16.
17. "17th World Sanskrit Conference First Circular," 4–5.
18. The 18th World Sanskrit Conference has announced twenty-two sessions, including repeating "History, Art and Architecture, Epigraphy" ("WSC 2021 First Circular," 3).
19. On this, see, e.g., Ali, "Royal Eulogy as World History," 227–29.
20. Wang, "Is There a Chinese Mode of Historical Thinking?," 204.
21. Thapar, "Some Reflections," 185.
22. Inden, "Philological to Dialogical Texts," 4–5.
23. Respectively, Kaul, *Making of Early Kashmir*, 3; Nandy, "History's Forgotten Doubles," 45. Also see Pollock, "Mīmāṃsā and the Problem of History," 604–5.
24. Talbot, *Last Hindu Emperor*, 12; for a similar point, see Chatterjee, "History in the Vernacular," 19.
25. Rao, Shulman, and Subrahmanyam, *Textures of Time*, 253; see pp. 1–11 for the authors' argument that a native reader/listener would recognize alleged changes in texture.

An additional issue is that there were arguably never native speakers, as we understand that category today, of premodern Sanskrit (Pollock, "Pretextures of Time," 376).

26. For criticisms of *Textures of Time*, see Chekuri, "Writing Politics Back Into History"; Mantena, "Question of History"; Pollock, "Pretextures of Time." On, e.g., earlier treatments of the *Rāyavācakamu*, see Wagoner, *Tidings of the King*, 5–6.
27. Pollock, "Pretextures of Time," 381; for a response, see, Rao, Shulman, and Subrahmanyam, "Pragmatic Response," 419.
28. Arondekar and Patel, "Area Impossible," 152.
29. Cf. Sumit Guha's approach of a sustained engagement with Western theory en route to recovering "socially recognized historical memory" in numerous linguistic traditions in South Asia between 1200 and 2000 CE (*History and Collective Memory*, chap. 1).
30. Halbfass, *India and Europe*, 182.
31. Ernst, *Eternal Garden*, 30.
32. Nicholson, *Unifying Hinduism*, 190–96.
33. Marshall Hodgson coined "Islamicate" in his *Venture of Islam*, 1:58–59. On the term's popularity today, consider that a search for "Islamicate" on Google Scholar produced nearly six thousand results in the past ten years (search conducted on October 17, 2019, with date range limited to 2010 and later).
34. On some of the assumptions and limits of "Islamicate," see Ahmed, *What Is Islam?*, 157–75. For an astute criticism of the limits of Ahmed's book, see Zaman, "An Islam of One's Own."
35. Some scholars (e.g., Flatt, *Courts of the Deccan Sultanates*, 17–18) distinguish the "Persianate world" from the "Persianate cosmopolis." It remains unclear to me if the "Persian cosmopolis" and the "Persianate cosmopolis" are supposed to be different from each other in some way. So far as I can tell, "Indo-Persianate" and "Indo-Persian" are complete synonyms (e.g., Arjomand, "A Decade of Persianate Studies," 313, 329, 331). The "Persian(ate) cosmopolis" (or any comparable formulation) has not been theorized in a manner approaching the deftness and sophistication of its model, namely Sheldon Pollock's "Sanskrit cosmopolis."
36. Ali, "Indian Historical Writing," 85–86 (mainly on purana); Fitzgerald, "History and Primordium" (distinguishing purana from itihasa); Pollock, "Mīmāṃsā and the Problem of History" (mainly on itihasa); Thapar, *Past Before Us*, 55–62; Thapar, "Society and Historical Consciousness." For other recent attempts to look to the itihasa-purana tradition to find written Sanskrit histories, see, e.g., Chatterjee, "History in the Vernacular," 1–4 and 12–13; Omvedt, *Buddhism in India*, 165.
37. Patrick Olivelle translates "itihasa" as "lore" in his rendering of Kautilya's *Arthaśāstra* (*King, Governance, and Law*, 70); for an overview of the changing meaning of "itihasa" over time, see Thapar, *Past Before Us*, 56–62. Wendy Doniger notes that puranas consist of myth, ritual, and history (*Hindus*, 701). Many modern thinkers continue to understand "itihasa" as history (e.g., Guha, *History and Collective Memory*, 22).
38. E.g., in the *Rājapraśasti*, Ranachoda Bhatta cites the *Vāyupurāṇa* (*Epigraphia Indica*, 29:9 of appendix); the text's modern editors identify the passage as from the *Ekaliṅgamāhātmya* (*Epigraphia Indica*, 30:92 of appendix).

39. My definition is similar to that offered by many historians: e.g., "The past itself is not a narrative. In its entirety, it is as chaotic, uncoordinated, and complex as life. History is about making sense of that mess, finding or creating patterns and meanings and stories from the maelstrom" (Arnold, *History*, 13); also see the first of five C's explained in Andrews and Burke, "What Does It Mean to Think Historically?"
40. Berkwitz, *Buddhist History*, 26 (italics in original).
41. Hegel quoted in Hayden White, *Content of the Form*, 11–12 (generally); Pollock, "Making History," 574 (on India, specifically on Chaulukyan historiography).
42. On shastra generally, see Pollock, "Idea of Śāstra," 17–26; Pollock, "Playing by the Rules," 301–12; Pollock, "Theory of Practice," 499–519. Others have noted the lack of a Sanskrit shastra on history (e.g., Bowles, "Historical Traditions in Hindu Texts").
43. Hardy, "Drāviḍa Temples," 41–54.
44. Pollock, "Social Aesthetic."
45. Witzel, "Indian Historical Writing," 40 (disrupted); Lal, *History of History*, 58–59 (willful amnesia).
46. Anandavardhana distinguished between invented (*utprekṣita*) and already-known (*vṛtta*) stories, the latter typically from the epics (*Dhvanyāloka*, ed. Durgaprasada and Panshikar, 3.10).
47. Thapar, *Past Before Us*, 6.
48. Nandy, "History's Forgotten Doubles," 47.
49. Pollock, "Making History," 575.
50. Cf. Rao, Shulman, Subrahmanyam, *Textures of Time*, 263.
51. *Poetics* of Aristotle, 28.
52. *Rājataraṅgiṇī* of Shrivara, 1.1.4. My translation of this verse benefited from a Twitter debate that I started in October 2019 about how to best capture it in English.
53. Taylor, *Catalogue Raisonnée*, iv.
54. Hegel, *Philosophy of History*, 162. For other modern attempts to cover this ground, see, e.g., Ali, "Royal Eulogy as World History," 167–68; Mantena, "Question of History," 397–98.
55. See, e.g., Michael Witzel's comments on hyperbole and flattery in "Indian Historical Writing," 5.
56. Hayden White, *Tropics of Discourse*, 99 (italics in original).
57. Dean, "*Metahistory*"; Spiegel, "Above, About and Beyond the Writing of History."
58. Spiegel, "Above, About and Beyond the Writing of History," 494.
59. Hobsbawm, *On History*, 270–77.
60. Chattopadhyaya, *Representing the Other?*, 25.
61. See Pollock, "Pretextures of Time," 376, on "factualizing tropes."
62. On the varying historical accuracy of Indo-Persian chronicles and other issues to consider when reading these materials, see Sunil Kumar, *Emergence of the Delhi Sultanate*, 20–45. As Walter Slaje notes, history writing in Mughal India is widely accepted as such, even though it is sometimes closer to literary fiction ("Guise of Poetry," 208).
63. See Walter Slaje's arguments on this point, specifically concerning Kashmiri sources, in *Medieval Kashmir*, 8–10.

64. The most egregious example is H. M. Elliot and John Dowson's *The History of India, as Told by Its Own Historians.*
65. For discussions of historical consciousness in Sanskrit, or the alleged lack thereof, that focus on Brahmins, see, e.g., Houben, "Brahmin Intellectual"; Mohanty, *Reason and Tradition*, 187–92; Pollock, "Mīmāṃsā and the Problem of History." Brahmin-centric tendencies also come out in other corners of South Asian Studies (see, e.g., Guha's discussion of caste in *Beyond Caste*, 38–41).
66. See, e.g., Ananya Vajpeyi's discussion of the "regressive face of Indology" on ugly display at the 17th World Sanskrit Conference held in 2018 in Vancouver, Canada ("How to Move a Mountain").
67. Novetzke, *Quotidian Revolution*, 25–26.
68. E.g., Kashi Gomez's forthcoming dissertation on female Sanskrit poets, Sarah Pierce Taylor's work on gender and emotion in premodern South India, and Anand Venkatkrishnan's research on Sanskrit and the American caste system.
69. Venkatkrishnan, "Hidden Mūrtis."
70. Mallette, "Sanskrit Snapshots," 133–34.
71. Ajay K. Rao, "Responses to the Conquests of Madurai," 1.
72. Zaman, "Cities"; Zaman, "Nostalgia."
73. Truschke, "Modern Politics in Premodern History"; Truschke, "Hate Male"; Vadukut, "Historian Who Engages."
74. For an analysis of the literary categories through which such poetry was understood, see Ali, "Violence, Gastronomy, and the Meanings of War."
75. Flood, *Objects of Translation*; note Ali Anooshahr's criticism of Flood in "Elephant and the Sovereign," 618.
76. E.g., Ernst, *Eternal Garden*, 22–24.
77. Eaton, *India in the Persianate Age*, 10–18.
78. Hobsbawm, *On History*, 7.
79. I borrow some language here from Hobsbawm, *On History*, 6.
80. Orsini, "How to Do Multilingual Literary History?," 243.
81. Richard Davis cautions, correctly in my view, against easily taking literary boasts as accurate representations of political reality in premodern Sanskrit works (*Lives of Indian Images*, 120–21, speaking of the *Madhurāvijaya*).

1. Before Indo-Persian Rule

1. Patel, "Mosque in South Asia," 3–6.
2. Eaton, "Temple Desecration in Pre-modern India," 63.
3. Maclean, *Religion and Society in Arab Sind.*
4. See, e.g., the discussion later in this chapter of Madhumati, who served the Rashtrakutas and is mentioned in the 926 Chinchani Rashtrakuta grant (*Epigraphia Indica*, 32:45–55).

5. (1) The 736 Kavi plate (Mirashi, *Inscriptions of the Kalachuri-Chedi Era*, 1:96–102); the contents are largely repeated in the 736 Prince of Wales plate, which also adds new descriptions of a few kings (Mirashi, *Inscriptions of the Kalachuri-Chedi Era*, 1:103–9). I do not list the 736 Prince of Wales plate separately because it does not offer new mentions of Muslim political figures beyond what is found in the 736 Kavi plate. (2) The 738 Navsari plate (Mirashi, *Inscriptions of the Kalachuri-Chedi Era*, 1:137–45); some read the plate's date as 739 (Mirashi, *Inscriptions of the Kalachuri-Chedi Era*, 1:139 and 1:139n2). (3) The ca. 750–800 fragmentary Hund inscription (*Epigraphia Indica*, 38:94–98; Prinsep, "Facsimiles of Ancient Inscriptions," 877–79). (4) The 795 Pratihara Vatsaraja inscription (*Epigraphia Indica*, 41:49–57). (5) The ca. 800s–early 900s Gwalior inscription of the Pratihara ruler Bhoja (*Epigraphia Indica*, 18:99–114). (6) The 926 Chinchani Rashtrakuta grant (*Epigraphia Indica*, 32:45–55). (7) The mid-900s Chinchani plate of the Rashtrakuta ruler Krishna II (*Epigraphia Indica*, 32:55–60).
6. The 738 Navsari plate and the 926 Chinchani Rashtrakuta grant contain slightly more detailed information about Muslims.
7. Of the seven inscriptions, two are from northwestern India, one is from Gujarat (near the coast), and two are from Thane district, in Maharashtra. The exception is one inscription found near Gwalior. The 736 Prince of Wales plate, which repeats the 736 Kavi plate, and the 738 Navsari plate are of unknown origin.
8. The royal subject of the ca. 750–800 fragmentary Hund inscription is unclear (Prinsep, "Facsimiles of Ancient Inscriptions," 878–79). K. V. Ramesh names the ruler as Anantadeva (*Epigraphia Indica*, 38:95), but the inscription is in Sharada script, which suggests an origin in or around Kashmir. Also note James Prinsep, who published about this inscription in the first half of the nineteenth century, read *udriktaturuṣka* (rising Turks) as modified by "flesh-eating" (from *puṣkalapala*) ("Facsimiles of Ancient Inscriptions," 878–79). Rama Shankar Avasthy and Amalananda Ghosh reexamined the original inscription and found this reading incorrect ("References to Muhammadans" [1937], 24n1).
9. The term "tajika" appears in two, nearly contemporary plates: the 736 Kavi plate, from Bharuch, and the 738 Navsari plate. On the Kavi plate, see Mirashi, *Inscriptions of the Kalachuri-Chedi Era*, 1:99, v. 2, and repeated in the 736 Prince of Wales plate (1:106, v. 2). Chattopadhyaya concurs on this being the earliest usage of "tajika," in *Representing the Other?*, 32. On the Navsari plate, see Mirashi, *Inscriptions of the Kalachuri-Chedi Era*, 1:141, line 33. The earliest use of "turushka" is probably Bana's *Harṣacarita*, ca. seventh century (Chattopadhyaya, *Representing the Other?*, 40; Prasad, "*Turuska* or Turks," 172); the first known appearance of "turushka" in an inscription is ca. 750–800 CE (*Epigraphia Indica*, 38:94–98).
10. "Tajika" was adapted from western Asia, although precisely how has been the subject of some debate (Chattopadhyaya, *Representing the Other?*, 32–33; Pingree, "Sanskrit Evidence for the Presence of Arabs," 172; Sundermann, "Name of the Tajiks").
11. Peter Jackson, "Turkish Slaves on Islam's Indian Frontier," 70–73.
12. In Persian, too, "Turk" was sometimes used as a "general ethnicon" that could include non-Turks (e.g., by Minhaj Siraj Juzjani in the thirteenth century, cited in Jackson, *Delhi Sultanate*, appendix 1).

13. The ca. 750–800 fragmentary Hund inscription (Prinsep, "Facsimiles of Ancient Inscriptions," 878; *Epigraphia Indica*, 38:97) and the ca. 800s–early 900s Gwalior inscription of the Pratihara ruler Bhoja (*Epigraphia Indica*, 18:108, v. 11) refer to "the Turks" (*turuṣka*). The 736 Kavi plate (Mirashi, *Inscriptions of the Kalachuri-Chedi Era*, 1:99) and the ca. mid-900s Chinchani plate of the Rashtrakuta ruler Krishna II (*Epigraphia Indica*, 32:59) refer to "the Tajikas" (*tājjika* or *tajjika*) (also see the 736 Prince of Wales plate, which repeats the verse including "tajika" from the 736 Kavi plate; cited in Mirashi, *Inscriptions of the Kalachuri-Chedi Era*, 1:106). The 738 Navsari plate refers to "the tajika army" (*tājikānīka*) (Mirashi, *Inscriptions of the Kalachuri-Chedi Era*, 1:141, line 33).
14. Wink, *Al-Hind*, 2:112, citing Bosworth on the ethnic-heterogeneity point.
15. Brajadulal Chattopadhyaya says that inscriptional references to tajikas cease after the tenth century, although he cites a use of *tājiya* from the mid-eleventh century (*Representing the Other?*, 39 and 37, respectively).
16. Pingree, *Jyotiḥśāstra*, 97–100. Also note the use of "tajika" as the name of a horse in the late fifteenth-century *Rājataraṅgiṇī* of Shrivara (Singh ed., 1.6.6).
17. For some examples, see Prasad, "*Turuska* or Turks," 171–73, and Chattopadhyaya, *Representing the Other?*, 40–43.
18. *Amarakoṣa* 2.6.128. Several puranas talk about turushkas, but these are hard to date precisely (Prasad, "*Turuska* or Turks," 171).
19. *Epigraphia Indica*, 18:108, v. 11.
20. *Epigraphia Indica*, 41:56, v. 9.
21. *Epigraphia Indica*, 32:59; see p. 58 for guesses on the identities of the dynasties and areas mentioned in this passage.
22. *Epigraphia Indica*, 32:52, v. 16.
23. Mirashi, *Inscriptions of the Kalachuri-Chedi Era*, 1:99, v. 2 (repeated in 736 Prince of Wales plate on 1:106, v. 2).
24. Mirashi, *Inscriptions of the Kalachuri-Chedi Era*, 1:140–41 (with correction on 1:140n17).
25. Mirashi, *Inscriptions of the Kalachuri-Chedi Era*, 1:141.
26. *anivarttakanivarttayitṛ* (Mirashi, *Inscriptions of the Kalachuri-Chedi Era*, 1:141, lines 34–35). The epithet comes at the end of a lengthy section about Pulakeshiraja opposing the tajika army.
27. I am grateful to Daud Ali for this point regarding the 738 Navsari plate in particular.
28. *Epigraphia Indica*, 32:52; on the reconstruction of the names, see Pingree, "Sanskrit Evidence for the Presence of Arabs," 176.
29. *Epigraphia Indica*, 32:45–55. Also see Chakravarti, "Monarchs, Merchants, and a Maṭha," 263–70.
30. In addition to the examples given in this paragraph, note the following examples. The ca. 800s–early 900s Gwalior inscription of the Pratihara ruler Bhoja, which refers to "Turks" (*turuṣka*) in v. 11, mentions an undefined *mlecchādipa* in v. 4 (*Epigraphia Indica*, 18:107). The ca. ninth-century Khalimpur plate of Dharmapala refers to a yavana (*Epigraphia Indica*, 4:243–54). Some scholars think that this could be a Muslim ruler (Chattopadhyaya, *Representing the Other?*, 42); others postulate that it refers to a foreign (non-Muslim) ruler in Central India (cited in Avasthy and Ghosh, "References to

Muhammadans" [1936], 164). An eleventh-century Chola inscription on Persian (*pārasī*) women singing praises presumably refers to Muslims, given the spread of Islam to Persia, but this is not entirely clear (*Epigraphia Indica*, 5:103–4; Chattopadhyaya, *Representing the Other?*, 32).

31. Avasthy and Ghosh, "References to Muhammadans" (1936), 164–65.
32. *Epigraphia Indica*, 32:59, v. 11.
33. The ca. 800–1000 CE *Devalasmṛti* refers to Muslims as *caṇḍāla* (Maclean, *Religion and Society in Arab Sind*, 78–80); see my discussion of the *Pṛthvīrājavijaya* in chapter 2.
34. Van der Kuijp, "Earliest Indian Reference to Muslims," 171. This supersedes the earlier view that the first use of "musalamana" in Sanskrit was from 1264 (Chattopadhyaya, *Representing the Other?*, 29).
35. The earliest mosques on the subcontinent are in Sindh, and there is physical evidence of a mosque in Gwalior by the late eighth century (Patel, "Mosque in South Asia," 8 [on Sindh] and 12 [on Gwalior]).
36. Flood, *Objects of Translation*, 279n190.
37. For an overview, see Avasthy and Ghosh, "References to Muhammadans" (1936), 166–75; Chattopadhyaya, *Representing the Other?*, 93–95.
38. On the 1059 plate: Moraes, *Kadamba Kula*, 394–400; on the family being involved in governance: Moraes, *Kadamba Kula*, 172. Also see Chattopadhyaya, *Representing the Other?*, 37.
39. Moraes, *Kadamba Kula*, 396.
40. For *hammīra*, see, e.g., the 1109 Etawah inscription of Madanapala and Govindrachandradeva (Kielhorn, "Copper-Plate Grants," 16); the 1167 Hansi inscription of the Chauhan ruler Prithviraj II (Bhandarkar, "Some Unpublished Inscriptions," 19, v. 4); the 1197 Machhlishahr Gahadavala plate (Prasad, *Sanskrit Inscriptions of Delhi Sultanate*, 58–70). For *haṃvīra*, see, e.g., the ca. early twelfth-century Mahoba Chandella inscription (*Epigraphia Indica*, 1:221, v. 17). For *hambīra*, see, e.g., the 1175 Benares plate of Jayachandra (Kielhorn, "Copper-Plate Grants," 130).
41. Avasthy and Ghosh, "References to Muhammadans" (1936), 170–71; Sten Konow in *Epigraphia Indica*, 9:321; D. R. Bhandarkar, "Slow Progress of Islam Power," 138–39. For a counterview, see Hirananda Sastri in *Epigraphia Indica* 13:296.
42. Flood, *Objects of Translation*, 114.
43. 1167 Jabalpur plate of the Kalachuri ruler Jayasimha (Mirashi, *Inscriptions of the Kalachuri-Chedi Era*, 1:328, v. 17); repeated in 1180–81 Kumbhi plates and 1193 Umariya plates (respectively, Mirashi, *Inscriptions of the Kalachuri-Chedi Era*, 2:649, v. 23; *Epigraphia Indica*, 41:45, v. 27). I read the verse as follows: *naṣṭaṃ gūrjjarabhujā bhujabalaṃ muktaṃ turuṣkena ca tyaktaḥ kuntalanāyakena sahasā kandarpakelikramaḥ / śrutvā śrijayasiṃhadevanṛpate rājyābhiṣekaṃ nṛpāḥ santrāsādapare 'pyapāsya jagatīṃ pāre yayur vāridheḥ.*
44. E.g., the early twelfth-century Nagpur inscription of the rulers of Malwa (*Epigraphia Indica*, 2:188 and 194, v. 54); the ca. twelfth-century fragmentary Jhansi inscription of Sallakshanasimha (*Epigraphia Indica*, 1:217, line 30).
45. Eaton, *India in the Persianate Age*, 21.

46. *Raghuvaṃśa* 4.67 and Avasthy and Ghosh, "References to Muhammadans" (1936), 168–69, citing D. R. Bhandarkar. In addition to sharing imagery, both sources use the phrase *kuṅkumakesara*.
47. On the completion dates of the *Kālacakratantra* and the *Vimalaprabhā*, see Newman, "Islam in the Kālacakra Tantra," 316. For an account of the major Kalachakra texts and translations, see Hammar, *Studies in the Kālacakra Tantra*, 68–73; John Newman lists the texts that refer to Islam ("Islam in the Kālacakra Tantra," 313).
48. E.g., Berzin, "Buddhist View of Islam"; Elverskog, *Buddhism and Islam*, 97–103; Hoffman, "Kālacakra Studies"; Newman, "Islam in the Kālacakra Tantra." More generally on the Kalachakra texts, see Hammar, *Studies in the Kālacakra Tantra*.
49. E.g., Brajadulal Chattopadhyaya does not mention the Kalachakra tradition in *Representing the Other?*
50. *iha mlecchadharme vedadharme 'pi devatāpitrartharṃ prāṇātipātaḥ kartavyaḥ kṣatradharme 'pi ca tarpayitvā pitṝn devān khādan māṃsaṃ na doṣabhāg iti brahmarṣivacanāt. tathā doṣaṃ tatra na paśyāmi yo duṣṭe duṣṭam ācared iti. evaṃ vedadharmaṃ pramāṇīkṛtya mlecchadharmaparigrahaṃ kariṣyanti* (quoted in Newman, "Islam in the Kālacakra Tantra," 347; I make some small corrections).
51. Noted in Newman, "Islam in the Kālacakra Tantra," 334 (quote 1). *Pañcatantra* 5.80 (I consulted the Romanized text on GRETIL) and *Garuḍapurāṇa* 1.115.47 (quote 2). Quote 2 also appears in other story collections (Schmidt-Madsen, "Repossessing the Past," 78–79).
52. *tena kāraṇenānāgate 'dhvani mlecchadharmāpraveśāya yuṣmadbhyo mayā niyamo dattaḥ. tasmād bhavadbhir mamājñā kartavyeti* (quoted in Newman, "Islam in the Kālacakra Tantra," 347).
53. Elverskog, *Buddhism and Islam*, 97.
54. Newman, "Islam in the Kālacakra Tantra," 328–29.
55. Elverskog, *Buddhism and Islam*, 97–98.
56. In this paragraph, I draw on Newman, "Islam in the Kālacakra Tantra."
57. The Kalachakra texts also call Muslims *tāyin*, an ethnonym akin to "tajika" (Newman, "Islam in the Kālacakra Tantra," 318).
58. Newman, "Islam in the Kālacakra Tantra," 317n11.
59. Newman, "Islam in the Kālacakra Tantra," 327.
60. Newman, "Islam in the Kālacakra Tantra," 327 and 327n30.
61. Newman, "Islam in the Kālacakra Tantra," 327–28.
62. Quoted, along with *Vimalaprabhā* commentary, in Newman, "Islam in the Kālacakra Tantra," 348 and 352; the author notes this error on p. 323. Also see Elverskog, *Buddhism and Islam*, 100.
63. The eight prophets listed are Adam, Noah, Ibrahim, Moses, Jesus, the White-Clad, Muhammad, and the Mahdi (*Critical Edition of the Śrī Kālacakratantra-Rāja*, 39, v. 153). For translations and comparison with the Tibetan version of the *Kālacakratantra*, see Hoffman, "Kālacakra Studies," 56–57; Newman, "Islam in the Kālacakra Tantra," 320 and 351–52. For theories on the origins of this list, see Elverskog, *Buddhism and Islam*, 98; Newman, "Islam in the Kālacakra Tantra," 321–23.

64. Elverskog, *Buddhism and Islam*, 99–100.
65. Newman, "Islam in the Kālacakra Tantra," 326.
66. Elverskog, *Buddhism and Islam*, 2.
67. Truschke, "Power of the Islamic Sword."
68. Thapar, *Somanatha*, 78–88.
69. Eaton, *India in the Persianate Age*, 19–21 and 23–29.
70. Eaton, *India in the Persianate Age*, 22.
71. Based on earlier works, Dhanapala was around seventy to seventy-five years old in 1025 (Andrew Ollett, private communication, and http://www.prakrit.info/blog/dhanapalas-satyapuriya-srimahavira-utsahaḥ/). I thank Ollett for bringing the "Saccaüriviīraucchāhu" to my attention. On the definition of Apabhramsha as "largely continuous with Prakrit," see Ollett, *Language of the Snakes*, 16.
72. *Satyapurīya-śrīmahāvīra-utsāhaḥ* vv. 3–4; translation lightly adapted from Andrew Ollett's translation in http://www.prakrit.info/blog/dhanapalas-satyapuriya-srimahavira-utsahaḥ/.
73. Maclean, *Religion and Society in Arab Sind*, 78–82.
74. John Newman cites Wilhelm Halbfass, Carl Ernst, and Sheldon Pollock on this point ("Islam in the Kālacakra Tantra," 312).
75. Hammar, *Studies in the Kālacakra Tantra*, 25; Newman, "Brief History of the Kalachakra," 76.
76. On silences at different moments in the production of history, see Trouillot, *Silencing the Past*, 51–66.
77. The 736 Kavi plate was found in a rubbish heap several hundred years ago and subsequently held by Kapila Brahmins (Mirashi, *Inscriptions of the Kalachuri-Chedi Era*, 1:96); the 926 Chinchani Rashtrakuta grant was found by a farmer plowing his field in 1955 (*Epigraphia Indica*, 32:45).
78. The ca. 750–800 fragmentary inscription found in Hund, near Attock (*Epigraphia Indica*, 38:94).

2. Difference That Mattered

1. For an overview of the Ghurids, see Bosworth, "Ghurids." For overviews of Ghurid raids from the 1170s through the 1190s, see Asher and Talbot, *India Before Europe*, 25–27; Eaton, *India in the Persianate Age*, 39–41; Peter Jackson, *Delhi Sultanate*, 7–12; Sunil Kumar, *Emergence of the Delhi Sultanate*, 51–52. Sunil Kumar mentions that Delhi was annexed later in 1192 (*Emergence of the Delhi Sultanate*, 110).
2. See, e.g., the three inscriptions mentioned in Avasthy and Ghosh, "References to Muhammadans" (1936), 172–73.
3. *Epigraphia Indica*, 1:26, v. 15; also quoted in Avasthy and Ghosh, "References to Muhammadans" (1936), 172. Rama Shankar Avasthy and Amalananda Ghosh identify this battle as Shihabuddin Muhammad Ghori's 1178 attack on Bhimadeva ("References to Muhammadans" [1936], 173), but Georg Bühler disagrees (*Epigraphia*

Indica, 1:22–23). See later in this chapter for a discussion of "turushka" as meaning "Ghurid" (*mlecchādhināthа* is used as a synonym two verses later in the same inscription, *Epigraphia Indica*, 1:27, v. 17).

4. *dalitadharaṇicakraṃ vīrahammīracakraṃ* (Avasthy and Ghosh, "References to Muhammadans" [1936], 173).
5. See, e.g., Aziz Ahmad's idea of a "Muslim epic of conquest" versus a "Hindu epic of resistance" ("Epic and Counter-Epic," 470–76). As Ajay Rao notes, Ahmad's article, published in 1963, "continues to haunt scholarly discussions of representations of Indo-Islamic conquests" ("Responses to the Conquests of Madurai," 1).
6. Eaton, *India in the Persianate Age*, 39.
7. Sanskrit poets often ended their works before the major central event, and so there is no reason why Jayanaka might not have done the same. One example is Kalidasa's *Kumārasambhava*, which ends before Kumara's birth.
8. If this is not the story about Prithviraj that you know, then you are not alone. The two major Persian-language histories usually relied upon for the 1192 battle of Tarain, Tajuddin Hasan Nizami's *Tāj al-Maʾāsir* (ca. 1217) and Minhaj Siraj Juzjani's *Ṭabaqāt-i Nāṣirī* (1259/1260), offer different accounts of Prithviraj's fate (Talbot, *Last Hindu Emperor*, 43–50). The *Ṭabaqāt-i Nāṣirī* says that Prithviraj fled during the 1192 battle, was captured, and then was executed. Here I follow the earlier source, the *Tāj al-Maʾāsir*, which says Prithviraj survived and became a short-lived vassal of the Ghurids before being replaced by his son. Coins bearing the names of both Muhammad Ghori and Prithviraj constitute further evidence for this vassal story line (Singh, "Coins Bearing the Names of Muhammad Bin Sam and Prithviraja III"). Both Persian and Sanskrit sources record Hariraja's role (Talbot, *Last Hindu Emperor*, 45n60). Works from other traditions offer further variations of Prithviraj's tale. For example, Merutunga's 1305 *Prabandhacintāmaṇi* (Wishing-stone of narratives) says that Muhammad Ghori planned to reinstate Prithviraj but then had him beheaded instead (Dasharatha Sharma, *Early Chauhān Dynasties*, 87; also see chapter 4).
9. E.g., Chattopadhyaya, *Representing the Other?*, 44; Lienhard, *History of Classical Poetry*, 219; Ojha, introduction to *Pṛthvīrājavijaya*, 3; Pathak, *Ancient Historians of India*, 98; Pollock, "Rāmāyaṇa and Political Imagination," 274; Prabha, *Historical Mahākāvyas in Sanskrit*, 146–47; Talbot, *Last Hindu Emperor*, 37. Note that many of these scholars give the date range 1191–1193, which is based, I believe, on a slight miscalculation of the date of the second Ghurid-Chauhan battle at Tarain. Har Bilas Sarda suggests a wider range, of 1178–1200 ("Prithviraja Vijaya," 261).
10. A Chauhan ruled Ajmer at least until 1194/1195; for a discussion of the Ghurid practice of relying upon Hindu vassal rulers, especially in the 1190s, see Flood, *Objects of Translation*, 111–12.
11. Siddiqui, *Indo-Persian Historiography*, 42–43; Talbot, *Last Hindu Emperor*, 44.
12. *Pṛthvīrājavijaya* 1.30 and 1.32, respectively.
13. *Pṛthvīrājavijaya* 1.31.
14. Bronner, "Poetics of Ambivalence," 458; Pollock, "Sanskrit Literary Culture from the Inside Out," 104.
15. *Pṛthvīrājavijaya* 1.34.

16. The *Harivijaya*, a fourth-century Prakrit *mahākāvya*, is lost. On the *Haravijaya*, see Smith, *Ratnākara's Haravijaya*. For other vijaya works that might be viewed as predecessors to Jayanaka's poem, see Pathak, *Ancient Historians of India*, 102.
17. For a brief history of the genre of "patron-sponsored court epics," see McCrea, "Poetry Beyond Good and Evil," 503–5; see the rest of the article for an analysis of the *Vikramāṅkadevacarita*.
18. Bronner, "Poetics of Ambivalence," 458; McCrea, "Poetry Beyond Good and Evil," 505.
19. Several scholars have noted similarities between the *Vikramāṅkadevacarita* and the *Pṛthvīrājavijaya*; e.g., Lienhard, *History of Classical Poetry*, 219; Sarda, "Prithviraja Vijaya," 260. Vishwambhar Sharan Pathak sees allusions to Bana's *Kādambarī*, Bharavi's *Kirātārjunīya*, and Kalidasa's *Raghuvaṃśa* (*Ancient Historians of India*, 98–99).
20. Jonaraja also wrote commentaries on two works with mythological themes: Bharavi's *Kirātārjunīya* and Mankha's *Śrīkaṇṭhacarita* (Obrock, "Translation and History," 76–80).
21. Thapar, "Presence of the Other."
22. Flood, *Objects of Translation*, 96–98.
23. Alka Patel gives examples of mosques in India dating back to the eighth century CE ("Mosque in South Asia," 6–14).
24. Flood, *Objects of Translation*, 139–41.
25. Patel, "Expanding the Ghurid Architectural Corpus," 51.
26. Patel, "Expanding the Ghurid Architectural Corpus," 41–42.
27. Ilyse R. Morgenstein Fuerst discusses the significant variations in the tales of how, when, and why Muinuddin Chishti came to Ajmer ("Space, Power, and Stories," 56–60); for an overview of historical sources on Muinuddin Chishti, see Currie, *Shrine and Cult*, 20–65. In the early thirteenth century, Muinuddin Chishti was buried in Ajmer; today, his tomb draws as many visitors on Muinuddin Chishti's death anniversary as the annual hajj to Mecca (Morgenstein Fuerst, "Space, Power, and Stories," 56n3).
28. On Pushkar's association with Brahma, see Zeitlyn, "Construction and Reconstruction of Pushkar." On the association of Brahma and Pushkar from the seventeenth century until the present, see Thomases, "Making Pushkar Paradise," 116–57. The association of Prithviraj with Delhi is a later development, which reflects the centrality of Delhi as the seat of political power in northern India from Delhi Sultanate–rule onward. On this, see Talbot, *Last Hindu Emperor*, chap. 3.
29. *Pṛthvīrājavijaya* 1.40.
30. *Pṛthvīrājavijaya* 1.44 and 1.46.
31. *Pṛthvīrājavijaya* 1.49. Also see verses 1.45 and 1.48, where Jayanaka criticizes the Buddha avatar.
32. *Pṛthvīrājavijaya* 1.50.
33. *Pṛthvīrājavijaya* 1.50.
34. *Pṛthvīrājavijaya* 1.51.
35. *Pṛthvīrājavijaya* 1.52.
36. *Pṛthvīrājavijaya* 1.53.
37. *Pṛthvīrājavijaya* 1.56, plus commentary.
38. *Pṛthvīrājavijaya* 1.57.

39. *Pṛthvīrājavijaya* 1.60.
40. *Pṛthvīrājavijaya* 1.61 (Kubera).
41. Especially *Pṛthvīrājavijaya* 1.64–72.
42. *Pṛthvīrājavijaya* 8.31, plus commentary. I think that Jonaraja is faithful to Jayanaka's meaning here.
43. *Pṛthvīrājavijaya* 8.9.
44. Respectively, *Pṛthvīrājavijaya* 8.1 and 8.11.
45. The relationship between Brahmins and Kshatriyas has occupied undue attention among Indologists, especially among an earlier generation; for a brief, recent take on some of this literature, see Upinder Singh, *Political Violence in Ancient India*, 12–13.
46. Respectively, see Bühler, "Origin of the Town of Ajmer," 52–53, and *Pṛthvīrājavijaya* 10.38 (translated in Pollock, "Rāmāyaṇa and Political Imagination," 276).
47. Flood, *Objects of Translation*, 139–41.
48. Eliade, *Sacred and the Profane*, chap. 1. I am grateful to Sudipta Kaviraj for this point and several others in this paragraph.
49. *Hammīramahākāvya* 1:14–17 (all citations in the book refer to both Kirtane and Jinavijaya editions unless otherwise specified); Kirtane, introduction to *Hammīramahākāvya*, 11–12; Sreenivasan, "Alauddin Khalji Remembered," 276. Sushila Zeitlyn notes a story that Brahma created the Chauhan lineage when he performed a sacrifice at Pushkar, but she gives neither a source nor a date for the tale ("Construction and Reconstruction of Pushkar," 47–48).
50. Pathak, *Ancient Historians of India*, 130–36; Pollock, "Rāmāyaṇa and Political Imagination," 274–77; Talbot, *Last Hindu Emperor*, 41–42. For a critical take on this argument, see Chattopadhyaya, *Representing the Other?*, 100–15.
51. See numerous examples cited in Granoff, "Holy Warriors," 291–95. For examples where the political enemy appears to be Muslim, see an Ajaygadh rock inscription (*Epigraphia Indica*, 1:327, v. 7) and a 1285 inscription at Mount Abu (Avasthy and Ghosh, "References to Muhammadans" [1936], 182).
52. The Pulindas were a tribe, often listed along with the *śabara* and *kirāta*. The meaning of "pulinda" as a synonym for "mleccha" was well established by this point in time. See, e.g., the sixth–eighth century CE *Amarakośa* (published as *Nāmaliṅgānuśāsana* of Amarasimha, 161, v. 21) and the eighth/ninth-century CE Vishvarupa commentary on *Yājñavalkyasmṛti* (Kane, *History of Dharmasastra*, 256).
53. Jonaraja also occasionally uses other common Sanskrit terms for Muslims, such as "yavana" (e.g., commentary on *Pṛthvīrājavijaya* 6.7). Luther Obrock argues for a fine distinction between Jonaraja's uses of "yavana" and "mleccha" ("Translation and History," 81–82; Cf. Ogura, "Incompatible Outsiders," 185–87); I find Obrock's argument untenable, given the multiple uses of "yavana" in critical statements in Jonaraja's *Rājataraṅgiṇī* (e.g., vv. 571, 575, 721, 745, and 834). Jonaraja's use of "yavana" to gloss verse 6.7 of the *Pṛthvīrājavijaya* (*yavanocitaṃ pretasaṃskāraṃ*) also echoes his own usage of *yavanapretasaṃskārān* (*Rājataraṅgiṇī* of Jonaraja, v. 476).
54. E.g., on Mahmud of Ghazni's incursions: *Rājataraṅgiṇī* of Kalhana, 7.51, 7.56, and 7.70 (turushka), 7.63 (chandala), and 7.53, 7.64 (hammira). For an example of "mleccha," see 8.2843.

55. *Pṛthvīrājavijaya* 10.37.
56. E.g., Sunil Kumar, *Emergence of the Delhi Sultanate*, 46–128.
57. Many have written on the term "mleccha," including Chattopadhyaya, *Representing the Other?*, chaps. 2 and 4; Halbfass, *India and Europe*, 175–89; Thapar, "Image of the Barbarian." Perhaps the most extensive study is Parasher, *Mlecchas in Early India*.
58. *Vaiṣṇavadharmaśāstra*, 444, 84.4 (my translation; for Olivelle's translation, see p. 146). I first found reference to this text in Upinder Singh, *Political Violence in Ancient India*, 377. On the date of the *Vaiṣṇavadharmaśāstra*, see Olivelle's introduction, 13–15.
59. *Pṛthvīrājavijaya* 1.54.
60. I am grateful to Finbarr Barry Flood for this point.
61. *Pṛthvīrājavijaya* 1.55.
62. *Pṛthvīrājavijaya* 10.38.
63. Sanderson, "Meaning in Tantric Ritual," 81–87; David Gordon White, "Tantra in Practice," 16.
64. *Pṛthvīrājavijaya* 6.6; this part of the verse does not survive, but the commentary attests to the idea (p. 149).
65. *Pṛthvīrājavijaya* 6.13.
66. This episode is narrated in *Pṛthvīrājavijaya* 6.1–27. In other Sanskrit texts that discuss battles with Muslim foes, enemy blood is said to soothe the earth's pain (e.g., *Madhurāvijaya* 8.33, speaking of an impending confrontation with the Sultanate of Madurai in the fourteenth century). All citations are to the Thiruvenkatachari edition of the *Madhurāvijaya* unless otherwise noted.
67. *Pṛthvīrājavijaya* 10.40.
68. D. N. Jha, *Myth of the Holy Cow*, 113.
69. D. N. Jha, *Myth of the Holy Cow*, 114–15.
70. *Pṛthvīrājavijaya* 10.39–40; for a translation, see Pollock, "Rāmāyaṇa and Political Imagination," 276.
71. *Pṛthvīrājavijaya* 10.40.
72. *Language of the Gods*, especially chaps. 3–6.
73. *Pṛthvīrājavijaya* 10.43–46; adapted from Sheldon Pollock's translation in "Rāmāyaṇa and Political Imagination," 276–77.
74. *Kāvyamīmāṃsā*, 50; Deshpande, *Sanskrit and Prakrit*, 92.
75. For a translation that attempts to replicate the absence of labials in English, see *What Ten Young Men Did*, 459–85.
76. Parasher, *Mlecchas in Early India*, 76–112.
77. Thapar, "Image of the Barbarian," 409.
78. *Tāj al-Ma'āṣir*, ms. India Office Islamic 15, fol. 38b; lightly adapted from Bhagwat Saroop's translation in *Tajud Din Hasan Nizami's Taj ul Ma'athir*, 53–54.
79. *Pṛthvīrājavijaya* 1.35.
80. McCarter, "Picture-Gallery Episode," 41–42.
81. *ṣaṇṇām saṃskṛtādīnāṃ ṣaṭsaṅkhyānāṃ vācām. bhāṣāṣaṭkasyetyarthaḥ* (*Pṛthvīrājavijaya*, p. 15).
82. Pollock, *Language of the Gods*, 89–105; also see Ollett, *Language of the Snakes*, chap. 5.
83. Excerpts translated in Pollock, *Language of the Gods*, 583; also see analysis on p. 111.

84. *Sarasvatīkaṇṭhābharaṇa*, 143. Pollock translates the same verse in *Language of the Gods*, 583.
85. *Kāvyamīmāṃsā*, 54–55 (chapter 10); quoted in translation in Smith, *Ratnākara's Haravijaya*, 87.
86. See F. Kielhorn's edition of the fragmentary *Lalitavigraharāja*, including facsimiles of the slabs on which it is preserved (*Bruchstücke Indischer Schauspiele in Inschriften zu Ajmere*); also see Kielhorn, "Sanskrit Plays, Partly Preserved as Inscriptions at Ajmere," 201–12.
87. On "hammira," see, e.g., *Lalitavigraharāja* as edited in Kielhorn, "Sanskrit Plays, Partly Preserved as Inscriptions at Ajmere," 208–9, and Kielhorn, *Bruchstücke Indischer Schauspiele in Inschriften zu Ajmere*, 13–14; on "king of the Turks," see Kielhorn, "Sanskrit Plays, Partly Preserved as Inscriptions at Ajmere," 206 and 208; Kielhorn, *Bruchstücke Indischer Schauspiele in Inschriften zu Ajmere*, 10–13 and 15.
88. Sheldon Pollock notes that the ambassador cites the puranas ("Rāmāyaṇa and Political Imagination," 276n17; for the passage, see Kielhorn, *Bruchstücke Indischer Schauspiele in Inschriften zu Ajmere*, 15). On the languages used by different characters in the *Lalitavigraharāja*, see Leclère, "Ambivalent Representations," 161–79.
89. Leclère, "Ambivalent Representations," 194.
90. Stone slabs containing part of the *Lalitavigraharāja* were recovered in what is now called the Adhai-din-ka-Jhompra mosque (Talbot, *Last Hindu Emperor*, 38; Kielhorn, "Sanskrit Plays, Partly Preserved as Inscriptions at Ajmere," 201).
91. Jayaratha cites *Pṛthvīrājavijaya* 5.50, 5.75, 5.91, 5.173, 5.177, 5.178, and 5.181 in his commentary on Ruyyaka's *Alaṃkārasarvasva*. For citations, see, respectively, *Alaṃkārasarvasva*, 64, 73, 82, 173, 180–1 (5.177), and 181 (5.178, with some variations, and 5.181); Jayaratha does not typically name the *Pṛthvīrājavijaya* as the source (although he does so on p. 64). I am indebted for these identifications to Ojha, introduction to *Pṛthvīrājavijaya*, 2n3.
92. *Pṛthvīrājavijaya* 5.70 (featuring Durlabharaja II) and 5.113 (featuring Ajayaraja).
93. Morison, "Some Account of the Genealogies," 189.
94. See Georg Bühler's description of the sole known manuscript of Jayanaka's *Pṛthvīrājavijaya* in *Tour in Search of Sanskrit Mss* (1877), 62–64.
95. In chronological order: 1178 Barla inscription, 1180 Phalodhi inscription, three 1183 Madanpur inscriptions, 1188 Udaipur inscription, and 1188 Visalpur inscription. On the 1178 Barla inscription, see *Epigraphia Indica*, 32:299–304. On the 1180 Phalodhi inscription, see Tessitori, "Progress Report," 85. On the 1183 Madanpur inscriptions, see Cunningham, *Report of Tours in Bundelkhand and Malwa in 1874–75 and 1876–77*, 98–100, and Cunningham, *Reports of a Tour in Bundelkhand and Rewa in 1883–84*, 171–75. On the 1188 Udaipur inscription, see Archaeological Survey of India, *Progress Report, 1905–1906*, 62, #2224. On the 1188 Visalpur inscription, see Carlleyle, *Report of a Tour in Eastern Rajputana in 1871–72 and 1872–73*, 154–56. I am indebted for these references to Talbot, *Last Hindu Emperor*, 38n29.
96. Kielhorn, "Delhi Siwalik Pillar Inscriptions of Visaladeva," 215–19. For a more recent translation of the relevant section of this inscription, see Pollock, "Rāmāyaṇa and Political Imagination," 278; on the inscription more generally, see Talbot, *Last Hindu Emperor*, 37–38 and 90.

97. The *Pṛthvīrājavijaya* mentions a bard, Prithvibhata (11.13), at court and names another poet, Vishvarupa, as also present in Ajmer (Dasharatha Sharma, *Early Chauhān Dynasties*, 88). As per Dasharatha Sharma, the early fourteenth-century *Kharataragacchapaṭṭāvalī* mentions Jains visiting Prithviraj's court (*Early Chauhān Dynasties*, 88).

3. Indo-Muslim Rulers

1. The dates for Gangadevi's *Madhurāvijaya* and Nayachandra's *Hammīramahākāvya* are necessarily approximate. Gangadevi must have written after 1371, the year of the major battle she describes in her work; her husband, King Kampan, died in 1374, but the poem may have been written after his death. Nayachandra wrote at the Gwalior court of King Virama Tomar, who ruled from 1402 until 1423.
2. Chaudhuri, *Contribution of Women*.
3. See chapter 1 for references on the earliest uses of "hammira," to refer to the Ghaznavids and others. Note that "hammira" may reflect the real usage of "amir" in Persian sources, such as al-Gardizi, to talk about the early Ghaznavids (Bosworth, "Titulature of the Early Ghaznavids," 223), and among Muslim rulers in Sindh (Flood, *Objects of Translation*, 255). An early use of "suratrana" is found in a 1273 inscription describing the destruction, several decades prior, of the city Nagada (Nagadraha) by a suratrana, probably referring to Shamsuddin Iltutmish (r. 1210–36) or his troops (Gulab Chandra Choudhary, *Political History of Northern India*, 176; Geiger, "Chîrwâ-Inschrift," 157, v. 16; Jackson, *Delhi Sultanate*, 133).
4. One also sees Sanskrit *suratāla* for "sultan," especially in Karnataka sources. E.g., a 1347 inscription of Harihara's brother Marappa (Eaton and Wagoner, *Power, Memory, Architecture*, 28; University of Mysore, *Annual Report of the Mysore Archaeological Department for the Year 1929*, 161) and a ca. 1408 inscription (*Epigraphia Carnatica*, 10:141; date given on p. xlvii).
5. For references, see Flood, *Objects of Translation*, 257. As Finbarr Barry Flood notes, the title hammira also appears in the names of rulers from later periods in other parts of India, such as *haṃvīra*, a Gajapati ruler of Orissa in mid-fifteenth century (*Objects of Translation*, 258).
6. Eaton and Wagoner, *Power, Memory, Architecture*, 28; University of Mysore, *Annual Report of the Mysore Archaeological Department for the Year 1929*, 161.
7. On Bukka being *hindūrāyasuratrāṇa* (Wagoner, "Sultan Among Hindu Kings," 862n8). Bukka is called a sultan (*suratālu*), without the prefix *hindūrāya-*, in at least two inscriptions, dated 1355 and 1356 (Wagoner, "Sultan Among Hindu Kings," 863).
8. For later uses of *hindūrāyasuratrāṇa*, see Wagoner, "Sultan Among Hindu Kings," 862n8. Kapaya Nayak, a Deccani rebel against the Delhi Sultanate during the 1360s, is referred as *andhrasuratrāṇa* (*Epigraphia Indica*, 13:264, v. 25; also see Flood, *Objects of Translation*, 258, and Wagoner, "Sultan Among Hindu Kings," 862n8). In subsequent centuries, the parallel title *urigōlasūratrāṇa* (sultan of Warangal) appeared (Wagoner, "Sultan Among Hindu Kings," 862n8).

9. Eaton, "Persian Cosmopolis."
10. Flood, *Objects of Translation*, 257.
11. Wagoner, "Sultan Among Hindu Kings," 856–67.
12. Bhavnagar Archaeological Department, *Collection of Prakrit and Sanskrit Inscriptions*, 113–14. The intended referent of the "sultan of Delhi and Gujarat" is not entirely clear. Two possibilities are Muhammad Shah (r. 1434–45), a Delhi Sultanate king of the Sayyid dynasty, and Ahmad Shah (r. 1411–42), sultan of Gujarat. In the *Rājavinoda*, Rana Kumbha is said to have served a later Gujarat sultan, Mahmud Begada (r. 1459–1511) (Gode, "Date of the Rājavinoda," 357–58; Kapadia, "Last Cakravartin?," 84).
13. Archaeological Survey of India, *Progress Report, 1912*, 53.
14. Wagoner, "Sultan Among Hindu Kings," 868–71.
15. For the date of the Varadaraja *kalyāṇa maṇḍapa* (marriage hall), see Michell, *Architecture and Art of Southern India*, 81–82. I am indebted to a Brahmin priest at the Varadaraja temple complex for pointing out the two-faced horse riders.
16. Wagoner, "Harihara, Bukka, and the Sultan," 304–5 (italics in original).
17. Cf. Talbot's argument that *hindū* here denotes an incipient Indian ethnicity (Talbot, "Inscribing the Other," 700).
18. *Vividhatīrthakalpa*, 95 and 97, respectively. Jinaprabha completed his sections of the *Vividhatīrthakalpa* in 1333; Jinaprabha's student, Vidyatilaka, added onto the work thereafter.
19. Flood, *Objects of Translation*, 117. There is also a bejeweled gold ring, probably dating from the twelfth or thirteenth century, that is inscribed with *śrīmad hamīra*; it is unclear whether the inscription dates to the same period as the ring.
20. Eaton, *India in the Persianate World*, 49; British Museum no. IOLC.7789.
21. The inscriptions are as follows: (1) 1276 Palam Baoli inscription (Prasad, *Sanskrit Inscriptions of Delhi Sultanate*, 3–15); (2) 1291 Delhi Museum stone inscription, originally from Sonepat (Prasad, *Sanskrit Inscriptions of Delhi Sultanate*, 15–18); (3) 1328 Sarban stone inscription (Prasad, *Sanskrit Inscriptions of Delhi Sultanate*, 27–31).
22. *Epigraphia Indica*, 12:17–27; Talbot, *Last Hindu Emperor*, 92.
23. Prasad, *Sanskrit Inscriptions of Delhi Sultanate*, 8, v. 3 (my translation; see p. 12 for Prasad's translation). Of the three other inscriptions, one also uses "shakendra" to refer to the sultans (Prasad, *Sanskrit Inscriptions of Delhi Sultanate*, 16), one uses "shaka" (*Epigraphia Indica*, 12:23, v. 6), and one uses the terms "mleccha" and "turushka" (Prasad, *Sanskrit Inscriptions of Delhi Sultanate*, 29, vv. 5 and 6). For recent discussions of the Palam Baoli inscription, see Eaton, *India in the Persianate Age*, 54–56; Veluthat, "Rise and Fall of the *Kāvya* Project," 12–15.
24. Respectively, *rājyaṃ nihatakaṇṭakaṃ* and *pratāpadahanadagdhāri* (Prasad, *Sanskrit Inscriptions of Delhi Sultanate*, 29, vv. 4–5).
25. *gajavājinarādhīśaiḥ . . . śakaiḥ* (*Epigraphia Indica*, 12:23, v. 6).
26. Talbot, *Last Hindu Emperor*, 69–106.
27. *Tārīkh-i hindūstān az rāja yūdhishtar tā humāyūn*, ms. no. 2264/5274 of the Punjab University Library of Lahore, fol. 2a (*prithbī rāj bar takht-i indarpathah nishasht*). The work must date to Humayun's reign or later.
28. *Tārīkh-i Fīrūzshāhī* of Barani, 272.

29. Pollock, *Language of the Gods*, 430–31.
30. For discussions of the *Jagaḍūcarita*, see, e.g., Chattopadhyaya, *Representing the Other?*, 61–63; Sheikh, *Forging a Region*, 119–23.
31. See *Jagaḍūcarita*, 58–65; *hariśaṅkaramandira* is mentioned in 6.50 and *masīti* in 6.64.
32. *Prabandhakośa*, 130.
33. For the Sanskrit inscription, see *Epigraphia Indica*, 34:140–50; for the Arabic inscription, see *Epigraphia Indica*, Arabic and Persian Supplement 1961:10–15. For discussions of the inscription, see, e.g., Chakravarti, *Trade and Traders*, 220–42; Thapar, *Somanatha*, 88–96.
34. The Sanskrit inscription is dated May 25, 1264, and the Arabic inscription is dated July 23, 1264 (Chakravarti, *Trade and Traders*, 226).
35. *Epigraphia Indica*, 34:146, lines 1–2.
36. Thapar, *Somanatha*, 89.
37. *Epigraphia Indica*, 4:298; for the Arabic inscription, see Blochmann, "Inscriptions from Ahmadâbâd," 367–68; Kapadia, *In Praise of Kings*, 113.
38. *Epigraphia Indica*, 34:146.
39. *Epigraphia Indica*, 34:144; omissions noted in *Epigraphia Indica*, Arabic and Persian Supplement 1961:12.
40. *Epigraphia Indica*, 34:149; Chakravarti, *Trade and Traders*, 237.
41. *Epigraphia Indica*, Arabic and Persian Supplement 1961:12–13.
42. Singh, *Political Violence in Ancient India*, 10.
43. Cf. Ahmad, "Epic and Counter-Epic," 472–76.
44. The year 1371 is the most common date given for the Vijayanagara overthrow of the Sultanate of Madurai. I allow for some flexibility here, because the campaign may have begun slightly earlier (Sudyka, *Vijayanagara*, 109n122), and because it may have taken several years for the Sultanate to fully die out (Husaini, "History of Madura Sultanate," 125–27).
45. On 1311: Shokoohy, "Architecture of the Sultanate of Ma'bar," 33, and Shokoohy, *Muslim Architecture of South India*, 25. S. A. Q. Husaini details the history from 1323 onward in "History of Madura Sultanate." On the territorial extent of the Sultanate of Madurai, see Husaini, "History of Madura Sultanate," 116–19. A contemporary, rhetorical account of the Khalji assault is found in Amir Khusrau's prose work *Khazāʾin al-Futūḥ* (Treasures of victories).
46. In 1333, Jalaluddin, the Tughluq governor, renamed himself Sultan Ahsan Shah and began minting coins in his own name (Shokoohy, "Architecture of the Sultanate of Ma'bar," 34; Husaini, "History of Madura Sultanate," 90–93). The exact extent of the Sultanate of Madurai varied over time (see maps in S. Selvin Kumar, *Madurai Sultanate*).
47. There is not agreement on the number of sultans who ruled from Madurai; for a few lists, see Husaini, "History of Madura Sultanate," 90–116; S. Selvin Kumar, *Madurai Sultanate*, 24; Shokoohy, "Architecture of the Sultanate of Ma'bar," 34–35; Thiruvenkatachari, introduction to *Madhurāvijaya*, 56. Mehrdad Shokoohy points out that the fourteenth-century city of Madurai may have been nearby modern-day Madurai rather than in the exact same location (Shokoohy, "Architecture of the Sultanate of Ma'bar," 42; Shokoohy, *Muslim Architecture of South India*, 28–32).

48. For a summary of editions of the *Madhurāvijaya* and some secondary scholarship, see Sudyka, *Vijayanagara*, 15–17. For a brief overview of the *Madhurāvijaya*'s contents, see Prabha, *Historical Mahākāvyas in Sanskrit*, 320–23. For the suggestion that Gangadevi was an eyewitness to the Vijayanagara takeover of Madurai, see Thiruvenkatachari, introduction to *Madhurāvijaya*, 1.

49. Gangadevi lists, in order: Valmiki, Vyasa, Kalidasa, Bana, Bharavi, Dandin, Bhavabhuti, "poet of Karṇāmṛta," and Tikkana (*Madhurāvijaya* 1.5–13; I discuss Tikkana below).

50. *Madhurāvijaya* 1.14–16. On these poets, see Sudyka, *Vijayanagara*, 33; Thiruvenkatachari, introduction to *Madhurāvijaya*, 3–5.

51. Eaton, *Social History of the Deccan*, 21.

52. Sudyka, *Vijayanagara*, 33–34.

53. Bala, "Madhurāvijaya of Gaṅgā Devī," 14–17.

54. On Tikkana, see Velcheru Narayana Rao, "Multiple Literary Cultures in Telugu," 393.

55. *Madhurāvijaya* 3.41–43.

56. Ajay Rao also makes this point in "Responses to the Conquests of Madurai," 5.

57. *Madhurāvijaya*, 124, 9.28 (for the identification of Champa in this verse, also see *Conquest of Madhurā*, 109). In his edition of the *Madhurāvijaya*, S. Thiruvenkatachari numbers chapter 9's verses in his English translation but not in the Sanskrit chapter. Moreover, he does not translate incomplete verses. Accordingly, for chapter 9 of the *Madhurāvijaya*, I give the page number for the Sanskrit text and the verse number based on Thiruvenkatachari's translation.

58. *Madhurāvijaya* 8.29.

59. *Madhurāvijaya* 4.1–4.51.

60. Ajay Rao, "Responses to the Conquests of Madurai," 7.

61. On tinkling anklets: *Madhurāvijaya* 8.9 and *Raghuvaṃśa* 16.12. On animals obscuring sculptures: *Madhurāvijaya* 8.10 (spiderwebs) and *Raghuvaṃśa* 16.17 (shed snake skins). On this section of the *Raghuvaṃśa*, see Winiarski, "Women's Town—Ghost Town." For the suggestion to compare the two passages, I am indebted to Sudyka, *Vijayanagara*, 111.

62. For another translation, see Richard H. Davis, *Lives of Indian Images*, 117.

63. See, e.g., Ajay Rao's discussion of Vedanta Deshika's *Abhītistava* ("Responses to the Conquests of Madurai," 2–5).

64. Richard H. Davis, *Lives of Indian Images*, 113. *Madhurāvijaya* 8.1 mentions *vyāghrapurī*, another name for Chidambaram (Sudyka, *Vijayanagara*, 110; on *vyāghrapura* as another name for Chidambaram generally, see Cox, *Modes of Philology*, 37). Note that the 1969 edition of the *Madhurāvijaya*, edited by Subrahmanyasastri, reconstructs the verse so that *vyāghrapurī* refers to Madurai (466), which I think is incorrect. William Jackson's summary leaves the referent of *vyāghrapurī* vague and appears to list Chidambaram separately (*Vijayanagara Voices*, 62).

65. *Madhurāvijaya* 8.6.

66. *Madhurāvijaya* 8.4.

67. *Pṛthvīrājavijaya* 1.52 and *Madhurāvijaya* 8.11.

68. Also see Ajay Rao's table in "Responses to the Conquests of Madurai," 6.
69. *Madhurāvijaya* 8.7.
70. *Madhurāvijaya* 8.8; for a brief discussion of the aesthetics of this verse, see Rajaraman and Kotamraju, "Sound Play," 8). While Gangadevi depicts impaled skulls as a negative development, impalement at Madurai had positive connotations in other contexts. Legend has it that, in the seventh century CE, Shaivites impaled thousands of Jains in Madurai. This story had been in circulation for centuries by Gangadevi's time and was typically told positively in Shaivite circles (Peterson, "Śramaṇas Against the Tamil Way," 181; Peterson, "Tamil Śaiva Hagiography," 208–9).
71. *Madhurāvijaya* 8.13. Kalidasa mentions the Tamraparni as well, although using different imagery (*Raghuvaṃśa* 4.50).
72. *Madhurāvijaya* 8.14–16. For the translation of verse 16, I found inspiration in the rendering by Shankar Rajaraman and Venetia Kotamraju in *Conquest of Madhurā*, 99.
73. *Madhurāvijaya* 8.17–28.
74. *Madhurāvijaya* 8.35.
75. According to the editor S. Thiruvenkatachari (*Madhurāvijaya*, 121n).
76. *Madhurāvijaya* 8.7 (men drinking alcohol) and 8.32 (women drinking alcohol).
77. *Madhurāvijaya* 8.7 (meat eating) and 8.13 (cow killing).
78. Talbot, "Inscribing the Other," 696–97.
79. Talbot, "Inscribing the Other," 697–99.
80. The two verses share similar imagery of a powerful hero wiping away drunkenness with his martial valor (*Madhurāvijaya* 8.32 and *Raghuvaṃśa* 4.61); for a translation of Kalidasa's verse, see Knutson, "Poetic Justice," 290.
81. *Madhurāvijaya* 8.31.
82. *Madhurāvijaya* 8.12. Ibn Battuta confirms that officials in the Sultanate of Madurai spoke Persian (Husaini, "History of Madura Sultanate," 120; Shokoohy, "Architecture of the Sultanate of Ma'bar," 34).
83. *vipinavihagavāśita . . .* (*Pṛthvīrājavijaya* 10.45).
84. Shokoohy, *Muslim Architecture of South India*, 23–24.
85. Compare to Ibn Battuta's discussion of the Sultanate of Madurai (Husaini, "History of Madura Sultanate," 120–23).
86. *Futūḥ al-Salāṭīn* of Isami, 405, 465. Also see discussion and citations in Eaton and Wagoner, *Power, Memory, Architecture*, 27–28, 37n81–82.
87. *Futūḥ al-Salāṭīn* of Isami, 10 (especially note references to *kishwar-i dīvgīr* and *zi khūn-i musulmān-i tawḥīd* in contrast to Zahhak).
88. *Madhurāvijaya* 8.24; also see 8.22 and 8.25.
89. *Madhurāvijaya*, 125, 9.36.
90. On the former, see *Madhurāvijaya* 4.32.
91. Richard H. Davis, *Lives of Indian Images*, 120–21. Also see Ajay Rao, "Responses to the Conquests of Madurai," 8–9.
92. *Madhurāvijaya* 4.83.
93. *Madhurāvijaya* 8.33.
94. S. Thiruvenkatachari notes the missing verses in *Madhurāvijaya*, 122n.

95. *Madhurāvijaya*, 122, 9.2; I borrow here from Shankar Rajaraman and Venetia Kotamraju's translation (*Conquest of Madhurā*, 105).

96. *Madhurāvijaya*, 123, 9.11; correct -*śorṣau* to -*śīrṣau* (my translation; Ajay Rao translates the same verse in "Responses to the Conquests of Madurai," 6).

97. On fighters going to heaven: *Madhurāvijaya* 4.61 and 9.9, 9.11 (p. 123); on rivers of blood: *Madhurāvijaya* 4.58 and 9.14–15 (p. 123).

98. *Madhurāvijaya* 4.60 and 9.6 (p. 122).

99. *Madhurāvijaya* 4.59 and 9.1 (p. 122).

100. *Madhurāvijaya* 9.21–40 (pp. 124–25) and 4.77–83, respectively.

101. *Madhurāvijaya* 2.23.

102. *Madhurāvijaya*, 125, 9.40.

103. *Tārīkh-i Fīrūzshāhī* of Shams Siraj Afif, 261–63. Shams Siraj Afif himself notes that some Muslims survived and went north to Delhi; he also mistakes other details of the conflict, such as naming Bukka as the overthrower rather than Kampan.

104. Shokoohy, *Muslim Architecture in South India*, 27.

105. Sultans Alauddin and Shamsuddin Adil Shah are purportedly buried in the Goripalayam Dargah (on this site, see Shokoohy, "Architecture of the Sultanate of Ma'bar," 44–66, and Shokoohy, *Muslim Architecture of South India*, 34–50); Sultan Alauddin Sikandar Shah, the last sultan of Madurai, is purportedly buried in the Thiruparankundram Dargah (on this site, see Shokoohy, "Architecture of the Sultanate of Ma'bar," 67–74 and Shokoohy, *Muslim Architecture of South India*, 57–65).

106. *Madhurāvijaya*, 124, 9.25 and 125, 9.36.

107. *Madhurāvijaya*, 124, 9.25.

108. *Madhurāvijaya*, 125, 9.38 and 9.39, respectively.

109. There has been some confusion about the date of the *Hammīramahākāvya*, with guesses spanning from the fourteenth to the late fifteenth century. The text is rightly placed in the early fifteenth-century Gwalior court during the reign of Virama Tomar (Bednar, "Mongol, Muslim, Rajput," 598n48; Hens, "In the Guise of Eulogy," 1n2; Pollock, *Language of the Gods*, 394n29). For an overview of the *Hammīramahākāvya*'s contents, see Kirtane, introduction to *Hammīramahākāvya*, 10–47; Prabha, *Historical Mahākāvyas in Sanskrit*, 293–301.

110. *Hammīramahākāvya* 14.43. Phyllis Granoff also cites this verse in "Mountains of Eternity," 42.

111. *Hammīramahākāvya* 14.26.

112. *Hammīramahākāvya* 14.43.

113. Many Jain merchant families and Digambara religious leaders moved to Gwalior in the aftermath of these events (de Clercq, "Bhaṭṭārakas and Digambara Monastic Lineages," 80); fifteenth-century Jains also wrote within Delhi Sultanate domains (de Clercq, "Apabhramsha as a Literary Medium," 343–46).

114. In 1401, the Tughluqs led an assault on Gwalior (Jackson, *Delhi Sultanate*, 321); Khizr Khan, a Sayyid, led attacks on Gwalior in 1416 and 1421.

115. On Vasudeva, see *Hammīramahākāvya* 1.27; for the lineage of kings as outlined by Nayachandra, see Kirtane, introduction to *Hammīramahākāvya*, 13–16. On Vasudeva

in other Sanskrit sources, see Sarda, "Prithviraja Vijaya," 263–64. Between his accounts of Vasudeva and Hammira, Nayachandra mentions numerous Chauhan conflicts with Muslims. For instance, a tenth-century Chauhan king, Simharaja, killed a *śakapati*, Muslim ruler or sultan, called Hatim (*Hammīramahākāvya* 1.104 in Jinavijaya ed.; 1.102 in Kirtane ed.; the name is *hetima* in Sanskrit; on Simharaja in other Sanskrit sources, see Sarda, "Prithviraja Vijaya," 268–69n3.). In the second chapter, two Muslims foes are mentioned by name: Hejamuddin and Shahabuddin (*hejamadīna* and *sahābadīna* in Sanskrit, respectively; *Hammīramahākāvya* 2.24 and 2.37). Much of chapters 3 and 4 concerns Chauhan conflicts with Muslim rulers, including Prithviraj's clashes with Muhammad Ghori and fights over Ranthambhor Fort.

116. E.g., the 1276 Palam Baoli inscription discussed earlier in this chapter. There is also a slightly later story about intermarriage between the two dynasties, which would make Hammira a Tomar in addition to being a Chauhan (Talbot, *Last Hindu Emperor*, 13–14).
117. Vrat, *Glimpses of Jaina Sanskrit Mahākāvyas*.
118. *Hammīramahākāvya* 14.26; *Hammīramahākāvya*, Jinavijaya ed., 9, 16, 23, 34, 40, 44, 54 (missing on p. 63, at the end of chapter 8), 77, 85, 92, 98, 114, and 120; Kirtane ed., 10, 18, 25, 38, 45, 50, 61, 72, 87, 95, 104, 111, 129, and 135.
119. *Hammīramahākāvya* 14.34; on Mammata's *rasadoṣas*, see *Kāvyaprakāśa* 7.60–62 and Pollock, *Rasa Reader*, 228–35.
120. Compare to other interpretations of the *Hammīramahākāvya*, including that it is a "proto-vernacular text" (Bednar, "Conquest and Resistance," 255) or an ironic narrative (Hens, "In the Guise of Eulogy"). Michael Bednar comments on Hens's theory in Bednar, "Mongol, Muslim, Rajput," 598–99, and Hens responds in "Beyond Power and Praise."
121. *Hammīramahākāvya* 13.224–25 in Kirtane ed. and 13.225–26 in Jinavijaya ed. This is preceded by a series of verses on Hammira fighting the Khalji army as a whole.
122. Michael Bednar has argued that Nayachandra promotes an early version of Rajput values (see, e.g., "Mongol, Muslim, Rajput"); Richard Eaton has argued, with more nuance, that Nayachandra's values of "loyalty, courage, and heroic martyrdom" would later be termed Rajput (*India in the Persianate World*, 130). I think that Eaton's formulation is more accurate, but both arguments strike me as slightly teleological. Moreover, emphasizing the later category of Rajput in analyzing Nayachandra's work fails to fully situate his depiction of Hammira against the deep tradition of Sanskrit thought on Indian kingship.
123. *Hammīramahākāvya* 4.143. The *Hammīramahākāvyadīpikā* glosses "shaka" as "turushka" (*Hammīramahākāvya*, Jinavijaya ed., 165).
124. *Hammīramahākāvya* 10.34 mentions "the eight" and 10.38–39 gives their names.
125. On this, also see Bednar, "Mongol, Muslim, Rajput," 600–2.
126. *Futūḥ al-Salāṭīn*, 254–55, and *Tārīkh-i Mubārakshāhī*, 75, on the new Muslims, including Muhammad Shah, rebelling and then taking refuge at Ranthambhor.
127. *Hammīramahākāvya*, chap. 10.

128. *Hammīramahākāvya* 13.25–38; this passage is translated in Bednar, "Conquest and Resistance," 195–96.
129. *Hammīramahākāvya* 10.21. This verse comes amid a series of verses that name other strengths of Hammira.
130. *Hammīramahākāvya* 11.61.
131. *Hammīramahākāvya* 13.81. Virama criticizes this behavior (*Hammīramahākāvya* 13.91–98). The section is translated in Bednar, "Conquest and Resistance," 198–200.
132. On Ratipala's name, see Hens, "Beyond Power and Praise," 9. "Rayapala" is found in the 1481 *Hammīrāyaṇa* (Bednar, "Mongol, Muslim, Rajput," 603), and "Ramapala" is found in the ca. 1412–16 *Puruṣaparīkṣā* (Hens, "Beyond Power and Praise," 17n66).
133. *Hammīramahākāvya* 14.16; also see 14.21.
134. *Hammīramahākāvya* 13.149–51. Michael Bednar also translates these verses in "Conquest and Resistance," 153 and 202.
135. *Hammīramahākāvya* 13.153.
136. *Hammīramahākāvya* 13.154–57; also see Bednar, "Mongol, Muslim, Rajput," 602.
137. *Hammīramahākāvya* 13.160b–161a.
138. *Hammīramahākāvya* 13.164.
139. Bednar, "Conquest and Resistance," 203–8; Bednar, "Mongol, Muslim, Rajput," 606–7.
140. Bednar "Mongol, Muslim, Rajput," 606.
141. *Hammīramahākāvya* 13.225 in Kirtane ed. and 13.226 in Jinavijaya ed. E.g., in the ca. 1590 *Surjanacarita*, Alauddin kills Hammira (12.76–77; all citations are to both the Sharma and Chaudhuri editions of the *Surjanacarita* unless otherwise noted).
142. *Hammīramahākāvya* 13.163 and 14.19, respectively.
143. Pollock, *Language of the Gods*, 240n25.
144. *Hammīramahākāvya* 13.150 and 13.163, respectively.
145. For example, a Buddhist text reports that Kambojas lacked the four-fold class system (Bronkhorst, *Greater Magadha*, 353); book 12 of the Mahabharata describes Kambojas as animal-like and evil-doers (*Mahābhārata* 12.200.40–41).
146. *Hammīramahākāvya* 13.208 in Kirtane ed. and 13.209 in Jinavijaya ed.
147. *Hammīramahākāvya* 14.20. For another interpretation of this verse, see *Hammīramahākāvya: Hindī Anuvād*, 172.
148. *Hammīramahākāvya* 14.20.
149. Eaton, *India in the Persianate Age*, 17.
150. *New Catalogus Catalogorum*, 18:141. The manuscript in Lahore has only seven cantos, and, so far as I can tell, it has not been consulted by anybody who has worked on the text (no. 4485 in Saith, *Catalogue of Sanskrit Manuscripts in the Punjab University Library*, 261).
151. The 1485 manuscript was copied in Firozpur; an earlier manuscript, dated 1429, is in Kota (Hens, "Beyond Power and Praise," 13n13). The commentary, the *Hammīramahākāvyadīpikā*, is printed in the *Hammīramahākāvya*, Jinavijaya ed., 122–74.
152. Pollock, "Death of Sanskrit," 400–404.
153. For a summary of the play, see Dalal, introduction to *Hammīramadamardana*, vi–x.

154. *Hammīramadamardana*, 34 and 55; also see discussion in Leclère, "Ambivalent Representations," 187–88.

155. Respectively, *abhinavarāmāvatāra* and *nikhilayavanakṣayakara* (*Rambhāmañjarī*, 12).

156. On Vidyapati's *Puruṣaparīkṣā*, see Pankaj Kumar Jha, "Beyond the Local and the Universal," and Pankaj Kumar Jha, *Political History of Literature*, 133–83.

4. Local Stories in Fourteenth-Century Gujarat and Fifteenth-Century Kashmir

1. This Rajashekhara should not be confused with the tenth-century theorist and poet of the same name.

2. *New Catalogus Catalogorum*, 10:41 (Kakka), 13:9–10 (Rajashekhara), 13:10 (Merutunga), 30:2 (Jinaprabha/Vidyatilaka).

3. *Rājataraṅgiṇī* of Kalhana, 1.21–23. Cf. to others who say, on the basis of 1.21, that Kalhana wrote for a royal audience (e.g., Roy, "Making of a Mandala," 63; Slaje, "In the Guise of Poetry," 232–33). Michael Witzel points to some possible revisions made by Kalhana to his *Rājataraṅgiṇī*, designed to make the text more appealing to royalty ("Indian Historical Writing," 45nn44–46).

4. Witzel, "Indian Historical Writing," 10. Kalhana identifies himself as the son of court minister Chanpaka at the end of each chapter (Knutson, "Poetic Justice," 281n1).

5. Jonaraja and Shrivara both label themselves as court poets (respectively, *Rājataraṅgiṇī* of Jonaraja, vv. 10–12, and *Rājataraṅgiṇī* of Shrivara, 1.1.11–12). Jonaraja wrote under the support of Zayn al-Abidin (r. 1418–19; 1420–70) (*Rājataraṅgiṇī* of Jonaraja, vv. 10–12). Shrivara mentions paying back a debt (*niṣkṛti*) to three successive Shah Miri kings: Zayn al-Abidin, Haydar Shah (r. 1470–72), and Hasan Shah (r. 1472–84) (On Zayn and Haydar Shah: *Rājataraṅgiṇī* of Shrivara, 1.1.12 and 1.1.17; also cited in Obrock, "History at the End of History," 231n23. On Hasan Shah: *Rājataraṅgiṇī* of Shrivara, 3.3; also cited in Slaje, "Note on the Genesis," 384). John Nemec identifies some of the ways that Jonaraja mirrors Kalhana ("Review of *Kingship in Kaśmīr*," 405). All Jonaraja citations refer to the Slaje edition. All citations to the *Rājataraṅgiṇī* of Shrivara correspond to both the Kaul and Singh editions, unless otherwise noted.

6. On Kalhana's knowledge of the Mahabharata, see, e.g., Stein, introduction to *Rājataraṅgiṇī* of Kalhana, 11; Kaul, "'Seeing' the Past," 203–4. On *śāntarasa* in Kalhana's chronicle and in the Mahabharata, as interpreted by Anandavardhana, see, e.g., McCrea, "Śāntarasa in the *Rājataraṅgiṇī*."

7. *bhāratamivābhirāmaṃ* (*Prabandhacintāmaṇi*, 1, v. 5; all citations are to the Jinavijaya edition).

8. *Prabandhacintāmaṇi*, 1, v. 6.

9. Thapar, *Past Before Us*, 608–9; Roy "Making of a Mandala," 53.

10. On the prabandha genre, see Cort, "Genres of Jain History," 486–88; Deleu, "Note on the Jain Prabandhas" (especially on the *Prabandhakośa*). Phyllis Granoff often

separates the genre of prabandhas from "sectarian" biographies (*paṭṭāvalī*, *gurvāvalī*; e.g., in "Religious Biography and Clan History," 196–97).

11. The *Prabandhacintāmaṇi* has been edited by Jinavijaya; there is an English translation by C. H. Tawney. The earliest prabandhas were written in the thirteenth century, the most well known of which is Prabhachandra's *Prabhāvakacaritra* (1277/1278), about twenty-two Shvetambara monks (Cort, "Genres of Jain History," 487; Vose, "Making of a Medieval Jain Monk," 325).
12. *Prabandhacintāmaṇi*, 1, v. 6.
13. *Prabandhacintāmaṇi*, 1, vv. 3–4.
14. E.g., Ali, "Temporality, Narration, and the Problem of History," 248 and 254; Pollock, "Pretextures of Time," 380; Sewell, "Dates in Merutunga's 'Prabandha Chintamani.'"
15. *Prabandhakośa*, 1, lines 18–20. See also Cort, "Genres of Jain History," 498n26; Vose, "Making of a Medieval Jain Monk," 326–27.
16. *śrotumarhanti bhavyāstat pāpanāśanakāmyayā* (*Vividhatīrthakalpa*, 1, v. 3). Also note the late thirteenth-century *Prabhāvakacaritra*, written for spiritual edification (Cort, "Genres of Jain History," 487). About two-thirds of the *Vividhatīrthakalpa* is in Prakrit (Vose, "Making of a Medieval Jain Monk," 11).
17. Ali, "Temporality, Narration, and the Problem of History," 249–56.
18. Meisami, "Past in Service of the Present."
19. For the modern assumption that there is a conflict between writing history and communicating moral lessons, see, e.g., Flügel, "Worshipping the Ideal King," 358–61.
20. Ali, "Indian Historical Writing," 92.
21. E.g., *Prabandhacintāmaṇi*, 107–9 (trans. Tawney, 172–76); *Vividhatīrthakalpa*, 29; *Prabandhakośa*, 23 (translated in Granoff, *Clever Adulteress*, 169–70).
22. Karna was unseated, again, during a 1310–11 Khalji-led assault. On these events and the somewhat conflicting accounts of them, see Peter Jackson, *Delhi Sultanate*, 195–96; Asoke Kumar Majumdar, *Chaulukyas of Gujarat*, 186–93.
23. Merutunga tells his readers that he wrote in Vardhamana, today known as Wadhwan (*Prabandhacintāmaṇi*, 125; trans. Tawney, 204). Toshikazu Arai observes that Merutunga focuses on Gujarati rulers ("Jaina Kingship," 93).
24. For a more robust description of the *Nābhinandanajinoddhāra*, see Qvarnström, "Story Behind the Story."
25. *Vividhatīrthakalpa*, 109, v. 3 (*śrīyoginīpattane*); *Prabandhakośa*, 131, v. 7 (*ḍhillyāṃ*).
26. Vose, "Making of a Medieval Jain Monk," 98.
27. Jinaprabha records that he wrote story #21 in Devagiri (*Vividhatīrthakalpa*, 44; Vose, "Making of a Medieval Jain Monk," 323); he tells the tale of how the king sent him to Devagiri in story #22 (*Vividhatīrthakalpa*, 45–46).
28. *Nābhinandanajinoddhāraprabandha* 3.129 (also noted in Qvarnström, "Story Behind the Story," 205); Kakka dates Javari's restoration to eight hundred years after Vikramaditya's reign in 3.148. Also see Phyllis Granoff's summary and discussion of Kakka's section on Javari in "Householder as Shaman," 305–8.
29. *Prabandhakośa*, 7–9.
30. Granoff, *Clever Adulteress*, 152 (149–53 for the full story).

31. *Prabandhakośa*, 8.

32. Jinaprabha often uses *suratāṇa/surattāṇa*, a Prakrit equivalent of Sanskrit "suratrana," in the *Vividhatīrthakalpa*; Merutunga uses *suratāṇa* in his *Prabandhacintāmaṇi*.

33. *Nābhinandanajinoddhāraprabandha* 3.1.

34. *Prabandhacintāmaṇi*, 103.

35. *Prabandhacintāmaṇi*, 117–18; trans. Tawney, 191.

36. *Prabandhacintāmaṇi*, 97; Mularaja is also known as Balamularaja and Mularaja II.

37. *Prabandhacintāmaṇi*, 97, vv. *144–45; C. H. Tawney omits these verses in his translation (*Prabandhacintāmaṇi*, trans. Tawney, 154).

38. *Kīrtikaumudī* 2.57–58. On the *Kīrtikaumudī* as history, see, e.g., Dasgupta and De, *History of Sanskrit Literature*, 678.

39. Bhavnagar Archaeological Department, *Collection of Prakrit and Sanskrit Inscriptions*, 210, v. 27 (on the inscription's date, see p. 208). Rama Shankar Avasthy and Amalananda Ghosh draw attention to this inscription and posit a connection with the story about Queen Naiki found in Merutunga's *Prabandhacintāmaṇi* ("References to Muhammadans" [1936], 172, and "References to Muhammadans" [1937], 24).

40. Asoke Kumar Majumdar, *Chaulukyas of Gujarat*, 131–37.

41. E.g., *Prabandhacintāmaṇi*, 97 (*mleccharājā*), 103 (*suratāṇa, mālima*), 117 (*mlecchapati, mleccharājā*).

42. *Prabandhakośa*, 130; compare to *Vividhatīrthakalpa*, 79.

43. Wang, "Is There a Chinese Mode of Historical Thinking?," 206–7.

44. *Nābhinandanajinoddhāraprabandha* 3.1–9 (3.1 contains an alliterative play on Alauddin's name: *alāvadīno nadīnavat*); also see Dasaratha Sharma's translation in "New Light," 96.

45. Kakka says that Shatrunjaya had been previously restored by Bharata, Sagara, the Pandavas, Javari, and Vagbhata (*Nābhinandanajinoddhāraprabandha*, 104–28); other authors, such as Jinaprabha, name sixteen restorations (Cort, *Framing the Jina*, 143–51).

46. *Prabandhacintāmaṇi*, 107–9; trans. Tawney, 172–76.

47. *śrīśilādityarājña utpattistathā raṅkotpattistatkṛto valabhībhaṅgaśceti prabandhatrayam* (*Prabandhacintāmaṇi*, 109).

48. *Prabandhacintāmaṇi*, 114; trans. Tawney, 185–86.

49. *Prabandhakośa*, 57–58; translated in Granoff, *Clever Adulteress*, 161–62.

50. The Kali Yuga is usually the final of four eras, whereas the Duhshama Kala (*duḥṣamā kāla*) is the fifth of six eras. The Duhshama Kala is followed by the even worse Duhshama-duhshama Kala, *duḥṣama-duḥṣamā kāla* (von Glasenapp, *Jainism*, 333–35).

51. Steven Vose counts a dozen mentions of the Duhshama Kala and more general references to the bad condition of the times in the *Vividhatīrthakalpa* ("Making of a Medieval Jain Monk," 345–46).

52. Vose, "Making of a Medieval Jain Monk," 352.

53. On kiratas: *Vividhatīrthakalpa*, 57–58; *Vividhatīrthakalpaḥ*, trans. Chojnacki, 412–18; Vose, "Making of a Medieval Jain Monk," 353. On the king of Malwa: *Vividhatīrthakalpa*, 77–78; Vose, "Making of a Medieval Jain Monk," 353.

54. *Vividhatīrthakalpa*, 57, #31; also see translation in Granoff, "Tales of Broken Limbs," 200.

55. *Nābhinandanajinoddhāraprabandha* 3.19–20. Other scholars have also drawn attention to this causality in Kakka's text (Dundas, *Jains*, 145, Qvarnström, "Story Behind the Story," 200).
56. *Vividhatīrthakalpa*, 106; also see Granoff, "Tales of Broken Limbs," 202, and Granoff, "Jina Bleeds," 132.
57. On this passage, see Asoke Kumar Majumdar, *Chaulukyas of Gujarat*, 158.
58. *Prabandhakośa*, 117, line 16. On Gardabhilla in earlier Jain works, such as the (twelfth century?) *Kālakācāryakathā*, see Brown, *Story of Kālaka*, 3 and 8–9.
59. John Cort, personal communication.
60. *Prabandhakośa*, 117, lines 16–18 (gives the name as *jayantacandra*).
61. Granoff, "Tales of Broken Limbs," 196n11.
62. *Vividhatīrthakalpa*, 45 (names given as *sāhavadīṇa* and *puhavirāya*); Vose, "Making of a Medieval Jain Monk," 383.
63. *Vividhatīrthakalpa*, 97; also see translation in Vose, "Making of a Medieval Jain Monk," 4, and Granoff's translation of the full passage in Granoff and Shinohara, *Speaking of Monks*, 12–17. This constitutes an early use of "Hindu" outside of Perso-Arabic texts, as I discuss in chapter 3.
64. *Vividhatīrthakalpa*, 45 (#22); Vose, "Making of a Medieval Jain Monk," 386 (see 383–91 on this episode). Phyllis Granoff translates this story in Granoff and Shinohara, *Speaking of Monks*, 3–7.
65. Richard H. Davis, *Lives of Indian Images*, chap. 2; Eaton, "Temple Desecration," 62–69.
66. *Vividhatīrthakalpa*, 45–46.
67. *Vividhatīrthakalpa*, 95–97; translated by Granoff in Granoff and Shinohara, *Speaking of Monks*, 12–17.
68. Eaton, *India in the Persianate Age*, 71.
69. Balbir, "À Propos des Hymnes Jaina Multilingues"; Banarsi Das Jain, "Persian of Jain Hymns," 47–49; Vose, "Making of a Medieval Jain Monk," 224–36.
70. For an overview of the authors and texts within the Kashmiri *Rājataraṅgiṇī* tradition, see, e.g., Slaje, *Medieval Kashmir*, 7.
71. Although lost today, Prajyabhatta's *Rājataraṅgiṇī* was still extant in the seventeenth century (*Kavīndrācāryasūcipatram*, #2049).
72. The text of Pseudo-Jonaraja is found in one manuscript among the roughly two dozen manuscripts of Jonaraja's work (Slaje, introduction to *Rājataraṅgiṇī* of Jonaraja, 38–47). The modern practice of printing the two together makes it easy to mistakenly read Pseudo-Jonaraja as part of Jonaraja's original work. But the two should be analyzed separately, due to the time gap and authorial difference. I decline to take up either Pseudo-Jonaraja or Shuka here due to space constraints, and I look forward to another scholar analyzing these important texts. While I cite Walter Slaje's edition of Jonaraja's chronicle, readers ought to be cautious about using Slaje's accompanying English translation, especially to investigate questions about religious identities. Slaje translates numerous Sanskrit terms as "Muslim," a choice that one reviewer characterized as "somewhat rash" (Nemec, "Review of *Kingship in Kaśmīr*," 406). Slaje also inserts the term "Hindu" in his translation in brackets when there is not a Sanskrit

equivalent, which adds a modern interpretative layer (e.g., *Rājataraṅgiṇī* of Jonaraja, 163, 169, 185, 187, and 203). Readers should see these translation choices as Slaje's interpretation rather than as a close rendering of Jonaraja's *Rājataraṅgiṇī*. I do not include here the nineteenth-century *Rājataraṅgiṇī* of Damodara Pandit.

73. For a summary of the debate on whether Kalhana wrote a work of history or poetry and some of its implications, see Zutshi, "Translating the Past." As Luther Obrock points out, the history-or-poetry question comes up in the work of Bernhard Kolver and of Shonaleekha Kaul, both of whom posit that Kalhana penned a work of poetry, not history ("Translation and History," 6).
74. For other criticisms of the history-or-poetry debate concerning Kalhana, see, e.g., Cox, "Literary Register and Historical Consciousness," 131–32; Kaul, *Making of Early Kashmir*, chap. 2; Kaul, "'Seeing' the Past"; Slaje, "In the Guise of Poetry," 207–12; Thapar, *Past Before Us*, 598–99.
75. Bronner, "From Conqueror to Connoisseur," 161.
76. E.g., *Rājataraṅgiṇī* of Kalhana, numerous mentions of kavi in 1.3–24 and colophon on 3:294 (also note mention of his work's rasa in 1.23); *Rājataraṅgiṇī* of Jonaraja, numerous mentions of kavi and kavya in vv. 5–26; *Rājataraṅgiṇī* of Shrivara, numerous mentions of kavi and kavya in 1.1.3–10 and 3.2.
77. Respectively, *Rājataraṅgiṇī* of Kalhana, 1.10; *Rājataraṅgiṇī* of Jonaraja, v. 7; *Rājataraṅgiṇī* of Shrivara, 3.2. Also see Shrivara's use of *rājyavṛtta* in 3.5 and *rājavṛtta* in 1.1.9.
78. *Rājataraṅgiṇī* of Shrivara, 3.2; reading *svavāgyogyaprakāreṇa* as printed in Kaul ed.
79. E.g. (to varying degrees), Asthana, *Indian View of History*, 22; Basham, "Kashmir Chronicle," 58; Brokaw and Busch, "Relating the Past," 139; Chatterjee, "History in the Vernacular," 1; R. C. Majumdar, "Ideas of History in Sanskrit Literature," 14, 25; Raina, "Kalhana," 167; Raje, *Biography and History*, 36; Rao, Shulman, and Subrahmanyam, *Textures of Time*, 259–60; Salomon, "Notes on the Translations of Kalhaṇa's Rājataraṅgiṇī," 149; Shulman, "Kalhaṇa's *Rājataraṅgiṇī*," 127.
80. I disagree with attributions of "scientific accuracy" to Kalhana (Knutson, "Poetic Justice," 282).
81. McCrea, "Śāntarasa in the *Rājataraṅgiṇī*," 180–81.
82. Pollock, "Death of Sanskrit," 397; also see Sukla Das's comments on Jonaraja being a lesser poet in comparison to Kalhana ("Jonarāja and Dvitīya Rājataranginī," 61).
83. Thapar, *Past Before Us*, 625.
84. Some thinkers also criticize Kalhana for having penned "relatively weak historiography" (Rao, Shulman, and Subrahmanyam, *Textures of Time*, 259), following Keith, *Classical Sanskrit Literature*, 66–69; for a response, see Pollock, "Pretextures of Time," 375–76.
85. E.g., *Rājataraṅgiṇī* of Kalhana, 7.175, about a group of *mlecchārāja* in the early to mid-eleventh century (also see Stein, introduction to *Rājataraṅgiṇī*, 109).
86. E.g., *Rājataraṅgiṇī* of Kalhana, 1.170, 8.3412 (for Indo-Scythian or Kushan kings, it seems, ca. second century CE); 4.179 (for ethnic Turks in the early to mid-eighth century); 5.152, 7.51, 7.56, 7.70, and 7.118 (for Muslims; on 5.152 usage, see Stein's note J in *Rājataraṅgiṇī* of Kalhana, 3:338–39).
87. *Rājataraṅgiṇī* of Kalhana, 2.6, 3.128.

88. E.g., *Rājataraṅgiṇī* of Kalhana, 8.2264 (yavana), 7.63 (chandala), 7.53 and 7.64 (hammira).

89. E.g., *Rājataraṅgiṇī* of Kalhana, 7.1149, 8.885–88, 8.919–23.

90. *Rājataraṅgiṇī* of Kalhana, 7.520 (concubines) and 7.528–31 (shifty craftsman).

91. *Rājataraṅgiṇī* of Kalhana, 7.1232.

92. McCrea, "Śāntarasa in the *Rājataraṅgiṇī*," 194; Kalhana devoted roughly twenty-five percent of his *Rājataraṅgiṇī* to Jayasimha (Witzel, "Indian Historical Writing," 10).

93. *Rājataraṅgiṇī* of Kalhana, 7.1146–48 (incest; also noted in McCrea, "Śāntarasa in the *Rājataraṅgiṇī*," 195) and 7.1149 (supporting turushka rulers; pork).

94. *Rājataraṅgiṇī* of Kalhana, 7.1089–94.

95. For guesses about the mendicants' identity, see, e.g., Basham, "Harṣa of Kashmir," 688–91.

96. *grāme puretha nagare prāsādo na sa kaścana / harṣarājaturuṣkeṇa na yo niṣpratimīkṛtaḥ* (*Rājataraṅgiṇī* of Kalhana, 7.1095; my translation).

97. *no puraṃ pattanaṃ nāpi na grāmo na ca tad vanam / yatra sūhaturuṣkeṇa surāgāram aśeṣyata* (*Rājataraṅgiṇī* of Jonaraja, v. 603; my translation).

98. *Rājataraṅgiṇī* of Jonaraja, vv. 308–976 concern the Shah Miris. More generally on the textual history of Jonaraja's work, see Obrock, "Translation and History," 84; Slaje, introduction to *Rājataraṅgiṇī* of Jonaraja, 37–47.

99. For other brief assessments of Jonaraja, see, e.g., Nemec, "Review of *Kingship in Kaśmīr*," 405; Obrock, "Translation and History," 83–92; Pollock, "Death of Sanskrit," 396–400.

100. Shrivara cited in Obrock, "History at the End of History," 231. Also note Jonaraja's mention of Zayn listening to Sanskrit shastras, discussed later in this chapter).

101. For mentions during Jayasimha's rule, see *Rājataraṅgiṇī* of Jonaraja, vv. 32–36.

102. *Rājataraṅgiṇī* of Jonaraja, vv. 193–94.

103. On Rinchen's conversion to Islam, see Walter Slaje's note in *Rājataraṅgiṇī* of Jonaraja, 265n206. Jonaraja calls Rinchen a "suratrana" (v. 174), which was perhaps a subtle nod to his conversion (although the term "suratrana" was not limited to Muslim kings by this point in Sanskrit literary history).

104. *Rājataraṅgiṇī* of Jonaraja, v. 308.

105. For a comprehensive list of Jonaraja's uses of these terms, see Ogura, "Incompatible Outsiders," 199–202. Jonaraja makes one mention of Persians ("parasika," v. 369).

106. Ogura, "Incompatible Outsiders," 185–86.

107. *Rājataraṅgiṇī* of Jonaraja, v. 116.

108. Slaje in *Rājataraṅgiṇī* of Jonaraja, 262n131. Amir Khusrau notes that Khajlak was part of a Mongol army that marched against the Delhi Sultanate around 1288 (Elliot and Dowson, *History of India*, 3:527–30).

109. *Rājataraṅgiṇī* of Jonaraja, v. 161 (*rākṣasa*) and vv. 598–99 (*mleccharāja* and Harsha).

110. *Rājataraṅgiṇī* of Jonaraja, vv. 571–76.

111. *Rājataraṅgiṇī* of Jonaraja, v. 600. Pseudo-Jonaraja adds a heavy interpretive layer here, which should not be read as part of Jonaraja's original text (printed in *Rājataraṅgiṇī* of Jonaraja, 168–69).

112. *Rājataraṅgiṇī* of Jonaraja, v. 762.

113. *Rājataraṅgiṇī* of Jonaraja, v. 820.

114. Other scholars have also noticed that Jonaraja does not call Zayn al-Abidin a "mleccha" (e.g., Mohammed, "Sultan Zain-ul-Abidin," 223).

115. *harāṃśajaḥ . . . yasyāsīc cakṣuṣāṃ trayam* (*Rājataraṅgiṇī* of Jonaraja, v. 134).

116. *Rājataraṅgiṇī* of Jonaraja, v. 132.

117. Deambi, *Corpus of Śāradā Inscriptions*, 114–15.

118. *Rājataraṅgiṇī* of Jonaraja, vv. 430–38.

119. *Rājataraṅgiṇī* of Jonaraja, vv. 455–57.

120. *Rājataraṅgiṇī* of Jonaraja, vv. 442 and 462, respectively. Earlier scholars have taken some liberties in their comments on the appearance of the term "hinduka," exactly twice, in Jonaraja's text. Some have broadened these two uses to the entire chronicle, saying that Jonaraja wrote about hinduka rule (Pollock, "Death of Sanskrit," 399–400) or a Hindu worldview (Nemec, "Review of *Kingship in Kaśmīr*," 405).

121. *Rājataraṅgiṇī* of Jonaraja, vv. 786–93 and 801–4 (giving justice), 817 (jizya), 889 (mathas and dharmashalas), and 898 (feeding yogis).

122. *Rājataraṅgiṇī* of Jonaraja, v. 841 (see vv. 841–56 for the entire episode).

123. *Rājataraṅgiṇī* of Jonaraja, v. 823. On this verse and the language used to describe Tilakacharya, see Slaje, "Last Buddhist of Kashmir," 188–91.

124. *Rājataraṅgiṇī* of Jonaraja, v. 824.

125. On the *Nīlamatapurāṇa*, see *Rājataraṅgiṇī* of Jonaraja, v. 907. For other references, see, e.g., Mohammed, "Sultan Zain-ul-Abidin," 220–22.

126. *Rājataraṅgiṇī* of Jonaraja, vv. 475–76.

127. *Rājataraṅgiṇī* of Jonaraja, vv. 695–713.

128. The *Bahāristān-i-Shāhī* mentions Ali Shah going on hajj at roughly the same time (*Bahāristān-i-Shāhī* 11.1; also noted by Walter Slaje in *Rājataraṅgiṇī* of Jonaraja, 282n564).

129. *Rājataraṅgiṇī* of Jonaraja, v. 247 (see variant readings noted in Srikanth Kaul's edition).

130. Walter Slaje notes a possible similarity between one verse by Jonaraja and two verses attributed to Lal Ded (*Rājataraṅgiṇī* of Jonaraja, 269n286). However, this suggestion, especially the idea that Jonaraja is echoing Lal Ded rather than the other way around, ought to be tempered by uncertainty about the age of verses attributed to Lal Ded in the *Lallāvākyāni* (Accardi, "Asceticism, Gender, and the State," appendix D; Accardi, "Orientalism and the Invention of Kashmiri Religion(s)"). More generally on Lal Ded and Sheikh Nooruddin, see, e.g., Zutshi, *Languages of Belonging*, 18–27; Khan, *Kashmir's Transition to Islam*. On memories and sociopolitical usages of these figures in the sixteenth and seventeenth centuries, see Accardi, "Asceticism, Gender, and the State."

131. *Rājataraṅgiṇī* of Jonaraja, vv. 586–87.

132. *Rājataraṅgiṇī* of Jonaraja, vv. 651–75; translated in Obrock, "Translation and History," 87–90. For a brief account of Suha Bhatta, see Slaje, "Three Bhaṭṭas," 332–33.

133. *Rājataraṅgiṇī* of Jonaraja, vv. 596 and 605, respectively.

134. *Rājataraṅgiṇī* of Jonaraja, vv. 659 (suicide) and 668 (dressed as Muslims).

135. *vicchettum icchatā vidyāṃ tenāpahatavṛttibhiḥ / laḍitaṃ prativeśmāgraṃ piṇḍīlobhād dvijaiś śvavat* (*Rājataraṅgiṇī* of Jonaraja, v. 669).

136. *Rājataraṅgiṇī* of Jonaraja, v. 670; also noted by Ogura, "Incompatible Outsiders," 189–90.

137. *Rājataraṅgiṇī* of Jonaraja, v. 651. The verse works better in Sanskrit, where several pairs of words echo one another, such as lion (*mṛgapati*) and other animals (*mṛgān*), *khātā* (earth) and *khanitrair* (spades).

138. Walter Slaje and, following him, Luther Obrock have argued that Shrivara wrote two independent chronicles: the *Jainataraṅgiṇī* (on Zayn and his son, Haydar Shah; books 1 and 2 of Shrivara's work as printed) and the *Rājataraṅgiṇī* (on Hasan Shah and Muhammad Shah; books 3 and 4 of Shrivara's work as printed) (Slaje, "Note on the Genesis"; Obrock, "History at the End of History," 223–24; Obrock, "Translation and History," 94–95). I think that the evidence furnished for this thesis, namely the use of two titles at different points and a benedictory verse in the opening of book 3, is suggestive but not definitive. Notably, Jonaraja offers a benedictory verse to begin his treatment of the Shah Miri dynasty slightly less than one-third of the way through his *Rājataraṅgiṇī*, which everyone takes as a single work (*Rājataraṅgiṇī* of Jonaraja, v. 308). In any case, other Kashmiri Sanskrit intellectuals soon understood Shrivara's work as a single unit. Writing in 1513, only a few decades after Shrivara completed his chronicle(s), Shuka referred to the *Rājataraṅgiṇī*s of Jonaraja and Shrivara as a pair (*dvayam*) (*Rājataraṅgiṇī* of Shuka, 1.6; also cited in Slaje, "Note on the Genesis," 385).

139. On these political events, see, e.g., Accardi, "Asceticism, Gender, and the State," 284.

140. For an analysis of the first book of Shrivara's *Rājataraṅgiṇī*, see Obrock, "History at the End of History."

141. *Rājataraṅgiṇī* of Shrivara, 1.4.5 (*harāṃśa* in Singh ed. and *śivāṃśa* in Kaul ed.); *Rājataraṅgiṇī* of Jonaraja, v. 134 (*harāṃśaja*).

142. *Rājataraṅgiṇī* of Shrivara, 1.1.52–55; I am grateful to Dean Accardi and Luther Obrock for drawing my attention to this passage.

143. E.g., *Rājataraṅgiṇī* of Shrivara, 1.6.22 (horses and Khurasan) and 1.6.26 (Mecca).

144. E.g., *merasaidamuhammada*, i.e., Amir Saida [Sayyid] Muhammad in the *Rājataraṅgiṇī* of Jonaraja, v. 573.

145. . . . *saidanāsīrādīn samāgatān paigambarānvaye jātān* . . . (*Rājataraṅgiṇī* of Shrivara, 3.153 in Kaul ed. and 3.154 in Singh ed.).

146. Accardi, "Asceticism, Gender, and the State," 257–58.

147. *Rājataraṅgiṇī* of Shrivara, 3.159 in Kaul ed. and 3.160 in Singh ed.

148. E.g., *Rājataraṅgiṇī* of Shrivara, 3.546 in Kaul ed. and 3.547 in Singh ed.

149. E.g., *saidās* . . . *turuṣkāśvastamānasāḥ* (*Rājataraṅgiṇī* of Shrivara, 3.449 in Kaul ed. and 3.450 in Singh ed.); *saidāḥ* . . . *turuṣkādṛtamānasāḥ* (*Rājataraṅgiṇī* of Shrivara, 3.526 in Kaul ed. and 3.527 in Singh ed.).

150. E.g., Shrivara calls the Saidas "turushka" in 3.337 in Kaul ed.

151. *Rājataraṅgiṇī* of Shrivara, 3.154 in Kaul ed. and 3.155 in Singh ed. (wives and estates). On Baihaqi Sayyid intermarriages with the Kashmiri Sultanate, see Accardi, "Asceticism, Gender, and the State," appendix B.

152. *Rājataraṅgiṇī* of Shrivara, 3.155–68 in Kaul ed. and 3.156–69 in Singh ed.

153. I am summarizing here based on *Rājataraṅgiṇī* of Shrivara, latter half of chapter 3.

154. *Rājataraṅgiṇī* of Shrivara, 4.1–3.

155. *Rājataraṅgiṇī* of Shrivara, chapter 4.

156. *Rājataraṅgiṇī* of Shrivara, 4.17.

157. *Rājataraṅgiṇī* of Shrivara, 4.16 (*deśyasaṃskṛtaśāstravidvat-*).
158. See, e.g., on hunting, *Rājataraṅgiṇī* of Shrivara, 3.501–13 (deer) and 4.21–23 (birds) in Kaul ed. Alcohol consumption and beef eating come up several times in books 3 and 4.
159. *Rājataraṅgiṇī* of Shrivara, 3.513 in Kaul ed.
160. *Rājataraṅgiṇī* of Shrivara, 3.546 in Kaul ed. and 3.547 in Singh ed.
161. Bakker, "Somaśarman, Somavaṃśa, and Somasiddhānta," 5–7.
162. *Rājataraṅgiṇī* of Shrivara, 1.1.45–50. For a list of Shrivara's use of "mausula," see Satoshi Ogura's chart in "Incompatible Outsiders," 202–5.
163. *Rājataraṅgiṇī* of Shrivara, 1.1.77 (on the exact Persian term used in this passage, see Obrock, "Translation and History," 98n189).
164. *Rājataraṅgiṇī* of Shrivara, 1.5.76. Later he describes Sikandar as "attached to Islamic teaching" (*yavanendramatapriya*) (*Rājataraṅgiṇī* of Shrivara, 3.265 in Kaul ed. and 3.267 in Singh ed.).
165. *Rājataraṅgiṇī* of Shrivara, 3.270 in Kaul ed. and 3.272 in Singh ed.; 4.504–5 in Kaul ed. and 4.506–7 in Singh ed.
166. *Rājataraṅgiṇī* of Shrivara, 3.224 in Kaul ed. and 3.226 in Singh ed., on the naming of Muhammad Khan (Sanskrit *mahmadakhāna*).
167. *Pṛthvīrājavijaya* 6.7.
168. *Rājataraṅgiṇī* of Shrivara, 2.88–97 (*durvyasanamātra* in 2.90 and *bahukāruṣu dattavittāḥ* in 2.89).
169. The more standard Sanskrit term is *prāḍvivāka* (e.g., *Dharmasūtra* of Gautama, 13.26, 13.27, and 13.31). All five printed editions of Shrivara's work that I consulted give the term as *prāḍviveka* (1.1.45 in ed. Dhar, eds. Durgaprasada and Peterson, ed. Kaul, and ed. Singh; p. 2 of Shrivara in Calcutta 1835). Srikanth Kaul notes a manuscript variant of *prāḍvivāka* (9n45a).
170. *Rājataraṅgiṇī* of Shrivara, 2.205 in Kaul ed. and 2.206 in Singh ed.
171. Nicholson, *Unifying Hinduism*, 192–96.
172. *svaveda*: *Rājataraṅgiṇī* of Shrivara, 3.559 in Kaul ed. and 3.560 in Singh ed.; *yacchāstra*: *Rājataraṅgiṇī* of Shrivara, 2.93 in Kaul ed., where *yac* refers to *mleccha* (2.90), and *mausula* (2.89).
173. *Rājataraṅgiṇī* of Shrivara, 3.277 in Kaul ed. and 3.279 in Singh ed.
174. *Rājataraṅgiṇī* of Shrivara, 3.286 in Kaul ed. and 3.288 in Singh ed.
175. *Rājataraṅgiṇī* of Shrivara, 3.279 in Kaul ed. and 3.281 in Singh ed. (reading *praṇatā* with Kaul).
176. *Rājataraṅgiṇī* of Shrivara, 3.282 in Kaul ed. and 3.284 in Singh ed. (*catuḥstambha*); *Rājataraṅgiṇī* of Shrivara, 3.184 in Kaul ed. and 3.185 in Singh ed., mentions building *masoda*s and *hujira*s or *hajira*s (Persian *ḥaẓīra*, I think) with wood and stone.
177. *Rājataraṅgiṇī* of Shrivara, 1.7.173 in Kaul ed. and 1.7.174 in Singh ed.
178. E.g., *Rājataraṅgiṇī* of Shrivara, 3.284 in Kaul ed. and 3.286 in Singh ed.
179. E.g., Khan, *Kashmir's Transition to Islam*, and Accardi, "Embedded Mystics," 247–48, respectively.
180. E.g., note Walter Slaje's easy assumption that "hinduka" means Hindu (*Medieval Kashmir*, 4).

181. *Rājataraṅgiṇī* of Shrivara, 2.122–23 in Kaul ed.

182. *Rājataraṅgiṇī* of Shrivara, 4.504–5 in Kaul ed. and 4.506–7 in Singh ed.

183. *Rājataraṅgiṇī* of Shrivara, 3.270 in Kaul ed. and 3.272 in Singh ed. (correcting Singh's error of *vablabha* for *vallabha*).

184. *Rājataraṅgiṇī* of Shrivara, 3.291 in Kaul ed. and 3.293 in Singh ed.

185. *Rājataraṅgiṇī* of Shrivara, 2.122–23 in Kaul ed.

186. *Rājataraṅgiṇī* of Shrivara, 3.205 in Kaul ed. and 3.206–7 in Singh ed.

187. *Rājataraṅgiṇī* of Shrivara, 3.216 in Kaul ed. and 3.218 in Singh ed. The simile is nice since *gul* in the queen's name means "rose."

188. *Rājataraṅgiṇī* of Shrivara 3.175 in Kaul ed. and 3.176 in Singh ed.

189. I refer to the first two terms earlier in this chapter. *madrasa*: *Rājataraṅgiṇī* of Shrivara, 3.175 in Kaul ed. and 3.176 in Singh ed.; *khāngāh* (Sanskrit *khānagāha*): *Rājataraṅgiṇī* of Shrivara, 3.177, 3.184, 3.193, 3.197, and 3.200 in Kaul ed.

190. *Rājataraṅgiṇī* of Shrivara, 4.153 (*yavanākṣara* . . .); *Rājataraṅgiṇī* of Shrivara, 2.132 in Kaul ed. and 2.133 in Singh ed. (*pārasībhāṣayā kāvya*).

191. *Rājataraṅgiṇī* of Shrivara, 1.4.39.

192. *Rājataraṅgiṇī* of Shrivara, 1.5.83 Compare to mentions during Akbar's period that Zayn al-Abidin had texts translated between four languages: Arabic, Persian, Kashmiri, and Hindi (*Āʾīn-i Akbarī*, 1:584).

193. In his Persian history completed in 1579, known as *Tārīkh-i Sayyid ʿAlī* or *Tārīkh-i Kashmīr*, Sayyid Ali also notes Persian translations of the Mahabharata and the *Rājataraṅgiṇī*, probably meaning Kalhana's text (*Tārīkh-i Sayyid ʿAlī*, 21 in Persian; suggestion of only Kalhana's text in Ogura, "Note on the Genesis," 135). Mulla Ahmad translated some of the rajataranginis and the Mahabharata into Persian (Shukla, "Persian Translations of Sanskrit Works," 188).

194. Shrivara calls vernaculars *deśādivāg* (*Rājataraṅgiṇī* of Shrivara, 1.5.83), *bhāṣā* (3.236 in Kaul ed. and 3.238 in Singh ed.), and *deśya* (4.16). Elsewhere in the text, Shrivara uses *deśa* to specify Persian (1.4.39), but context makes it clear that the term also doubles as a reference to non-Persian vernaculars used in Kashmir. E.g., 1.5.83 lists *deśa* and *pārasī* separately; 3.236 in Kaul ed. mentions songs being translated between *bhāṣā* and *pārasī*; 4.16 says that the Persian-speaking Saida jeered at people who knew *deśya*. Cf. Pollock, "Sanskrit Literary Culture," 93n117, and Eaton, *India in the Persianate World*, 119 (both based on applying the usage in 1.4.39 to Shrivara's entire chronicle).

195. Truschke, *Culture of Encounters*, 104–6.

196. *Rājataraṅgiṇī* of Shrivara, 3.236–38 in Kaul ed. and 3.238–40 in Singh ed.

197. *Rājataraṅgiṇī* of Shrivara, 3.256–7 in Kaul ed. and 3.258–9 in Singh ed. (*bharataśāstrādeḥ*); *deśabhāṣā* cannot refer to Persian here since Shrivara says that the sultan does not know *deśabhāṣā*.

198. *Rājataraṅgiṇī* of Shrivara, 3.245 in Kaul ed. and 3.247 in Singh ed.

199. E.g., see Rattan Lal Hangloo's "Kashmiriyat," which offers an overview of different definitions of the term, an argument that it existed in premodernity, and in conclusion proclaims that, despite the region's current difficulties, "*Kashmiriyat* will never die" (62).

200. For a thought-provoking attempt to think about the possible relationships of history to political presents and contemporary communities, see Scott, "Dehistoricising History."
201. *Rājataraṅgiṇī* of Shuka, 1.10; compare to *Rājataraṅgiṇī* of Jonaraja, v. 7, and *Rājataraṅgiṇī* of Shrivara, 1.1.9, 3.2, 3.5.
202. Ogura, "Note on the Genesis," 135–46; Ogura, "Transmission Lines of Historical Information," 33–44; Ogura, "Turning *Taraṅgiṇī* into *Tārīḫ*."
203. Abul Fazl, *Āʾīn-i Akbarī*, 1:578.
204. See Satoshi Ogura's table 7 in "Transmission Lines of Historical Information," 55; see p. 53 for the suggestion that the author of *Bahāristān-i Shāhī* may have worked directly from the Sanskrit rajataranginis. On some Kashmiri Persian tarikhs dating to the seventeenth century and later, see Zutshi, "Past as Tradition."
205. Satoshi Ogura discusses this in his "Note on the Genesis," 144–45 (pp. 138–39 for *tarjuma*).
206. *Kavīndrācāryasūcipatram*, #2046 (Kalhana), #2047 (Jonaraja?), #2048 (Shrivara), and #2049 (Prajyabhatta).
207. See the table of contents as listed in the introduction to *Purātanaprabandhasaṅgraha*, 4–6. For a discussion on Padalipta's historicity from our vantage point, see Vose, "Making of a Medieval Jain Monk," 341–42.
208. *Purātanaprabandhasaṅgraha*, 82–83; *Prabandhacintāmaṇi*, 107–9.
209. John Cort speaks of "localized histories" ("Genres of Jain History," 480–90); for more on how the local concerns of specific Jain communities intersected with Indo-Muslim politics, see chapter 5.

5. Meeting the Mughals and Reformulating Jain Identity

1. Truschke, *Culture of Encounters*, chap. 1.
2. Steven Vose mentions the substitution of Firuz Shah ("Making of a Medieval Jain Monk," 412). Also, an early seventeenth-century *Kharataragacchapaṭṭāvalī* dubs Jinaprabha "the awakener of glorious Alauddin Padshah" (*śrīallāvadīnapātisāhipratibodhaka*) (*Kharataragacchapaṭṭāvalīsaṅgraha*, 54; also cited in Vose, "Making of a Medieval Jain Monk," 417).
3. On Sanskrit texts sponsored by or dedicated to the Mughals, see Truschke, *Culture of Encounters*, chap. 2.
4. The four known manuscripts of Padmasagara's *Jagadgurukāvya* are all in Jain bhandars (libraries), three in Patan and one in Chani. Several manuscripts of Jayasoma's *Mantrikarmacandravaṃśāvalīprabandha* are in bhandars. D. N. Marshall lists eight manuscripts of Devavimala's *Hīrasaubhāgya*, most of which are in bhandars (*Mughals in India*, 133, #422). The single printed edition of Devavimala's *Hīrasundaramahākāvya* lists three manuscripts, all in bhandars (introduction to *Hīrasundaramahākāvya*, 8). Siddhichandra's *Bhānucandragaṇicarita* is found in a single manuscript, which was in a private Jain

collection in Bikaner as of 1941 (preface to *Bhānucandragaṇicarita*, v–vi). Hemavijaya and Gunavijaya's *Vijayapraśastimahākāvya* exists in at least ten manuscripts, about half of which are in bhandars (Marshall, *Mughals in India*, 185, #632). Many of the listed copies of Vallabha Pathaka's *Vijayadevamāhātmya* are in bhandars (Marshall, *Mughals in India*, 473, #1819; *New Catalogus Catalogorum*, 29:43).

5. The exception is Jayasoma's *Mantrikarmacandravaṃśāvalīprabandha*. On links between Jain monks and the laity regarding interactions with Mughal elites, see Shalin Jain's substantial work (e.g., *Identity, Community, and State*, "Interaction of the 'Lords,'" "Jain Elites and the Mughal State," "Merchants and the Rulers," "Piety, Laity, and Royalty"). Also see Surendra Gopal's many essays on Jains in Mughal India, collected in *Jains in India*.
6. The year 1667 is the latest date that I see in the *Tapāgacchapaṭṭāvalī* of Meghavijaya, and he died in 1704.
7. I thank Andrew Ollett for some of these suggestions.
8. Dundas, *History, Scripture and Controversy*, 7–8. On forms of Gujarati in premodernity, see Yashaschandra, "Hemacandra to *Hind Svarāj*," 574–81.
9. Yashaschandra, "Hemacandra to *Hind Svarāj*," 572–73.
10. Muniraj Vidyavijayji draws upon and discusses *Lābhodayarāsa*, *Vijayatilakasūrirāsa*, and *Hīravijayasūrirāsa* (*Monk and a Monarch*). Mohanlal Dalichand Desai mentions Gunavinaya's *Karmacandravaṃsaprabandha* in the introduction to *Bhānucandragaṇicarita*, 12.
11. For more on Karmachandra's time at court, see Shalin Jain, "Centre and the 'Locality.'"
12. A solid starting point for thinking about connections between Sanskrit and vernacular traditions for early modern Jain thinkers is given by John Cort in his "Defense of Icons in Three Languages," on one Jain author who wrote on the same subject in Prakrit, Sanskrit, and a vernacular.
13. Pollock, *Language of the Gods*, chaps. 8–10.
14. E.g., Cort, "Genres of Jain History," 483.
15. Carr, *What Is History?*, 10.
16. Shvetambara writers also do not seem to reflect on the apparent lack of relations between the Mughals and Digambara Jains. The absence of Mughal-Digambara relations is a tad surprising, given the Mughal interest in Shvetambara monks and that between three and five Digambara bhattaraka seats were located in Agra during the reigns of Akbar and Jahangir (Detige, "Digambara Renouncers").
17. On the Nagapuriya, see Shivprasad, *Jain Shvetambar Gaccho ka Samkshipt Itihas*, 2:672–92.
18. Truschke, *Culture of Encounters*, 31–32 and 69–74; *Akbarasāhiśṛṅgāradarpaṇa* 1.1 (Rahman) and 4.27, 4.44, and 4.83–85 (addressed to Akbar, who is named in the vocative in four of these verses).
19. *Bhānucandragaṇicarita* 2.140–68; the story also appears in the *Hīravijayasūrirāsa* (Vidyavijayji, *Monk and a Monarch*, 42).
20. Dundas, *History, Scripture and Controversy*, 134; Granoff in Granoff and Shinohara, *Speaking of Monks*, 39 and 89n68.
21. Dundas, *History, Scripture and Controversy*, 224n88.

22. Dharmasagara's *Tapāgacchapaṭṭāvalī* consists of twenty Prakrit verses accompanied by a Sanskrit autocommentary.
23. *Tapāgacchapaṭṭāvalī* of Dharmasagara, 70 (Anandavimala's sultan), 71 (Sultan Mahmud), and 72 (Akbar). Note a report that a Berlin manuscript of Dharmasagara's work names Anandavimala's sultan as *suratrāṇa-mahimūda* (Weber, *Handschriften-Verzeichnisse de Königlichen Bibliothek zu Berlin*, 1014). Dharmasagara does not specify further the identities of the two sultans. The Berlin catalogue proposes that Anandavimala's sultan was Mahmud II of Malwa (Weber, *Handschriften-Verzeichnisse de Königlichen Bibliothek zu Berlin*, 1014n3). My best guess for Vijayadana's sultan is Mahmud III (r. 1536–54) of Gujarat's Muzaffarid dynasty.
24. Padmasagara's *Jagadgurukāvya* v. 138; Siddhichandra's *Bhānucandragaṇicarita* 1.96; Devavimala's *Hīrasaubhāgya* 11.18. Only Hemavijaya, writing in the 1620s and 1630s, specifies that the governor's name was Itimad Khan (*atimetakhāna*; *Vijayapraśastimahākāvya* 9.15).
25. Verses printed in introduction to *Akbarasāhiśṛṅgāradarpaṇa*, xx.
26. R. G. Bhandarkar, *Report on the Search for Sanskrit Mss.*, 42–44; I also discuss this passage in Truschke, *Culture of Encounters*, 32.
27. Also note Nayasundara's *Bṛhatpośālikapaṭṭāvalī*, on a branch of the Tapa Gaccha, which describes relations between Jain monks and the rulers of Gujarat going further back in time (see, e.g., pp. 31–32).
28. *Epigraphia Indica*, 1:324.
29. *Tapāgacchapaṭṭāvalī* of Dharmasagara, 73. Dharmasagara's reference attests that the *Hīrasaubhāgya* existed, at least in a draft form, by 1592; accordingly, I have expanded its composition date range as compared to Truschke, *Culture of Encounters*, 167. The work was likely written over a period of years, perhaps a few decades (Dundas, *History, Scripture and Controversy*, 59).
30. *Tapāgacchapaṭṭāvalī* of Meghavijaya, 88 (text named as *Vijayapraśastikāvya*).
31. *Digvijayamahākāvya* 4.22.
32. *Rājataraṅgiṇī* of Kalhana, 1.11–15; see Stein's discussion in introduction to *Rājataraṅgiṇī* of Kalhana, 24–27.
33. *Tapāgacchapaṭṭāvalī* of Dharmasagara, 73.
34. *Epigraphia Indica*, 2:59–60, no. 13 (*ṣāṇmāsikasakalajantujātābhayadānapravarttana*); *Epigraphia Indica*, 2:52–53, no. 12, v. 17 (*ṣaṇmāsābhayadānapuṣṭa*) and v. 18 (jizya); *Kṛpārasakośa* v. 126 (jizya) and v. 127 (*jantujātamabhayaṃ pratimāsaṣaṭkaṃ*).
35. *Hīrasaubhāgya* 14.195; *Jagadgurukāvya* vv. 182 and 185.
36. 1594 Patan inscription in *Epigraphia Indica*, 1:324; *Mantrikarmacandravaṃśāvalīprabandha* vv. 446.
37. Vrat, *Glimpses of Jaina Sanskrit Mahākāvyas*, 91–108.
38. Dundas, *History, Scripture and Controversy*, 59.
39. E.g., John Cort divides history writing by genre in his "Genres of Jain History"; Phyllis Granoff contrasts different genres in "Biographies of Siddhasena," 331.
40. *Bhānucandragaṇicarita* 1.14.
41. *Hīrasaubhāgya* 10.1–10; 10.1 (Shri: *kelinilayo nalinālayāyāḥ*), 10.7 (thunderbolt), and 10.8 (Alaka).

42. *Vijayapraśastimahākāvya* 9.20 (9.20–23 on Fatehpur Sikri).

43. *Hīrasaubhāgya* 10.71–72.

44. Mishra, *Inscriptions of Rājasthān*, 3:28, lines 22–23. Since the inscription is fragmentary, we may be missing some of the place names in this list. The temple's main icons were installed by Indra of the Shrimal community (Mishra, *Inscriptions of Rājasthān*, 3:27). Also cited in Sreenivasan, "Rethinking Kingship and Authority," 557–58.

45. *Tapāgacchapaṭṭāvalī* of Dharmasagara, 73.

46. *Ā'īn-i Akbarī*, 1:386.

47. E.g., *lābhapura* in *Bhānucandragaṇicarita* 2.34; *Digvijayamahākāvya* 4.25 (*lābhapurī*); *Mantrikarmacandravaṃśāvalīprabandha* v. 381; *Tapāgacchapaṭṭāvalī* of Meghavijaya, 89.

48. *Kṛpārasakośa* vv. 66–86; Truschke, *Culture of Encounters*, 75–76. Also see the full translation of the *Kṛpārasakośa* in Truschke, "Mughal Sanskrit Literature," 457–73.

49. *gūrjaraṃ deśaṃ svargakhaṇḍamivāparam* (*Bhānucandragaṇicarita* 1.64).

50. E.g., *Mantrikarmacandravaṃśāvalīprabandha* vv. 372 and 386.

51. *Bhānucandragaṇicarita* 3.43. For the episode more broadly, see *Bhānucandragaṇicarita* 1.9 (*śatruñjayakṣoṇībhṛtkaramocana*) and 3.32–71. Siddhichandra reports on several other disputes over Shatrunjaya, including a time when Tapa Gaccha Jains blocked Kharatara Gaccha affiliates from building a temple there (*Bhānucandragaṇicarita* 4.119–22; also see 4.163–67.). Siddhichandra also mentions Bhanuchandra nullifying a Shatrunjaya-related tax in the colophon of his commentary on Bana's *Kādambarī* (p. 609).

52. *Epigraphia Indica*, 2:50–59.

53. *suratāṇanūradījahāṅgīrasavāīvijayirājye* (*Epigraphia Indica*, 2:60–67, nos. 15, 17, 18, 19, 20, 23, and 24; no. 15 has *nūradīna* for *nūradī*); *pātasāhāśrīśāhājyāhāṃvijayarājye* (*Epigraphia Indica*, 2:72, no. 30).

54. *Epigraphia Indica*, 2:61–63, nos. 17–20.

55. *Jagadgurukāvya* vv. 168–70; *Hīrasaubhāgya* 14.6–13.

56. *Jagadgurukāvya* v. 170.

57. *Hīrasaubhāgya* 14.7 and 14.9, respectively.

58. *Vividhatīrthakalpa*, 45–46; translated by Granoff in Granoff and Shinohara, *Speaking of Monks*, 3–7.

59. *Hīrasaubhāgya* 14.91–128.

60. *Hīrasaubhāgya* 14.93.

61. Leaving aside the question of whether Akbar was illiterate, we have no direct evidence that Akbar could speak or understand Sanskrit, Prakrit, or Gujarati.

62. *Hīrasaubhāgya* 14.101 notes Akbar's persistent offers.

63. There is fairly extensive scholarship on gift giving in Mughal India and perceptions thereof across cultural boundaries. E.g., Gordon, *Robes of Honour*; Loomba, "Of Gifts, Ambassadors, and Copy-Cats"; Siebenhüner, "Approaching Diplomatic and Courtly Gift-Giving."

64. Cort, "Jain Knowledge Warehouses" (laymen and bhandars); Granoff, "Authority and Innovation," 49–50 (monks at court).

65. E.g., 1584 Akbar farman against animal slaughter during Paryushan (Desai, introduction to *Bhānucandragaṇicarita*, 77–78); 1591 Akbar farman on temple construction (Desai,

introduction to *Bhānucandragaṇicarita*, 78–79; Vidyavijayji, *Monk and a Monarch*, 95–99); 1601 confirmation of 1591 farman (Desai, introduction to *Bhānucandragaṇicarita*, 79–81; Vidyavijayji, *Monk and a Monarch*, 100–4); 1605 order prohibiting animal slaughter for six months annually (Desai, introduction to *Bhānucandragaṇicarita*, 82–83; Vidyavijayji, *Monk and a Monarch*, 110–14).

66. *Bhānucandragaṇicarita* 4.93–101. Mohanlal Dalichand Desai notes that the stupa still stands in Diu and gives a Sanskrit inscription found on the stupa that mentions Akbar (introduction to *Bhānucandragaṇicarita*, 41–42n58a).
67. Prakrit *phuramāṇa* appears in the *Vividhatīrthakalpa* (E.g., pp. 46, 95, 96, 106). In Jain Sanskrit texts, the term sometimes appears as *sphuranmāna* (e.g., *Hīrasaubhāgya* 11.18). Devavimala defines *sphuranmāna* as *pharamāna iti yavanabhāṣayā lekhākhyā* in *Hīrasaubhāgya*, commentary on 11.18.
68. *Mantrikarmacandravaṃśāvalīprabandha* vv. 396–98.
69. *Vijayadevamāhātmya* 6.15.
70. *Bhānucandragaṇicarita* 2.121.
71. See Truschke, *Culture of Encounters*, chap. 1.
72. *Bhānucandragaṇicarita* 2.67–71 and 2.106–9.
73. *Muntakhab al-Tavārīkh*, 2:260–61 and 2:322; *Commentary of Father Monserrate*, 184.
74. *Mantrikarmacandravaṃśāvalīprabandha* vv. 359–65; *Bhānucandragaṇicarita* 2.140–68.
75. On the Mughals' Brahmin astrologers, see Minkowski, "Learned Brahmins and the Mughal Court."
76. *Hīrasaubhāgya* 13.137–43. Also see the translation of the same passage in Dundas, "Jain Perceptions of Islam," 38. This passage is also found in Devavimala's *Hīrasundaramahākāvya* 13.136–42. On this text, see Dundas, *History, Scripture and Controversy*, 59.
77. Truschke, "Dangerous Debates," 1321–22.
78. *Hīrasaubhāgya*, commentary on 11.18 (*khāna iti nāma yavanajātau prasiddham*).
79. *Hīrasaubhāgya* 13.144–51 (also see the translation of the same passage in Paul Dundas, "Jain Perceptions of Islam," 39). This passage is also found in Devavimala's *Hīrasundaramahākāvya* 13.143–50. I have added the names of Hiravijaya and Abul Fazl for clarity at several places.
80. *Hīrasaubhāgya* 17.186–97; also noted in Dundas, *History, Scripture and Controversy*, 70.
81. *Bhānucandragaṇicarita* 4.124–29. Note a similar scene of Akbar becoming filled with compassion (*kāruṇya*) at Chittor and so releasing the captured Rajput king (*Jagadgurukāvya* vv. 118–20; discussed in chapter 7).
82. Truschke, "Dangerous Debates," 1338–39; *Bhānucandragaṇicarita* 4.301–05.
83. For scholarly takes on Jain theism, see, e.g., Balbir, "Deities"; Cort, *Jains in the World*, 91–99. For practitioner takes on the same subject, see, e.g., Cort, "Jain Questions and Answers"; JAINA, "Concept of God."
84. *Hīrasaubhāgya* 14.26–27 (*parameśitā*, glossed in commentary as "parameshvara"); *Tapāgacchapaṭṭāvalī* of Dharmasagara, 73 (parameshvara).
85. Truschke, *Culture of Encounters*, 45–46.
86. *Epigraphia Indica*, 2:54, v. 29, reading the suggested alternative of *pratyakṣa* (n. 10).

87. *Bhānucandragaṇicarita* 4.42.
88. *Vijayapraśastimahākāvya* 12.216.
89. Meghavijaya mentions some Brahmins (*kenacidbhaṭṭena*, *Tapāgacchapaṭṭāvalī*, p. 89).
90. *Vijayadevamāhātmya* 6.27.
91. *Vijayapraśastimahākāvya* 12.178, and *Tapāgacchapaṭṭāvalī* of Meghavijaya, p. 89.
92. Fisher, *Hindu Pluralism*, 32 and 206n1 (as the author notes, the verse often has slight variants).
93. *Vijayadevamāhātmya* 6.28.
94. *Vijayadevamāhātmya* 6.28–40.
95. *Vijayadevamāhātmya* 6.97–106.
96. Pierce Taylor, "Jaina *Maṭha*." I am also grateful to John Cort for this point.
97. Pierce Taylor, "Jaina *Maṭha*."
98. *Jagadgurukāvya* vv. 188–91.
99. Dundas, *History, Scripture and Controversy*, 59.
100. *Vijayapraśastimahākāvya*, commentary on 3.29; also noted in Granoff, "Authority and Innovation," 50.
101. Paul Dundas also makes this point in *History, Scripture and Controversy*, 24.
102. Most notably, the beginning of chapter 2 of the *Bhānucandragaṇicarita* narrates Bhanuchandra's lineage.
103. *Bhānucandragaṇicarita* 1.39.
104. *Bhānucandragaṇicarita* 4.179–81.
105. *Bhānucandragaṇicarita* 4.180.
106. *Bhānucandragaṇicarita* 4.259–68.
107. *Bhānucandragaṇicarita* 1.68–71.
108. Siddhichandra's enumeration of Sanskrit knowledge systems mastered by Abul Fazl contains some curious omissions. He does not include Nyaya, an exclusion for which I have no explanation (I thank Satoshi Ogura for pointing out this omission). Nor does Siddhichandra include the Vedas (unless they are included in Vedanta), which may reflect his grounding in Jain thought (I thank Kiyokazu Okita for pointing out this omission).
109. *Bhānucandragaṇicarita* 4.85.
110. *Bhānucandragaṇicarita* 4.90 and 4.104.
111. *Bhānucandragaṇicarita* 4.271.
112. Parikh, introduction to *Kāvyaprakāśakhaṇḍana*, 6.
113. *Vasatanrājaśākuna*, 1.
114. Truschke, *Culture of Encounters*, 27–54.
115. I discuss the only major exception to the first point, the *Kavīndracandrodaya*, in Truschke, "Contested History."
116. Trouillot, *Silencing the Past*, 51.
117. See Truschke, "Dangerous Debates," 1335–41 (discussion); Truschke, "Mughal Debate about Jain Asceticism," 112–20 (translation).
118. *Jahāngīrnāma*, ed. Hashim, 249–50; *Jahangirnama*, ed. Thackston, 250–51.
119. *Majālīs-i Jahāngīrī*, 111.

6. Rajput and Maratha Kingships in an Indo-Persian Political Order

1. As noted by Pushkar Sohoni, all three successor sultanates kept alive the myth of Bahmani sovereignty through acts such as minting Bahmani coinage (*Architecture of a Deccan Sultanate*, 29 and 56–57).
2. At Amer: Muraridasa's *Mānaprakāśa* (ca. 1610). At Baglan: *Rāṣṭrauḍhavaṃśamahākāvya* (see this chapter). At Bundi: *Surjanacarita* (see this chapter) and *Śatruśalyacarita* (ca. 1635). At Mewar: Sadashiva's *Rājaratnākara* (1677); Ranachoda Bhatta's *Amarakāvya* and *Rājapraśasti*. I expect that this is a highly incomplete list.
3. Talbot, "Mewar Court's Construction of History," 16; *Epigraphia Indica*, 29:1–90 of appendix (a summary of the text is given in *Epigraphia Indica*, 30:91–123 of appendix).
4. E.g., Talbot, "Poetic Record of the Rajput Rebellion" and "Mewar Court's Construction of History" (Sanskrit texts: Sadashiva's 1677 *Rājaratnākara* and Ranachoda Bhatta's 1676 *Rājapraśasti*); Sreenivasan, "Rethinking Kingship and Authority" (Sanskrit, Persian, and vernacular inscriptions).
5. Talbot, "Elephants, Hunting and Mughal Service."
6. Joffee, "Art, Architecture and Politics in Mewar," 109–23.
7. E.g., on "Rajput," see Kolff, *Naukar, Rajput, and Sepoy*, chaps. 3–4, and Kothiyal, *Nomadic Narratives*, chap. 2; on "Maratha," see Gordon, *Marathas*, 13–17, and Kulkarni, *Marathas*, part 1, section 3.
8. Eaton, *India in the Persianate Age*, 351.
9. In secondary literature, the Rathods are sometimes called Rathors or Rathores; the Hadas are also called Haras.
10. Talbot, *Last Hindu Emperor*, 158. Gordon notes a few earlier indications that Shivaji claimed to be a Rajput (*Marathas*, 88n44).
11. For an overview of Shivaji's military alliances, see Gordon, *Marathas*, 59–90, and Kulkarni, *Marathas*, part 1, section 5.
12. Ziegler, "Notes on Rajput Loyalties."
13. E.g., on the Amer court, see Sreenivasan "Rethinking Kingship and Authority," 565–66; on the Mewar court, see Talbot, "Poetic Record of the Rajput Rebellion," and Tiwari, "Historiography of Mewar." The available evidence suggests that the Bundi court only commissioned Braj works some years after sponsoring Sanskrit histories (Busch, "Classical Past in the Mughal Present," 677). Elsewhere, Allison Busch writes about Keshavdas's Hindi historical poems at the Orchha court ("Literary Responses to the Mughal Imperium" and *Poetry of Kings*, chap. 1).
14. *Rājapraśasti* 1.16; I take inspiration for the translation from *Epigraphia Indica*, 30:91 of appendix. Ironically, Ranachoda ends with several vernacular verses in chapter 24 (*Epigraphia Indica*, 30:114 of appendix; *Rājapraśasti*, pp. 89–90). Cf. Jnandev's comparison of Marathi and Sanskrit, ca. thirteenth century, quoted in Novetzke, *Quotidian Revolution*, 233.
15. On Jayarama's *Rādhāmādhavavilāsacampū*, see Busch, "Listening for the Context," 271–74, and Guha, "Transitions and Translations," 25–28. P. K. Gode dates the work between 1653 and 1658 (*Studies in Indian Cultural History*, 2:108).

16. *Parṇālaparvatagrahaṇākhyāna* 1.32 ("Hindustan" is *hindusthāna*), and 2.2 (twelve languages).
17. *Parṇālaparvatagrahaṇākhyāna* 2.2.
18. Talbot, *Last Hindu Emperor*, 72 and 100–2; on the *Pṛthvīrāj Rāso*'s complex textual history, see pp. 277–90.
19. *Rājapraśasti* 3.27; Talbot, *Last Hindu Emperor*, 151.
20. James Laine discusses Agrindas's 1659 *povāḍa* in Laine, *Epic of Shivaji*, 5–6. On *bakhars*, see Prachi Deshpande, *Creative Pasts*; Guha, *History and Collective Memory*, chap. 3; Guha, "Speaking Historically," 1084–103; Herwadkar, *Forgotten Literature*. On *bāt*, *khyāt*, and *vigat*, see Ziegler, "Marvari Historical Chronicles" (I borrow the terms' translations from Talbot, *Last Hindu Emperor*, 163).
21. For instance, some authors contributed verses to the praise poems *Kavīndracandrodaya* and *Kavīndracandrikā*—composed in Sanskrit and Hindi, respectively—that commemorated Kavindracharya Sarasvati convincing Shah Jahan to cancel some pilgrimage taxes (Truschke, *Culture of Encounters*, 304n146; Truschke, "Contested History," 441 on Hirarama Kavi).
22. The *Maṇḍalīkacarita* has been edited from five manuscripts and printed by H. D. Velankar in two journal articles: "Maṇḍalika Mahākāvya of Gaṅgādhara Kavi" (chapters 1–5) and "Śrīgaṅgādharakavikṛtaṃ Śrīmaṇḍalīkamahākāvyam" (chapters 6–10); I cite the text using the title *Maṇḍalīkacarita*. For estimates of the text's composition date, see Velankar, "Maṇḍalīka, the Last Great King," 37, and Sandesara and Bhojak, introduction to *Gaṅgadāsapratāpavilāsanāṭakam*, ii. Gangadhara's authorship is mentioned in *Maṇḍalīkacarita* 1.2. For secondary scholarship, see Kapadia, *In Praise of Kings*, 76–102, and Velankar, "Maṇḍalīka, the Last Great King."
23. Teuscher, "Kingship and Genealogy," 72–77.
24. In sequential verses, Khangara conquers the Gohilas and Jhallas (*Maṇḍalīkacarita* 1.68) and *yavanabhūpatīn* (1.69). Other early mentions of yavanas include that Khangara's son Jayasimha routed a *yāvanarāja* (1.77); Meliga gave protection to a Jhalla chief named Krishna who had fled from a *yavanendra* (1.87) and fought a Sultan Ahmed (*ahammadasuratrāṇa*, 1.88).
25. *Maṇḍalīkacarita* 3.38. On this passage, also see Kapadia, *In Praise of Kings*, 91–92; Sheikh, "Alliance, Genealogy and Political Power," 40–41.
26. *Maṇḍalīkacarita* 3.11; others have translated this as "Western ocean" (Kapadia, *In Praise of Kings*, 92; Sheikh, *Forging a Region*, 117; Velankar, "Maṇḍalīka, the Last Great King," 43).
27. *Gazetteer of the Bombay Presidency* (Kathiawar), 590–92. I decline to call Sangan a pirate owing to the various assumptions attached to that label; on the history of piracy in India as conceptualized through the colonial lens, see Subramanian, *Sovereign and the Pirate*, especially 3–24.
28. *Maṇḍalīkacarita* 10.4. This verse has attracted the attention of several scholars, who have generally cited it with the assumption that "mleccha" means "Muslim" and, quite problematically, outside its literary context as some sort of metacommentary on Mandalik killing all Muslims (Granoff, "Mountains of Eternity," 42–43; Sheikh, *Forging a Region*, 116). This reading makes little sense in the context of the *Maṇḍalīkacarita*, and it is a reminder of the need to read texts holistically.

29. Sheikh, *Forging a Region*, 117; Cf. Hodivala, *Studies in Indo-Muslim History*, 661–62.

30. *Gaṅgadāsapratāpavilāsanāṭakam*, 18 (Gangadhara names a "Gujarat sultan," *gūrjarasuratrāṇa*; I surmise the identity from context and the play's 1449 composition date); also noted in Kapadia, *In Praise of Kings*, 1.

31. Kapadia, *In Praise of Kings*, 103–28; Obrock, "Muslim *Mahākāvyas*," 61–64.

32. On the *Kānhaḍade Prabandha*'s date, see Bhatnagar, introduction to *Padmanābha's Kānhaḍade Prabandha*, vii. For discussions of the work, see, e.g., Raeside, "Gujarati Bardic Poem"; Sreenivasan, "Medieval Rajput Histories of Jalor," 87–108.

33. Sheikh, *Forging a Region*, 136; Sreenivasan, "Medieval Rajput Histories of Jalor," 88.

34. The only known surviving manuscript of the *Gaṅgadāsapratāpavilāsa* is undated, but it centers around a 1449 conflict and was likely composed shortly thereafter (Sandesara and Bhojak, introduction to *Gaṅgadāsapratāpavilāsanāṭakam*, i–ii; Kapadia, *In Praise of Kings*, 83). The play is sometimes wrongly described as about Gangadasa's defeat (e.g., Granoff, "Mountains of Eternity," 42). In the drama, Gangadasa defeats Sultan Muhammad II with the assistance of another Muslim ruler based in Mandu (*Gaṅgadāsapratāpavilāsanāṭakam*, act 8; also noted in Sandesara and Bhojak, introduction to *Gaṅgadāsapratāpavilāsanāṭakam*, x, and Leclère, "Ambivalent Representations," 194–95).

35. Talbot also notes the contemporaneity of *Surjanacarita* and *Akbarnāma*, in "Justifying Defeat," 332; I borrow much from Talbot's excellent analysis of the *Surjanacarita*.

36. Magha's *Śiśupālavadha* also contains twenty chapters; J. L. de Bruyne compares the *Rāṣṭrauḍhavaṃśamahākāvya* and the *Śiśupālavadha* several times in his translation of the former text (*Rudrakavi's Great Poem*).

37. *Rāṣṭrauḍhavaṃśamahākāvya* 3.11. Note the similar mention of Khadgasena's victory over the yavana lord Malik and over the Mongol heroes (*mugūlavīra*) at Lalingachala (3.39).

38. *vīrasenaḥ . . . yāvane lohapure samantādakālaholotsavamātatāna* (*Rāṣṭrauḍhavaṃśamahākāvya* 3.42).

39. Talbot, "Elephants, Hunting and Mughal Service," 81.

40. *Surjanacarita* 13.49.

41. Accounts differ on what exactly happened, but on early Bundi-Mewar relations, see Hooja, *History of Rajasthan*, 359–64 and 512–16; Mathur, *Relations of Hadas with Mughal Emperors*, 1–49.

42. Talbot, "Justifying Defeat," 342.

43. *Surjanacarita* 16.5 on Akbar.

44. *Surjanacarita* 13.72–80; Cynthia Talbot describes this section as formulaic ("Justifying Defeat," 343). On the military history of Surjan's recovery of Kota, see Mathur, *Relations of Hadas with Mughal Emperors*, 47–49. Bundi and Kota are about 40 kilometers apart.

45. *Surjanacarita* 17.54–55; in 17.54, the two editions of the text differ in naming Akbar as *hūmātmaja* (Chaudhuri ed.) and *hūmāyuñja* (Sharma ed.).

46. Talbot, "Justifying Defeat," 344.

47. *Surjanacarita* 18.7–9; reading *mahīśitṛ* with Chaudhuri ed. (*śakeśitṛ* in Sharma ed.). I have added Akbar's name for clarity.

48. *adhikatarastava lābhaḥ* (*Surjanacarita* 18.16 in Chaudhuri ed. and 18.15 in Sharma ed.). For the envoy's full speech, see *Surjanacarita* 18.1–22 in Chaudhuri ed. and 18.1–21 in Sharma ed.
49. Talbot, "Justifying Defeat," 351, citing *Akbarnāma*.
50. Busch, "Classical Past in the Mughal Present," 682.
51. *Surjanacarita* 18.24ff. in Chaudhuri ed. and 18.23ff. in Sharma ed.
52. *Surjanacarita* 19.30–31.
53. "Justifying Defeat," 351–54.
54. *Surjanacarita* 19.49. On this verse, see Talbot, "Justifying Defeat," 355–56.
55. *Surjanacarita* 12.77.
56. Hammira's story is narrated in chapters 11–12 of the *Surjanacarita*.
57. *Surjanacarita* 18.17 in Chaudhuri ed. and 18.16 in Sharma ed. Cynthia Talbot offers a few solutions to resolve what she sees as a disconnect between the work's earlier praise of Hammira and its later condemnation ("Justifying Defeat," 346–47 and 351).
58. Talbot makes a similar argument in "Justifying Defeat," 357.
59. Guha, *Environment and Ethnicity in India*, 65–66.
60. *Rāṣṭrauḍhavaṃśamahākāvya* 1.11 on patronage. The bulk of the *Rāṣṭrauḍhavaṃśamahākāvya* has been translated by J. L. de Bruyne under the title *Rudrakavi's Great Poem*; I offer my own translations here.
61. *Rāṣṭrauḍhavaṃśamahākāvya* 20.100 (Lakshmana as verbal source) and 9.71–74 (Lakshmana at Narayan's consecration).
62. Truschke, *Culture of Encounters*, 65 and 81–88; three of the works have been edited by J. B. Chaudhuri under the title *Works of Rudra Kavi*.
63. *Rāṣṭrauḍhavaṃśamahākāvya* 1.38, 2.56, 3.50, 4.39, 5.41, 6.44, 7.68, 8.66, 9.80, 10.39, 11.47, 12.77, 13.38, 14.67, 15.56, 16.55, 17.40, 18.81, 19.71, 20.101.
64. *Rāṣṭrauḍhavaṃśamahākāvya*, chap. 11 (11.1 for southern king).
65. *dakṣiṇadeśalabdhyai* (*Rāṣṭrauḍhavaṃśamahākāvya* 13.29) and *dakṣiṇadigjayāya* (19.5).
66. *Rāṣṭrauḍhavaṃśamahākāvya* 13.29–32.
67. . . . *niśśeṣapurāṇyaluṇṭhat* (*Rāṣṭrauḍhavaṃśamahākāvya* 13.35) and *sāṃrājya* (*Rāṣṭrauḍhavaṃśamahākāvya* 13.37; note the correction suggested by J. L. de Bruyne in *Rudrakavi's Great Poem*, 108n1, citing the same verse as 13.38).
68. de Bruyne, preface to *Rāṣṭrauḍhavaṃśamahākāvya*, xii.
69. . . . *śrīśāhanārāyaṇasphūrjatkīrtticaritra* . . . (*Rāṣṭrauḍhavaṃśamahākāvya* 1.38, 2.56, 3.50, 4.39, 5.41, 6.44, 7.68, 8.66, 9.80, 10.39, 11.47, 12.77, 13.38, 14.67, 15.56, 16.55, 17.40, 18.81, 19.71, 20.101).
70. Respectively, *kuberadigbhūmipati* (*Rāṣṭrauḍhavaṃśamahākāvya* 19.38), *kuberadiññiyantṛ* (19.64), and *kuberadiññātha* (20.2).
71. *dillīpati* (*Rāṣṭrauḍhavaṃśamahākāvya* 19.23, 19.25, 20.1, 20.6), *dillīśa* (19.52, 20.28).
72. *Rāṣṭrauḍhavaṃśamahākāvya* 20.3–4; 20.4 contains a play on the word *pratāpa*, which I translate here as "your brilliance and your son."
73. *Rāṣṭrauḍhavaṃśamahākāvya* 20.21.
74. *Rāṣṭrauḍhavaṃśamahākāvya* 20.22–25. Also note mentions of the Mughals giving gifts to Narayan Shah (19.36–37, 19.62–63).
75. E.g., *Rāṣṭrauḍhavaṃśamahākāvya* 20.30–31.

76. *Rāṣṭrauḍhavaṃśamahākāvya* 20.79–83 for the pilgrimage.
77. E.g., see the pilgrimage in chapter 20 of the *Rāṣṭrauḍhavaṃśamahākāvya*.
78. E.g., Pillai, *Rebel Sultans*, 140–46.
79. *Rāṣṭrauḍhavaṃśamahākāvya* 20.85 (*illakhāna*); de Bruyne also mentions this (*Rudrakavi's Great Poem*, 128).
80. *Rāṣṭrauḍhavaṃśamahākāvya* 20.57; J. L. de Bruyne also notes Chand Bibi's absence (*Rudrakavi's Great Poem*, 127).
81. *Ma'āṣir al-Umarā*, 2:113–16.
82. Asher, "Architecture of Rāja Mān Singh," 191; Sreenivasan, "Rethinking Kingship and Authority," 559.
83. Talbot, "Elephants, Hunting and Mughal Service," 84.
84. On the patronage of Shivaji (*Śivabhārata* 1.24–27) and of Sambhaji (Gode, "Harikavi Alias Bhānubhaṭṭa," 283, v. 10). Rajaram's patronage is less clear, but it seems likely given the text's subject matter and the ties between the family of Keshava Pandit, the author, and the Bhonsles (Bendrey, introduction to *Rājārāmacarita*, 2–3).
85. Many later Maratha-sponsored works also focus on these earlier leaders. Govinda II, Paramananda's grandson, penned a continuation of the *Sūryavaṃśa* that focuses on the reign of Sambhaji, of which 5 cantos survive (printed as section 5 of *Paramānandakāvya*; Sarkar, *House of Shivaji*, 291–92). The 1718 *Śivadigvijaya* focuses on Shivaji (note that its authenticity is debated as per the discussion between Jadunath Sarkar and Govind Sakharam Sardesai discussed in Chakrabarty, *Calling of History*, 158–60). Purushottam's early nineteenth-century *Śivakāvya*, on Shivaji, contains color illustrations (Gode, *Studies in Indian Cultural History*, 2:99).
86. E.g., *Parṇālaparvatagrahaṇākhyāna* 3.1.
87. The *Sūryavaṃśa* and the *Paramānandakāvya* have quite different takes on Shivaji and were never integrated, hence the uncertainty about whether they were authored by the same man.
88. The work has been edited by Govind Sakharam Sardesai in *Paramānandakāvya*, 33–102. The majority of the chapters' colophons identify the author as *kavīndraparamānanda* (pp. 41, 56, 60, 76, 79, 85, 88, 95, 102), and others say simply *kavīndra* (pp. 36, 39, 51). Chapter 7's colophon does not name an author (p. 68). The pro-Sambha bent of the *Paramānandakāvya*, including criticisms of Shivaji, indicate that the work was likely composed during Sambha's reign and mark it as rather distinct from the *Sūryavaṃśa*. Whoever wrote it never got around to formally numbering the chapters (Sarkar, *House of Shivaji*, 289–90). Sardesai summarizes the text in his introduction to *Paramānandakāvya*, 20–27.
89. V. G. Khobrekar lists the military activities narrated in the poem (foreword to *Parṇālaparvatagrahaṇākhyāna*, 1–2).
90. *Rājārāmacarita* 1.3.
91. *Rājārāmacarita* 1.4; on the date see Bendrey, introduction to *Rājārāmacarita*, 5.
92. O'Hanlon, "Contested Conjunctures," 776–78.
93. *Śivabhārata* 7.36 (*bālalīlā*) and 8.1–3 (pandits' question).
94. *Śivabhārata* 9.72–74 and 10.1–4.
95. *Rājārāmacarita* 1.11ff.

96. *Paramānandakāvya*, chapters 4–6.
97. Gode, "Harikavi Alias Bhānubhaṭṭa."
98. The title resonance is noted by Jadunath Sarkar, foreword to *Paramānandakāvya*, 1; Varnekar, "Shivaji's Patronage to Sanskrit Learning," 89. James Laine and S. S. Bahulkar note the resonance of a few individual verses (*Epic of Shivaji*, 178 and 351).
99. Also note *purāṇamiva nūtanam* in *Sūryavaṃśa* 1.18; some modern scholars have taken *anupurāṇa* as part of the work's title (e.g., Kruijtzer, *Xenophobia*, 158).
100. Chakrabarti, *Religious Process*, 44.
101. Kruijtzer, *Xenophobia*, 162.
102. *Parṇālaparvatagrahaṇākhyāna* 1.53. For Mainaka's story, see *Rāmāyaṇa* 5.56.
103. *Rājārāmacarita* 1.8–9.
104. Ziegler, "Notes on Rajput Loyalties," 235.
105. Eaton, *Social History of the Deccan*, 89–90; as Eaton notes, Krishna Raya's more well known modern name, Krishnadeva Raya, is a nineteenth-century invention (80n2).
106. *Śivabhārata* 5.19–20.
107. Gijs Kruijtzer also notes the frequency of "yavana" in the *Śivabhārata* (*Xenophobia*, 158–59). To further complicate matters, in one case, Paramananda also refers back to the older meaning of "yavana" as "Greek" in a reference to one of Krishna's exploits (*Śivabhārata* 18.2–3; Laine and Bahulkar, *Epic of Shivaji*, 231).
108. *Śivabhārata* 18.52. Several chapters later, Shaista Khan, Aurangzeb's uncle, is described as smashing temples and monasteries (25.60).
109. *Śivabhārata* 17.12. For more on Shivaji's alleged intolerance toward Islam, see, e.g., 19.28–31.
110. *Śivabhārata* 17.56–57.
111. As Bendrey notes, both "mleñccha" and "mleccha" appear in the *Rājārāmacarita* (note on p. 50).
112. *Śivabhārata* 11.40, 22.32, 29.77, 31.36.
113. *Śivabhārata* 14.83 (*paṭhāṇa*), 22.14 (*paṭhāna*), 25.36 (*paṭāna*), 25.39 (*paṭhāṇa*), 25.38 (*ujabakha*), and 28.53 (*ajabaḍānvaya*); for another use of *ujabakha* in Sanskrit see *Sarvadeśavṛttāntasaṅgraha*, 101, translating Persian *ūzbak* (*History of Akbar*, 1:422).
114. E.g., *Śivabhārata* 4.6, 4.8, 4.52, and 9.22 (*tāmra*); 4.51 and 9.24 (*tāmrānana*); *Parṇālaparvatagrahaṇākhyāna* 1.33, 2.5, 5.5, 5.9 (*tāmra*). For Marathi usages, see under *tāmra* in Date, *Maharashtra Sabdakosa*.
115. *Parṇālaparvatagrahaṇākhyāna* 1.33; also, 5.9 identifies Shaista Khan as the "best" (*mahattara*) of the *tāmra*.
116. *jahānagīrastāmrāṇāmadhipastīvravikramaḥ* (*Śivabhārata* 4.8).
117. Sanskrit *tāmradvīpa* used to be used for Ceylon (Sri Lanka), but I do not see traces of that here. Sircar, *Geography of Ancient and Medieval India*, 316.
118. *Śivabhārata* 4.49 (*śyāmānana*); also see uses of *śyāmāsya* in *Parṇālaparvatagrahaṇākhyāna* 2.13, 3.8.
119. *Śivabhārata* 1.59–60. Mustafa Khan is later described as *adharmātma* (devoid of dharma; 13.2), so apparently Muslims, just like Hindus, could be good or bad.
120. E.g., see James Laine's trouble explaining this description in "Resisting My Attackers," 155.

121. James Laine and S. S. Bahulkar use the word "Muslim" more than seventy-five times in the *Epic of Shivaji*, often to translate "yavana."

122. E.g., James Laine and S. S. Bahulkar use "Hindu" to translate *kṣatriya* and *bāhuja* in *Epic of Shivaji*, 5.31, 15.4, and 25.21. A relatively rare Sanskrit use of the term "Hindu" is found in the *Parṇālaparvatagrahaṇākhyāna*, where it says that it is written in the Hindus' shastra (*hindūnāṃ śāstre*) that Vishnu's tenth avatar, Kalki, will come down and rescue the earth overtaken by yavanas (5.6–5.7).

123. *paddhatiṃ varṇadharmāṇāṃ rodhduṃ yo hi vyavasthitaḥ* (*Śivabhārata* 18.21).

124. As Govind Sakharam Sardesai put it, "The orthodox Brahman opinion was not favourable to Shivaji's claim to be recognised as a Kshatriya by blood" (*New History of the Marathas*, 1:216); as Jadunath Sarkar put it, "The Bhonslas were popularly known to be neither Kshatriyas nor of any other twice-born caste, but mere tillers of the soil" (*Shivaji and His Times*, 240). More recently, André Wink has written, "[Shivaji being of kshatriya lineage] was a claim which, despite repeated attempts to prove genealogically its correctness, was destined to remain disputed forever" (*Land and Sovereignty*, 36).

125. The term "fabricated" belongs to Jadunath Sarkar (*Shivaji and His Times*, 241).

126. Deshpande, "Kṣatriyas in the Kali Age?," 98 on the 1664 *Śyenavījātidharmanirṇaya.*

127. Sarkar, *Shivaji and His Times*, 243–46; Vajpeyi, "Excavating Identity Through Tradition," 244.

128. Vajpeyi, "Excavating Identity Through Tradition," 243.

129. Bendrey, *Coronation of Shivaji*, 40–44; Gordon, *Marathas*, 87–89; Sarkar, *Shivaji and His Times*, 243–46; Vajpeyi, "Excavating Identity Through Tradition," 242.

130. Shivaji's first coronation also involved non-Sanskrit-based ideas that we must look beyond the Sanskrit tradition to recover (Guha, "Conviviality and Cosmopolitanism," 280); the Englishman Henry Oxinden witnessed parts of the ceremony (*English Records on Shivaji*, 369–76).

131. Bendrey, *Coronation of Shivaji*, 53–55; Laine in Laine and Bahulkar, *Epic of Shivaji*, 24–25; Sardesai, *New History of the Marathas*, 1:224–25; Sarkar, foreword to *Paramānandakāvya*, 4–5.

132. See discussion and edition in Salomon, "Śivarājarājyābhiṣekakalpataru."

133. Paramananda and Shivaji met sometime before 1666, when, according to Dingal letters, Paramananda accompanied Shivaji to Aurangzeb's court and, after leaving, was detained for several months by officials in Amer due to suspicions about the amount of wealth he was carrying. After being released, Paramananda went to Benares (Sarkar, *House of Shivaji*, 287–89). At some point, he returned to Maharashtra, because, as per the *Parṇālaparvatagrahaṇākhyāna* (4.16–19), Shivaji met Paramananda there in 1673. Shivaji died in 1680.

134. *sargabandho mahākāvyaṃ tatraiko nāyakaḥ suraḥ sadvaṃśaḥ kṣatriyovāpi dhīrodāttaguṇānvitaḥ* (*Sāhityadarpaṇa*, chap. 6, p. 365); on the *Sāhityadarpaṇa*'s date and translation of the title, see Pollock, *Rasa Reader*, 261.

135. Quoted in Busch, *Poetry of Kings*, 191.

136. *Muntakhab al-Tavārīkh*, 2:326; *Pārasīprakāśa* of Krishnadasa vv. 2–4.

137. *Parṇālaparvatagrahaṇākhyāna* 1.18.

138. Salomon, "Śivarājarājyābhiṣekakalpataru," 75, v. 28 and 78, v. 68.

139. *Śivabhārata* 21.47–48 (will not fight a Brahmin); 26.54–55 (hosts Brahmins in his army).

140. *Śivabhārata* 21.83–84.

141. *mahārāṣṭro janapadastadānīṃ tatsamāśrayāt*, where *tat* = Shivaji (*Śivabhārata* 10.32), and *śailādhipati* (27.37).

142. Eaton, *India in the Persianate Age*, 318.

143. Sarkar, *House of Shivaji*, 143.

144. Shaista Khan's advance on Panhal Fort contains some notably strong praise regarding military might (*Śivabhārata*, chap. 25).

145. Faruqui, "Awrangzīb."

146. *Śivabhārata* 10.15.

147. *Śivabhārata* 6.69–75.

148. *Śivabhārata* 29.23 (*daṇḍahastādapi krūraṃ*).

149. *Śivabhārata* 27.18 (*yavanāntakara*) and 1.15 (*yavanāntaka*). As Gijs Kruijtzer notes, Europeans (*phairaṅga*; *Śivabhārata* 30.2) are described as worse than yavanas (*yavanāvara*), so there seems to be a hierarchy at play here (*Xenophobia*, 159). That said, Europeans are mentioned in only one section, consisting of few verses (30.1–4), which I do not think compares to the text's repeated mentions of yavanas.

150. Novetzke, "Laine Controversy."

151. Truschke, "Censoring Indian History," 14–17; both the Stanford University Press and Oxford University Press Pakistan editions of *Aurangzeb* contain no censorship regarding Shivaji.

152. On the many modern Shivajis, see Jasper, "Commemorating Shivaji."

153. Ghadyalpatil, "Modi Lays Foundation of Shivaji Statue." For some of the other ways that the modern-day Shivaji is honored, see Jasper, "Commemorating Shivaji," 1–4.

154. Jayarama wrote for Ekoji in Thanjavur, and Keshava Pandit appears to have been at Jinji with Rajaram. On manuscripts, see *New Catalogus Catalogorum*, 11:237 and 23:296, respectively.

155. The still-unprinted *Kosalabhosalīya* of Sheshacalapati (ca. 1700), a shlesha poem about Thanjavur-based Shahji (r. 1684–1711) and Rama (Bronner, *Extreme Poetry*, 127–28 and 270); Venkatesha's *Bhosalavaṃśāvalī*, on Sarabhoji (r. 1712–1727) and his ancestors, and Gangadhara's *Bhosalavaṃśāvalī* (Krishnamachariar, *History of Classical Sanskrit Literature*, 246–47).

156. *Rājapraśasti* 1.9; *Epigraphia Indica*, 29:2 of appendix.

157. *Surjanacarita* 20.64 (misprinted in Chaudhuri ed.; note correction on p. 28).

158. *New Catalogus Catalogorum*, 6:368–69; Chaudhuri, introduction to *Surjanacarita* (3); the second (handwritten) manuscript copy, in Pune, dates to 1912.

7. Mughal Political Histories

1. Gode, review of *Vīrabhānūdayakāvya*, 163–65; Shastri, "Critical Analysis of the *Virabhanudaya-kavyam*," in *Vīrabhānūdayakāvya*, 1–28.

2. R. N Choudhary, *Political History of Khandavala*, 12–40.
3. *Jagadgurukāvya* vv. 40–121. I have written elsewhere about Padmasagara's rewriting of Mughal history; see Truschke, *Culture of Encounters*, 195–97, and Truschke, "Setting the Record Wrong," 375–81.
4. Sunil Sharma, "History of Akbar."
5. All three works have been edited and translated by Wheeler Thackston in *Three Memoirs of Homayun*.
6. Vann, "Hayden White and Non-Non-Histories," 186.
7. *Akbarasāhiśṛṅgāradarpaṇa* 1.2; *Kṛpārasakośa* vv. 18–20.
8. Padmasagara refers to Sher Shah Suri as *sūra*; his identity is made clear by military feats attributed to him (see, e.g., *Jagadgurukāvya* v. 45).
9. *Jagadgurukāvya* vv. 44 and 82, respectively.
10. *Jagadgurukāvya* v. 59.
11. Sheikh, *Forging a Region*, 139–43 and 153–54.
12. *Jagadgurukāvya* v. 74.
13. On this sort of truth in roughly contemporary European materials, see Natalie Zemon Davis, *Fiction in the Archives*, 3–4.
14. *Jagadgurukāvya* v. 76.
15. See, especially, *Jagadgurukāvya* vv. 77–82.
16. *Jagadgurukāvya* vv. 84–85. Note that the *Sarvadeśavṛttāntasaṅgraha* glosses *cāturvarṇya* as *hindūka* (ms. 2775 of India Office Collection, fol. 222a and 23n1 of printed edition).
17. See, especially, *Jagadgurukāvya* vv. 111–15; for the full account of Chittor, see *Jagadgurukāvya* vv. 96–120.
18. Zaman, "Mughal Conquest of Chittor," 287–97.
19. Victoria and Albert Museum, IS.2:69-1896; http://collections.vam.ac.uk/item/O9614/.
20. *Jagadgurukāvya* v. 112 (*jālmahṛdīva dhārmikahṛdīva*).
21. *Jagadgurukāvya* vv. 116–18 (v. 116: gives the order to massacre).
22. Using this Jain-friendly trait as a transition may also explain why Padmasagara temporally inverts the siege of Chittor and the founding of Fatehpur Sikri.
23. *Jagadgurukāvya* vv. 43 and 50, respectively.
24. *Jagadgurukāvya* vv .46 and 49, respectively.
25. *Jagadgurukāvya* vv. 41–42. *Madhyadeśa* literally means "middle region," but it generally refers to an area of land closer to what we call northern India or what the Mughals called Hindustan. On changing ideas about *madhyadeśa*, see Deshpande, *Sanskrit and Prakrit*, especially chap. 6.
26. E.g., *Kṛpārasakośa* vv. 8–17 (Sanskrit text; on Kabul); Dale, *Garden of the Eight Paradises*, chaps. 5–6, and Dale, *Babur*, chap. 5 (on place in Babur's memoirs); Faruqui, "Forgotten Prince," 490n8 (on Kabul versus Hindustan in historiography in Akbar's time).
27. *Jagadgurukāvya* vv. 118–20.
28. *Jagadgurukāvya* v. 84.
29. Between vv. 87–92 of *Jagadgurukāvya*, "Hindu" is used five times (in every verse except v. 91).
30. *Jagadgurukāvya* vv. 88 and 90, respectively.

31. *Jagadgurukāvya* vv. 42 and 87, respectively.
32. *Jagadgurukāvya* v. 89.
33. For a brief overview, see Eaton, *India in the Persianate Age*, 217–18.
34. *parairhindubhiryaddattāḥ svasutāḥ svarājyavibhavakṣemāya nābhyarthitaiḥ* (*Jagadgurukāvya* v. 92; vv. 91–92 for the emissary's full speech).
35. *Jagadgurukāvya* v. 94; *Śatakatrayam* v. 73 of *Nītiśataka*.
36. Eaton, *India in the Persianate Age*, 248–49.
37. *Sarvadeśavṛttāntasaṅgraha*, 166 and noted by Chaudhuri, introduction to *Sarvadeśavṛttāntasaṅgraha*, xvii (unless otherwise noted, all citations to the *Sarvadeśavṛttāntasaṅgraha* are page numbers). This ending corresponds with Wheeler Thackston's edition of the *Akbarnāma* (*History of Akbar*, 2:112; all citations to Thackston's *History of Akbar* refer to the Persian text, and all translations are my own).
38. On the *Sulaimaccaritra*, see Minkowski, "King David in Oudh," and Obrock, "Muslim *Mahākāvyas*," 64–67. It has been translated by A. N. D. Haksar under the title *Suleiman Charitra* (Gurgaon: Penguin, 2015).
39. The *Kathākautuka* is printed, edited by Mahamahopadhyaya Pandit Sivadatta and Kasinath Pandurang Parab (Bombay: Tukaram Javaji, 1901). For secondary scholarship, see Rani Majumdar, "Kathakautuka"; Obrock, "Muslim *Mahākāvyas*," 67–70; Obrock, "Translation and History," chap. 7.
40. D'Hubert, *Shade of the Golden Palace*, 94, and Obrock, "Muslim *Mahākāvyas*," 64–65 (Lal Khan); Obrock, "Muslim *Mahākāvyas*," 67 (Muhammad Shah).
41. *History of Akbar*, 1:2.
42. *Sarvadeśavṛttāntasaṅgraha* vv. 11–12a.
43. *Sarvadeśavṛttāntasaṅgraha* v. 27, and *History of Akbar*, 1:2.
44. *History of Akbar*, 1:80–144; omitted in *Sarvadeśavṛttāntasaṅgraha*, 19–20.
45. *Sarvadeśavṛttāntasaṅgraha*, 159; *History of Akbar*, 2:50–70.
46. *Sarvadeśavṛttāntasaṅgraha*, 20; *History of Akbar*, 1:148 (wet nurses). *Sarvadeśavṛttāntasaṅgraha*, 22–23; *History of Akbar*, 1:164 (ancestors). *Sarvadeśavṛttāntasaṅgraha*, 164–65; *History of Akbar*, 2:94–102 (Humayun's companions).
47. *Sarvadeśavṛttāntasaṅgraha*, 88; *History of Akbar*, 1:376.
48. *Sarvadeśavṛttāntasaṅgraha*, 53; *History of Akbar*, 1:282 (half-sister); also note the death of Faruq, Humayun's brother, as a young child (*Sarvadeśavṛttāntasaṅgraha*, 74; *History of Akbar*, 1:336). *Sarvadeśavṛttāntasaṅgraha*, 129; *History of Akbar*, 1:504 (elephant).
49. E.g., *Sarvadeśavṛttāntasaṅgraha*, 72 and 82; *History of Akbar*, 1:332 and 1:362 (Kanauj). E.g., *Sarvadeśavṛttāntasaṅgraha*, 91; *History of Akbar*, 1:394 (Chunnar).
50. E.g., *Sarvadeśavṛttāntasaṅgraha*, 25 (*madhyadeśa*, for *hindūstān* as per *History of Akbar*, 1:178).
51. On folio 21a of ms. 2775 in the India Office Collection in London, the scribe mistakenly wrote *hindusthāne* just beneath *madhyadeśa*; *hindusthāne* is crossed out as a correction (I viewed a photostat of this manuscript in the Punjab University Library of Lahore, no. 6619).
52. *Sarvadeśavṛttāntasaṅgraha*, 61; *History of Akbar*, 1:302.
53. *Sarvadeśavṛttāntasaṅgraha*, 106; *History of Akbar*, 1:436.

54. *Sarvadeśavṛttāntasaṅgraha*, 25; *History of Akbar*, 1:178. Also, e.g., the title of *Tārīkh-i Fīrūzshāhī* is omitted (*Sarvadeśavṛttāntasaṅgraha*, 150, *History of Akbar*, 2:22).
55. *Sarvadeśavṛttāntasaṅgraha*, 51; *History of Akbar*, 1:276 (*Shāhnāma*). *Sarvadeśavṛttāntasaṅgraha*, 88; *History of Akbar*, 1:378 (*Vāqi'āt-i Bāburī*). *Sarvadeśavṛttāntasaṅgraha*, 130, *History of Akbar*, 1:508 (*Tārīkh-i Rāshīdī*).
56. *Sarvadeśavṛttāntasaṅgraha*, 54; *History of Akbar*, 1:282 (Sikander and Feraydun). *Sarvadeśavṛttāntasaṅgraha*, 106; *History of Akbar*, 1:436 (librarian). *Sarvadeśavṛttāntasaṅgraha*, 123 and 154; *History of Akbar*, 1:482 and 2:32, respectively (khutba).
57. *Sarvadeśavṛttāntasaṅgraha*, 23; *History of Akbar*, 1:166.
58. *Sarvadeśavṛttāntasaṅgraha*, 107; *History of Akbar*, 1:438–440. On Humayun's clothing, see Moin, *Millennial Sovereign*, 121–22.
59. *Sarvadeśavṛttāntasaṅgraha*, 27; *History of Akbar*, 1:186.
60. *Sarvadeśavṛttāntasaṅgraha*, 90; *History of Akbar*, 1:390.
61. *Sarvadeśavṛttāntasaṅgraha*, 90; *History of Akbar*, 1:390.
62. *Sarvadeśavṛttāntasaṅgraha*, 88; *History of Akbar*, 1:378 (divan). *Sarvadeśavṛttāntasaṅgraha*, 89; *History of Akbar*, 1:382 (versified prabandha).
63. *Sarvadeśavṛttāntasaṅgraha* v. 25.
64. *Sarvadeśavṛttāntasaṅgraha* v. 29.
65. *Sarvadeśavṛttāntasaṅgraha*, 23–24; *History of Akbar*, 1:166–74. Incidentally, Mahesh Thakur was renowned as a Naiyayika (Kroll, "Logical Approach to Law," 14n53).
66. A modern handwritten copy of the premodern manuscript is also extant (introduction to *Sarvadeśavṛttāntasaṅgraha*, ii).
67. Hasan Ali Khan / Abdulla is also known as Qutb al-Mulk; Husain Ali Khan is also known as Imam al-Mulk.
68. The *Nṛpatinītigarbhitavṛtta* was edited by Jatindra Bimal Chaudhuri; the work's title is based on its colophon (*Nṛpatinītigarbhitavṛtta*, 75; Eggeling, *Catalogue of the Sanskrit Manuscripts in the Library of the India Office*, part 7, 1515). Aside from Chaudhuri's introduction, I am not aware of secondary scholarship on this text.
69. The *Ābdullacarita* was edited by Jatindra Bimal Chaudhuri. The work has prose passages and, in Chaudhuri's edition, the verse numbers start over at 1,000; for clarity, I cite by page number and, where applicable, verse number. Secondary scholarship on this work is limited, but includes Chaudhuri, *Muslim Patronage to Sanskritic Learning*, 80–84, and Mohan, *Ābdullāh-carita*. I found Khalid Hasan Abbasi's 1992 thesis from Aligarh Muslim University, titled "Laksmipati's Abdullahcarita," but the online PDF was too low resolution for me to read.
70. Faruqui, *Princes of the Mughal Empire*, 320–21; Fisher, *Short History of the Mughal Empire*, 214–15; Richards, *Mughal Empire*, 272–73.
71. Faruqui, *Princes of the Mughal Empire*, 321.
72. *Nṛpatinītigarbhitavṛtta*, 1, v. 1. Jagacchandra is sometimes named as Jagat Chand or Jnanacandra. Gazetteers say that Jagacchandra ruled 1708–1720, but I am unclear about the source of that information (*Uttar Pradesh District Gazetteers*, 15:32).
73. Eggeling, *Catalogue of the Sanskrit Manuscripts in the Library of the India Office*, part 6, 1404–5; Mohan, *Ābdullāh-carita*, 34–35.

74. Lakshmipati identifies himself as a Brahmin (*dvijāgrya*) in the *Nṛpatinītigarbhitavṛtta* (1, v. 2) and gives his lineage in the *Ābdullacarita* (71, vv. 805–7).

75. *Ābdullacarita*, 71, vv. 801–4.

76. *Nṛpatinītigarbhitavṛtta*, 1, v. 3 (*sarveṣāṃ bhūmipālānāmupadeśāya*).

77. Jahandar Shah.

78. *Nṛpatinītigarbhitavṛtta*, 1, vv. 6–9 (read correction of *drutaṃ*); Azimuddin is more commonly known as Azimusshan. The phrase "Aurangzeb's line" (*auraṅgajevabhūmīndratanaya*) for the Mughals is repeated later (e.g., *auraṅgajevatanaya*, on p. 22).

79. Chaudhuri, *Muslim Patronage to Sanskritic Learning*, 83; Mohan, *Ābdullāh-carita*, 164–216.

80. *Nṛpatinītigarbhitavṛtta*, 3; *Ābdullacarita*, 1, vv. 6 and 11.

81. *Nṛpatinītigarbhitavṛtta*, 1, vv. 16–17.

82. *Nṛpatinītigarbhitavṛtta*, 1, v. 18.

83. *Ābdullacarita*, 54, vv. 411–427.

84. *Ābdullacarita*, 54, v. 423.

85. *Nṛpatinītigarbhitavṛtta*, 3.

86. Quoted in Busch, *Poetry of Kings*, 98.

87. *Nṛpatinītigarbhitavṛtta*, 20.

88. *Nṛpatinītigarbhitavṛtta*, 3.

89. I think *arśas* here likely referred to hemorrhoids, but it could have been an anal fistula or rectal prolapse.

90. I have no explanation for the name being given as Makara.

91. I am grateful to Erica Wald for this information.

92. *Nṛpatinītigarbhitavṛtta*, 31–32. Hamilton appears to be mentioned again on p. 69. Lakshmipati also says that Rafi-ud-Daulat was impotent (*Ābdullacarita*, 1, v. 18; Mohan, *Ābdullāh-carita*, 129).

93. For Persian texts, see, e.g., Kaicker, "Unquiet City," 248–49 (on Khush Hal), and Chaudhuri, introduction to *Nṛpatinītigarbhitavṛtta*, 18n1 (on Kamwar Khan). For early East India Company records, see, e.g., Wilson, *Early Annals of the English in Bengal*, 103, and Wheeler, *Early Records of British India*, 177, which both quote from relevant records.

94. Kaicker, "Unquiet City," 232–37.

95. *Nṛpatinītigarbhitavṛtta*, 76–84.

96. *Nṛpatinītigarbhitavṛtta*, 60.

97. *Nṛpatinītigarbhitavṛtta*, 60.

98. *Nṛpatinītigarbhitavṛtta*, 50 (also note the section on p. 60, where nearly every line begins with a Persian word or phrase).

99. *Ābdullacarita*, 2, v. 34.

100. I am grateful to Corinne Lefèvre for this observation; see Allison Busch's astute analysis of such intermixing in *Poetry of Kings*.

101. *Nṛpatinītigarbhitavṛtta*, 1, vv. 4–5a (read *samudīraṇam*, as per the correction on p. 86).

102. Note in *Nṛpatinītigarbhitavṛtta*, 85; Mohan, *Ābdullāh-carita*, 124.

103. *Agarvi* (for Persian *agar* or *agarchih*) and *vejarda* (whose origins remain obscure to me). On *vejarda*, also see *Nṛpatinītigarbhitavṛtta*, 67; on its meaning as "forbidden," see p. 83.

There remains far more to say about Lakshmipati's skillful use of Persian than I have hazarded here. For instance, he opens his *Nṛpatinītigarbhitavṛtta* with lines studded with Sanskrit references but then towards the work's close has a section heavily laden with Persian vocabulary. The mixed language of this text deserves further study.

104. *Dhvanyāloka* of Anandavardhana, 98 (Ingalls translation).
105. Pollock, "Death of Sanskrit," 392–426. For other criticisms (to varying degrees), see Bronner and Shulman, "Cloud Turned Goose"; Hanneder, "On 'The Death of Sanskrit' "; Hatcher, "Sanskrit and the Morning After."
106. Kaviraj, "Modernity, State, and Toleration," 262n5.
107. Chhabra, *Antiquities of Chamba State*, 2:108; cited in Sharma, "State Formation," 424.
108. E.g., the *Rāmaprakāśa* (1799), mentioned and quoted in Eggeling, *Catalogue of the Sanskrit Manuscripts in the Library of the India Office*, part 3, 502.

Epilogue

1. Chakrabarti, *Religious Process*. Bengal also featured in works of political history produced elsewhere, such as Vakpatiraja's eighth-century Prakrit *Gauḍavaho* (Bengal's demise; ca. 725), on Yashovarman of Kanauj (Smith, "History of the City of Kanauj," 777–82).
2. Knutson, *Into the Twilight*, chap. 3.
3. Eaton, Ansari, and Qasemi, "Bengal."
4. Eaton, *Rise of Islam*, 33–34.
5. Eaton, *India in the Persianate World*, 111–13.
6. The *Sekaśubhodayā* is ascribed, falsely, to Halayudha Mishra, a minister of Lakshmana Sena who died in the early thirteenth century (Dey, "Imagery and the Representation," 403–4). The *Sekaśubhodayā* changes so many details about Shaykh Tabrizi's life that the text's modern translator muses whether the work might be about a different Jalaluddin altogether (Sen, introduction to *Sekaśubhodayā*, xvii). It is also not entirely in Sanskrit, but rather mixes in Bengali verses.
7. Eaton, *Rise of Islam*, 215–18.
8. Eaton, *India in the Persianate World*, 364.
9. Talbot, "Justifying Defeat," 343.
10. Chaudhuri, introduction to *Surjanacarita*, 3; Chaudhuri, *Muslim Patronage to Sanskritic Learning*, 80n2 on the *Ābdullacarita*.
11. Pollock, *Language of the Gods*, chap. 10. Note Allison Busch's arguments about the rise of history writing in Hindi as tied to Mughal rule ("Poetry of History," 163–64).
12. Guha, *History and Collective Memory*, 72 (pp. 71–82 on history writing in Bengal more broadly).
13. In the course of presenting aspects of this book project between 2016 and 2019, several scholars asked me about connections between Sanskrit histories on Indo-Persian rule and earlier Sanskrit writers, such as Bilhana and Bana. We might ask the same question for less well-known works, such as Parimala Padmagupta's

Navasāhasāṅkacarita (Navasahasankha's Deeds, c. 1000 CE) or Hemachandra's twelfth-century *Kumārapālacarita* (Kumarapala's Deeds). For one attempt to position Bana's *Harṣacarita* within a larger series of Sanskrit histories, see Kulke, "Historiography in Early Medieval India," 79.

14. Gode, "Harikavi alias Bhānubhaṭṭa," 262 (manuscript found in Surat) and 271 (text authored in Surat).
15. Wujastyk, "Indian Manuscripts," 3; on premodern Indian manuscript culture, also see Pollock, "Literary Culture and Manuscript Culture," 83–90.
16. Wujastyk, "Indian Manuscripts," 5.
17. Bronner and Shulman, "Cloud Turned Goose," 6.
18. Hobsbawm, *On History*, 23.
19. Norton, "Assessing Women's History"; also see Norton's comments on this subject in "History on the Diagonal."
20. For a small taste of this, see the "Statements, Standards, and Guidelines of the Discipline" section of the American Historical Association's website.
21. Nandy, "History's Forgotten Doubles," 47.
22. Busch, "Poetry of History," 162.
23. On saffron attacks on knowledge, see the introduction. For recent documentation and overviews of saffron violence, see Bajoria, "Violent Cow Protection in India," and Griswold, "Violent Toll of Hindu Nationalism."
24. Ricoeur, *Memory, History, Forgetting*, 178.
25. Mukherjee, "What Made the East India Company So Successful?"
26. On Islam and the end of Indian Buddhism, see Truschke, "Power of the Islamic Sword."
27. White, *Metahistory*, 2.

Appendix

1. Reading the correction in Mirashi, *Inscriptions of the Kalachuri-Chedi Era*, 1:140n17, after *tarala-*, *tāratarāsidāritodita*, followed by *-saindhava*.
2. Jayanaka plays on the name of Pushkar throughout this passage. I give the Sanskrit terms where appropriate so that readers can glimpse this aspect of the text.
3. According to the *Pṛthvīrājavijaya* commentator Jonaraja, Karttikeya's peacock lives on divine water (*mayūrā hi divyajalajīvakāḥ*).
4. Chidambaram.
5. This verse is incomplete; my reading of the extant portion remains tentative.
6. A Vaghela king.
7. A lay Jain leader; his name is also spelled Desala in the passage.
8. Literally "weighing 32 *maṇ*as," which I take to be 32 man, a unit of measurement in Akbar's period equaling 55.32 pounds (Habib, *Atlas of the Mughal Empire*, xiv).
9. This verse is adapted slightly, in both grammar and vocabulary, from a *nīti* verse in Bhartrhari's *Śatakatrayam* (v. 73 of *Nītiśataka*).

10. In the *Hīrasaubhāgya*'s autocommentary, Devavimala explains why Allah will refute "the false construction of mine versus another's," by citing a famous Sanskrit sentiment that the entire world is a single family: "Only narrow-minded people make the distinction of mine versus another's. For the right-minded, the whole world is a family." *ayaṃ nijaḥ paro veti gaṇanā laghucetasām / udāracaritānāṃ tu vasudhaiva kuṭumbakaṃ* (commentary on v. 13.139). On the provenance of this verse and its modern resonances, see Hatcher, "Cosmos Is One Family."
11. In the text's autocommentary, Devavimala connects the description of hell's vicious guards with a Prakrit verse from Dharmadasa's *Vidagdhamukhamaṇḍana* (Ornament of the clever-mouthed), a popular work of riddles dating to mid-eleventh century or earlier.
12. The same passage is found in *Hīrasundaramahākāvya*, 13.136–50.
13. I omit verse 42; something is wrong with this verse as printed.
14. I decline to literally translate a bit on sesame seeds in this verse because it is nonsensical in English.
15. *śeṣūjīpāhaḍīdānaśāha*. Pahari = Shah Murad.
16. Mohanlal Dalichand Desai lists these eight in the introduction to *Bhānucandragaṇicarita* (24n4).
17. *abalātphajalaḥ śekhaḥ*.
18. I have no explanation for *makara* here.
19. Exactly who is speaking and when in this passage is not entirely clear to me; my translation reflects my current best guesses.

Bibliography

Primary Sources

Ābdullacarita of Lakshmipati, published as *The Ābdullāh-carita by Lakṣmīdhara*. Ed. Jatindra Bimal Chaudhuri. Calcutta: Pracyavani, 1947.

Āʾīn-i Akbarī of Abul Fazl ibn Mubarak. Ed. H. Blochmann. 2 vols. Calcutta: Asiatic Society of Bengal, 1867–77.

Akbarasāhiśṛṅgāradarpaṇa of Padmasundara. Ed. K. Madhava Krishna Sarma. Bikaner: Anup Sanskrit Library, 1943.

Alaṃkārasarvasva of Ruyyaka, with the commentary of Jayaratha. Ed. Mahamahopadhyaya Pandit Durgaprasad and Kashinath Pandurang Parab. Bombay: Tukaram Javaji, 1893.

Amarakoṣa of Amarasimha. Ed. Haragovinda Shastri. Varanasi: Chowkhamba Sanskrit Series Office, 1968.

Bahāristān-i-Shāhī: A Chronicle of Mediaeval Kashmir. Trans. K. N. Pandit. Calcutta: Firma KLM Private Limited, 1991.

Bhānucandragaṇicarita of Siddhichandra. Ed. Mohanlal Dalichand Desai. Ahmedabad-Calcutta: Sanchalaka Singhi Jain Granthamala, 1941.

Bṛhatpośālikapaṭṭāvalī of Nayasundara, published in *Vividhagacchīyapaṭṭāvalīsaṃgraha*, ed. Muni Jinavijaya. Bombay, Singhi Jain Series, 1961.

The Commentary of Father Monserrate, S. J., on His Journey to the Court of Akbar of Antoni de Monserrat. Trans. John S. Hoyland and S. N. Banerjee. London: Humphrey Milford; Oxford University Press, 1922.

The Conquest of Madhurā by Gaṅgādevī. Trans. Shankar Rajaraman and Venetia Kotamraju. Bangalore: Rasala, 2013.

A Critical Edition of the Śrī Kālacakratantra-Rāja (Collated with the Tibetan Version). Ed. Biswanath Banerjee. Calcutta: Asiatic Society, 1985.

Dharmasūtra of Gautama, published as *Śrīgautamadharmaśāstram: The Institutes of Gautama.* Ed. Adolt Friedrich Stenzler. London: Trübner, 1876.

Dhvanyāloka of Anandavardhana, with the commentary of Abhinavaguptacarya. Ed. Mahamahopadhyaya Pandit Durgaprasada and Wasudev Laxman Shastri Panshikar. Bombay: Pandurang Jawaji, 1928.

The *Dhvanyāloka* of Anandavardhana, with the *Locana* of Abhinavagupta. Trans. Daniel H. H. Ingalls, Jeffrey Moussaieff Masson, and M. V. Patwardhan. Cambridge, MA: Harvard University Press, 1990.

Digvijayamahākāvya of Meghavijaya. Ed. Ambalal Premchand Shah. Bombay: Bharatiya Vidya Bhavan, 1945.

English Records on Shivaji (1659–1682). Poona: Shiva Charitra Karyalaya, 1931.

Epigraphia Carnatica. Bangalore and Mysore: Government Press, 1886–1919.

Epigraphia Indica of the Archaeological Survey of India. Calcutta and Delhi: Asiatic Society, 1892–.

Futūḥ al-Salāṭīn of Isami. Ed. A. S. Usha. Madras: University of Madras, 1948.

Gaṅgadāsapratāpavilāsanāṭakam of Gangadhara. Ed. Bhogilal Jayachandbhai Sandesara and Amritlal Mohanlal Bhojak. Baroda: Oriental Institute, 1973.

Garuḍapurāṇa. Ed. Jivananda Vidyasagara Bhattacarya. Calcutta: Sarasvatiyantra, 1890.

Hammīramahākāvya of Nayachandra. Ed. Nilkanth Janardan Kirtane. Bombay: Education Society's Press, 1879.

Hammīramahākāvya of Nayachandra. Ed. Jinavijaya. Jodhpur: Rajasthan Prachyavidya Pratisthan, 1968.

Hammīramahākāvya: Hindī Anuvād. Trans. Nathulal Trivedi Madhukar Shastri. Jodhpur: Rajasthan Oriental Research Institute, 1997.

Hammīramadamardana of Jayasimhasuri. Ed. Chimanlal D. Dalal. Baroda: Central Library, 1920.

Hīrasaubhāgya of Devavimala, with his own gloss. Ed. Mahamahopadhyaya Pandit Sivadatta and Kashinath Pandurang Parab. Bombay: Tukaram Javaji, 1900.

Hīrasundaramahākāvya of Devavimala, published as *Śrīhīrasundaramahākāvyam.* Ed. Muni Ratnakirtivijaya. 2 vols. Khambhat: Shri Jain Granthaprakashan Samiti, 1996.

The History of Akbar of Abul Fazl ibn Mubarak. Ed. and trans. Wheeler M. Thackston. 5 vols. Cambridge, MA: Harvard University Press, 2015–2019.

Jagadgurukāvya of Padmasagara. Ed. Hargovinddas and Becardas. Benares: Harakhchand Bhurabhai, 1910.

Jagaḍūcarita of Sarvananda, published as *The Jagaḍûcharita of Sarvâṇanda: A Historical Romance from Gujarât.* Ed. Georg Bühler. Wien: Akademie der Wissenschaften, 1892.

The Jahangirnama: Memoirs of Jahangir, Emperor of India. Ed. and trans. Wheeler M. Thackston. Washington, DC: Freer Gallery of Art, Arthur M. Sackler Gallery; New York: Oxford University Press, 1999.

Jahāngīrnāma yā Tūzuk-i Jahāngīrī. Ed. Muhammad Hashim. Tehran: Bunyad-i Farhang-i Iran, 1980.

The Kādambarī of Banabhatta and His Son (Bhushanabhatta), with the Commentaries of Bhanuchandra and His Disciple Siddhichandra. Ed. Kashinath Pandurang Parab. Bombay: Pandurang Javaji, 1912.

Kavīndrācāryasūcipatram. Ed. R. Ananta Krishna Sastry. Baroda: Central Library, 1921.

Kāvyamīmāṃsā of Rajashekhara. Ed. C. D. Dalal and R. A. Sastry. Revised and enlarged by K. S. Ramaswami Sastri Siromani. Baroda: Oriental Institute, 1934.

Kāvyaprakāśa of Mammata, with *Saṅketa* of Manikyachandra, *Madhumatī* of Ravi Bhattacharya, and *Bhāvukapriya*. Ed. N. S. Venkatanathacharya. 2 vols. Mysore: Oriental Research Institute, 1977.

Kharataragacchapaṭṭāvalī. In *Kharataragacchapaṭṭāvalīsaṅgraha*.

Kharataragacchapaṭṭāvalīsaṅgraha. Ed. Jinavijaya. Calcutta: Puran Chand Nahar, 1932.

King, Governance, and Law in Ancient India: Kauṭilya's Arthaśāstra. Trans. Patrick Olivelle. New York: Oxford University Press, 2013.

Kīrtikaumudī of Someshvaradeva. Ed. Abaji Vishnu Kathavate. Bombay: Government Central Book Depot, 1883.

Kṛpārasakośa of Shantichandra. Ed. Muni Jinavijaya. Bhavnagar: Shri Jain Atmanand Sabha, 1917.

Ma'āṣir al-Umarā of Shahnavaz Khan. Ed. Maulavi ʿAbdur Rahim and Maulavi Mirza Ashraf ʿAli. 3 vols. Calcutta: Asiatic Society of Bengal, 1888–1891.

Madhurāvijaya of Gangadevi. Ed. S. Thiruvenkatachari. Annamalainagar: Annamalai University, 1957.

Madhurāvijaya of Gangadevi. Ed. Potukucci Subrahmanyashastri. Guntur: Ajanta Artu Printers, 1969.

Mahābhārata, published as *The Mahābhārata, for the First Time Critically Edited*. Ed. Vishnu S. Sukthankar et al. 19 vols. Poona: Bhandarkar Oriental Research Institute, 1933–1966.

Majālīs-i Jahāngīrī of Abdus Sattar ibn Qasim Lahawri. Ed. ʿArif Nawshahi and Muʿin Nizami. Tehran: Miras-i Maktub, 2006.

Maṇḍalīkacarita of Gangadhara. See Velankar, "Maṇḍalika Mahākāvya of Gaṅgādhara Kavi" (chapters 1–5) and "Śrīgaṅgādharakavikṛtaṃ Śrīmaṇḍalīkamahākāvyam" (chapters 6–10).

Mantrikarmacandravaṃśāvalīprabandha of Jayasoma, with the commentary of Gunavinaya. Ed. Acharya Muni Jinavijaya. Bombay: Bharatiya Vidya Bhavan, 1980.

Muntakhab al-Tavārīkh of Abdul Qadir Badauni. Ed. Captain W. N. Lees and Munshi Ahmad Ali. Vol. 2. Calcutta: College Press, 1865.

Nābhinandanajinoddhāraprabandha of Kakka. Ed. and trans. (into Gujarati) Bhagvandas Harakhchand. Limdi: Shri Hemachandracharya Jain Granthamala, 1929.

Nāmaliṅgānuśāsana of Amarasimha, with the commentary of Kshirasvamin. Ed. Krishnaji Govind Oka. Poona: D. G. Khandekar, 1913.

Nṛpatinītigarbhitavṛtta of Lakshmipati. Ed. Jatindra Bimal Chaudhuri. Calcutta: Pracyavani, 1959.

Pañcatantra. Ed. Ramchandra Jha. Varanasi: Chowkhamba Vidyabhavan, 1991.

Paramānandakāvya of Kavindra Paramananda. Ed. Govind Sakharam Sardesai, with a foreword by Jadunath Sarkar. Baroda: Oriental Institute, 1952.

Pārasīprakāśa of Krishnadasa. Ed. Vibhuti Bhushan Bhattacharya. Varanasi: Varanaseya Sanskrit Vishvavidyalaya, 1965.

Parṇālaparvatagrahaṇākhyāna of Jayarama Pindye. Ed. Devsingh Venkatsingh Chauhan, with a foreword by V. G. Khobrekar. Pune: Maharashtra Rashtrabhasha Sabha, 1970.

Poetics of Aristotle. Trans. Anthony Kenny. Oxford: Oxford University Press, 2013.

Prabandhacintāmaṇi of Merutunga. Ed. Jinavijaya Muni. Shantiniketan: Adhisthata Singhi Jaina Jnanapitha, 1933.

The Prabandhacintāmaṇi, or Wishing-Stone of Narratives of Merutunga. Trans. C. H. Tawney. Calcutta: Asiatic Society, 1901.

Prabandhakośa of Rajashekhara. Ed. Jinavijaya. Shantiniketan: Adhisthata Singhi Jaina Jnanapitha, 1935.

Pṛthvīrājavijaya of Jayanaka, with the commentary of Jonaraja. Ed. Gaurishankar Hirachand Ojha and Chandradhar Sharma Guleri. Ajmer: Vedic Yantralaya, 1941.

Purātanaprabandhasaṅgraha. Ed. Jinavijaya Muni. Ahmedabad: Sangalaka Singhi Jaina Granthamala, 1931.

Raghuvaṃśa of Kalidasa, with the *Sañjīvinī* commentary of Mallinatha. Ed. H. D. Velankar. Bombay: Nirnaya Sagar Press, 1948.

Rājapraśasti of Ranachoda Bhatta. Ed. N. P. Chakravarti and B. Ch. Chhabra. In *Epigraphia Indica*, 29:1–20. Calcutta: Government of India Press, 1952.

Rājārāmacarita, published as *Keshavpandit's Rajaram-Charitram, or Shri Chhatrapati Rajaram's Journey to Jinji.* Ed. V. S. Bendrey. Poona: Bharat Itihas Samshodhak Mandal, 1931.

Rājataraṅgiṇī of Kalhana, published as *Kalhaṇa's Rājataraṅgiṇī: A Chronicle of the Kings of Kaśmīr.* Ed. March Aurel Stein. 3 vols. Reprint, Delhi: Motilal Banarasidass, 1989.

Rājataraṅgiṇī of Jonaraja. Ed. Srikanth Kaul. Hoshiarpur: Vishveshvaranand Institute, 1967.

Rājataraṅgiṇī of Jonaraja, published as *Kingship in Kaśmīr (AD 1148–1459): From the Pen of Jonarāja, Court Paṇḍit to Sulṭān Zayn al-'Ābidīn.* Ed. Walter Slaje. Halle: Universitätsverlag Halle-Wittenberg, 2014.

Rājataraṅgiṇī of Shrivara. In *Rājataraṅgiṇī.* Calcutta: Baptist Mission Press, 1835.

Rājataraṅgiṇī of Shrivara, published as *Rājataraṅgiṇī: Volume 3.* Ed. Durgaprasada and P. Peterson. Bombay: Government Central Book Depot, 1896.

Rājataraṅgiṇī of Shrivara. In *Rājataraṅgiṇī of Śrīvara and Śuka.* Ed. Srikanth Kaul. Hoshiarpur: Vishveshvaranand Institute, 1966.

Rājataraṅgiṇī of Shrivara, published as *Jaina-Rājataraṅgiṇī.* Ed. Raghunath Singh. 2 vols. Varanasi: Chaukhamba Amarabharati Prakashan and Krishnadas Academy, 1977.

Rājataraṅgiṇī of Shrivara, published as *Śrīvara's Zaina Rājataraṅgiṇī.* Ed. and trans. Kashi Nath Dhar. Delhi: Indian Council of Historical Research and People's Publishing House, 1994.

Rājataraṅgiṇī of Shuka. In *Rājataraṅgiṇī of Śrīvara and Śuka.* Ed. Srikanth Kaul. Hoshiarpur: Vishveshvaranand Institute, 1966.

Rāmāyaṇa of Valmiki. Ed. G. H. Bhatt et al. 7 vols. Baroda: Oriental Institute, 1960–1975.

Rambhāmañjarī of Nayachandra. Ed. and trans. Ram Prakash Poddar. Vaishali: Research Institute of Prakrit Jainology and Ahimsa, 1976.

Rāṣṭrauḍhavaṃśamahākāvya of Rudrakavi. Ed. Embar Krishnamacharya, with an introduction by C. D. Dalal. Baroda: Central Library, 1917.

Rudrakavi's Great Poem of the Dynasty of Rāṣṭrauḍha: Cantos 1–13 and 18–20. Trans. J. L. de Bruyne. Leiden: Brill, 1968.

Sāhityadarpaṇa of Vishvanatha, with the commentaries of Anantadasa and Bhattacharya Maheshvara Tarkalankara. Lahore: Motilal Banarsidass, 1938.

Sarasvatīkaṇṭhābharaṇa of Bhoja, with the commentaries of Ramasimha and Jagaddhara. Ed. Kedarnath Sharma and Wasudev Laxman Shastri Panshikar. Bombay: Pandurang Jawaji, 1934.

Sarvadeśavṛttāntasaṅgraha. British Library, London, manuscript India Office 2775.

Sarvadeśavṛttāntasaṅgraha, or Akbarnāma: Being an Abridged Sanskrit Rendering of the Persian Akbarnāma. Ed. Subhadra Jha. Patna: Patna University, 1962/1963.

Śatakatrayam of Bhartrhari. Ed. D. D. Kosambi and K. V. Krishnamoorthi Sharma. Bombay: Bharatiya Vidya Bhavan, 1946.

Satyapurīya-śrīmahāvīra-utsāhaḥ of Dhanapala. Ed. Jinavijaya Muni. *Jaina Sahitya Samshodhak* 3 (1927): 241–43.

Sekaśubhodayā of Halayudha Misra. Ed. and trans. Sukumar Sen. Calcutta: Asiatic Society, 1963.

Śivabhārata of Paramananda. Ed. Sadashiva Mahadeva Divekar. Poona: Ganesh Printing Press, 1927.

Śrīpaṭṭāvalīsamuccaya. Ed. Muni Darshanavijaya. Viramgam: Shri Charitra Smaraka Granthamala, 1933.

Surjanacarita of Chandrashekhara, published as *The Śūrjana-carita (Historical Sanskrit Mahākāvya)*. Ed. Jatindra Bimal Chaudhuri. Calcutta: Pracyavani, 1951.

Surjanacarita of Chandrashekhara, published as *Surjanacaritamahākāvyam*. Ed. and trans. (into Hindi) Chandradhara Sharma. Kashi: Chandradhara Sharma, 1952.

Tāj al-Maʾāsir of Tajuddin Hasan Nizami. British Library, London, manuscript India Office Islamic 15.

Tajud Din Hasan Nizami's Taj ul Ma'athir (The Crown of Glorious Deeds). Trans. Bhagwat Saroop. Delhi: Saud Ahmad Dehlavi, 1998.

Tapāgacchapaṭṭāvalī of Dharmasagara, published as *Śrītapāgacchapaṭṭāvalīsūtra* in *Śrīpaṭṭāvalīsamuccaya*.

Tapāgacchapaṭṭāvalī of Meghavijaya, published as *Śrītapāgacchapaṭṭāvalīsūtravṛtanusandhānam* in *Śrīpaṭṭāvalīsamuccaya*.

Tārīkh-i Fīrūzshāhī of Shams Siraj Afif. Ed. Maulavi Vilayat Husain. Calcutta: Asiatic Society of Bengal, 1891.

Tārīkh-i Fīrūzshāhī of Ziauddin Barani. Ed. Saiyid Ahmad Khan, under the supervision of Captain W. Nassau Lees. Calcutta: Asiatic Society of Bengal, 1860.

Tārīkh-i hindūstān az rāja yūdhishtar tā humāyūn. Punjab University Library, Lahore, manuscript no. 2264/5274.

Tārīkh-i Mubārakshāhī of Yahiya bin Ahmad bin Abdullah Sirhindi. Trans. K. K. Basu. Baroda: Oriental Institute, 1932.

Tārīkh-i Sayyid ʿAlī, published as *Tarikh-i-Sayyed Ali: History of Kashmir 1374–1570*. Ed. Zubida Jan. Srinagar: Jay Kay Book Shop, 2009.

Three Memoirs of Homayun: Gulbadan Begim's Humáyunnáma; Jawhar Áftábachi's Tadhkiratu'l-wáqíat; Báyazíd Bayát's Táríkh-i Humáyun. Ed. and trans. Wheeler M. Thackston. Costa Mesa, CA: Mazda, 2009.

Vaiṣṇavadharmaśāstra, published as *The Law Code of Viṣṇu: A Critical Edition and Annotated Translation of the Vaiṣṇava-Dharmaśāstra*. Ed. and trans. Patrick Olivelle. Cambridge, MA: Department of Sanskrit and Indian Studies at Harvard University, 2009.

Vasantarājaśākuna with *Ṭīkā* of Bhanuchandra. Mumbai: Khemraj Sri Krishnadas Shreshthina, 1987.
Vijayadevamāhātmya of Vallabha Pathaka. Ed. Bhikshu Jinavijaya. Ahmedabad: K. P. Modi, 1928.
Vijayapraśastimahākāvya of Hemavijaya, with the commentary of Gunavijaya. Mumbai: Shri Jinashasan Aradhana Trust, 1988.
Vikramāṅkadevacarita of Bilhana. Ed. Georg Bühler. Bombay: Government Central Book Depot, 1875.
Vīrabhānūdayakāvya of Madhava. Ed. and trans. K. K. Lele and Anant Shastri Upadhyaya, with critical analysis by Hirananada Shastri. Rewa: Rewa Darbar, 1938.
Vividhatīrthakalpa of Jinaprabhasuri and Vidyatilaka. Ed. Jinavijaya. Shantiniketan: Adhisthata Singhi Jaina Jnanapitha, 1934.
Vividhatīrthakalpaḥ: Regards sur le Lieu Saint Jaina. Trans. Christine Chojnacki. Vol. 1. Pondichery: Institute Français de Pondichéry, École Française d'Extrême-Orient, 1995.
What Ten Young Men Did of Dandin. Trans. Isabelle Onians. New York: New York University Press, 2005.

Secondary Sources

Accardi, Dean. "Asceticism, Gender, and the State: Saints of the Kashmiri Sultanate, 1550–1650." PhD diss., University of Texas at Austin, 2014.
——. "Embedded Mystics: Writing Lal Ded and Nund Rishi into the Kashmiri Landscape." In *Kashmir: History, Politics, Representation*, ed. Chitralekha Zutshi, 247–64. Cambridge: Cambridge University Press, 2018.
——. "Orientalism and the Invention of Kashmiri Religion(s)." *International Journal of Hindu Studies* 22 (2018): 411–30.
Ahmad, Aziz. "Epic and Counter-Epic in Medieval India." *Journal of the American Oriental Society* 83, no. 4 (1963): 470–76.
Ahmed, Shahab. *What Is Islam? The Importance of Being Islamic*. Princeton, NJ: Princeton University Press, 2016.
Ali, Daud. "Indian Historical Writing, c. 600–c. 1400." In *400–1400*, ed. Sarah Foot and Chase F. Robinson, 80–101. Vol. 2 of *The Oxford History of Historical Writing*. Oxford: Oxford University Press, 2012.
——. "Royal Eulogy as World History: Rethinking Copper-Plate Inscriptions in Cōḻa India." In *Querying the Medieval: Texts and the History of Practices in South Asia*, ed. Ronald Inden, Jonathan Walters, and Daud Ali, 165–229. New York: Oxford University Press, 2000.
——. "Temporality, Narration, and the Problem of History: A View from Western India c. 1100–1400." *Indian Economic and Social History Review* 50, no. 2 (2013): 237–59.
——. "Violence, Gastronomy and the Meanings of War in Medieval South India." *Medieval History Journal* 3, no. 2 (2000): 261–89.

Andrews, Thomas, and Flannery Burke. "What Does It Mean to Think Historically?" *Perspective on History* 45, no. 1 (January 2007). https://www.historians.org/publications-and-directories/perspectives-on-history/january-2007/what-does-it-mean-to-think-historically.

Anooshahr, Ali. "The Elephant and the Sovereign: India circa 1000 CE." *Journal of the Royal Asiatic Society*, 3rd ser., 28, no. 4 (2018): 615–44.

Arai, Toshikazu. "Jaina Kingship in the *Prabandhacintāmaṇi*." In *Kingship and Authority in South Asia*, ed. John F. Richards, 92–132. Delhi: Oxford University Press, 1998.

Archaeological Survey of India. *Progress Report of the Archaeological Survey of India, Western Circle, for the Months July 1905 to March 1906, Inclusive*. Bombay: Government of Bombay, 1906.

——. *Progress Report of the Archaeological Survey of India, Western Circle, for the Year Ending 31st March 1912*. Bombay: Government of Bombay, 1912.

Arjomand, Saïd Amir. "A Decade of Persianate Studies." *Journal of Persianate Studies* 8, no. 2 (2015): 309–33.

Arnold, John H. *History: A Very Short Introduction*. Oxford: Oxford University Press, 2000.

Arondekar, Anjali, and Geeta Patel. "Area Impossible: Notes Toward an Introduction." *GLQ: A Journal of Lesbian and Gay Studies* 22, no. 2 (2016): 151–71.

Asher, Catherine B. "The Architecture of Rāja Mān Singh: A Study of Sub-Imperial Patronage." In *The Powers of Art: Patronage in Indian Culture*, ed. Barbara Stoller Miller, 183–201. Delhi: Oxford University Press, 1992.

Asher, Catherine B., and Cynthia Talbot. *India Before Europe*. Cambridge: Cambridge University Press, 2006.

Asthana, Pratima. *The Indian View of History*. Agra: M. G., 1992.

Avasthy, Rama Shankar, and Amalananda Ghosh. "References to Muhammadans in Sanskrit Inscriptions in Northern India—A.D. 730 to 1320." *Journal of Indian History* 15, no. 2 (1936): 161–84.

——. "References to Muhammadans in Sanskrit Inscriptions of Northern India." *Journal of Indian History* 16 (1937): 24–26.

Bajoria, Jayshree. "Violent Cow Protection in India: Vigilante Groups Attack Minorities." Human Rights Watch, February 18, 2019. https://www.hrw.org/report/2019/02/18/violent-cow-protection-india/vigilante-groups-attack-minorities.

Bakker, Hans. "Somaśarman, Somavaṃśa, and Somasiddhānta: A Pāśupata Tradition in Seventh-Century Dakṣiṇa Kosala." In *Harānandalaharī: Volume in Honour of Professor Minoru Hara on His Seventieth Birthday*, ed. Minoru Hara, Ryutaro Tsuchida, and Albrecht Wezler, 1–19. Reinbek: I. Wezler Verlag, 2000.

Bala, Mudigonda. "The Madhurāvijaya of Gaṅgā Devī: A Study." PhD diss., Aligarh Muslim University, 1989.

Balbir, Nalini. "Deities." In *Jainpedia*. Institute of Jainology, 2009–. Accessed October 12, 2019. http://www.jainpedia.org/themes/practices/deities.html.

——. "À Propos des Hymnes Jaina Multilingues (Sanskrit, Prakrit, Persan)." In *Indica et Tibetica Festschrift für Michael Hahn*, ed. Konrad Klaus and Jens-Uwe Hartmann, 39–61. Wien: Arbeitskreis für Tibetische und Buddhistische Studien, 2007.

Basham, A. L. "Harṣa of Kashmir and the Iconoclast Ascetics." *Bulletin of the School of Oriental and African Studies, University of London* 12, no. 3/4 (1948): 688–91.

———. "The Kashmir Chronicle." In *Historians of India, Pakistan and Ceylon*, ed. Cyril Henry Philips, 57–65. London: Oxford University Press, 1961.

Bednar, Michael Boris. "Conquest and Resistance in Context: A Historiographical Reading of Sanskrit and Persian Battle Narratives." PhD diss., University of Texas at Austin, 2007.

———. "Mongol, Muslim, Rajput: Mahimāsāhi in Persian Texts and the Sanskrit *Hammīra-Mahākāvya*." *Journal of the Economic and Social History of the Orient* 60 (2017): 585–613.

Bendrey, V. S. *Coronation of Shivaji the Great, or The Procedure of the Religious Ceremony Performed by Gagabhatta for the Consecration of Shivaji as a Hindu King*. Bombay: P. P. H. Bookstall, 1960.

Berkwitz, Stephen C. *Buddhist History in the Vernacular: The Power of the Past in Late Medieval Sri Lanka*. Boston: Brill, 2004.

Berzin, Alexander. "A Buddhist View of Islam." In *Islam and Inter-Faith Relations: The Gerald Weisfeld Lectures 2006*, ed. Perry Schmidt-Leukel and Lloyd Ridgeon, 225–51. London: SCM Press, 2007.

Bhandarkar, D. R. "Slow Progress of Islam Power in Ancient India." *Annals of the Bhandarkar Oriental Research Institute* 11, no. 2 (1930): 128–48.

———. "Some Unpublished Inscriptions." *Indian Antiquary* 41 (1912): 17–21.

Bhandarkar, R. G. *Report on the Search for Sanskrit Mss. in the Bombay Presidency During the Year 1882–83*. Bombay: Government Central Press, 1884.

Bhatnagar, V. S. Introduction to *Padmanābha's Kānhaḍade Prabandha (India's Greatest Patriotic Saga of Medieval Times)*, vii–xxiv. New Delhi: Voice of India, 1991.

Bhavnagar Archaeological Department. *A Collection of Prakrit and Sanskrit Inscriptions*. Bhavnagar: State Printing Press, 1894.

Blochmann, H. "Inscriptions from Ahmadâbâd." *Indian Antiquary* 4 (1875): 367–68.

Bosworth, C. Edmund. "Ghurids." In *Encyclopædia Iranica*, ed. Ehsan Yarshater. Last updated February 9, 2012. http://www.iranicaonline.org/articles/ghurids.

———. "The Titulature of the Early Ghaznavids." *Oriens* 15 (1962): 210–33.

Bowles, Adam. "Historical Traditions in Hindu Texts." In *Oxford Bibliographies: Hinduism*, ed. Tracy Coleman. Last modified May 23, 2012. https://www.oxfordbibliographies.com/view/document/obo-9780195399318/obo-9780195399318-0054.xml.

Bronkhorst, Johannes. *Greater Magadha: Studies in the Culture of Early India*. Leiden: Brill, 2007.

Bronner, Yigal. *Extreme Poetry: The South Asian Movement of Simultaneous Narration*. New York: Columbia University Press, 2010.

———. "From Conqueror to Connoisseur: Kalhaṇa's Account of Jayāpīḍa and the Fashioning of Kashmir as a Kingdom of Learning." *Indian Economic and Social History Review* 50, no. 2 (2013): 161–77.

———. "The Poetics of Ambivalence: Imagining and Unimagining the Political in Bilhaṇa's *Vikramāṅkadevacarita*." *Journal of Indian Philosophy* 38 (2010): 457–83.

Bronner, Yigal, and David Shulman. "'A Cloud Turned Goose:' Sanskrit in the Vernacular Millennium." *Indian Economic and Social History Review* 43, no. 1 (2006): 1–30.

Brown, W. Norman. *The Story of Kālaka: Texts, History, Legends, and Miniature Paintings of the Śvetāmbara Jain Hagiographical Work, the Kālakācāryakathā (with 15 Plates)*. Baltimore: Lord Baltimore Press, 1933.

Bühler, Georg. *Detailed Report of a Tour in Search of Sanskrit Mss Made in Kaśmír, Rajputana, and Central India*. Bombay: Society's Library, Town Hall, 1877.

——. "Origin of the Town of Ajmer and of Its Name." *Wiener Zeitschrift für die Kunde des Morgenlandes* 11 (1897): 51–56.

Busch, Allison. "The Classical Past in the Mughal Present: The Brajbhasha *Rīti* Tradition." In *Innovations and Turning Points: Toward a History of Kavya Literature*, ed. Yigal Bronner, David Shulman, and Gary Tubb, 648–90. Oxford: Oxford University Press, 2014.

——. "Listening for the Context: Tuning in to the Reception of Riti Poetry." In *Tellings and Texts: Music, Literature, and Performance in North India*, ed. Francesca Orsini and Katherine Butler Schofield, 249–82. Cambridge: Open Book, 2015.

——. "Literary Responses to the Mughal Imperium: The Historical Poems of Keśavdās." *South Asia Research* 25, no. 1 (2005): 31–54.

——. "The Poetry of History in Early Modern India." *Proceedings of the British Academy* 207 (2017): 161–80.

——. *Poetry of Kings: The Classical Hindi Literature of Mughal India*. New York: Oxford University Press, 2011.

Busch, Allison, and Cynthia Brokaw. "Relating the Past: Writing (and Rewriting) History." In *What China and India Once Were: The Pasts That May Shape the Global Future*, ed. Sheldon Pollock and Benjamin Elman, 127–64. New York: Columbia University Press, 2018.

Carlleyle, A. C. L. *Report of a Tour in Eastern Rajputana in 1871–72 and 1872–73*. Calcutta: Office of the Superintendent of Government Printing, 1878.

Carr, Edward Hallett. *What Is History? The George Macaulay Trevelyan Lectures Delivered in the University of Cambridge, January–March 1961*. New York: Knopf, 1965.

Certeau, Michel de. *The Writing of History*. Trans. Tom Conley. New York: Columbia University Press, 1988.

Chakrabarti, Kunal. *Religious Process: The* Purāṇas *and The Making of a Regional Tradition*. New Delhi: Oxford University Press, 2001.

Chakrabarty, Dipesh. *The Calling of History: Sir Jadunath Sarkar and His Empire of Truth*. Chicago: University of Chicago Press, 2015.

Chakravarti, Ranabir. "Monarchs, Merchants, and a Maṭha in Northern Konkan (c. AD 900–1053)." In *Trade in Early India*, ed. Ranabir Chakravarti, 257–81. New Delhi: Oxford University Press, 2001.

——. *Trade and Traders in Early Indian Society*. 2nd ed. New Delhi: Manohar, 2007.

Chatterjee, Partha. "Introduction: History in the Vernacular." In *History in the Vernacular*, ed. Raziuddin Aquil and Partha Chatterjee, 1–24. Ranikhet: Permanent Black, 2008.

Chattopadhyaya, Brajadulal. *Representing the Other? Sanskrit Sources and the Muslims, Eighth to Fourteenth Century*. New Delhi: Manohar, 1998.

Chaudhuri, Jatindra Bimal. *The Contribution of Women to Sanskrit Literature*. Calcutta: Oriental Press, 1943.

——. *Muslim Patronage to Sanskritic Learning*. Delhi: Ibadah-i Adabiyat-i Delli, 1942.

Chekuri, Christopher. "Writing Politics Back Into History." *History and Theory* 46, no. 3 (2007): 384–95.

Chhabra, B. Ch. *Antiquities of Chamba State*. Vol. 2. Delhi: Manager of Publications, 1957.

Choudhary, Gulab Chandra. *Political History of Northern India From Jain Sources (c. 650 A.D. to 1300 A.D.)*. Amritsar: Sohanlal Jaindharma Pracharak Samiti, 1963.

Choudhary, R. N. *Political History of Khandavala Dynasty in Mithila: 1556–1793*. Delhi: Capital Publishing House, 1987.

Chowdhury, Shreya Roy. "Inspired by the RSS, Dictated by BJP Minister: The Inside Story of Rajasthan's Textbook Revisions." Scroll.In, November 15, 2018. https://scroll.in/article/901314/inspired-by-the-rss-dictated-by-bjp-minister-the-inside-story-of-rajasthans-textbook-revisions.

de Clercq, Eva. "Apabhramsha as a Literary Medium in Fifteenth-Century North India." In *After Timur Left: Culture and Circulation in Fifteenth-Century North India*, ed. Francesca Orsini and Samira Sheikh, 339–64. Oxford: Oxford University Press, 2014.

——. "Bhaṭṭārakas and Digambara Monastic Lineages of Fifteenth Century Gwalior: Glimpses from Raïdhū's Writings." *Journal of Asian History* 45, no. 1/2 (2011): 63–83.

Cort, John E. "In Defense of Icons in Three Languages: The Iconophilic Writing of Yaśovijaya." *International Journal of Jaina Studies* 6, no. 2 (2010): 1–45.

——. *Framing the Jina: Narratives of Icons and Idols in Jain History*. New York: Oxford University Press, 2010.

——. "Genres of Jain History." *Journal of Indian Philosophy* 23, no. 4 (1995): 469–506.

——. "The Jain Knowledge Warehouses: Traditional Libraries in India." *Journal of the American Oriental Society* 115, no. 1 (1995): 77–87.

——. "Jain Questions and Answers: Who Is God and How Is He Worshiped?" In *Religions of India in Practice*, ed. Donald S. Lopez, 598–608. Princeton, NJ: Princeton University Press, 1995.

——. *Jains in the World: Religious Values and Ideology in India*. New York: Oxford University Press, 2001.

Cox, Whitney. "Literary Register and Historical Consciousness in Kalhaṇa: A Hypothesis." *Indian Economic and Social History Review* 50, no. 2 (2013): 131–60.

——. *Modes of Philology in Medieval South India*. Leiden: Brill, 2017.

Cunningham, Alexander. *Report of Tours in Bundelkhand and Malwa in 1874–75 and 1876–77*. Calcutta: Office of the Superintendent of Government Printing, 1880.

——. *Reports of a Tour in Bundelkhand and Rewa in 1883–84; and of a Tour in Rewa, Bundelkhand, Malwa, and Gwalior, in 1884–85*. Calcutta: Superintendent of Government Printing, 1885.

Currie, P. M. *The Shrine and Cult of Muʿīn al-Dīn Chishtī of Ajmer*. New Delhi: Oxford University Press, 2006.

Dale, Stephen F. *Babur: Timurid Prince and Mughal Emperor, 1483–1530*. Cambridge: Cambridge University Press, 2018.

——. *The Garden of the Eight Paradises: Bābur and the Culture of Empire in Central Asia, Afghanistan and India (1483–1530)*. Leiden: Brill, 2004.

Das, Sukla. "Jonarāja and Dvitīya Rājataranginī." In *Indological Studies: Prof. D. C. Sircar Commemoration Volume*, ed. Sachindra Kumar Maity and Upendra Thakur, 61–64. New Delhi: Abhinav Publications, 1987.

Dasgupta, S. N., and S. K. De. *A History of Sanskrit Literature: Classical Period*. Vol. 1. Calcutta: University of Calcutta, 1947.

Date, Yasavanta Ramakrshna. *Maharashtra Sabdakosa*. Pune: Maharashtra Kosamandala, 1932–1950.

Davis, Natalie Zemon. *Fiction in the Archives: Pardon Tales and Their Tellers in Sixteenth-Century France*. Stanford, CA: Stanford University Press, 1987.

Davis, Richard H. *Lives of Indian Images*. Princeton, NJ: Princeton University Press, 1997.

Deambi, B. K. Kaul. *Corpus of Śāradā Inscriptions in Kashmir, with Special Reference to Origin and Development of Śāradā Script*. Delhi: Agam Kala Prakashan, 1982.

Dean, Carolyn J. "*Metahistory: The Historical Imagination in Nineteenth-Century Europe*, by Hayden White." *American Historical Review* 124, no. 4 (2019): 1337–50.

Deleu, J. "A Note on the Jain Prabandhas." In *Studien zum Jainismus und Buddhismus: Gedenkschrift für Ludwig Alsdorf*, ed. Klaus Bruhn and Albrecht Wezler, 61–72. Wiesbaden: Franz Steiner Verlag, 1981.

Deshpande, Madhav M. "Kṣatriyas in the Kali Age? Gāgābhaṭṭa and His Opponents." *Indo-Iranian Journal* 53 (2010): 95–120.

——. *Sanskrit and Prakrit: Sociolinguistic Issues*. Delhi: Motilal Banarsidass, 1993.

Deshpande, Prachi. *Creative Pasts: Historical Memory and Identity in Western India, 1700–1960*. New York: Columbia University Press, 2007.

Detige, Tillo. "Digambara Renouncers in Western and Central India (c. 1200–1800)." In *Encyclopedia of Jainism*, ed. John E. Cort, Paul Dundas, Kristi L. Wiley, and Knut A. Jacobsen. Leiden: Brill, forthcoming.

Dey, Gitanjali. "The Imagery and the Representation of Shaikh Jalaluddin Tabrezi in '*Seka Subhodaya*' of Halayudha Mishra." *Proceedings of the Indian History Congress* 67 (2006–2007): 401–17.

D'Hubert, Thibaut. *In the Shade of the Golden Palace: Ālāol and Middle Bengali Poetics in Arakan*. New York: Oxford University Press, 2018.

Doniger, Wendy. *The Hindus: An Alternative History*. New York: Oxford University Press, 2009.

Dundas, Paul. *History, Scripture and Controversy in a Medieval Jain Sect*. New York: Routledge, 2007.

——. *The Jains*. 2nd ed. London: Routledge, 2002.

——. "Jain Perceptions of Islam in the Early Modern Period." *Indo-Iranian Journal* 42 (1999): 35–46.

Eaton, Richard M. *India in the Persianate Age, 1000–1765*. Oakland: University of California Press, 2019.

——. "Persian Cosmopolis." In *Oxford Research Encyclopedia of Asian History*. Oxford: Oxford University Press, forthcoming.

——. *The Rise of Islam and The Bengal Frontier, 1204–1760*. Berkeley: University of California Press, 1993.

——. *A Social History of the Deccan, 1300–1761: Eight Indian Lives*. Cambridge: Cambridge University Press, 2005.

——. "Temple Desecration in Pre-modern India." *Frontline*, December 22, 2000.

Eaton, Richard M., N. H. Ansari, and S. H. Qasemi. "Bengal." In *Encyclopædia Iranica*, ed. Ehsan Yarshater. Last updated December 15, 1989. http://www.iranicaonline.org/articles/bengal.

Eaton, Richard M., and Phillip B. Wagoner. *Power, Memory, Architecture: Contested Sites on India's Deccan Plateau, 1300–1600*. New Delhi: Oxford University Press, 2014.

Eggeling, Julius. *Catalogue of the Sanskrit Manuscripts in the Library of the India Office*. 7 parts. London: Gilbert and Rivington, 1887–1904.

Eliade, Mircea. *The Sacred and the Profane: The Nature of Religion*. Trans. Willard R. Trask. New York: Harcourt, 1957.

Elliot, H. M., and John Dowson. *The History of India, as Told by Its Own Historians*. 8 vols. London: Trübner, 1867–1877.

Elverskog, Johan. *Buddhism and Islam on the Silk Road*. Philadelphia: University of Pennsylvania Press, 2010.

Ernst, Carl W. *Eternal Garden: Mysticism, History, and Politics at a South Asian Sufi Center*. Albany: State University of New York Press, 1992.

Faruqui, Munis D. "Awrangzīb." In *Encyclopaedia of Islam*, 3rd ed., ed. Kate Fleet, Gudrun Krämer, Denis Matringe, John Nawas, and Everett Rowson. Leiden: Brill, 2011. http://dx.doi.org/10.1163/1573-3912_ei3_COM_23859.

——. "The Forgotten Prince: Mirza Hakim and the Formation of the Mughal Empire in India." *Journal of the Economic and Social History of the Orient* 48, no. 4 (2005): 487–523.

——. *The Princes of the Mughal Empire, 1504–1719*. New York: Cambridge University Press, 2012.

Fisher, Elaine M. *Hindu Pluralism: Religion and the Public Sphere in Early Modern South India*. Oakland: University of California Press, 2017.

Fisher, Michael H. *A Short History of the Mughal Empire*. London: I. B. Tauris, 2016.

Fitzgerald, James L. "History and Primordium in Ancient Indian Historical Writing: *Itihāsa* and *Purāṇa* in the *Mahābhārata* and Beyond." In *Thinking, Recording, and Writing History in the Ancient World*, ed. Kurt A. Raaflaub, 41–60. Malden, MA: Wiley-Blackwell, 2014.

Flatt, Emma J. *The Courts of the Deccan Sultanates: Living Well in the Persian Cosmopolis*. Cambridge: Cambridge University Press, 2019.

Flood, Finbarr B. *Objects of Translation: Material Culture and Medieval "Hindu-Muslim" Encounter*. Princeton, NJ: Princeton University Press, 2009.

Flügel, Peter. "Worshipping the Ideal King: On the Social Implications of Jaina Conversion Stories." In *Geschichten und Geschichte: Historiographie und Hagiographie in der Asiatischen Religionsgeschichte*, ed. Peter Schalk, 357–432. Uppsala: Uppsala University, 2010.

Gazetteer of the Bombay Presidency. Vol. 8: Kathiawar. Bombay: Government Central Press, 1884.

Geiger, Bernhard. "Chîrwâ-Inschrift aus der Zeit des Guhila-Fürsten Samarasiṁha. [Vikrama-]Saṁvat 1330 [A. D. 1273]." *Wiener Zeitschrift für die Kunde des Morgenlandes* 21 (1907): 143–62.

Ghadyalpatil, Abhiram. "Modi Lays Foundation of Shivaji Statue, Rs1.06 Trillion Worth of Infra Projects." *LiveMint*, December 24, 2016. https://www.livemint.com/Politics/kXqmnXhYbJMdFwEn4IUhzI/Narendra-Modi-lays-foundation-of-Shivaji-statue-off-Mumbai-c.html.

Glasenapp, Helmuth von. *Jainism: An Indian Religion of Salvation*. Trans. Shridhar B. Shrotri. Delhi: Motilal Banarsidass, 1999.

Gode, P. K. "Date of the Rājavinoda of Udayarāja, a Hindu Court-Poet of Mahamūda Begaḍā—Between A.D. 1458 and 1469." In *Studies in Indian Literary History*, 1:346–63. Bombay: Bharatiya Vidya Bhavan, 1953.

——. "Harikavi Alias Bhānubhaṭṭa: A Court-Poet of King Sambhāji and His Works: (1) Śambhurājacarita Composed in A.D. 1685; (2) Haihayendracarita and Its Commentary; (3) Subhāṣitahārāvali." *Annals of the Bhandarkar Oriental Research Institute* 16, no. 3/4 (1934–1935): 262–91.

——. "Review of Vīrabhānūdayakāvya." *Annals of the Bhandarkar Oriental Research Institute* 27, no. 1/2 (1946): 163–65.

——. *Studies in Indian Cultural History*. Vol. 2. Poona: Prof. P. K. Gode Collected Works Publication Committee, 1960.

Gopal, Surendra. *Jains in India: Historical Essays*. Delhi: Manohar, 2019.

Gordon, Stewart. *The Marathas 1600–1818*. Vol. 2, part 4, of *The New Cambridge History of India*, ed. Gordon Johnson. Cambridge: Cambridge University Press, 1993.

——, ed. *Robes of Honour: Khil'at in Pre-Colonial and Colonial India*. New Delhi: Oxford University Press, 2003.

Granoff, Phyllis. "Authority and Innovation: A Study of the Use of Similes in the Biography of Hiravijaya to Provide Sanction for the Monk at Court." *Jinamanjari* 1 (1990): 48–60.

——. "The Biographies of Siddhasena: A Study in the Texture of Allusion and the Weaving of a Group-Image." *Journal of Indian Philosophy* 17, no. 4 (1989): 329–84.

——, ed. *The Clever Adulteress and Other Stories: A Treasury of Jain Literature*. Oakville, Ontario: Mosaic Press, 1990.

——. "Holy Warriors: A Preliminary Study of Some Biographies of Saints and Kings in the Classical Indian Tradition." *Journal of Indian Philosophy* 12 (1984): 291–303.

——. "The Householder as Shaman: Jain Biographies of Temple Builders." *East and West* 42, no. 2/4 (1992): 301–17.

——. "The Jina Bleeds: Threats to the Faith and the Rescue of the Faithful in Medieval Jain Stories." In *Images, Miracles, and Authority in Asian Religious Traditions*, ed. Richard H. Davis, 121–40. Boulder, CO: Westview Press, 1998.

——. "Mountains of Eternity: Raidhū and the Colossal Jinas of Gwalior." *Rivista di studi sudasiatici* 1 (2006): 31–50.

——. "Religious Biography and Clan History Among the Śvetāṃbara Jains in North India." *East and West* 39 (1989): 195–215.

——. "Tales of Broken Limbs and Bleeding Wounds: Responses to Muslim Iconoclasm in Medieval India." *East and West* 41, no. 1/4 (1991): 189–203.

Granoff, Phyllis, and Koichi Shinohara. *Speaking of Monks: Religious Biography in India and China*. Oakville, Ontario: Mosaic Press, 1993.

Griswold, Eliza. "The Violent Toll of Hindu Nationalism in India." *New Yorker*, March 5, 2019. https://www.newyorker.com/news/on-religion/the-violent-toll-of-hindu-nationalism-in-india.

Guha, Sumit. *Beyond Caste: Identity and Power in South Asia, Past and Present*. Leiden: Brill, 2013.

——. "Conviviality and Cosmopolitanism: Recognition and Representation of 'East' and 'West' in Peninsular India, c. 1600–1800." In *South Asian Cosmopolitanisms: Sources, Itineraries, Languages (16th–18th Century)*, ed. Corinne Lefèvre, Ines G. Županov, and Jorge Flores, 275–92. Paris: Éditions de l'école des hautes études en sciences sociales, 2015.

——. *Environment and Ethnicity in India, 1200–1991*. Cambridge: Cambridge University Press, 1999.

——. *History and Collective Memory in South Asia, 1200–2000*. Seattle: University of Washington Press, 2019.

——. "Speaking Historically: The Changing Voices of Historical Narration in Western India, 1400–1900." *American Historical Review* 109, no. 4 (2004): 1084–103.

——. "Transitions and Translations: Regional Power and Vernacular Identity in the Dakhan, 1500–1800." *Comparative Studies of South Asia, Africa, and the Middle East* 24, no. 2 (2004): 23–31.

Habib, Irfan. *An Atlas of the Mughal Empire: Political and Economic Maps, with Detailed Notes, Bibliography and Index*. Aligarh: Centre of Advanced Study in History, Aligarh Muslim University, 1982.

Halbfass, Wilhelm. *India and Europe: An Essay in Understanding*. Albany: State University of New York Press, 1988.

Hammar, Urban. *Studies in the Kālacakra Tantra: A History of the Kālacakra Tantra in Tibet and a Study of the Concept of Ādibuddha, the Fourth Body of the Buddha and the Supreme Unchanging*. Stockholm: Stockholms Universitet, 2005.

Hangloo, Rattan Lal. "Kashmiriyat: The Voice of the Past Misconstrued." In *The Parchment of Kashmir: History, Society, and Polity*, ed. Nyla Ali Khan, 37–68. New York: Palgrave Macmillan, 2012.

Hanneder, J. "On 'The Death of Sanskrit.'" *Indo-Iranian Journal* 45 (2002): 293–310.

Hardy, Adam. "Drāviḍa Temples in the Samarāṅgaṇasūtradhāra." *South Asian Studies* 25 (2009): 41–62.

Hatcher, Brian A. "'The Cosmos is One Family' (*vasudhaiva kutumbakam*): Problematic Mantra of Hindu Humanism." *Contributions to Indian Sociology* 28, no. 1 (1994): 149–62.

——. "Sanskrit and the Morning After: The Metaphorics and Theory of Intellectual Change." *Indian Economic and Social History Review* 44, no. 3 (2007): 336–61.

Hegel, Georg. *The Philosophy of History*. Trans. J. Sibree. New York: Cosimo, 2007.

Hens, Sander. "Beyond Power and Praise: Nayacandra Sūri's Tragic-Historical Epic *Hammīra-mahākāvya* as a Subversive Response to Hero Glorification in Early Tomar Gwalior." *South Asia History and Culture* 11, no. 1 (2020): 1–20.

——. "In the Guise of Eulogy: Nayacandra Sūri's *Hammīramahākāvya* as an Ironic Reworking of the Hammīra Legend." Revised MA thesis, Ghent University, 2016.

Herwadkar, R. V. *A Forgotten Literature: Foundations of Marathi Chronicles*. Bombay: Popular Prakashan, 1994.

Hobsbawm, Eric. *On History*. New York: New Press, 1997.

Hodgson, Marshall G. S. *The Venture of Islam: Conscience and History in a World Civilization*. Vol. 1, *The Classical Age of Islam*. Chicago: University of Chicago Press, 1974.

Hodivala, Shahpurshah Hormasji. *A Critical Commentary on Elliot and Dowson's "History of India as Told by Its Own Historians."* Vol. 2 of *Studies in Indo-Muslim History*. Bombay, 1939.

Hoffman, Helmut H. R. "Kālacakra Studies 1: Manichaeism, Christianity, and Islam in the *Kālacakra Tantra*." *Central Asiatic Journal* 13, no. 1 (1969): 52–73.

Hooja, Rima. *A History of Rajasthan*. New Delhi: Rupa, 2006.

Houben, Jan E. M. "The Brahmin Intellectual: History, Ritual and 'Time Out of Time.'" *Journal of Indian Philosophy* 30 (2002): 463–79.

Husaini, S. A. Q. "The History of Madura Sultanate." *Journal of the Asiatic Society of Pakistan* 2 (1957): 90–130.

Inden, Ronald. "Introduction: Philological to Dialogical Texts." In *Querying the Medieval: Texts and the History of Practices in South Asia*, ed. Ronald Inden, Jonathan Walters, and Daud Ali, 3–28. New York: Oxford University Press, 2000.

Jackson, Peter. *The Delhi Sultanate: A Political and Military History*. Cambridge: Cambridge University Press, 1999.

——. "Turkish Slaves on Islam's Indian Frontier." In *Slavery and South Asian History*, ed. Indrani Chatterjee and Richard M. Eaton, 63–82. Bloomington: Indiana University Press, 2006.

Jackson, William J. *Vijayanagara Voices: Exploring South Indian History and Hindu Literature*. Aldershot, Hampshire, UK: Ashgate, 2015.

Jain, Banarsi Das. "The Persian of Jain Hymns." In *Siddha-Bhāratī, or The Rosary of Indology: Presenting 108 Original Papers on Indological Subjects in Honour of the 60th Birthday of Dr. Siddheshwar Varma*, ed. Vishva Bandhu, 47–49. Hoshiarpur: Vishveshvaranand Vedic Research Institute, 1950.

Jain, Rupam, and Tom Lasseter. "By Rewriting History, Hindu Nationalists Aim to Assert Their Dominance over India." Reuters, March 6, 2018. https://www.reuters.com/investigates/special-report/india-modi-culture/.

Jain, Shalin. "The Centre and the 'Locality' in Mughal India: The Case of Mantri Karam Chand Bachhawat of Bikaner." In *Proceedings of the Indian History Congress*, 332–39. 68th Session. Delhi: Indian Council of Historical Research, 2007.

——. *Identity, Community and State: The Jains Under the Mughals*. Delhi: Primus Books, 2018.

——. "Interaction of the 'Lords': The Jain Community and the Mughal Royalty under Akbar." *Social Scientist* 40, no. 3–4 (2012): 33–57.

——. "Jain Elites and the Mughal State under Shahjahan." *Indian Historical Review* 42, no. 2 (2015): 210–25.

——. "The Merchants and the Rulers: The Jain Traders in the Early Seventeenth Century Agra." In *Transformations in Indian History*, ed. Pratima Asthana and S. Z. H. Jafri, 290–98. Delhi: Anamika, 2009.

——. "Piety, Laity and Royalty: Jains Under the Mughals in the First Half of the Seventeenth Century." *Indian Historical Review* 40, no. 1 (2013): 67–92.

JAINA. "The Concept of God in Jainism." JAINA: Federation of Jain Associations in North America. Accessed September 4, 2019. https://www.jaina.org/page/ConceptofGod.

Jasper, Daniel Alan. "Commemorating Shivaji: Regional and Religious Identity in Maharashtra, India." PhD diss., New School University, 2002.

Jha, D. N. *The Myth of the Holy Cow.* London: Verso, 2002.

Jha, Pankaj Kumar. "Beyond the Local and the Universal: Exclusionary Strategies of Expansive Literary Cultures in Fifteenth-Century Mithila." *Indian Economic and Social History Review* 51, no. 1 (2014): 1–40.

——. *A Political History of Literature: Vidyapati and the Fifteenth Century.* Delhi: Oxford University Press, 2019.

Joffee, Jennifer Beth. "Art, Architecture and Politics in Mewar, 1628–1710." PhD diss., University of Minnesota, 2005.

Jolly, Julius. *Georg Bühler, 1837–1898.* Strassburg: Trübner, 1899.

Kaicker, Abhishek. "Unquiet City: Making and Unmaking Politics in Mughal Delhi, 1707–39." PhD diss., Columbia University, 2014.

Kane, Pandurang Vaman. *History of Dharmasastra: Ancient and Mediaeval Religious and Civil Law.* Vol. 1. Poona: Bhandarkar Oriental Research Institute, 1930.

Kapadia, Aparna. "The Last Cakravartin? The Gujarat Sultan as 'Universal King' in Fifteenth Century Sanskrit Poetry." *Medieval History Journal* 16, no. 1 (2013): 63–88.

——. *In Praise of Kings: Rajputs, Sultans and Poets in Fifteenth-Century Gujarat.* Cambridge: Cambridge University Press, 2018.

Kaul, Shonaleeka. *The Making of Early Kashmir: Landscape and Identity in the Rajatarangini.* New Delhi: Oxford University Press, 2018.

——. "'Seeing' the Past: Text and Questions of History in the *Rājataraṅgiṇī*." *History and Theory* 53, no. 2 (2014): 194–211.

Kaviraj, Sudipta. "Modernity, State, and Toleration in Indian History: Exploring Accommodations and Partitions." In *Boundaries of Toleration*, ed. Alfred Stepan and Charles Taylor, 233–66. New York: Columbia University Press, 2014.

Keith, A. Berriedale. *Classical Sanskrit Literature.* London: Oxford University Press, 1923.

Khan, Mohammad Ishaq. *Kashmir's Transition to Islam: The Role of Muslim Rishis (15th–18th Century).* New Delhi: Manohar, 1994.

Kielhorn, F. *Bruchstücke Indischer Schauspiele in Inschriften zu Ajmere.* Berlin: Weidmannsche Buchhandlung, 1901.

——. "Copper-Plate Grants of the Kings of Kanauj." *Indian Antiquary* 18 (1889): 9–146.

——. "Delhi Siwalik Pillar Inscriptions of Visaladeva; The Vikrama Year 1220." *Indian Antiquary* 19 (1890): 215–19.

——. "Sanskrit Plays, Partly Preserved as Inscriptions at Ajmere." *Indian Antiquary* 20 (1891): 201–12.

Knutson, Jesse. *Into the Twilight of Sanskrit Court Poetry: The Sena Salon of Bengal and Beyond.* Berkeley: University of California Press, 2014.

——. "Poetic Justice: On Kalhaṇa's Historical Aesthetics." *Comparative Studies of South Asia, Africa, and the Middle East* 35, no. 2 (2015): 281–93.

Kolff, Dirk H. A. *Naukar, Rajput, and Sepoy: The Ethnohistory of the Military Labour Market in Hindustan, 1450–1850.* Cambridge: Cambridge University Press, 1990.

Kothiyal, Tanuja. *Nomadic Narratives: A History of Mobility and Identity in the Great Indian Desert*. Delhi: Cambridge University Press, 2016.

Krishnamachariar, M. *History of Classical Sanskrit Literature*. Madras: Tirumalai-Tirupati Devasthanams Press, 1937.

Kroll, Ethan Saul. "A Logical Approach to Law." PhD diss., University of Chicago, 2010.

Kruijtzer, Gijs. *Xenophobia in Seventeenth-Century India*. Leiden: Leiden University Press, 2009.

Kulkarni, A. R. *The Marathas*. Pune: Diamond Publications, 2008.

Kulke, Hermann. "Historiography in Early Medieval India." In *Explorations in the History of South Asia: Essays in Honour of Dietmar Rothermund*, ed. Georg Berkemer, Tilman Frasch, Hermann Kulke, and Jürgen Lütt, 71–83. New Delhi: Manohar, 2001.

Kumar, S. Selvin. *Madurai Sultanate*. Madurai: Kamaraj University, 1990.

Kumar, Sunil. *The Emergence of the Delhi Sultanate, 1192–1286*. Delhi: Permanent Black, 2007.

Laine, James W. "Resisting My Attackers; Resisting My Defenders: Representing the Shivaji Narratives." In *Engaging South Asian Religions: Boundaries, Appropriations, and Resistances*, ed. Matthew N. Schmalz and Peter Gottschalk, 153–72. Albany: State University of New York Press, 2011.

Laine, James W., trans., in collaboration with S. S Bahulkar. *The Epic of Shivaji: Kavindra Paramananda's Śivabhārata*. Hyderabad, India: Orient Longman, 2001.

Lal, Vinay. *The History of History: Politics and Scholarship in Modern India*. New Delhi: Oxford University Press, 2003.

Larson, Gerald James. "Karma as a 'Sociology of Knowledge' or 'Social Psychology' of Process/Praxis." In *Karma and Rebirth in Classical Indian Traditions*, ed. Wendy Doniger O'Flaherty, 303–16. Berkeley: University of California Press, 1980.

Leclère, Basile. "Ambivalent Representations of Muslims in Medieval Indian Theatre." *Studies in History* 27, no. 2 (2011): 155–95.

Lienhard, Siegfried. *History of Classical Poetry: Sanskrit, Pali, Prakrit*. Wiesbaden: Otto Harrassowitz, 1984.

Lohuizen-de Leeuw, J. E. van. "India and Its Cultural Empire." In *Orientalism and History*, ed. Dénis Sinor, 34–56. Cambridge: W. Heffer and Sons, 1954.

Loomba, Ania. "Of Gifts, Ambassadors, and Copy-Cats: Diplomacy, Exchange, and Difference in Early Modern India." In *Emissaries in Early Modern Literature and Culture: Mediation, Transmission, Traffic, 1550–1700*, ed. Brinda Charry and Gitanjali Shahani, 41–75. Farnham, Surrey, UK: Ashgate, 2009.

MacDonell, Arthur A. *A History of Sanskrit Literature*. New York: D. Appleton, 1900.

Maclean, Derryl N. *Religion and Society in Arab Sind*. Leiden: Brill, 1989.

Majumdar, Asoke Kumar. *Chaulukyas of Gujarat: A Survey of the History and Culture of Gujarat from the Middle of the Tenth to the End of the Thirteenth Century*. Bombay: Bharatiya Vidya Bhavan, 1956.

Majumdar, R. C. "Ideas of History in Sanskrit Literature." In *Historians of India, Pakistan and Ceylon*, ed. C. H. Philips, 13–28. London: Oxford University Press, 1961.

Majumdar, Rani. "The Kathakautuka: A Persian Love Poem in Sanskrit Garb." *Journal of the Oriental Institute, M. S. University of Baroda* 47, no. 3–4 (1998): 283–87.

Mallette, Karla. "Sanskrit Snapshots." *Comparative Studies of South Asia, Africa, and the Middle East* 38, no. 1 (2018): 127–35.

Mantena, Rama. "The Question of History in Precolonial India." *History and Theory* 46, no. 3 (2007): 396–408.

Marshall, D. N. *Mughals in India: A Bibliographical Survey*. Vol. 1, *Manuscripts*. Bombay: Asia Publishing House, 1967.

Mathur, R. S. *Relations of Hadas with Mughal Emperors: 1568–1720 A.D.* Delhi: Deputy Publications, 1986.

McCarter, Elliott Craver. "The Picture-Gallery Episode of the *Pṛthvīrājavijaya Mahākāvya*: Translation of the Eleventh *Sarga* and Analysis of Its Political Application." MA thesis, University of Texas at Austin, 2005.

McCrea, Lawrence. "Poetry Beyond Good and Evil: Bilhaṇa and the Tradition of Patron-Centered Court Epic." *Journal of Indian Philosophy* 38 (2010): 503–18.

——. "Śāntarasa in the *Rājataraṅgiṇī*: History, Epic, and Moral Decay." *Indian Economic and Social History Review* 50, no. 2 (2013): 179–99.

Meisami, Julie Scott. "The Past in Service of the Present: Two Views of History in Medieval Persia." *Poetics Today* 14, no. 2 (1993): 247–75.

Michell, George. *Architecture and Art of Southern India: Vijayanagara and the Successor States*. Cambridge: Cambridge University Press, 1995.

Minkowski, Christopher. "King David in Oudh: A Bible Story in Sanskrit and the Just King at an Afghan Court." Inaugural Lecture for the Boden Professorship, University of Oxford, March 7, 2006.

——. "Learned Brahmins and the Mughal Court: *The Jyotiṣas*." In *Religious Interactions in Mughal India*, ed. Vasudha Dalmia and Munis D. Faruqui, 102–34. New Delhi: Oxford University Press, 2014.

Mirashi, Vasudev Vishnu, ed. *Inscriptions of the Kalachuri-Chedi Era*. Vol. 4. Ootacamund: Government Epigraphist for India, 1955.

Mishra, Ratanlal. *Inscriptions of Rājasthān*. Vol. 3. Udaipur: Himanshu Publication, 2006.

Mohammed, Jigar. "Sultan Zain-ul-Abidin (1420–70) in the Sanskrit Sources of Kashmir: A Study of the *Rajatarangini*'s [*sic*] of Jonaraja and Srivara." *Proceedings of the Indian History Congress* 58 (1997): 218–25.

Mohan, V. *The Ābdullāh-Carita of Laksmipati: A Study*. Chennai: C. P. R. Publications, 2015.

Mohanty, Jitendra Nath. *Reason and Tradition in Indian Thought: An Essay on the Nature of Indian Philosophical Thinking*. Oxford: Clarendon Press, 2002.

Moin, A. Azfar. *The Millennial Sovereign: Sacred Kingship and Sainthood in Islam*. New York: Columbia University Press, 2012.

Moraes, George M. *The Kadamba Kula: A History of Ancient and Mediaeval Karnataka*. Bombay: B. X. Furtado and Sons, 1931.

Morgenstein Fuerst, Ilyse R. "Space, Power, and Stories: Hagiography, Nationalist Discourse, and the Construction of Sacred Space at the Khwaja Sahib in Ajmer, India." *Symposia* 3, no. 1 (2011): 55–69.

Morison, James. "Some Account of the Genealogies in the Pṛithvîrâjavijaya." *Wiener Zeitschrift für die Kunde des Morgenlandes* 7 (1893): 188–92.

Mukherjee, Rudrangshu. "What Made the East India Company So Successful?" *India Forum*, November 1, 2019. https://www.theindiaforum.in/article/what-made-east-india-company-so-successful.

Nandy, Ashis. "History's Forgotten Doubles." *History and Theory* 34, no. 2 (1995): 44–66.

Nemec, John. "Review of *Kingship in Kaśmīr (AD 1148–1459), from the Pen of Jonarāja, Court Paṇḍit to Sulṭān Zayn al-ʿĀbidīn, Critically Edited with Annotated Translation, Indexes, and Maps.* By Walter Slaje." *Journal of the American Oriental Society* 137, no. 2 (2017): 404–6.

Newman, John. "A Brief History of the Kalachakra." In *The Wheel of Time: The Kalachakra in Context*, ed. Geshe Lhundub Sopa, Roger Jackson, and John Newman, 51–90. Ithaca, NY: Snow Lion Publications, 1991.

——. "Islam in the Kālacakra Tantra." *Journal of the International Association of Buddhist Studies* 21, no. 2 (1998): 311–71.

Nicholson, Andrew J. *Unifying Hinduism: Philosophy and Identity in Indian Intellectual History.* New York: Columbia University Press, 2010.

Norton, Mary Beth. "Assessing Women's History from a Personal Angle." *Perspectives on History* 56, no. 8 (October 25, 2018). https://www.historians.org/publications-and-directories/perspectives-on-history/november-2018/assessing-womens-history-from-a-personal-angle.

——. "History on the Diagonal." *American Historical Review* 124, no. 1 (February 2019): 1–19.

Novetzke, Christian Lee. "The Laine Controversy and the Study of Hinduism." *International Journal of Hindu Studies* 8, no. 1–3 (2004): 183–201.

——. *The Quotidian Revolution: Vernacularization, Religion, and the Premodern Public Sphere in India.* New York: Columbia University Press, 2016.

Obrock, Luther. "History at the End of History: Śrīvara's *Jainataraṅgiṇī*." *Indian Economic and Social History Review* 50, no. 2 (2013): 221–36.

——. "Muslim *Mahākāvyas*: Sanskrit and Translation in the Sultanates." In *Text and Tradition in Early Modern North India*, ed. Tyler Williams, Anshu Malhotra, and John Stratton Hawley, 58–76. Delhi: Oxford University Press, 2018.

——. "Translation and History: The Development of a Kashmiri Textual Tradition from ca. 1000–1500." PhD diss., University of California–Berkeley, 2015.

Ogura, Satoshi. "Incompatible Outsiders or Believers of a Darśana? Representations of Muslims by Three Brahmans of Šāhmīrid Kašmīr." *Rivista degli studi orientali* 88, no. 1–4 (2015): 179–211.

——. "A Note on the Genesis and Character of a So-Called 'Persian Translation of the *Rājataraṅgiṇīs*' in Maulana Azad Library and Rampur Raza Library." In *History, Literature, and Scholarly Perspectives: South and West Asian Context; Festschrift Presented in Honor of Moinuddin Aqeel*, ed. Jawed Ahmed Khursheed and Khalid Amin, 135–46. Karachi: Islamic Research Academy, 2016.

——. "Transmission Lines of Historical Information on Kašmīr: From *Rājataraṅgiṇīs* to the Persian Chronicles in the Early Muġal Period." *Journal of Indological Studies* 22–23 (2010–11): 23–59.

——. "Turning *Taraṅgiṇī* into *Tārīḫ*: A Comparative Study on Jonarāja's *Rājataraṅgiṇī* and Its Persian Translation Composed at the Court of Akbar." Paper presented at the Sixteenth World Sanskrit Conference, Bangkok, June 29, 2015.

O'Hanlon, Rosalind. "Contested Conjunctures: Brahman Communities and 'Early Modernity' in India. *American Historical Review* 118, no. 3 (2013): 765–87.

Ollett, Andrew. *Language of the Snakes: Prakrit, Sanskrit and the Language Order of Premodern India.* Oakland: University of California Press, 2017.

Omvedt, Gail. *Buddhism in India: Challenging Brahmanism and Caste.* New Delhi: Sage, 2003.

Orsini, Francesca. "How to Do Multilingual Literary History? Lessons from Fifteenth- and Sixteenth-Century North India." *Indian Economic and Social History Review* 49, no. 2 (2012): 225–46.

Parasher, Aloka. *Mlecchas in Early India: A Study in Attitude Towards Outsiders Up to AD 600.* New Delhi: Munshiram Manoharlal, 1991.

Parikh, Rasikalal Chotalal. Introduction to *Kāvyaprakāśakhaṇḍana* of Siddhichandra, 6–20. Singhi Jain Shastra Shikshapith, Bharatiya Vidya Bhavan: Bombay, 1953.

Patel, Alka. "Expanding the Ghurid Architectural Corpus East of the Indus: The Jāgeśvara Temple at Sādaḍi, Rajasthan." *Archives of Asian Art* 59 (2009): 33–56.

——. "The Mosque in South Asia: Beginnings." In *Piety and Politics in the Early Indian Mosque.* Ed. Finbarr Barry Flood, 3–26. Oxford: Oxford University Press, 2008.

Pathak, Vishwambhar Sharan. *Ancient Historians of India: A Study in Historical Biographies.* Bombay: Asia Publishing House, 1966.

Perrett, Roy W. "History, Time, and Knowledge in Ancient India." *History and Theory* 38, no. 3 (1999): 307–21.

Peterson, Indira Viswanathan. "Śramaṇas Against the Tamil Way: Jains as Others in Tamil Śaiva Literature." In *Open Boundaries: Jain Communities and Cultures in Indian History,* ed. John E. Cort, 163–85. Albany: State University of New York Press, 1998.

——. "Tamil Śaiva Hagiography." In *According to Tradition: Hagiographical Writing in India,* ed. Winand M. Callewaert and Rupert Snell, 191–228. Wiesbaden: Harrassowitz Verlag, 1994.

Pierce Taylor, Sarah. "The Jaina *Maṭha* and the Rhetoric of Empire." In *Beyond the Monastery: The Entangled Institutional History of the South Asian Maṭha*, ed. Caleb Simmons and Sarah Pierce Taylor. Forthcoming.

Pillai, Manu S. *Rebel Sultans: The Deccan from Khilji to Shivaji.* New Delhi: Juggernaut, 2018.

Pingree, David. *Jyotiḥśāstra.* Wiesbaden: Otto Harrassowitz, 1981.

——. "Sanskrit Evidence for the Presence of Arabs, Jews, and Persians in Western India: Ca. 700–1300." *Journal of the Oriental Institute, M. S. University of Baroda* 31, no. 1 (1981): 172–82.

Pollock, Sheldon. "The Death of Sanskrit." *Comparative Studies in Society and History* 43, no. 2 (2001): 392–426.

——. "The Idea of Śāstra in Traditional India." In *Shastric Traditions in Indian Arts,* ed. Anna Libera Dallapiccola, Christine Walter-Mendy, and Stephanie Zingel-Avé Lallemant, 17–26. Stuttgart: Franz Steiner Verlag, 1989.

——. *The Language of the Gods in the World of Men: Sanskrit, Culture, and Power in Premodern India.* Berkeley: University of California Press, 2006.

——. "Literary Culture and Manuscript Culture in Precolonial India." In *Literary Cultures and the Material Book*, ed. Simon Eliot, Andrew Nash, and Ian Willison, 77–94. London: British Library, 2007.

——. "Making History: Kalyāṇi A.D. 1008." In *Śrī Nāgābhinandanam: Dr. M. S. Nagaraja Rao Festschrift: Essays on Art, Culture, History, Archaeology, Epigraphy and Conservation of Cultural Property of India and Neighbouring Countries*, ed. L. K. Srinivasan and S. Nagaraju, 2:559–76. Bangalore: M. S. Nagaraja Rao Felicitation Committee, 1995.

——. "Mīmāṃsā and the Problem of History in Traditional India." *Journal of the American Oriental Society* 109, no. 4 (1989): 603–10.

——. "Playing by the Rules: Śāstra and Sanskrit Literature." In *Shastric Traditions in Indian Arts*, ed. Anna Libera Dallapiccola, Christine Walter-Mendy, and Stephanie Zingel-Avé Lallemant, 301–12. Stuttgart: Franz Steiner Verlag, 1989.

——. "Pretextures of Time." *History and Theory* 46, no. 3 (2007): 364–81.

——. "Rāmāyaṇa and Political Imagination in India." *Journal of Asian Studies* 52, no. 2 (1993): 261–97.

——, ed. and trans. *A Rasa Reader: Classical Indian Aesthetics*. New York: Columbia University Press, 2016.

——. "Sanskrit Literary Culture from the Inside Out." In *Literary Cultures in History: Reconstructions from South Asia*, ed. Sheldon Pollock, 39–130. Berkeley: University of California Press, 2003.

——. "The Social Aesthetic and Sanskrit Literary Theory." *Journal of Indian Philosophy* 29, no. 1/2 (2001): 197–229.

——. "The Theory of Practice and the Practice of Theory in Indian Intellectual History." *Journal of the American Oriental Society* 105, no. 3 (1985): 499–519.

——. "We Need to Find What We Are Not Looking For." *International Institute for Asian Studies Newsletter* 43 (Spring 2007): 3–5.

Prabha, Chandra. *Historical Mahākāvyas in Sanskrit (Eleventh to Fifteenth Century A.D.)*. New Delhi: Shri Bharat Bharati, 1976.

Prasad, Pushpa. *Sanskrit Inscriptions of Delhi Sultanate, 1191–1526*. Delhi: Oxford University Press, 1990.

——. "The *Turuska* or Turks in Late Ancient Indian Documents." In *Proceedings of the Indian History Congress: 55th Session, Aligarh, 1994*, 170–75. Delhi: Indian History Congress, 1995.

Prinsep, James. "Facsimiles of Ancient Inscriptions." *Journal of the Asiatic Society of Bengal* 67 (1837): 869–87.

Qvarnström, Olle. "The Story Behind the Story: Jain Identity and Patronage as Narrated by Kakkasūri in the Nābhinandanajinoddhāraprabandha." In *The Gift of Knowledge: Patterns of Patronage in Jainism; Essays in Honour of Prof. Hampa Nagarajaiah's Promotion of Jain Studies*, ed. Christine Chojnacki and Basile Leclére, 196–208. Bangalore: Sapna Book House, 2018.

Raeside, I. M. P. "A Gujarati Bardic Poem: The *Kānhaḍade-Prabandha*." In *The Indian Narrative: Perspectives and Patterns*, ed. Christopher Shackle and Rupert Snell, 137–53. Wiesbaden: O. Harrassowitz, 1992.

Raghavan, V., et. al., eds. *New Catalogus Catalogorum: An Alphabetical Register of Sanskrit and Allied Works and Authors*. University of Madras. Madras, 1949–.

Raina, L. N. "Kalhana—The Great Chronicler." In *Kashmiri Pandits: A Cultural Heritage*, ed. Saligram Bhatt, 167–70. New Delhi: Lancers Books, 1995.

Rajaraman, Shankar, and Venetia Kotamraju. "Sound Play and the *Madhurā Vijaya* of Gaṅgādevī." *Asian Literature and Translation* 1, no. 4 (2013): 1–17.
Raje, Chandrakant Gajanan. *Biography and History in Sanskrit Literature*. Bombay: Bombay University Press, 1958.
Rao, Ajay K. "From Fear to Hostility: Responses to the Conquests of Madurai." *South Asian Studies* 32, no. 1 (2016): 1–12 (digital offprint).
Rao, Velcheru Narayana. "Multiple Literary Cultures in Telugu: Court, Temple, and Public." In *Literary Cultures in History: Reconstructions from South Asia*, ed. Sheldon Pollock, 383–436. Berkeley: University of California Press, 2003.
Rao, Velcheru Narayana, David Shulman, and Sanjay Subrahmanyam. *Textures of Time: Writing History in South India, 1600–1800*. New York: Other Press, 2003.
——. "A Pragmatic Response." *History and Theory* 46, no. 3 (2007): 409–27.
Richards, John F. *The Mughal Empire*. Cambridge: Cambridge University Press, 1995.
Ricoeur, Paul. *Memory, History, Forgetting*. Trans. Kathleen Blamey and David Pellauer. Chicago: University of Chicago Press, 2004.
Roy, Kumkum. "The Making of a Mandala: Fuzzy Frontiers of Kalhana's Kashmir." In *Negotiating India's Past: Essays in Memory of Partha Sarathi Gupta*, ed. Biswamoy Pati, Bhairabi Prasad Sahu, and T. K. Venkatasubramanian, 52–66. New Delhi: Tulika Books, 2003.
Said, Edward W. *Orientalism*. New York: Random House, 1978.
Saith, Shanti Saroop. *Catalogue of Sanskrit Manuscripts in the Punjab University Library*. Lahore: University of the Panjab, 1941.
Salomon, Richard. "Notes on the Translations of Kalhaṇa's Rājataraṅgiṇī (I–IV)." *Berliner Indologische Studien* 3 (1987): 147–79.
——. "The Śivarājarājyābhiṣekakalpataru: A Sanskrit Text on Śivājī." *Journal of the Oriental Institute, M. S. University of Baroda* 28 (1979): 70–89.
Sanderson, Alexis. "Meaning in Tantric Ritual." In *Essais sur le rituel*, ed. Anne-Marie Blondeau and Kristofer Schipper, 3:15–95. Louvain-Paris: Peeters, 1995.
Sarda, Har Bilas. "The Prithviraja Vijaya." *Journal of the Royal Asiatic Society of Great Britain and Ireland* (1913): 259–81.
Sardesai, Govind Sakharam. *New History of the Marathas*. Vol. 1, *Shivaji and His Line [1600–1707]*. Bombay: Dhawale, 1957.
Sarkar, Jadunath. *House of Shivaji: Studies and Documents on Maratha History, Royal Period*. New Delhi: Orient Longman, 1978.
——. *Shivaji and His Times*. London: Longmans, Green, 1920.
Schmidt-Madsen, Jacob. "Repossessing the Past: Authorial Tradition and Scribal Innovation in Śivadāsa's Vetālapañcaviṃśatikā." MA thesis, University of Copenhagen, 2014.
Scott, David. "Dehistoricising History." In *Unmaking the Nation: The Politics of Identity and History in Modern Sri Lanka*, ed. Pradeep Jeganathan and Qadri Ismail, 20–33. Colombo: Social Scientists' Association, 1995.
Sewell, Robert. "The Dates in Merutunga's 'Prabandha Chintamani.'" *Journal of the Royal Asiatic Society of Great Britain and Ireland*, no. 3 (1920): 333–41.
Sharma, Dasaratha. "New Light on Alāuddīn Khaljī's Achievements." *Indian Historical Quarterly* 32, no. 1 (1956): 96–98.

Sharma, Dasharatha. *Early Chauhān Dynasties: A Study of Chauhān Political History, Chauhān Political Institutions, and Life in the Chauhān Dominions from c. 800 to 1316 A.D.* Delhi: S. Chand, 1959.

Sharma, Mahesh. "State Formation and Cultural Complex in Western Himalaya: Chamba Genealogy and Epigraphs—700–1650 C. E." *Indian Economic and Social History Review* 41, no. 4 (2004): 387–432.

Sharma, Shalini. "India: How Some Hindu Nationalists Are Rewriting Caste History in the Name of Decolonisation." *The Conversation*, May 9, 2019. https://theconversation.com/india-how-some-hindu-nationalists-are-rewriting-caste-history-in-the-name-of-decolonisation-114133.

Sharma, Sunil. "The History of Akbar: Indo-Persian for a New Audience." *Mizan* (blog), April 28, 2016. http://mizanproject.org/the-history-of-akbar/.

Sheikh, Samira. "Alliance, Genealogy and Political Power: The Cūḍāsamās of Junagadh and the Sultans of Gujarat." *Medieval History Journal* 11, no. 1 (2018): 29–61.

——. *Forging a Region: Sultans, Traders, and Pilgrims in Gujarat, 1200–1500.* Delhi: Oxford University Press, 2010.

Shivprasad. *Jain Shvetambar Gaccho ka Samkshipt Itihas.* Vol. 2. Surat: Omkarsuri Jnan Mandir, 2009.

Shokoohy, Mehrdad. "Architecture of the Sultanate of Ma'bar in Madura, and Other Muslim Monuments in South India." *Journal of the Royal Asiatic Society*, 3rd ser., 1, no. 1 (1991): 31–92.

——. *Muslim Architecture of South India: The Sultanate of Ma'bar and the Traditions of Maritime Settlers on the Malabar and Coromandel Coasts (Tamil Nadu, Kerala and Goa).* London: Routledge Curzon, 2013.

Shukla, N. S. "Persian Translations of Sanskrit Works." *Indological Studies: Journal of the Department of Sanskrit, University of Delhi* 3, no. 1–2 (1974): 175–91.

Shulman, David. "Preface: Kalhana's *Rājataraṅgiṇī*: What Is It?" *Indian Economic and Social History Review* 50, no. 2 (2013): 127–30.

Siddiqui, Iqtidar Husain. *Indo-Persian Historiography to the Fourteenth Century: Enlarged Edition.* Delhi: Primus Books, 2014.

Siebenhüner, Kim. "Approaching Diplomatic and Courtly Gift-Giving in Europe and Mughal India: Shared Practices and Cultural Diversity." *Medieval History Journal* 16, no. 2 (2013): 525–46.

Singh, P. N. "Coins Bearing the Names of Muhammad Bin Sam and Prithviraja III: A Reappraisal." *Israel Numismatics Journal* 10 (1988): 113–16.

Singh, Upinder. *Political Violence in Ancient India.* Cambridge, MA: Harvard University Press, 2017.

Sircar, D. C. *Studies in the Geography of Ancient and Medieval India.* New Delhi: Motilal Banarsidass, 1971.

Slaje, Walter. "In the Guise of Poetry—Kalhaṇa Reconsidered." In *Śāstrārambha: Inquiries into the Preamble in Sanskrit*, ed. Walter Slaje, 207–44. Wiesbaden: Harrassowitz Verlag, 2008.

——. "The Last Buddhist of Kashmir as Recorded by Jonarāja." In *Sanskrit Studies*, ed. Wagish Shukla, 2:185–93. New Delhi: DK Printworld, 2007.

——. *Medieval Kashmir and the Science of History*. Austin: South Asia Institute, University of Texas at Austin, 2004.
——. "A Note on the Genesis and Character of Śrīvara's So-Called 'Jaina-Rājataraṅgiṇī.'" *Journal of the American Oriental Society* 125, no. 3 (2005): 379–88.
——. "Three Bhaṭṭas, Two Sulṭāns, and the Kashmirian Atharvaveda." In *The Atharvaveda and Its Paippalādaśākhā: Historical and Philological Papers on a Vedic Tradition*, ed. Arlo Griffiths and Annette Schmiedchen, 329–53. Aachen: Shaker, 2007.
Smith, David. *Ratnākara's Haravijaya: An Introduction to the Sanskrit Court Epic*. New Delhi: Oxford University Press, 1985.
Smith, Vincent A. "The History of the City of Kanauj and of King Yasovarman." *Journal of the Royal Asiatic Society of Great Britain and Ireland*, 1908, 765–93.
Sohoni, Pushkar. *The Architecture of a Deccan Sultanate: Courtly Practice and Royal Authority in Late Medieval India*. London: I. B. Tauris, 2018.
Spiegel, Gabrielle M. "Above, About and Beyond the Writing of History: A Retrospective View of Hayden White's *Metahistory* on the 40th Anniversary of its Publication." *Rethinking History* 17, no. 4 (2013): 492–508.
Sreenivasan, Ramya. "Alauddin Khalji Remembered: Conquest, Gender, and Community in Medieval Rajput Narratives." *Studies in History* 18, no. 2 (2002): 275–96.
——. "The 'Marriage' of 'Hindu' and 'Turak': Medieval Rajput Histories of Jalor." *Medieval History Journal* 7, no. 1 (2004): 87–108.
——. "Rethinking Kingship and Authority in South Asia: Amber (Rajasthan), ca. 1560–1615." *Journal of the Economic and Social History of the Orient* 57 (2014): 549–86.
Stabler, Karen Chittick. "A Brief History of Interlibrary Loan with Special Reference to Indiana." *Indiana Libraries* 2, no. 2 (1982): 42–53.
Subramanian, Lakshmi. *The Sovereign and the Pirate: Ordering Maritime Subjects in India's Western Littoral*. Delhi: Oxford University Press, 2016.
Sudyka, Lidia. *Vijayanagara: A Forgotten Empire of Poetesses*. Part 1, *The Voice of Gaṅgādevī*. Kraków: Ksiegarnia Akademicka, 2013.
Sundermann, W. "An Early Attestation of the Name of the Tajiks." In *Medioiranica: Proceedings of the International Colloquium Organized by the Katholieke Universiteit Leuven from the 21st to the 23rd of May 1990*, ed. Wojciech Skalmowski and Alois van Tongerloo, 163–71. Leuven: Uitgeverij Peeters en Departement Orientalistiek, 1993.
Talbot, Cynthia. "Elephants, Hunting and Mughal Service: The Martial Lordship of Rao Ratan." In *Bundi Fort: A Rajput World*, ed. Milo Cleveland Beach, 80–95. Mumbai: Marg, 2016.
——. "Inscribing the Other, Inscribing the Self: Hindu-Muslim Identities in Pre-colonial India." *Comparative Studies in Society and History* 37, no. 4 (1995): 692–722.
——. "Justifying Defeat: A Rajput Perspective on the Age of Akbar." *Journal of the Economic and Social History of the Orient* 55 (2012): 329–68.
——. *The Last Hindu Emperor: Prithviraj Chauhan and the Indian Past, 1200–2000*. Cambridge: Cambridge University Press, 2016.
——. "The Mewar Court's Construction of History." In *Kingdom of the Sun: Indian Court and Village Art from the Princely State of Mewar*, ed. Joanna Gottfried Williams, 12–33. San Francisco, CA: Asian Art Museum, 2007.

——. "A Poetic Record of the Rajput Rebellion, c. 1680." *Journal of the Royal Asiatic Society*, 3rd ser., 28, no. 3 (2018): 461–83.

Taylor, William. *A Catalogue Raisonnée of Oriental Manuscripts in the Library of the (Late) College Fort Saint George*. Madras: Fort St. George Gazette Press, 1857.

Tessitori, L. P. "A Progress Report on the Preliminary Work Done During the Year 1915 in Connection with the Proposed Bardic and Historical Survey of Rajputana." *Journal of the Asiatic Society of Bengal* 12, no. 2 (1916): 57–116.

Teuscher, Ulrike. "Kingship and Genealogy in Mediaeval Western India." In *Sharing Sovereignty: The Little Kingdom in South Asia*, ed. Georg Berkemer, Margret Frenz, and Hermann Kulke, 63–80. Berlin: Klaus Schwarz, 2003.

Thaker, Aria. "The Latest Skirmish in California's Textbooks War Reveals the Mounting Influence of Hindutva in the United States." *Caravan*, February 6, 2018. https://caravanmagazine.in/vantage/californias-textbooks-war-reveals-mounting-influence-hindutva-united-states.

Thapar, Romila. "The Image of the Barbarian in Early India." *Comparative Studies in Society and History* 13, no. 4 (1971): 408–36.

——. *The Past Before Us: Historical Traditions of Early North India*. Cambridge, MA: Harvard University Press, 2013.

——. "The Presence of the Other: Religion and Society in Early North India." Nemi Chand Jain Memorial Lecture, Delhi, August 16, 2019. https://guftugu.in/2019/09/the-presence-of-the-other-religion-and-society-in-early-north-india/.

——. "Society and Historical Consciousness: The Itihāsa-Purāṇa Tradition." In *Situating Indian History for Sarvepalli Gopal*, ed. Sabyasachi Bhattacharya and Romila Thapar, 353–83. Delhi: Oxford University Press, 1986.

——. *Somanatha: The Many Voices of a History*. New Delhi: Penguin, 2004.

——. "Some Reflections on Early Indian Historical Thinking." In *Western Historical Thinking: An Intercultural Debate*, ed. Jörn Rüsen, 178–86. New York: Berghahn Books, 2002.

——. "They Peddle Myths and Call It History." *New York Times*, May 17, 2019. https://www.nytimes.com/2019/05/17/opinion/india-elections-modi-history.html.

"The 17th World Sanskrit Conference First Circular." October 2016. https://wsc.ubcsanskrit.ca/wsc2018-circulars.

Thomases, Drew. "Making Pushkar Paradise: Religion, Tourism, and Belonging in a North Indian Pilgrimage Town." PhD diss., Columbia University, 2015.

Tiwari, Arya R. C. G. "Historiography of Mewar—Its Sources, Problems, and Difficulties," *Poona Orientalist* 22, no. 1–2 (1957): 12–36.

Traub, Alex. "India's Dangerous New Curriculum." *New York Review of Books*, December 6, 2018. https://www.nybooks.com/articles/2018/12/06/indias-dangerous-new-curriculum/.

Trouillot, Michel-Rolph. *Silencing the Past: Power and the Production of History*. Boston: Beacon Press, 1995.

Truschke, Audrey. "Censoring Indian History." *History Today* 67, no. 8 (2017): 14–17.

——. "Contested History: Brahmanical Memories of Relations with the Mughals." *Journal of the Economic and Social History of the Orient* 58 (2015): 419–52.

——. *Culture of Encounters: Sanskrit at the Mughal Court.* New York: Columbia University Press, 2016.

——. "Dangerous Debates: Jain Responses to Theological Challenges at the Mughal Court." *Modern Asian Studies* 49, no. 5 (2015): 1311–44.

——. "Hate Male." *The Revealer*, July 14, 2020. https://therevealer.org/hate-male/.

——. "Modern Politics in Premodern History." *Stanford University Press Blog*, May 23, 2017. https://stanfordpress.typepad.com/blog/2017/05/modern-politics-in-premodern-history.html.

——. "A Mughal Debate about Jain Asceticism." In *The Empires of the Near East and India: Source Studies of the Safavid, Ottoman, and Mughal Literate Communities*, ed. Hani Khafipour, 107–23. New York: Columbia University Press, 2019.

——. "Mughal Sanskrit Literature: The *Book of War* and the *Treasury of Compassion*." In *The Empires of the Near East and India: Source Studies of the Safavid, Ottoman, and Mughal Literate Communities*, ed. Hani Khafipour, 450–77. New York: Columbia University Press, 2019.

——. "The Power of the Islamic Sword in Narrating the Death of Indian Buddhism." *History of Religions* 57, no. 4 (2018): 406–35.

——. "Setting the Record Wrong: A Sanskrit Vision of Mughal Conquests." *South Asian History and Culture* 3, no. 3 (2012): 373–96.

——. "Silencing Scholarly Voices, One Event at a Time." *The Wire*, August 20, 2018. https://thewire.in/communalism/silencing-scholarly-voices-audrey-truschke.

University of Mysore. *Annual Report of the Mysore Archaeological Department for the Year 1929, with the Government Review Thereon.* Bangalore: Government Press, 1931.

Uttar Pradesh District Gazetteers: Chamoli. Vol. 15. Lucknow: Government of Uttar Pradesh, 1979.

Vadukut, Sidin. "Audrey Truschke: The Historian Who Engages." *LiveMint*, October 14, 2017. https://www.livemint.com/Sundayapp/GjK6sLgFpFbYNKWKCshf9N/Audrey-Truschke—The-historian-who-engages.html.

Vajpeyi, Ananya. "Excavating Identity Through Tradition: Who Was Shivaji?" In *Traditions in Motion: Religion and Society in History*, ed. Satish Saberwal and Supriya Varma, 240–71. New Delhi: Oxford University Press, 2005.

——. "How to Move a Mountain." *The Hindu*, August 14, 2018. https://www.thehindu.com/opinion/op-ed/how-to-move-a-mountain/article24682600.ece.

Van der Kuijp, Leonard W. J. "The Earliest Indian Reference to Muslims in a Buddhist Philosophical Text of *Circa* 700." *Journal of Indian Philosophy* 34 (2006): 169–202.

Vann, Richard T. "Hayden White and Non-Non-Histories." In *Philosophy of History After Hayden White*, ed. Robert Doran, 183–199. New York: Bloomsbury Academic, 2013.

Varnekar, S. B. "Shivaji's Patronage to Sanskrit Learning." In *Chhatrapati Shivaji: Coronation Tercentenary Commemoration Volume*, ed. B. K. Apte, 85–91. Bombay: University of Bombay, 1975.

Velankar, H. D. "Maṇḍalika Mahākāvya of Gaṅgādhara Kavi." *Bharatiya Vidya* 15, no. 1 (1954): 35–57.

——. "Maṇḍalīka, the Last Great King of Independent Saurāṣṭra." *Bharatiya Vidya* 14 (1953): 36–61.

——. "Śrīgaṅgādharakavikṛtaṃ Śrīmaṇḍalīkamahākāvyam." *Bharatiya Vidya* 15, no. 2 (1954): 13–40.

Veluthat, Kesavan. "The Rise and Fall of the *Kāvya* Project." *Studies in People's History* 6, no. 1 (2019): 5–15.

Venkatkrishnan, Anand. "Hidden Mūrtis: The Sanskrit Students of Radcliffe College." *Schlesinger Library Blog*, March 21, 2019. https://www.radcliffe.harvard.edu/schlesinger-library/blog/hidden-murtis-sanskrit-students-radcliffe-college.

Veyne, Paul. *Writing History: Essay on Epistemology*. Trans. Mina Moore-Rinvolucri. Middletown, CT: Wesleyan University Press, 1984.

Vidyavijayji, Muniraj. *A Monk and a Monarch*. Trans. Dolarrai R. Mankad. Baroda: Deepchandji Banthia, 1944.

Vose, Steven M. "The Making of a Medieval Jain Monk: Language, Power, and Authority in the Works of Jinaprabhasūri (c. 1261–1333)." PhD diss., University of Pennsylvania, 2013.

Vrat, Satya. *Glimpses of Jaina Sanskrit Mahākāvyas*. Jaipur: Raj Publishing House, 2003.

Wagoner, Phillip B. "Harihara, Bukka, and the Sultan: The Delhi Sultanate in the Political Imagination of Vijayanagara." In *Beyond Turk and Hindu: Rethinking Religious Identities in Islamicate South Asia*, ed. David Gilmartin and Bruce B. Lawrence, 300–26. Gainesville: University Press of Florida, 2000.

——. " 'Sultan Among Hindu Kings': Dress, Titles, and the Islamicization of Hindu Culture at Vijayanagara." *Journal of Asian Studies* 55, no. 4 (1996): 851–80.

——. *Tidings of the King: A Translation and Ethnohistorical Analysis of the* Rāyavācakamu. Honolulu: University of Hawaii Press, 1993.

Wang, Q. Edward. "Is There a Chinese Mode of Historical Thinking? A Cross-Cultural Analysis." *History and Theory* 46, no. 3 (2007): 201–9.

Warder, A. K. *An Introduction to Indian Historiography*. Bombay: Popular Prakashan, 1972.

Weber, A. *Die Handschriften-Verzeichnisse de Königlichen Bibliothek zu Berlin*. Vol. 2, part 3. Berlin: A. Asher, 1892.

Wheeler, J. Talboys. *Early Records of British India: A History of the English Settlements in India as Told in the Government Records, the Works of Old Travellers, and Other Contemporary Documents, from the Earliest Period Down to the Rise of British Power in India*. London: Trübner, 1878.

White, David Gordon. "Tantra in Practice: Mapping a Tradition." In *Tantra in Practice*, ed. David Gordon White, 3–38. Princeton, NJ: Princeton University Press, 2000.

White, Hayden. *The Content of the Form: Narrative Discourse and Historical Representation*. Baltimore: Johns Hopkins University Press, 1987.

——. *Metahistory: The Historical Imagination in Nineteenth-Century Europe*. Baltimore: Johns Hopkins University Press, 1973.

——. *Tropics of Discourse: Essays in Cultural Criticism*. Baltimore: Johns Hopkins University Press, 1986.

Wilson, C. R. *The Early Annals of the English in Bengal, Being the Bengal Public Consultations for the First Half of the Eighteenth Century*. Vol. 2, part 2. Calcutta: The Bengal Secretariat Book Depot, 1911.

Winiarski, Tomasz. "Women's Town—Ghost Town: A Picture of a Dying City in the *Raghuvaṃśa*." *Cracow Indological Studies* 15 (2013): 37–66.

Wink, André. *Al-Hind: The Making of the Indo-Islamic World*. Vol. 2, *The Slave Kings and the Islamic Conquest, 11th–13th Centuries*. Leiden: Brill, 2002.

——. *Land and Sovereignty in India: Agrarian Society and Politics under the Eighteenth-Century Maratha Svarājya*. Cambridge: Cambridge University Press, 1986.

Witzel, Michael. "On Indian Historical Writing: The Role of the Vamçâvalîs." *Journal of the Japanese Association for South Asian Studies* 2 (1990): 1–57.

"WSC 2021 First Circular and Call for Abstracts." January 2019. https://www.wsc2021.com.au/activity/conference-circulars/.

Wujastyk, Dominik. "Indian Manuscripts." Prepublication draft of an article distributed under a Creative Commons license. University of Vienna, 2011.

Yashaschandra, Sitamshu. "Hemacandra to *Hind Svarāj*: Region and Power in Gujarati Literary Culture." In *Literary Cultures in History: Reconstructions from South Asia*, ed. Sheldon Pollock, 567–611. Berkeley: University of California Press, 2003.

Zaman, Taymiya. "Cities, Time, and the Backward Glance." *American Historical Review* 123, no. 3 (June 2018): 699–705.

——. "An Islam of One's Own." *Comparative Studies of South Asia, Africa, and the Middle East* 40, no. 1 (May 2020): 214–19.

——. "The Mughal Conquest of Chittor: Study of Akbar's Letter of Victory." In *The Empires of the Near East and India: Source Studies of the Safavid, Ottoman, and Mughal Literate Communities*, ed. Hani Khafipour, 287–300. New York: Columbia University Press, 2019.

——. "Nostalgia, Lahore, and the Ghost of Aurangzeb." *Fragments* 4 (2015): 1–27.

Zeitlyn, Sushila. "The Construction and Reconstruction of Pushkar." *South Asian Studies* 4, no. 1 (1988): 41–50.

Ziegler, Norman P. "Marvari Historical Chronicles: Sources for the Social and Cultural History of Rajasthan." *Indian Economic and Social History Review* 13 (1976): 219–50.

——. "Some Notes on Rajput Loyalties During the Mughal Period." In *Kingship and Authority in South Asia*, ed. John F. Richards, 215–51. Madison: South Asian Studies, University of Wisconsin–Madison, 1978.

Zutshi, Chitralekha. *Languages of Belonging: Islam, Regional Identity, and the Making of Kashmir*. Oxford: Oxford University Press, 2004.

——. "Past as Tradition, Past as History: The *Rajatarangini* Narratives in Kashmir's Persian Historical Tradition." *Indian Economic and Social History Review* 50, no. 2 (2013): 201–19.

——. "Translating the Past: Rethinking *Rajatarangini* Narratives in Colonial India." *Journal of Asian Studies* 70, no. 1 (2011): 5–27.

Index

Page numbers in *italics* indicate figures, tables, or photographs.

Ābdullacarita (Lakshmipati), *191*, 203–7, 213, 242–44, 300n69

Abdulla Khan (Sayyid brother), *191*, 203–5, 206, 242–44, 300n67

Abul Fazl, 143–44, 289n108; *Ā'īn-i Akbarī* by, 143, 210; Akbar and, 191; *Akbarnāma* by, 24, 168, 189, 191, 198–203; description of by Siddhichandra, 157, 239–40; Hiravijaya and, 146, 148–50, 235–36; historical accuracy of, 18; on rajataranginis, 130

Adam (first man), 259n63

Adhai-din-ka-Jhompra mosque, 49, *50*, 265n90

adhama (vile), 55

adharmadharma (corrupt dharma), 84

Adichie, Chimamanda Ngozi, 27

Adil Shahi dynasty, 161, 174, 179–80, 186; Mughals and, 163; Shahji and, 181

Adishvara inscription (circa 1595), 152

Afif, Shams Siraj, 271n103; *Tārīkh-i Fīrūzshāhī* by, 86

Aftabachi, Jawhar, 192

Afzal Khan (Adil Shahi general), 181, 183, 185

Agra, 139, 142–43, 146, 156, 200, 236; bhattaraka seats in, 285n16

ahimsa (nonviolence), 145, 245

Ahmadnagar, 173

Ahmadnagar Sultanate. *See* Nizam Shahis

Ahmad Shah (Gujarat ruler), 267n12

Ahmadshahi Sultanate. *See* Muzaffarid Sultanate

Ahmed, Riz, 133

Ahsan Shah (Madurai sultan), 268n46

Aibak, Qutbuddin (Ghurid general), 53

Ā'īn-i Akbarī (Abul Fazl), 143, 210. *See also* Akbarnāma; Sarvadeśavṛttāntasaṅgraha

Ajayadeva (king), 105

Ajmer, 49–50, *50*, 53–54, 62, 73

Akbar, 134, 143, 161, 168, 174, 200, 232–35, 283n192, 285n18; Abul Fazl and, 168, 191, 236–40; animal slaughter and, 141–42, 287n65; Chittor and, 194–95, *196*, 197–98, 288n81; divine light attributed to, 202; Hiravijaya and, 140,

Akbar (*continued*)
141–42, 145–46, 150, 154–56; Humayun and, 192–93, 292n45; illiteracy of, 287n61; Jains and, 25, 133, 140, 141–42, 144, 147, 150–53, 156, 285n16; Jinachandra and, 142; Padmasagara and, 192–98, 232–35; Padmasundara and, 139–40, 146; Shantichandra and, 144; Siddhichandra and, 150–51, 156–57, 236–39; sun veneration by, 148; Surjan and, 169–72, *176*, 177, 188; translations and, 130; as Vishnu avatar, 184
Akbarasāhiśṛṅgāradarpaṇa (Padmasundara), 139, 140
Akbarnāma (Abul Fazl), 24, 189, 190, 191, 198–203. *See also Ā'īn-i Akbarī; Sarvadeśavṛttāntasaṅgraha*
Akheraj (Gujarati ruler), 167
akhyayika (Sanskrit genre), 14
Alaka, 78, 143
Alaṃkārasarvasva (Ruyyaka), 46, 63, 265n91
Alauddin Khalji, 167; description of in Sanskrit, 105, 107–8, 229–32; Hammira Chauhan and, 89–90, 91–96, 273n141, 276n44; Jinaprabha and, 284n2; Karna of Gujarat and, 107, 108, 229, 275n22; Madurai and, 77; in *Puruṣaparīkṣā*, 98
Alauddin Sikandar Shah (Madurai sultan), *88*, 271n105
Ali, Daud, 12, 102
alim (learned man), 106
Ali Shah (Kashmiri ruler), 120, 280n128
Allah (God), 74, 75, 120, 139, 304n10. *See also* khudā; Rahman
Allahabad, 143
Alp Khan (Khalji governor), 108, 230
Amarakośa, 31
Amer, 162, 290n2
amir, 35, 245; hammira and, 62, 68, 266n3
Anandavardhana, 254n46; *Dhvanyāloka* by, 208
Anandavimala (Tapa Gaccha leader), 140
Andhra, 31, 69, 82, 108
animal slaughter: Akbar and, 141–42, 287n65; of cows, 57, 82; Kalachakra and, 38; in Paryushan festival, 147
anupurana (new purana), 13, 179, 245
Apabhramsha, 61, 138
arhat, 117, 153, 245
Aristotle, 16
Arjuna (epic character), 119
Arnoraja (Chauhan ruler), 36, 57
Arondekar, Anjali, 9
artha (wealth), 120
Artharatnāvalī (Samayasundara), 151
Arthaśāstra (Kautilya), 253n37
Aryans: land of, 64; rule of, 110–11. *See also* non-Aryans
asceticism, 51, 122, 226; of Jains, 111, 154, 157, 159, 160
Ashoka (Maurya king), 104
Ashvins (Hindu gods), 175
asura (demon), 55, 90, 245
Aurangzeb Alamgir, 185, 186–87, 191, 205, 296n133, 301n78, xvii–xviii
avatar (incarnation), 245; of Rama, 98; of Vishnu, 50–51, 54, 166, 184, 185, 195, 225–26, 262n31, 296n122
avīci. See Hell
aviddha (unpierced), 181–82
Ayodhya, 79

Babruvahana (epic character), 119
Babur, 140, 190, 192, 200, 201; Firdaus-Makani as post-death name, 200
Badakhshan, 143
Badauni, Abdul Qadir, 130
Baglan, 162–63, 168, 172–75. *See also* Rathods
Bahāristān-i Shāhī, 123, 280n128, 284n204
Bahmani Sultanate, 161, 180, 290n1
Baihaqi Sayyids, 123–24, 126–27, 131, 281n151
bakhars (histories), 164
Balabhadra of Chamba (ruler), 210
Bana, 114, 200, 262n19, 269n49, 302n13; *Harṣacarita* by, 215, 256n9

Baroda, 103
bāts (biographical tales), 164
Bayazid Bayat, 192
beef eating, 57, 82; by Hindus, 57; by non-Aryans, 55, 81–82, 115, 124, 125, 127, 210, 228, 282n158
Begada, Mahmud, 75, 167, 267n12
Benares, 109, 168, 170, 296n133; Brahmins from, 178–79, 183, 185
Bengal, 19, 26; Chandrashekhara and, 187; lack of Sanskrit histories written in, 212–14; Pala kingdom of, 39; Sufis in, 213
Bhagavadgita, 205, 245
Bhagiratha (legendary figure), 119
Bhānucandragaṇicarita (Siddhichandra), *136*, 144, 156, 158, 159–60, 236–40, 284n4, 287n51
Bhanuchandra, 139, 144, 147, 148, 156, 158–60
Bharavi, 76
Bhartrhari, 198, 234, 303n9
Bhattaraka (title for a Digambara Jain leader), 245, 285n16
Bhattavatara, 128
Bhavabhuti, 76, 269n49
bhaya (fear), 22
Bhimadeva (ruler), 45, 106
Bhoja (Chauhan defector), 91, 92
Bhoja (Pratihara ruler), *29*, 31, 257n13, 257n30
Bhoja (*Sarasvatīkaṇṭhābharaṇa*), 61
Bhonsle. *See* Maratha Bhonsle family
bībhatsa (macabre), 22
Bilhana, 302n13; *Vikramāṅkadevacarita* by, 47, 48, 66, 215, 252n8, 262n19
biographies, by Jains, 74, 106, 133–60, *136*, 274n10
bismillah (in God's name), 37
Brahma (Hindu god), 75, 117, 153; Chauhans and, 263n49; Ghurids and, 49–54, 224–27; Pushkar and, 50, 262n28
Brahmins, 6, 19, 53, 245, 255n65; of Benares, 178–79, 183, 185; Ghurids and, 51–53, 56, 64, 121, 224–27; as hinduka, 127; Jains and, 148, 152, 158–59; in Kashmir, 99–100, 116, 119–22, 124; Kshatriyas and, 53, 263n45; in Madurai, 80–81; Mughals and, 148, 151–52, 158–59, 190; Muslims and, 33, 40, 82, 126–28, *see also specific topics*; as Muslims converts, 36–37, 116, 120–22; privilege of, 20, 49–54, 82, 119, 120–22, 184–85; Zayn al-Abidin and, 119–20
Braj Bhasha, 170, 184, 206, 207
Bṛhatpośālikapaṭṭāvalī (Nayasundara), 286n27
Bronner, Yigal, 113, 216
Buddha, 50, 117, 153, 225
Buddhists, 24, 28; Kalachakra and, 24, 28, 36–41, 126, 149; Muslims and, 27, 36–43; Zayn al-Abidin and, 119
Bühler, Georg, 5, 216, 252n8
Bukka (Vijayanagara ruler), 271n103; Kampan and, 78–79; as suratrana, 69, 70, 266n7; turushkas and, 85–86
Bundelkhand, 64, 68
Bundi, 162, 168, 169, 170, 172, 213, 290n13, 292n41. *See also* Surjan of Hada

caliph, 98
Carr, E. H., 139
caste. *See* jati; varna
Champa (Sambuvaraya king), 78, 85, 269n57
champu (prose-verse mixture), 203, 245
chandala (low caste group), 33, 40, 55, 197, 245; Ghaznavids as, 55, 263n54; Ghurids as, 57
Chandrashekhara, 20; Bengal and, 187, 213; on Kshatriya kingship, 175–77; *Surjanacarita* by, 168–72, 187, 213, 293n57
Char Bagh garden, 200
charita (Sanskrit narrative genre), 14, 142, 245. *See also specific texts*
Chattopadhyaya, Brajadulal, 18, 257n15

Chaudhuri, J. B., 207, 300n68
Chauhan dynasty, 2, 271n115; Ajmer and, 73; Brahma and, 263n49; Delhi and, 70–73, 89–96; Ghaznavids and, 57; Ghurids and, 44, 45–65, 164; Hada branch, 162, 168, 169; Khaljis and, 91; Kshatriya heroism of, 90–91; *Pṛthvīrājavijaya* on, 25, 44–65; Sarban stone inscription (1328) on, 73; Tomars and, 70–73, 90. *See also* Hammira Chauhan; Prithviraj Chauhan
Chaulukya dynasty, of Gujarat, 29, 32, 45, 106; Muhammad Ghori and, 106; Pulakeshiraja of, 32, 223–24
Chidambaram, 80, 269n64
Chinchani Rashtrakuta grant (926 CE), *29*, 255n4, 256nn5–6, 260n77
Chinchani Rashtrakuta plate (circa mid-900s CE), *29*, 33, 256n5, 257n13
Chishti, Muinuddin, 48, 262n27
Chittor, 108, 195–98, *196*
Chola dynasty, 31, 86; inscriptions and, 257n30; Sambuvarayas and, 78; temple desecration by, 39
chronicles. *See specific texts*
Chudasamas, 165–66. *See also* Mandalik
Cort, John, 284n209, 285n12
cow slaughter, 57, 82; by Hindus, 57; by non-Aryans, 55, 81–82, 115, 124, 125, 127, 210, 228, 282n158

Dalca (Mongol warrior), 118
Dandin, 59–60, 76, 269n49
dargahs, of Sufis, 49, 86, *87*, *88*, 271n105
darśana (philosophical view), 126; of Muslims, 118, 121, 126
Darshanavijaya, 137
Daśakumāracarita (Dandin), 59
Davis, Richard, 84, 255n81
Dayakushala, 137
Deccan, 2, 172–75, 187
Delhi, 2, 214; Ajmer and, 73; Ghaznavids in, 44; Ghurids in, 44, 46, 49, 73; Jain intellectuals in, 111, 134, 140; kings of, 73; Mughals and, 143, 174, 175, 178, 192–95, 211; Prithviraj Chauhan and, 262n28; Sanskrit descriptions of, 142–43; suratrana of, 69, 70, 73; Timur's sack of, 90, 165
Delhi Sultanate, 2, 66; Bengal Sultanate and, 212; Chauhans and, 89–96; inscriptions about, 70–73; Jain intellectuals and, 103–4, 111, 134, 140–41; Jinaprabha in, 104; Madurai and, 76; Mongols and, 279n108; Muzaffarid Sultanate and, 165; as shaka, 73; Timur and, 90; Vijayanagara and, 70. *See also specific dynasties*
Desala (lay Jain), 230–31
Devagiri (Daulatabad), 108, 275n27
Devalasmṛti, 40
Devanagari script, 70, 212
Devavimala, 235–36, 288n67; Delhi and, 143; Fatehpur Sikri and, 143; *Hīrasaubhāgya* by, *136*, 141, 142, 148–50, 155–56, 157, 235–36, 284n4, 286n29, 304nn10–11; *Hīrasundaramahākāvya* by, *136*, 142, 284n4, 288n79; Hiravijaya and, 146; Mughals and, 151; Prakrit and, 149
Dhanapala, 260n71; *Saccaürivīraucchāhu* by, 39–40
dharma, 120, 180, 245; corruption and, 184; Muslims and, 37–39, 181, 182; varna and, 84, 93–94, 171–72, 183
Dharmadasa, 304n11
Dharmasagara, 140; Hiravijaya and, 141; Mughals and, 143–44; *Tapāgacchapaṭṭāvalī* by, 135, 140, 286n23, 286n29
dharmashala (pilgrim shelter), 119, 245
Dhruva, 227
dhvani (suggestion), 208
Dhvanyāloka (Anandavardhana), 208
Dickinson, Emily, 212
Digambara Jains, 245; in Gwalior, 271n113; Mughals and, 285n16. *See also* Bhattaraka
digvijaya (conquest of the directions), 91, 144, 156, 246

Digvijayamahākāvya (Meghavijaya), 156
divan (poetry collection), 202, 246
diversity, 67–68, 97; of "Hindu"-led polities, 91, 177, 190; as modern value, 20–21, 26, 219; of Muslim-led polities, 4, 67, 97; in production of history, 7, 24, 28, 42–43, 132, 219, 221; of Sanskrit intellectuals, 19–20, 67–68
Dowson, John, 253n64
dramida (southerner), 81, 83, 246
Duda (Gohil chieftain), 165
Duhshama-duhshama Kala, 276n50
Duhshama Kala, 109, 246, 276nn50–51. *See also* Kali Yuga
Durga (Hindu goddess), 79
Dushyanta (legendary king), 119
Dvapar Yuga, 52
Dvaraka, 194, 232
dvija (twice-born), 127, 246. *See also* Brahmins; Kshatriyas

Eaton, Richard, 23, 69, 185
Eid celebrations, in mosques, 126
Ekoji (Maratha ruler), 164, 177, 297n154
Elliot, H. M., 253n64
Elverskog, Johan, 39
Ernst, Carl, 10

farmans, 133, 144–47, 246, 287n65. *See also* sphuramana
Farrukh Siyar, 203, 206–7, 240–42
Fatehpur Sikri, 140, 142, 232–35; Devavimala and, 143; Hemavijaya and, 143
Fathnāma, 194
Fath Shah (Kashmiri ruler), 133
Firdaus-Makani. *See* Babur
Firdawsi (Persian poet), 128
Firishta, 18
Firuz, Nuruddin (trader), 74, 75
Firuz Shah (Tughluq ruler), 90, 134, 284n2
Fitzgerald, James, 12
Flood, Barry, 35
gadyakavya (prose poetry), 200, 246
Gagabhatta (Benares Brahmin), 183–84
Gahadavala dynasty, 109–10; inscriptions of, 35
Gajamalladeva (Rathod ruler), 168
Gangadasa of Champaner (ruler), 167
Gaṅgadāsapratāpavilāsa (Gangadhara), 167, 292n34
Gangadevi, 24, 138; as female writer, 19, 67, 79; on Hindus and Muslims, 96; *Madhurāvijaya* by, 19, 25, 67, 76–89, 97–98, 227–29, 266n1, 269, 269n57, 270nn69–82; Vijayanagara and, 269n48
Gangadhara, 77, 188; *Gaṅgadāsapratāpavilāsa* by, 167, 292n34; *Maṇḍalīkacarita* by, 162, 165–66, 168
Gardabhilla (ruler), 110
Garuḍapurāṇa, 37
Gautama (sage), 52
Gehlot clan, 69
genre: historical truth and, 254n46; history writing and, 8, 12–15, 102–3, 142; vernacular texts and, 164. *See also* Merutunga; *specific topics*
Ghaznavids: Chauhans and, 57; in Delhi, 44; Ghurids and, 58; as hammira, 266n3; Kalhana on, 55
Ghori, Shihabuddin Muhammad, 44, 53, 260n3, 261n8; Chaulukyas and, 106; Gahadavalas and, 109; as hammira, 70; Jayanaka on, 57, 58–59, 60; Prithviraj Chauhan and, 105, 110; in *Puruṣaparīkṣā*, 98; Samar Singh and, 164; Sarban stone inscription (1328) and, 73
Ghosh, Amalananda, 256n8, 276n39
Ghurids, 2, 3, 109; Brahma and, 49–54; Brahmins and, 121; Chauhans and, 44, 45–65, 164; Chaulukyas and, 45; in Delhi, 46, 73; Ghaznavids and, 58; mosques of, 48, *50*, 53–54; as outcastes, 54–58, 66–67; *Pṛthvīrājavijaya* on, 24–25, 30, 45–67; in Punjab, 44; as turushkas, 260n3; varna and, 64

Gītagovinda (Jayadeva), 212
Gohilas, 165, 291n24
Golkhatun (Gul Khatun), 127–28
Gori (Sanskrit for Ghori), 57
Goripalayam Dargah, 86, *87*
Greek (people), 33, 82–84, 249, 295n107
Guha, Sumit, 253n29
Gujarat, 19, 25; Chaulukyas of, 29, 32, 45, 106; Jains in, 74, 134, 135–38, 193–94; Jayasoma and, 144; Kashmir and, 99–132; local stories of fourteenth-century in, 99–132; mosques in, 74–75; prabandhas of, 14, 99–100; Somanatha temple in, 39; suratrana of, 69; Vaghelas in, 98, 103, 229, 275n22
Gulbadan Begum (Mughal princess), 192
Gumani Ram Kayasth, 210
Gunavijaya, 284n4; *Vijayapraśastimahākāvya* by, *136*, 141, 143, 152–53, 155, 284–85n5, 286n24
Gunavinaya, 137, 285n10
Gurjara-Pratihara dynasty, 29, 31–32, 35
Gwalior: Digambara Jains in, 271n113; *Hammīramahākāvya* and, 271n109; inscriptions and, *29*, 31, 256n5, 257n13; Jains in, 89–96, 271n113; mosques in, 258n35; Siddhichandra and, 150–51; Tughluqs at, 271n114

Hada Chauhans, 162, 169
hajj (pilgrimage to Mecca), 105, 246, 280n128
Halayudha Mishra (Sena minister), 302n6
Halbfass, Wilhelm, 9–10
Hamilton, William, 206, 240–42, 301n90
Hamiradevi, 69
hammira, 11, 35, 96, 116, 124, 229, 246, 258n40, 265n87, 266n3; as *haṃvīra*, 266n5; as Hindu kings, 68–70; in *Lalitavigraharāja*, 62; as Muslim rulers, 68
Hammira Chauhan, 67, 69, 89–96, 171–72; Alauddin Khalji and, 90, 91–96; Mahimasahi and, 91–96; Mongols and, 91–93; as a Tomar, 272n166
Hammīramadamardana (Jayasimhasuri), 98, 167
Hammīramahākāvya (Nayachandra), 67, 89–98, 175, 188, 263n49, 266n1, 271n109
Hariharan, Githa, 99
Harikavi (*Śambhurājacarita*), 177, 178, 216
Harir, Bai, 75
Hariraja (Chauhan ruler), 261n8
Harivijaya, 49
Harṣacarita (Bana), 200, 215, 302–3n13; "turushka" in, 256n9
Harsha (Kashmiri king), 100, 115–16
Hasan Shah (Kashmiri ruler), 123, 124, 128–29, 133
Haydar Shah (Kashmiri ruler), 125, 133
heaven, 37, 52, 85, 144, 149–50; moksha and, 171–72
Hegel, Georg Wilhelm Friedrich, 16–17
hell, 37, 149, 235; as *avīci*, 52; as *narakaviśeṣa*, 52
Hemavijaya, 143, 152–53, 284n4; *Vijayapraśastimahākāvya* by, *136*, 141, 143, 152–53, 155, 284–85n5, 286n24
hemorrhoids, of Farrukh Siyar, 240–42, 301n89
Hijri calendar, 34, 75, 200
Hindavi, 158, 246. *See also* Braj Bhasha
Hinduism, anachronism of, 57–58, 111, 183
hinduka, 127, 246; customs of, 128; as Hindu, 282n180; Jonaraja and, 280n120
Hindu-Muslim violence, 23, 39; and anachronism, 84, 129, 183
Hindus, 210, 246; Alauddin Khalji and, 91–92; Buddhists and, 38, 119–20; cow slaughter and, 57; as "hammira," 68–70; hinduka as, 282n180; Ideality of, 16–17; as meaning Indians, 84; Jains and, 39–41, 104–5, 158–59; in Kashmir, 121; Mongols and, 84; Muslims and, 3, 21–23, 27, 84, 96; as

Persian term, 23, 49; in Sanskrit usage, 68–70, 210; as "suratrana," 68–70; temple desecration and, 111; Vijayanagara and, 69–70; Zayn al-Abidin and, 120
Hindustan, 195, 201, 246, 291n16, 298n25
Hindutva, 1, 21–22, 23, 32, 251n3; academia and, 218; as distinct from Hinduism, 246
Hīrasaubhāgya (Devavimala), *136*, 141, 142, 148–50, 155–56, 157, 235–36, 284n4, 286n29, 304nn10–11
Hīrasundaramahākāvya (Devavimala), *136*, 142, 284n4, 288n79
Hiravijaya: Abul Fazl and, 148–50, 235–36; in Agra, 139; Akbar and, 140, 141–42, 145–46, 156; Devavimala and, 146; Dharmasagara and, 141; in *Jagadgurukāvya*, 191; Mughals and, 140; Padmasagara and, 154–55. *See also* *Hīrasaubhāgya*; *Hīrasundaramahākāvya*
Hīravijayasūrirāsa (Rishabhadas), 137
History of India, as Told by Its Own Historians (Elliot and Dowson), 255n64
history writing, 2; modern definitions of, 8–9, 13, 14–15, 219–21; Persian and, 18–19, 214; poetry and, 16–19, 131; Sanskrit and, 28, 100–101, 112–14, 130–32, 138, 141–42, 215–17; selectivity in, 139. *See also* genre; local histories
Hobsbawm, Eric, 217
Hodgson, Marshall, 253n33
Humayun, 73, 140, 192–93, 195, 198, 200, 201–2
Hunas, 31
Husain, M. F., 1
Husain Ali Khan (Sayyid brother), 203, 300n67
Husaini, S. A. Q., 268n45

Ibrahim (prophet), 259n63
Ibrahim ibn Adham (renunciant king of Balkh), 157–58
Iltutmish, Shamsuddin (king), 70, 98, 266n3
Inden, Ronald, 7
Indology, 20; Brahmin bias and, 19, 36, 41, 220; denial of Sanskrit histories, 5–8, 113–14; sexism and, 20–21, 218–19
Indo-Persian rule, 4, 14, 24, 218; before, 27–43; historical writing on, 46, 48, 98; Persian historiography of, 18, 168, 191, 218, 283n193; Rajput and Maratha kingships and, 161–88; Sanskrit histories on, 161, 203–11, 216, 217, 302n13, *see also specific texts and topics*
Indo-Turkic, 10–11
Indra (Hindu god), 50, 52, 157
Indraprastha, 73
In Praise of Kings (Kapadia), 165
inscriptions: Adishvara inscription (circa 1595 CE), 152; bilingual inscriptions, 74–75, 177; Chinchani plate of the Rashtrakuta ruler Krishna II (circa mid-900s CE), *29*, 33, 257n13; Chinchani Rashtrakuta grant (926 CE), *29*, 256nn5–6, 257n13; Gahadavala inscriptions on *turuṣkadaṇḍa*, 35; Gwalior inscription of the Pratihara ruler Bhoja (circa 800s–early 900s CE), *29*, 257n13; as historical sources, 7; Hund fragmentary inscription (circa 750–800 CE), *29*, 256n5, 256n8, 257n13; Jabalpur plate of the Kalachuri ruler Jayasimha (1167 CE), 35, 258n43; by Jains, 135, 138, 141–42, 143, 144, 152; Jodhpur Khatri inscription (1316 CE), 73; Kavi plate (736 CE), *29*, 31–32, 256n5, 256n7, 256n9, 257n13, 260n77; Khalimpur plate of Dharmapala (circa ninth century CE), 257n30; by Muslims, 74–75, 119; Muslims in, 27–43, 45, 70–73, 86, 106, 141–42, 143, 144, 152; Navsari plate (738 CE), *29*, 32–33, 34, 256n9, 256nn5–7; Palam Baoli (1276 CE), 73,

inscriptions (*continued*)
267n21, 267n23, 271n116; Prince of Wales plate (736 CE), 256n5, 256n7, 256n9; on Prithviraj Chauhan, 64, 265n96; Sarban stone inscription (1328 CE), 73, 267n21; on Shah Miris, 119; Veraval bilingual inscription, 74–75
Islam. *See specific topics*
Islamicate, 10, 253n33
Islam Shah (Sur ruler), 190
itihasa (lore), 12–13, 246; in *Arthaśāstra*, 253n37; purana and, 12–13, 253n36

Jadu (Bengal ruler), 212
Jagacchandra of Kumaon (ruler), 191, 204, 209
Jagadgurukāvya (Padmasagara), *136*, 142, *191*, 191–98, 232–35, 284n4
Jagadu (trader), 74
Jagaḍūcarita (Sarvananda), 74
Jahandar Shah (Mughal king), 205–6
Jahangir: Jains and, 25, 134, 144, 148, 182; Siddhichandra and, 151, 157–60
Jainataraṅgiṇī (Shrivara), 281n138. *See also Rājataraṅgiṇī* (Shrivara)
Jainavilāsa (Bhattavatara), 128
Jains, 19, 287n51; agency of, 90, 145–48; Akbar and, 25, 133, 152–53; asceticism of, 111, 154, 157, 159, 160; biographies by, 135, *136*, 138, 141, 147, 154; Brahmins and, 148, 158–59; Buddhists and, 38; chronicles by, 135, 138, 141; Cort on, 285n12; at Fatehpur Sikri, 232; in Gujarat, 134, 135–38, 193–94; in Gwalior, 90, 271n113; innovative writing by, 158–60; inscriptions by, 135, 138, 141–42, 143, 144, 152; Jagadu as, 74; Jahangir and, 25, 134, 144, 148, 151, 157–60, 182; local histories by, 138–45; Mughals and, 25, 133–60, 285n5, 285n16; Muslim-led raids and, 27; as Other, 154–58; prabandhas of, 14, 99–112, *103*, 130–31; in Rajasthan, 69; theology of, 148–54. *See also* Digambara Jains; Kharatara Gaccha; Nagapuriya Gaccha; Shvetambara Jains; Tapa Gaccha
Jai Singh (Mewar ruler), 162
Jalaluddin Muhammad. *See* Jadu
Jami (Persian poet), 199
janangama (low caste group), 11, 51, 246; Ghurids as, 55
Jangnāmā (Shridhar), 206
Jaswant Singh (Marwar ruler), 185
jati, 246; threats to, 120–21; yavana as, 104, 149, 180
jauhar, 94, 194, 246
Jayabhata IV (Gurjara ruler), 32
Jayachandra (Gahadavala ruler), 109, 110
Jayadeva (*Gītagovinda*), 212
Jayanaka, 80, 214–15; Kalhana and, 55; *Pṛthvīrājavijaya* by, 24–25, 30, 45–67, 83, 121, 215, 216, 224–27, 264n66; Pushkar and, 303n2. *See also Pṛthvīrājavijaya*
Jayarama Pindye: Adil Shahis and, 179–80; *Parṇālaparvatagrahaṇākhyāna* by, 164, 177, 178, *178*, 187; *Rādhāmādhavavilāsacampū* by, 164, 290n15; Shivaji and, 179–80
Jayaratha, 46, 63, 265n91
Jayasimha (Kalachuri ruler), 35, 258n43
Jayasimha (Kashmiri king), 116, 279n92
Jayasimhasuri, 98, 167
Jayasoma: Gujarat and, 144; *Mantri-karmacandravaṃśāvalīprabandha* by, *136*, 137, 147, 284nn4–5
Jesus (prophet), 259n63
Jhallas, 165, 291n24
Jinachandra, 141; Akbar and, 142
Jinamanikya, 141
Jinaprabha, 102, *103*, 284n2; in Delhi, 104; Devagiri and, 104, 275n27; Persian and, 111; Prithviraj Chauhan and, 110; Tughluqs and, 134, 146; *Vividhatīrthakalpa* by, 102, *103*, 104, 109, 110–12, 137, 146
jizya tax, 35, 141–42

Jnandev, 290n14
Jonaraja, 52, 166, 263n53; as court poet, 100, 274n5; hinduka and, 119, 280n120; Jayanaka and, 63; Kalhana and, 115–16, 274n5, 278n82; Kashmir and, 116–22; Lal Ded and, 120, 280n130; *Pṛthvīrājavijaya* commentary by, 48, 51, 52, 55, 61, 63–64, 121; *Rājataraṅgiṇī* by, 48, 63, 100, 112–14, *113*, 116–22, 130–32, 278n76, 279nn97–99, 280n130. *See also* Pseudo-Jonaraja
jugupsā (revulsion), 22
Juzjani, Minhaj Siraj, 256n12, 261n8

Kachhwahas, 162, 169, 177
Kadamba dynasty, 35
Kakatiya dynasty, 77
Kakka: *Nābhinandanajinoddhāra* by, *103*, 103–4, 107–9, 229–32, 277n55; Shatrunjaya and, 109, 276n45
Kalachakra Tantra, 24, 28, 36–41, 149; Buddhists of, 126; *Vimalaprabhā* commentary of, 36, 37
Kalakācārya, 110
Kalhana, 31; history-or-poetry debate on, 112–13, 278nn73–74; Jayanaka and, 55; Jonaraja and, 115–16, 274n5, 278n82; Mahabharata and, 100–101, 274n6; *Rājataraṅgiṇī* by, 5, 25, 55, 99–101, 112–14, *113*, 114–16, 130–32, 141, 274n3, 278nn76–78, 278nn85–96
Kalidasa, 114; *Kumārasambhava* by, 261n7; *Raghuvaṃśa* by, 14, 36, 79, 83, 179, 215, 262n19, 269n61, 270n71
Kali Yuga, 179, 246, 276n50; Jain prabandhas and, 109; Vishnu and, 52. *See also* Duhshama Kala
Kalki, 166, 296n122
Kalyanamalla (*Sulaimaccaritra*), 199
kalyana mandapa (marriage hall), *71*, *72*
kāma (desire), 120
Kambojas, 94–95, 273n145
Kampan (Vijayanagara ruler), 76–86, 266n1, 271n103; Gangadevi and, 76, 79, 266n1; Madurai and, 85–86; Madurai sultan and, 86; Sambuvarayas and, 77–79, 84, 85
Kam Raj (eighteenth-century author), 207
Kamsa, 78
Kanauj, 172, 201
Kanchi (Kanchipuram), 70, *71*, *72*, 77–80, 84, 267n15
Kānhaḍade Prabandha (Padmanabha), 167, 292n32
Kapadia, Aparna, 165
karma (action), 117, 150, 153, 236, 246
Karmacandravaṃsaprabandha (Gunavinaya), 137, 285n10
Karmachandra, *136*, 137, 139, 147, 148, 285n11
Karna (Vaghela ruler), 103, 107, 108, 229, 275n22
Karnataka, 107–8, 129, 153, 181, 230, 266n4
Karramiya (Muslim group): Ghurids as, 45
Karttikeya, 60–61, 225, 303n3
kāruṇya (compassion), 194, 288n81
Kashmir, 19, 25, 118; Brahmins in, 99–100, 116, 119–22, 124; Gujarat and, 99–132; Jonaraja and, 116–22; local stories of fourteenth century in, 99–132; modern politics in, 126, 129; *Pṛthvīrājavijaya* in, 63–64; rajataranginis of, 14, 99–101, 112–32, *113*
Kashmiriyat, 126, 129, 283n199
kathā (story), 101–2
Kathākautuka (Shrivara), 199
Kautilya (*Arthaśāstra*), 253n37
kavi (poet), 113, 246, 278n76
Kavīndracandrikā, 291n21
Kavīndracandrodaya, 291n21
Kavindracharya Sarasvati, 130, 291n21
Kavi plate (736 CE), 29, 31–32, 256n5, 256n7, 256n9, 257n13, 260n77
Kaviraj, Sudipta, 209
kavya (poetry), 14, 113, 170, 185, 200, 246, 278n76; Persian and, 128, 202

Kāvyamīmāṃsā (Rajashekhara, tenth century), 59, 61
Kerala, 181
Keshava Pandit, 178, 180–81, 294n84
Keshavdas, 290n13
Khadgasena (king), 292n37
Khajlak (Mongol leader), 118, 279n108
Khaljis, 66, 167, 278n22; Chauhans and, 91–92; Jains and, 140; Madurai and, 75–77, 268n45; Mahimasahi and, 95–96; Malik Kafur of, 79–80; Mongols and, 108; Vaghelas and, 103. *See also* Alauddin Khalji; Muhammad bin Bakhtiyar Khalji
khāngāh (Sufi lodge), 128
Khangara (king), 291n24
Kharatara Gaccha (Jain lineage), 134–35, 139, 141, 142, 144–45, 148, 158, 246, 287n51; competition with the Tapa Gaccha, 139, 142, 287n51
Kharataragacchapaṭṭāvalī, 284n2
Khasas, 31
Khizr Khan (Sayyid dynasty ruler), 271n114
khudā (God), 148, 235. *See also* Allah; Rahman
Khurram (Mughal prince), 144
khushfahm (wise man), 157, 247
Khusrau (Mughal prince), 144
Khusrau, Amir (Persian poet), 144, 279n108
khutba (Friday sermon), 201, 247
khyāts (lineage narratives), 164
kinnari (celestial musicians), 157, 247
kirata (forest dwelling people), 109, 247, 263n52
kīrti (fame), 171
Kīrtikaumudī (Someshvaradeva), 106
Kosalabhosalīya (Sheshacalapati), 297n155
Krishna (Vishnu avatar), 15, 238; Akbar and, 157, 238; Dvaraka and, 194, 232; Kamsa and, 78
Krishnadeva Raya. *See* Krishna Raya
Krishna II (Rashtrakuta ruler), 31, 33, 257n13
Krishna Raya (Vijayanagara ruler), 180–81, 296n98
Kṛpārasakośa (Shantichandra), 144
Kshatriyas, 247; Brahmins and, 53, 263n45; Chandrashekhara on, 175–77; of Chauhans, 90–91; dharma of, 37, 93–94; Gangadhara and, 188; in Gujarat, 165; kingship, 20, 25, 89–96, 161–88; Mahimasahi and, 91–96; Marathas and, 161–62, 190; as Muslim converts, 36–37; Rajputs as, 161–62, 163, 167–77, 190; Rudrakavi and, 188; Shivaji as, 183–87, 296n124; in *varṇāśramadharma*, 53
Kubera, 52, 143
Kumārasambhava (Kalidasa), 261n7
Kurukshetra, 94, 247
Kuru Shah (Shah Miri ancestor), 118–19

Lābhodayarāsa (Dayakushala), 137
Lahore, 44, 97, 143; as *lābhapura*, 144; as *lāhura*, 144, 201
Lahori, Muhammad Qasim, 207
Laine, James, 291n20
Lakshmana Sena (ruler), 302n6
Lakshmi (Hindu goddess), 56, 157
Lakshmipati, 24, 190–91; *Ābdullacarita* by, *191*, 203–7, 213, 242–44, 300n69; Jagacchandra of Kumaon and, 191, 209; *Nṛpatinītigarbhitavṛtta* by, *191*, 204–7, 240–42, 300n68
Lal Ded (Kashmiri mystic), 120, 280n130
Lalitavigraharāja (Somadeva), 62–63, 167, 265n90
Lal Kunwar, 206
Lallāvākyāni (Lal Ded), 280n130
local histories, 131–32, 138–45, 284n209
Lodi dynasty, 140, 141
Lolaka (military leader in Kashmir), 120

Ma'āsir al-Umarā, 175
Ma'bar. *See* Madurai
MacDonell, Arthur, 6

Madhumati (Rashtrakuta administrator), 33, 255n4
Madhurāvijaya (Gangadevi), 19, 25, 67, 76–89, 97–98, 227–29, 266n1, 269n57, 270n69–82
madhyadeśa (northern India), 195, 201, 298n25
madrasa (school), 128, 247
Madurai Sultanate, *87*, 268nn44–47, 270n82; Brahmins in, 80–81; cow slaughter in, 82; Gangadevi on, 75–89, 227–29; Goripalayam Dargah and, 86, *87*; Kampan and, 85–86; Thiruparankundram Dargah and, 86, *88*; Vijayanagara and, 66, 76, 85, 268n44
Mahabharata, 13, 14, 119, 163, 179, 247; Duryodhana in, 94; Kalhana and Merutunga on, 100–101, 274n6; Kambojas in, 95, 273n145; Yudhishthira in, 171. *See also* Bhagavadgita
mahakavya (great poem), 90, 170, 185, 247
mahatmya (genre of religious texts), 247202
Mahavira, 40, 111
Mahdi (Islamic figure), 259n63
Mahesh Thakur, 190, 198
Mahimasahi (Muhammad Shah), 91–96
Mahmud of Ghazni, 34, 36, 38, 39–40
Makara. *See* Hamilton, William
Malik Kafur (Khalji general), 79–80
Mallette, Karla, 21
Malwa, 36, 107–8, 109, 143, 192, 193, 230
Mammata, 90–91
Mandalik (Chudasama ruler), 165–66, 291n28
Maṇḍalīkacarita (Gangadhara), 162, 165–66, 168, 291n22, 291n28
Man Singh Kachhwaha, 177
Mantrikarmacandravaṃśāvalīprabandha (Jayasoma), *136*, 137, 147, 284nn4–5
Marappa (Vijayanagara founder), 69, 266n4
Maratha Bhonsle family, 3, 25–26, 162, 294n85; Kshatriyas and, 161–62, 163, 190; Other and, 179–83; political histories for, 177–79, *178*; Rajputs and, 161–88; unpopular narratives of, 186–88. *See also specific people*
Marathas. *See* Maratha Bhonsle family
Marathi, 164, 181–82 290n14
masjid (mosque), 126, 128, 247
masnavi (versified poem), 202, 247
matanga (low-caste group), 51–52, 55, 247
matha (Brahmin monastery), 33, 119, 247
mausula (Muslim), 122–26, 247. *See also* musula
mausulaveda. *See* Quran
Mecca, 37, 38; Merutunga on, 105; tirtha of, 105, 120, 206, 242–44; Zayn al-Abidin and, 119
Meghavijaya, 141, 152–53; *Digvijayamahākāvya* by, 156; *Tapāgacchapaṭṭāvalī* by, 135, 285n6
Merutunga, 261n8; on history, 100–101; on Mecca, 105; *Prabandhacintāmaṇi* by, 100–101, 102, 103, *103*, 105–6, 275n11, 276n39; on Valabhi, 108–9; Vardhamana and, 275n23
Metahistory (White), 17, 221
Mewar, 162, 163; Chittor and, 194–97; Rana Kumbha of, 69; Rana Uday Singh of, 233; Sisodiyas of, 169
Mir Khan (Shah Miri prince), 120
Mirza Muhammad (eighteenth-century author), 207
mleccha, 11, 30, 33, 38, 40, 118, 181, 247, 257n30, 264n57, 267n23; dharma of, 37–38, 181; Ghurids as, 52, 55, 60, 109; homeland of, 114–16; in Jain prabandhas, 105; Jonaraja and, 263n53; Kalki and, 166; Mughals as, 180–81; in *Prabandhacintāmaṇi*, 106; pulindas and, 263n52; in *Rājataraṅgiṇī* (Kalhana), 114–16; Scythians as, 110
Mohan, V., 207
moksha (liberation), 171–72, 247

Mongols, 20; Alauddin Khalji and, 91; Delhi and, 279n108; Hammira Chauhan and, 91–93, 91–96; Indians and, 84; Khalji and, 108. *See also* Dalca; Khajlak
Morgenstein Fuerst, Ilyse R., 262n27
Moses, 259n63
mosques, 34, 262n23; Eid celebrations in, 126; of Ghurids, 49, *50*, 53–54; in Gujarat, 74–75, 107; in Gwalior, 258n35; Jagadu and, 74; in Kashmir, 126; Maratha destructions of, 181; in Sindh, 258n35. *See also* masjid
mudgala (Mughal), 92, 192, 195, 247
Mughals, 2, 3, 26; Brahmins and, 148, 151–52, 158–59, 190; Dharmasagara and, 143–44; Digambara Jains and, 285n16; Hiravijaya and, 139–40, 141–42, 145–47, 148–51, 154–56, 191, 195, 235–36; Jains and, 25, 133–60, 285n5, 285n16; political histories of, 186–211, *192*; Rajputs and, 194–98, *196*, 232–35; reimaging political history of, 191–98; Shvetambara Jains and, 133–60; Siddhichandra and, 143, 147–48, 150–52, 156–60, 236–40
Muhammad (prophet), 37, 123, 259n63
muhammad (name), as rendered in Sanskrit, 33, 35
Muhammad bin Bakhtiyar Khalji, 212
Muhammad bin Tughluq (Muhammad Shah), 84, 104 111; Jinaprabha and, 134. *See also* Ulugh Khan
Muhammad Ibrahim (Mughal prince), 242–44
Muhammad Khan (Shah Miri prince), 120
Muhammad Shah (Shah Miri ruler), 123–24
Muhammad Shah II (Muzaffarid ruler), 165–67
Muhammad Shah Rangila (Mughal king), 203, 211, 242–44
Mularaja (king), 105–6, 276n36
musalman (Muslim), 124; as Sanskrit *musalamana*, 34, 75, 247, 258n34
Muslims. *See specific topics*
musula (muslim), 124, 247. *See also* mausula
Muzaffarid Sultanate, 165, 167
Muzaffar Shah (Muzaffarid ruler), 165

Nābhinandanajinoddhāra (Kakka), *103*, 103–4, 107–9, 229–32, 277n55
Nadir Shah (Persian ruler), 211
Nagabhata II (ruler), 31
Nagapuriya Gaccha (Jain lineage), 140–41
Nagarjuna (Chauhan ruler), 55
Naiki (Queen), 105–6, 276
Nainsi, 169
Naiṣadhīyacarita, 142
Nandy, Ashis, 219
Narayan Shah (Baglan ruler), 172, 173–75
Nāṭyaśāstra (Bharata), 129
Navsari plate (738 CE), *29*, 32–33, 34, 256n9, 256nn5–7
Nayachandra, 20, 138, 271n115; *Hammīramahākāvya* by, 67, 89–98, 175, 188, 263n49, 266n1, 266n 1, 271n109; on heroism, 89–96; modern interpretations of, 272n122; *Rambhāmañjarī* by, 98
Nayasundara (*Bṛhatpośālikapaṭṭāvalī*), 286n27
Nicholson, Andrew, 125–26
Nīlamatapurāṇa, 120, 280n125
Nītiśataka (Bhartrhari), 198, 234, 303n9
Nizam Shahis, 161, 172, 173–75, 182
Nizamuddin Ahmad, 168
Noah (prophet), 259n63
Nöldeke, Theodor, 5
non-Aryans, 70, 82, 110–11
Nooruddin, Sheikh, 120
Norton, Mary Beth, 218
Nṛpatinītigarbhitavṛtta (Lakshmipati), *191*, 204–7, 240–42, 300n68
Nur Jahan, 157, 159
nyaya, 289n108

Obrock, Luther, 281n138
Odras, 31
Olivelle, Patrick, 253n37
Orientalists, 6, 114; racism and, 16–17
Orsini, Francesca, 23
Other, 4, 154–58, 251n7; Maratha Bhonsle family and, 179–83
othering, 54, 64, 97, 179, 205; extreme, 58–59; harsh, 63, 210

Padmanabha (*Kānhaḍade Prabandha*), 167, 292n32
Padmasagara: Akbar as described by, 194–95; *Jagadgurukāvya* by, *136*, 142, 154–55, 191, *191*, 232–35, 284n4; on Mughal political history, *192*, 192–98
Padmasundara, 146; *Akbarasāhiśṛṅgāradarpaṇa* by, 139, 140
paighambar (prophet), 123, 128, 201, 247
Paishachi, 61
Palam Baoli inscription (1276 CE), 73, 267n21, 267n23, 271n116
Pañcatantra, 37
Pandavas (mythological family), 119, 276n45. *See also* Arjuna; Yudhishthira
Pandya dynasty, 31, 77, 84, 86, 107, 230
Paramananda, 13, 20; Afzal Khan, and, 183; Shivaji and, 184–86, 187, 188, 296n133; *Sūryavaṃśa* by, 13, *178*, 179, 180–85, 294n87
Paramānandakāvya, 177–78, *178*, 179, 183, 294nn87–88, 295n98
Paramardi (ruler), 64, 105
parameshita (God), 151, 288n84
parameshvara (God), 151–52, 200, 247, 288n84
parasi. *See* Persian (language); Persian (people)
parasika. *See* Persian (people)
Parṇālaparvatagrahaṇākhyāna (Jayarama Pindye), 164, 177, 178, *178*, 182, 184, 187, 296n122
Paryushan, 247, 287n65; animal slaughter and, 147
Pashupatas, 124
Patel, Geeta, 9
pattavali (lineage), 14, 247, 274–75n10. *See also specific texts*
Persian (language), 11, 73, 97, 123, 128–29, 157, 209, 247; "hindu" and, 23, 49; historiography and, 18, 177, 191–92, 206, 214, 254n62, 261n8, 284n204; Jinaprabha and, 111; as represented in Sanskrit texts, 18, 23–24, 58–61, 83, 125, 197, 207–8, 214, 228, 283n194; terms imported to Sanskrit, 30, 68–69, 75, 123, 124, 143, 147, 182, 207, 266n3, 282n176, 295n113, 301–2n103, 301n98; translation and, 130, 198–203
Persian (people), 31, 33, 247, 257–58n30, 279n105, 283n194
Persianate, 10–11, 12, 23, 154–58, 247, 253n35
Philosophy of History (Hegel), 16–17
poetry (Sanskrit), 14, 91, 125, 126, 157, 216; competition and, 47, 89; conventions of, 79, 169, 170; fear and, 80; God and, 74–75; gore and, 22, 32–33, 85, 223, 255n74; Hasan Shah's knowledge of, 128–29; history and, 8, 16–19, 36, 53, 112–13, 179, 190, 278nn73–74; Jains and, 90; languages of, 61, 128; power of, 66; shastra and, 14; tropes and, 52, 59, 77, 80–83, 86, 127, 186, 188, 208; violence and, 76, 194
political violence, 21–22, 75–88, 194, 214
Pollock, Sheldon, 9, 12, 58, 265n88
povāḍas (ballads), 164
prabandha (narrative), 14, 176, 247, 274–75nn10–11; of Gujarati Jains, 14, 99–100, 101–12, *103*, 130–31; as masnavi, 202; of Merutunga, 100–101. *See also specific texts*
Prabandhacintāmaṇi (Merutunga), 100–103, *103*, 105–6, 107–9, 261n8, 275n11, 276n39

Prabandhakośa (Rajashekhara, fourteenth century), 74, 102, *103*, 104–5, 107, 109, 110
Prajyabhatta, 112, *113*, 277n71
Prakrit, 19, 59, 61, 137, 247; Devavimala and, 149; Muslims and, 167; Prithviraj Chauhan and, 61; in *Vividhatīrthakalpa*, 102. *See also* Apabhramsha
Pratap Rudra (Kakatiya ruler), 77
Pratap Shah (Baglan king), 172, 174–75
Pratiharas. *See* Gurjara-Pratihara dynasty
Prayag, 143, 243
Prince of Wales plate (736 CE), 256n5, 256n7, 256n9
Prithvibhata (bard), 266n97
Prithviraj Chauhan, 47–49, 55; as Brahmin protector, 64; Delhi and, 262n28; fate of, 261n8; historical memory of, 73; Jayanaka on, 45–67; Jinaprabha on, 110; Karttikeya and, 60–61; Merutunga on, 105; patronage of, 64–65; Rama and, 54; Vishnu as, 52
Pṛthvīrājavijaya (Jayanaka), 24–25, 30, 45–67, 121, 215, 216, 264n66; Jayaratha cites, 265n91; Jonaraja's commentary on, 48, 51, 52, 55, 61, 63–64, 121; *Madhurāvijaya* and, 80; Prithvibhata in, 266n97
Pṛthvīrāj Rāso, 164, 291n18
Pseudo-Jonaraja, 277n72, 279n111; *Rājataraṅgiṇī* and, 112, *113*, 114
Pulakeshiraja (Chaulukya king), 32, 223–24
pulinda (outcaste tribe), 11, 55, 247, 263n52
Punjab, 44
purana (mythology), 12–13, 157, 205, 212, 239, 247, 265n88; anupurana and, 179; itihasa and, 12–13, 253n36; Muslims and, 62; "turushka" in, 257n18. *See also specific texts*
Purātanaprabandhasaṅgraha, 130–31
Puruṣaparīkṣā (Vidyapati), 98
Pushkar, 49–55, 206; Brahma and, 50, 262n28; description of, 224–27; Jayanaka and, 303n2; as *tripuṣkara*, 52, 224

Quran, 37, 125–26 (as *mausulaveda*), 149–50, 202, 235–36
Qutb Mosque, 49
Qutb Shahis, 161

Radha Devi, 92
Rādhāmādhavavilāsacampū (Jayarama Pindye), 164, 290n15
Raghuvaṃśa (Kalidasa), 14, 36, 79, 83, 179, 215, 262n19, 269n61, 270n71
Rahman (God), 37, 247; as Sanskrit *rahamān*, 139. *See also* Allah; *khudā*
Raidhu, 138
raja (king), 11, 116, 130, 248; in *rājaturuṣka*, 115
Rājapraśasti (Ranachoda Bhatta), 162, 163, 187, 253n38, 290n14
Rajaram (Maratha ruler), 177, 178, 294n84; Sambhaji and, 183
Rājārāmacarita (Keshava Pandit), 178, 179, 180, 182, 187
Rajashekhara (tenth century), 59–60, 61, 274n1
Rajashekhara (fourteenth century), 74, 102, *103*, 104–5, 107, 109, 110; in Delhi, 104
Rajasthan, 40, 49, *50*, 69, 89, *93*, 143
Rajasthani (language), 169, 180
Rājataraṅgiṇī (Jonaraja), 48, 100, 112–14, *113*, 116–22, 278n76, 279nn97–99, 280n130; as historical text, 130–32; *Pṛthvīrājavijaya* and, 63
Rājataraṅgiṇī (Kalhana), 5, 25, 55, 99–101, 112–14, *113*, 141, 274n3, 278nn76–78, 278nn85–96; as historical text, 130–32; Muslims in, 114–16
Rājataraṅgiṇī (Shrivara), 100, 112–14, *113*, 122–32, 281n138, 283n194
Rājataraṅgiṇī (Shuka), 112, *113*, 114
rajataranginis, 248; of Kashmir, 14, 99–101, 112–14, *113*; as tarikh, 130

rajavali (line of kings), 14, 248
Rājavinoda (Udayaraja), 167, 267n12
Rajendra Chola I (king), 39
Rajputs, 3, 25–26, 49; at Chittor, 194, *196*; Kshatriya kingship of, 161–62, 163, 167–77, 190; Marathas and, 161–88; Mughals and, 232–35; Muslims as, 180, 181; Nayachandra and, 272n122; Shivaji and, 184–85
rakshasa (demon), 55, 118, 205
Rama (epic character), 66, 119, 184, 226, 236, 248; Akbar and, 156; Jains and, 153; kingdom of, 181; lineage of, 184; as world-savior, 54, 78, 98
Ramayana, 15, 47, 54, 194, 248
Rambhāmañjarī (Nayachandra), 98
Ramrajya (Rama's rule), 181, 248
Ranachoda Bhatta, 162, 163, 187, 253n38, 290n14
Rana Kumbha (Mewar ruler), 69
Ranamalla (Chauhan defector), 91
Ranka (eighth-century merchant), 109
Ranthambhor, 89, 92, *93*, 95–96, 108, 169–72, 272n115; Hammira Chauhan at, 89–96
Rao, Ajay, 21
Rao, Velcheru Narayana, 8
rasa (aesthetic emotion), 57, 100, 248, 278n76. *See also specific named rasas*
Rashtrakutas, 29, 31, 33, 34, 255n4
Rāṣṭrauḍhavaṃśamahākāvya (Rudrakavi), 168, 172–77, 292n36, 293n60
Ratan, Rao (ruler), 162
Rathods, 290n9; of Baglan, 163, 168; of Kanauj, 172. *See also* Rāṣṭrauḍhavaṃśamahākāvya
Ratipala (Chauhan defector), 91, 92–93; as Rayapala, 92
Rinchen (Ladakhi king), 117, 279n103
Rishabhadas (*Hīravijayasūrirāsa*), 137
Rudrakavi: Kshatriya kingship and, 188; *Rāṣṭrauḍhavaṃśamahākāvya* by, 168, 172–77, 292n36, 293n60
Ruyyaka, 46, 63, 265n91
"Saccaürivīraucchāhu" (Strength of Satyapuri's Mahavira) (Dhanapala), 39–40
saffron terror. *See* Hindutva
Sagara (legendary king), 119, 276n45
Sahib Khan (Mughal governor), 140
saida: to refer to Baihaqi Sayyids, 123–24, 126; as Sanskrit word, 122–23, 248, 283n194
Saifuddin, Malik. *See* Suha Bhatta
Salman, Masud Saad, 161
Samara Shah (lay Jain), 103–4, 108
Samar Singh (Mewar ruler), 164
Samayasundara, 151
Sambhaji (Maratha ruler), 177, 183, 294n84
Śambhurājacarita (Harikavi), 177, 178, 179, 216
Sambuvaraya dynasty, 77–79, 84, 85
Samyan (place), 33
Sangan (ruler), 166, 291n27
Sanskrit language. *See specific topics*
Sanskrit literary culture, 4, 83, 118, 208, 212–14
śāntarasa (quiescence), 100
Sarasvatīkaṇṭhābharaṇa (Bhoja), 61
Sarban stone inscription (1328 CE), 73, 267n21
Sardesai, Govind Sakharam, 294n85, 294n88, 296n124
Sarkar, Jadunath, 183, 294n85, 295n98, 296n124
Sarvadeśavṛttāntasaṅgraha, *191*, 198–203, 209, 215, 299n37
Sarvananda (*Jagaḍūcarita*), 74
Śatakatrayam (Bhartrhari). *See* Nītiśataka
sati, 69, 248
Śatruśalyacarita, 162, 177
saubhāgya, 155
Sayyid brothers. *See* Abdulla Khan; Husain Ali Khan
Sayyids, 123, 248; at Gwalior, 271n114. *See also* Baihaqi Sayyids; saida
Scythians, 110, 115
Sekaśubhodayā, 213, 302n6

Shahabadi, Muhammad, 130
Shahi Khan (Shah Miri prince), 120. *See also* Zayn al-Abidin
Shah Jahan, 144, 162, 205, 291n21
Shahji (Shivaji's father), 164, 178–79, 181–82, 186
Shah Miri dynasty, 100, 112, 116–22, 128–29, 205, 279n98, 281n139, 291n21; princesses of, 123
Shāhnāma (Firdawsi), 128, 201
Shahrazuri, 201
shaka, 73, 90, 91, 114–16, 248, 267n23
shakendra, 248, 267n23
Shamsuddin Adil Shah (Madurai sultan), 271n105
Shamsuddin Shah Mir, 117, 118
Shantichandra (*Kṛpārasakośa*), 144
shastra (technical treatise), 13–14, 120, 157, 202, 239, 248, 254n42, 279n100, 296n122
Shatrunjaya, 102, 104, 108, 109, 135, 142, 144, 147, 231–32, 276n45, 287n51
Shatrushalya (Hada leader), 162
Shiladitya (ruler of Valabhi), 110
Shishunaga (Magadha ruler), 59
Shiva (Hindu god), 74, 113, 117, 153, 224–25, 226, 227; Pushkar and, 50–51; Shah Miris and, 118, 122; Shivaji and, 179, 185; temples to, 39, 80; texts on, 48; Vijayanagara and, 84; Yagishvara linga of, 204
Shivaji (Maratha ruler), 25, 163, 177, 178–87, 294n84, 294nn87–88, 296n130; Gagabhatta and, 183–84; Jayarama Pindye and, 179–80; as Kshatriya, 183–87, 296n124; Paramananda and, 184–86, 187, 188, 296n133; popular perceptions of, 186–87; as Shudra, 20, 183, 185–86, 290n10, 296n124
shlesha (double entendre), 61, 248, 297n155
Shridhar, 206
Shrivara, 16, 209; as court poet, 274n5; *Jainataraṅgiṇī* by, 281n138; *Kathākautuka* by, 199; *Rājataraṅgiṇī* by, 100, 112–14, *113*, 116, 122–32, 281n138, 283n194
Shrivarmaka (ruler), 31
Shudra, Shivaji as, 20, 183, 185–86, 290n10, 296n124
Shuka, 112, *113*, 114, 130, 281n138
Shulman, David, 8, 216
Shvetambara Jains, 99–100, 111–12, 133–60, 248, 285n16; in Gujarat, 138; Mughals and, 133–60; in Tapa Gaccha, 190
Siddhasuri (Jain leader), 232
Siddhichandra, 152, 289n108; Abul Fazl and, 157, 239–40, 289n108; Agra and, 143, 236; Akbar and, 150–51, 156–57, 236–39; *Bhānucandragaṇicarita* by, *136*, 144, 156, 158, 159–60, 236–40, 284n4, 287n51; Bhanuchandra and, 144, 147, 148, 156, 158–60; Gwalior Fort and, 150–51; Jahangir and, 157–60; Shatrunjaya and, 144, 287n51
siddhis, 122
Sikandar Shah (Kashmir ruler), 118, 120–21
Sikander Lodi (ruler), 141
Simharaja (Chauhan king), 271n115
Sindh, 27, 32, 223, 266n3; *Devalasmṛti* and, 40; mosques in, 258n35
Singh, Upinder, 75–76
Sinhalas, 31
Sisodiya dynasty, 163, 169; Mughals and, 197–98; Shivaji and, 183–84. *See also* Mewar; *specific rulers*
Śivabhārata. *See Sūryavaṃśa*
Slaje, Walter, 277n72, 280n130, 281n138, 282n180
Sohoni, Pushkar, 290n1
Somadeva, 62–63, 167, 265n90
Somasaubhāgya, 155
Someshvaradeva, 106
sphuramana ("farman" in Sanskrit), 147, 248; as *phuramāṇa* and *sphuranmāna*, 288n67
Spiegel, Gabrielle, 17

Sreenivasan, Ramya, 162
Srirangam temple, 79–80, 227
śṛṅgāra (erotic love), 139
suba (province), 143–44, 248
Subrahmanyam, Sanjay, 8
Sufis, 49, 248; in Bengal, 213; dargahs and, 86, *87*, *88*, 271n105; at Fatehpur Sikri, 194, 232
Suha Bhatta, 116, 121–22; as Malik Saifuddin, 122
Sulaimaccaritra (Kalyanamalla), 199
"sultan among Hindu kings": *hindurāyasuratāla*, 69; *hindūrāyasuratrāṇa*, 70, 266n7
Sunnis, 45
Sur Adali, 190
suratrana, 96, 124, 147, 248; Bukka as, 69, 70; of Delhi, 69, 73; of Gujarat, 69; as Hindu kings, 68–70; in Jain prabandhas, 104–5; Kampan and, 86; as Muslim rulers, 68, 70, 86, 104–5, 110, 140, 230, 266n3, 279n103, 286n23, 291n24, 292n30; as *suratāla*, 69, 266nn4–5. *See also* "sultan among Hindu kings"
Surjanacarita (Chandrashekhara), 164, 168–72, 175, 187, 213, 273n141, 292n35 293n57
Surjan of Hada, 168–72, 175, *176*, 177
Sūryasahasranāma (Thousand Names of the Sun), 148
Sūryavaṃśa (Paramananda), 13, 177, *178*, 179, 180–82, 184–85, 294n85, 294n87; yavana in, 181
svami, 32, 34, 223, 224, 248
syadvada (relativism), 151, 158, 248

Ṭabaqāt-i Akbarī (Nizamuddin Ahmad), 168
Ṭabaqāt-i Nāṣirī (Juzjani), 261n8
Tabrizi, Shaykh Jalaluddin, 213, 302n6
tajika, 29–33, 34, 124, 248; as adaptation from Pahlavi, 29, 256n10; cessation of term in inscriptions, 257n15; hammira and, 68; on Kavi plate (736 CE), 256n9; on Navsari plate (738 CE), 256n9; on Prince of Wales plate (736 CE), 256n9; Pulakeshiraja and, 223–24
Talbot, Cynthia, 73, 82, 162, 171, 267n17, 292n35, 292n44, 293n57
Tamil Nadu, 66, 75, 83, 84, 138, 187
tamra (reddish), 182, 248
tamranana (red-faced), 182, 249
Tamraparni River, 81, 228, 270n71
Tapa Gaccha (Jain lineage), 134–35, 137, 139–60, 190–98, 249, 286n27; competition with the Kharatara Gaccha, 139, 142, 287n51
Tapāgacchapaṭṭāvalī (Dharmasagara), 135, 140, 286n29, 286nn22–23
Tapāgacchapaṭṭāvalī (Meghavijaya), 135, 141, 152–53, 285n6
tapas (ascetic practices), 122
Tarain, Ghurid-Chauhan battles at, 44, 46–47, 52, 105, 261nn8–9
tarikh (history), 102, 130, 249
Tārīkh al-Ḥukamā (Shahrazuri), 201
Tārīkh-i Alfī, 168
Tārīkh-i Fīrūzshāhī (Barani), 73
Tārīkh-i Fīrūzshāhī (Shams Siraj Afif), 85, 271n103
Tārīkh-i Sayyid ʿAlī (Sayyid Ali), 283n193
Tawney, C. H., 5, 276n37
Tejahpala (Vaghela minister), 74, 107
Telangana, 107, 187, 230
Telugu, 77, 84, 138
Textures of Time (Rao, Shulman, and Subrahmanyam), 8
Thanjavur, 177, 187, 287n154
Thapar, Romila, 7, 12, 48
Thiruparankundram Dargah, 86, *88*, 271n105
Tikkana (Telugu poet), 77
Tilakacharya (Shah Miri minister), 119–20
Timur, 165
tirtha, 54, 102, 249; of Mecca, 105, 120, 206, 242–44; Surjan and, 170, 171–72

Tomar dynasty, 67, 70, 73, 89–96, 90, 266n1, 271n109, 272n166
translation, 210, 218; of Indo-Persian histories in modernity, 18; of Sanskrit and Persian texts in premodernity, 128–29, 130, 198–203; of Sanskrit texts in modernity, 105, 174, 181, 183, 197, 302n6. *See also specific topics and texts*
Tughluqs, 66; at Gwalior, 271n114; Jains and, 104, 111, 134, 140, 145–46; Jinaprabha and, 111, 134, 145–46; Madurai Sultanate and, 76, 268n46; southern India and, 76–77, 82, 84. *See also* Muhammad bin Tughluq
turushka, 11, 29–31, 34, 80, 82, 124, 181, 249, 267n23; alleged violence of, 111; earliest use of, 256nn8–9; Ghurids as, 55, 260n3; hammira and, 68; in Jain prabandhas, 105; Mahmud of Ghazni as, 40; raja and, 116; in *Rājataraṅgiṇī* (Kalhana), 114–16; rule of, 130; tax on, 35; as *tulushka*, 81, 85–86, 227

Udayaraja, 166–67
Udayashri (Shah Miri minister), 119
Uday Singh (Mewar ruler), 195, 197–98, 233–34
Ujjain, 110
Ulugh Khan (Tughluq general), 77. *See also* Muhammad bin Tughluq

Vaghelas, 106, 190; Iltutmish and, 98; Khaljis and, 103, 107–8, 229; literary patronage of, 110; mosques supported by, 74, 107. *See also* Tejahpala; Vastupala
vaideshika (outsider), 94, 249
Vaiṣṇavadharmaśāstra, 56, 264n58
Vajpeyi, Ananya, 184, 255n66
Vajrayana Buddhists, 36. *See also* Kalachakra Tantra
Valabhi, 32, 103, 108–9, 110, 130
Vallabha Pathaka, 139, 147, 152, 153; Vijayadeva and, 139; *Vijayadevamāhātmya* by, *136*, 147, 152–53, 284n4
Valmiki (purported Ramayana author), 47, 66, 76, 269n49
Van der Kuijp, Leonard, 34
Vāqi'āt-i Bāburī, 201
Varadaraja temple, 70, *71*, *72*, 267n15
varna, 20, 243, 245, 246, 247, 249; dharma and, 53, 84, 183; kings as upholding, 53, 84, 183; Muslims and, 40, 55, 64, 115, 127, 180, 186; Shivaji and, 20, 183, 185–86, 290n10, 296n124; in *varṇāśramadharma*, 53, 84. *See also* Brahmins; jati; Kshatriyas; Shudra
Vastupala (Vaghela minister), 74, 106–7
Veda, 37, 81–82, 202, 225, 227, 229, 243, 249; of Muslims, 125–26; Siddhichandra and, 289n108
Venkatkrishnan, Anand, 21
Veraval bilingual inscription, 74–75
vernacular language choice, 23–24, 77, 138, 163–64, 210, 283n194
Vidagdhamukhamaṇḍana (Dharmadasa), 304n11
Vidyapati, 138; *Puruṣaparīkṣā* by, 98
Vidyatilaka, *103*, 104, 110–11
vigats (clan chronicles), 164
Vigraharaja IV (Chauhan ruler), 62, 64
vijaya (victory text), 14, 46, 48, 85, 249. *See also* individual texts
Vijayadana (Tapa Gaccha leader), 140
Vijayadeva (Tapa Gaccha leader), *136*, 139
Vijayadevamāhātmya (Vallabha Pathaka), *136*, 147, 152–53, 284n4
Vijayanagara dynasty, 3, 98, 180; Gangadevi and, 67, 269n48; Hindu kings and, 69–70; Kakatiya dynasty and, 77; Madurai and, 66, 76, 77, 85, 268n44; Pandyas and, 77, 84, 86; Tamil Nadu and, 84. *See also* Gangadevi; Kampan; "sultan among Hindu kings"
Vijayapraśastimahākāvya (Hemavijaya and Gunavijaya), *136*, 141, 143, 152–53, 155, 284–85n5, 286n24

Vijayasena (Tapa Gaccha leader), *136*, 141, 147, 151–53
Vijayatilakasūrirāsa (Darshanavijaya), 137
Vikramaditya (legendary king, circa first century BCE), 61, 105, 275n28
Vikramaditya VI (Chaulukya ruler), 48
Vikramāṅkadevacarita (Bilhana), *Pṛthvīrājavijaya* and, 47, 48, 66, 215, 252n8, 262n19
Vikram samvat calendar, 110
Vimalaprabhā. *See* Kalachakra Tantra
Vindhya mountains, 187
violence: anachronism of Hindu-Muslim violence in premodernity, 84, 129, 183; modern Hindu-Muslim, 23, 39; political, 21–22, 75–88, 194, 214; of turushka, 111
vīra (hero), 89, 90–91, 96, 171; Mongols as, 292n38
Vīrabhānūdayakāvya, 190
Virama (Hammira Chauhan's brother), 91, 95, 273n131
Virama (Tomar king), 89, 90, 266n1, 271n109
Virasena (Baglan ruler), 168
Vishnu, 48, 79, 117, 195, 227; asceticism and, 51, 226; avatars of, 166, 296n122; Buddha as, 50–51, 225; footprints of in Mecca, 206, 243; Prithviraj Chauhan as, 52–54, 62; Pushkar and, 50–54, 224–27; Shivaji as, 184, 185; Zayn al-Abidin and, 118;
Vishvanatha (God), 77
Vishvanatha (*Sāhityadarpaṇa*), 184
Vividhatīrthakalpa (Jinaprabha and Vidyatilaka), 102, *103*, 104, 109, 110–12, 137, 146, 267n18, 275n16 276n51
Vose, Steven, 276n51, 284n2
vṛtta (story), 14, 101, 113, 130, 254n46

White, Hayden, 17, 192, 221
Wittig, Monique, 189
Wolpé, Sholeh, 44
World Sanskrit Conference, 6, 255n66

Yājñavalkyasmṛti, 37
yavana, 3, 11, 30, 33, 98, 149, 165, 249, 257n30, 297n149; Ghurids as, 55; in Jain prabandhas, 105; Jonaraja and, 263n53; Madurai sultans as, 83–84; in *Rājataraṅgiṇī* (Kalhana), 114–16; in *Sūryavaṃśa*, 181; in *yavanadarśana*, 118, 126; in *yavanarājya*, 180–81, 249
Yudhishthira (epic character), 73, 171
Yūsuf va Zulaykhā (Jami), 199

Zafar Khan (Tughluq governor), 165
Ẓafarnāma, 201
Zayn al-Abidin, 116–20, 122, 128–29, 274n5; as a non-mleccha, 118, 280n114; Saida and, 123; Sanskrit and, 116, 128–29, 279n100; translations sponsored by, 128, 283n192

GPSR Authorized Representative: Easy Access System Europe, Mustamäe tee 50, 10621 Tallinn, Estonia, gpsr.requests@easproject.com

www.ingramcontent.com/pod-product-compliance
Lightning Source LLC
Chambersburg PA
CBHW021930290426
44108CB00012B/796
* 9 7 8 0 2 3 1 1 9 7 0 5 2 *